108
8
20

Rookies Rated

Rookies Rated

Baseball's Finest Freshman Seasons

by

Warren N. Wilbert

FOREWORD BY KEN TATUM

McFarland & Company, Inc., Publishers
Jefferson, North Carolina, and London

Front cover photos: Left to right: Curt Davis (Brace Photo), Kid Nichols (Brace Photo), Kenny Lofton (Dennis Colgin), Nomar Garciaparra (Dennis Colgin). Fielder's glove image courtesy of Nokona Quality Athletic Goods.

Library of Congress Cataloguing-in-Publication Data

Wilbert, Warren N., 1927–
 Rookies rated : baseball's finest freshman seasons / by Warren N.
Wilbert ; foreword by Ken Tatum.
  p. cm.
 Includes bibliographical references and index.
 ISBN 0-7864-0739-5 (illustrated case binding : 50# alkaline paper) ∞
 1. Rookie baseball players — Rating of — United States. 2. Rookie
baseball players — United States — Statistics. I. Title.
GV865.A1W53 2000
796.357'0973 — dc21   00-24772

British Library cataloguing data are available

Manufactured in the United States of America

*McFarland & Company, Inc., Publishers
 Box 611, Jefferson, North Carolina 28640
  www.mcfarlandpub.com*

To Ginny
God's Very Special Gift to Me

Soli Deo Gloria

Acknowledgments

I've come to understand over the years that the realization of personal goals or achievements, however ambitious or modest, can usually be credited to many helpful people who patiently informed and corrected, encouraged, made suggestions, and otherwise supported our pet projects and even some of our indulgences. This book is no exception.

A select group of willing and very able helpers deserve my sincere thanks. Let these few words set that record straight, and permit me to salute each of you in turn as I recognize your timely and capable assistance in completing this book.

To my fellow saberites Bob Hoie, Dave Smith and the recently deceased Ralph Horton, each of whom provided valuable information that would otherwise have escaped me, thanks for listening and helping.

Walt Wilson, a friend indeed, went far beyond my requests for help to provide not only the box scores I requested, but also the extras that provided a human touch to some of those special rookie moments.

Correspondence with Johnny Pesky and Ken Tatum was a delight. I'm appreciative of the time they took to look back, providing both interesting and inspirational flashbacks.

Jim Meier, at that treasure house of baseball lore, *The Sporting News*, was most cooperative and cheerfully helpful in digging nuggets out of the past from *TSN*'s vast files.

Pete Palmer, who, in the midst of who knows how many projects of his own, was once again kind enough to provide the sabermetrician's touch, adding razor-sharp precision to the mountain of statistics that give meaning and insight into what happened on the field of play. I'm much obliged.

The photos in this book are the work of two very capable and treasured resources. George Brace and his able daughter Mary are wonderful people who happen to be the possessors of one of the finest baseball photo collections in existence, and it's always a pleasure to work with them. Then, too, there is Dennis Colgin, who has provided a significant number of the illustrations we've used. My "California Connection" came through when the chips were down. I'm grateful.

My coauthor in past writing ventures, Bill Hageman of the *Chicago Tribune*, who, like Charles Dickens' Barcus, was "always willin'," once again lent his capable and very professional hand as the rookie lineup moved through the "innings" of this book with encouragement and apt support. Thanks a million, Bill.

And finally, there was the blessing of

a loving and supportive family, all of whom chipped in the necessary doses of love, guidance and patience that mean so much. Especially Karen, who was ceaselessly on the lookout for books and articles that add the little extras, and made certain to check now and then to see how those rookies were coming along. To all of you — my love and heartfelt gratitude.

Table of Contents

PART III. From the First in 1880 to the Last in 1999   227

PART IV. The Honorable Mentions   313

Foreword
by Ken Tatum

"Holy Cow!" This well known exclamation by the late Harry Carey captures the true emotions of a rookie in the major leagues: anxiety, anticipation, self-doubt, determination.

Reflecting on my rookie year brings to mind the excitement and the sense of adventure that I felt. Playing with and against baseball players that I had watched on television was an awesome experience! I had climbed the ladder: A ball, AA, AAA, and finally, the majors! Most rookies can recall someone who made a significant impact on his career and on his advancement to the majors. In the minors, I gave it 110 percent every time I was asked to perform. My won-loss record in the minors and the influence of my manager, Rocky Bridges, were the two primary factors that enabled me to become a major league ballplayer. Rocky encouraged me, put me through the rigors of numerous pitching drills, and designed an exercise program to get me into top physical condition. I played winter ball for Rocky in Ponce, Puerto Rico, in 1968. This experience was a critical factor in my success. Being able to hold my own with major league players gave me the confidence that I would later need in big league competition. The following year Rocky became a coach on the California

Angels' major league staff, and I was called up to the majors.

Spring training with the big club is an experience I will never forget. When a player goes to the majors, he has the challenge of impressing the managers and the coaches and proving to them that he is good enough to stay. Being in a major league spring training enabled me to gain knowledge and experience that would help me to be successful in the big leagues.

Two times I was in spring training with the big club, and both times I was sent back to the minor leagues. In 1969, I was in Hawaii when I was called up to the majors. It was in the evening when my manager told me; within three hours I was on a plane headed for Anaheim, California, leaving behind my wife and young son.

Upon arriving at the stadium for the first time, I was overwhelmed with the immaculate condition of the field and the clubhouse. The locker room was spacious and clean, with cubicles for each player. Uniforms were cleaned and shoes were polished each day by the club staff. In the minor leagues players had to perform these tasks.

Meeting with the players and the managers was exciting, but I knew I would have to perform to stay. The first time I came out of the bullpen and took the mound was both thrilling and nerve-racking. There is no better feeling than pitching a successful game and, conversely, no worse feeling than letting the team down.

After each ball game we would go back to the locker room, where the locker boy would have a spread of food for our supper. In the minor leagues, players would shower and then go out and eat at a greasy spoon because they were given only $5 a day for meal money. Also, in the minors travel was by bus, not by air, and travel attire consisted of slacks and a nice shirt. Players took care of their own luggage and stayed in average hotels.

Traveling in the major leagues was different. On my first road trip, the team dressed up in coats and ties and rode in a nice bus to the airport. Our luggage was taken care of by our traveling secretary. While I was sitting on the plane, the traveling secretary came by and gave each player an envelope. I asked him what it contained, and he told me it was the meal money for our road trip. Compared to the minor league allotment, I thought I had enough money to last me a month! I soon learned how much meals and tips cost.

As my rookie year progressed, I was amazed at the difference between the big club and the minors. One thing that I had to adjust to was the umpire's throwing out brand new baseballs all the time. In the minor league the umpire was much less liberal with new baseballs. There was also a difference in the calls made in the big leagues. Major league umpires were very precise and consistent. As I pitched, I learned how each umpire called pitches and adjusted my target accordingly. Another difference was that big league umpires allowed no fraternizing between opposing clubs before games. In the minors the umpires did not prohibit conversations between the opposing players.

My rookie season in major league baseball was one of the most exciting and adventurous years of my life! It was a year of mixed emotions: anxiety, anticipation; self-doubt, determination; growth, and success. "Holy Cow!" I actually made it to the big leagues!

Introduction

Each season they head north, some for what merely amounts to baseball's "cup o' coffee," some for a spin around the league before being "sent down," and, among the legions of other players bent on making it in the Bigs, a precious few who not only make it, but make it big time. These are the rookies whose first full major league campaign is studded with Hall of Fame numbers and eye-popping plays. They "came up" performing like seasoned veterans, and quite often shouldered aside some of the game's great and proud old warriors.

Among baseball's precocious freshmen brought together in *Rookies Rated* you're going to find players like Joe Morgan, Christy Mathewson, Grover Cleveland Alexander and Ted Williams, Hall of Famers all, alongside a few of the "who are they?" types like Joe Berry, Reb Russell, Mitchell Page and Jimmy Williams. They all have at least one thing in common: a spot on the honor roll of the greatest rookie seasons in the game's history.

These extraordinary rookie years are lined up for a closer look to discover what the Dick Allens, Freddie Lynns or Tony Olivas achieved, each in his special year, that was worthy of a Rookie of the Year Award, or still other honors. It's a different mix of ballplayers, some of whom shot across the baseball firmament like a meteor in their rookie year only to fade away

into obscurity soon after, and others who moved on from outstanding debut seasons to long term careers of exceptional achievement.

There is no lack of surprise entries on this list — beginning with Curt Davis, who broke in with the Phillies in 1934 and put together the greatest rookie season in the game's history. You're going to want to check out this relatively unknown and little remembered pitcher whose rookie season in a four-team, 13 year career during the '30s and '40s passed by without the rave notices lavished on contemporaries like Rudy York, Hal Trosky, "Milkman" Jim Turner, and others, most of whom enjoyed outstanding freshman campaigns that captured the imagination of sportswriters around the major leagues.

Starting pitchers Cy Blanton of the Pirates (1935 rookie) and Ken Tatum of the Angels (1969) and reliever Doug Corbett of the Twins (1980) are other rookie phenoms no doubt even lesser known than Davis, which probably makes them all but forgotten by now. But each had *his year*, a season to remember, when hitting, pitching, stealing bases, chasing down hot smashes and winning ball games brought on the special rush that goes with making it in a big way under the Big Tent.

Baseball buffs today look forward to the annual Rookie of the Year (RY) awards.

Each year since 1949 the Baseball Writers Association of America (BBWAA) has honored one player in each league. (The award was actually initiated in 1947 when Jackie Robinson was named the first RY. That was followed by another single award in 1948 to Alvin Dark of the Boston Braves.) In its debut year of dual awards in 1949, RY honors were presented to Don Newcombe of the Brooklyn Dodgers and Roy Sievers of the St. Louis Browns. Each year since, BBWAA scribes in the various franchise cities of the major leagues have voted an American and a National Leaguer to this prestigious award.

It may seem a bit strange to Joe Baseball Fan that the BBWAA's annual RY awards don't always coincide with the listing presented here. Didn't the BBWAA name the right rookie? Or is the *Rookies Rated* list off base? Well, yes might be at least partially right for both questions. But just to set things straight up front, I'm going to contend that, in fact, the BBWAA did *not* always pick the rookie player who made *the most valuable contribution to his team's success*. And in this book, that's the key to the award. For instance, Jim Gilliam of the Dodgers, who was voted the National League RY, did not make as valuable a contribution to Brooklyn's 1953 success as Harvey Haddix, who finished a distant second in the voting, made to the St. Louis Cardinals that same year. And that's the reason the 1953 National League award should have been given to Haddix. (More on that later.)

The whys and wherefores supporting this contention may be found in the linear weights measurements of sabermetri-

cians,* whose calculations have transformed the way a player's performance may be examined, rated and evaluated. The bottom-line and most significant of their many new designations is the Total Player Rating (TPR), the ultimate sabermetric measure, which puts a numerical value on a player's contribution to his team's success in a given season. (The sabermetric numbers used in this book are explained in the Glossary.)

The best rookie seasons in the history of organized baseball as presented in *Rookies Rated* are ranked in priority order according to Total Player Ratings. Accordingly, the basis for sorting out the many exceptional rookie seasons in the game's history has gone beyond the usual comparison standards† to take a comprehensive, all-things-considered look at the *overall* performance of a Christy Mathewson or an Ozzie Smith, whether 1901 or 1978, as in the case of "Matty" or "The Wizard of Oz," was the year under scrutiny.

Harvey Haddix's great 1953 rookie season (above) has also been sabermetrically analyzed, as have the '53 rookie seasons of Jim Gilliam, Reuben Gomez, and the other players listed in the chart on page 5 with some of their more significant statistics for 1953.

In 1953 each franchise in the league was granted three votes from among the BBWAA writers covering each team, for a total of 24 possible votes. Gilliam attracted 11 votes for RY honors. Haddix, with four, finished second in the voting. The 3.6 difference in the TPRs of Haddix and Gilliam represents upwards of a four-game difference in the two players' contribution

---

*Sabermetrician *is the name given baseball researchers who are members of SABR, the Society for American Baseball Research, founded in 1971. The sabermetric analysis of baseball productivity and performance is based on mathematical and statistical records. The goal is to produce objective evaluations of baseball performance.*

†The usual comparison standards for pitchers rely heavily on ERAs, won-loss records and strikeouts for pitchers, and batting averages, runs batted in, home runs and slugging averages for position players. While these are important statistics, by themselves they simply do not reveal the full context of player performance, nor do they take into account the player's home field (e.g.: Wrigley Field or Fenway Park) or many other factors that affect statistics or the player's total contribution to his team's record.

Player/Tm	*RY Votes*				*Selected 1953 Statistics*				
Haddix, StL	4	W 20, L 9	19 CG	6 SH	3.06 ERA	10 PHI	34 PR	1 DEF	4.7 TPR
R. Gomez, NY	0	W 13, L 9	13 CG	3 SH	3.40 ERA	.208 OBA	20 PR	2 DEF	2.3 TPR
Buhl, Mil	0	W 13, L 8	8 CG	3 SH	2.97 ERA	154.1 IP	16 PR	1 DEF	1.8 TPR
Gilliam, Brk	11	.278 BA	125 R	17,3 BH	100 BB	21 SB	8 BR	3 FR	1.7 TPR
Baczewski, Cin	1	W 11, L 4	10 CG	1 SH	3.64 ERA	138.1 IP	12 PR	-3DEF	1.1 TPR

Ray Jablonski, St. Louis, received three RY votes. TPR rating: -3.0
Rip Repulski, St. Louis, received two RY votes. TPR rating: -2.3
Jim Bruton, Milwaukee, received two RY votes. TPR rating: -2.3
Jim Greengrass, Cincinnati, received one RY vote. TPR rating: 0.2

to their team's record in 1953, indicating a far stronger and more productive year for Haddix than for Gilliam. Haddix is profiled as one of the players tied for the number 13 position among the game's best rookie seasons.

What makes this TPR category such a valuable statistic? TPR is calculated by using an equation that takes several sabermetric measures into consideration: Batting Runs (BR), Fielding Runs (FR), Base Stealing Runs (BSR) and Runs Per Win (RPW). The formula: add a player's BR plus FR plus BSR, adjust for his position, and divide by RPW (usually around 10). The individual equation factors are, in turn, calculated by using a mathematical formula for FR or BR, as needed. The sabermetrician uses Pitching Runs (PR), Fielding Runs (FR) adjusted to the pitcher's position, Pitcher As Batter (PB) and Runs Per Win in computing the pitcher's rating (relief pitchers have an adjusted formula).

Consequently, each player is rated on each phase of play, presenting a total, or all-encompassing numerical value that more accurately reflects his contribution to the team's success during the course of the season. More precisely, the TPR number represents the number of wins the player might have contributed beyond that of an average player in a given season (average rated at 0.0). In Harvey Haddix's case in 1953 a 4.7 TPR would represent 4.7 (or 5) wins above average. Total Player Ratings range from negative readings of -10 and below to above +10. An example: Curt Davis' 1934 TPR was 7.8, the highest ever recorded by a rookie. The highest pitcher rating was Guy Hecker's 12.6 in 1884, and the highest position player's rating was Babe Ruth's 10.6 in 1923.

All that seems to be a tortuous, terribly convoluted way to get at who's better than whom. It's a long way from BAs and ERAs. But — and this is the point of it all — if one is to make judgments about who's better, Haddix or Gilliam, the standard cannot be shifting from statistic to statistic according to personal preference. The only way to level the playing field is to use a standard that gets at the heart of the game: scoring runs (or causing runs to be scored) or preventing runs from being scored. The former has to do with the offensive part of the game, the latter with defense.

So, the rookies presented in this review of baseball's greatest freshman seasons are rated according to their TPRs, from top to bottom. Davis' 7.8 is the high-water mark, and the review moves on down through the ten Honorable Mention rookies, each of whom registered a 3.3. The listing includes many ties, as might be expected out of a game that presses on toward its 200th anniversary. These ties are listed chronologically. For example, Win Mercer (1894), Joe McGinnity (1899), and Mark Fidrych (1976), each sporting a 5.0 TPR, are listed in that order at the number ten spot.

Now that you've passed Sabermetrics 101 with flying colors, it's time to move on to those talented young players (and some golden oldie rookies like Jittery Joe Berry, who at 39 debuted for Connie Mack's wartime A's with a snappy 3.6 TPR) who started their major league careers in a blaze of frosh pizzazz. Let's celebrate their achievements and salute them as baseball's finest rookies.

Glossary

This glossary and abbreviation key defines terms and designations used throughout this book that may not be familiar to all readers.

Abbrev. *Explanation*

A — Assists: an important category for catchers. Assists in the 90 to 100 range and above are indicative of active and accurately throwing catchers. Here are the best single season numbers for some of the catchers in the Hall of Fame: Ray Schalk, 183; Buck Ewing, 149; Gabby Hartnett, 114; Johnny Bench, 102; Mickey Cochrane, 94; and Roy Campanella, 72.

BR — Batting Runs: a statistic indicating the number of runs contributed beyond those of a league-average (defined as zero) player. Babe Ruth's 119 is the all-time single-season record, set in 1921. The formula for this stat includes the hitter's basehits, walks, times hit by the pitcher, and at bats, thus taking all offensive possibilities into consideration. (All BRs cited in this book are adjusted to league and park factors,

as are all other sabermetric terms.)

BSR — Base Stealing Runs: a statistic indicating the runs contributed beyond those of a league-average (defined as zero) player. The number is calculated on the basis of a 66.7 success rate, below which a runner hinders, rather than helps, his team's efforts. In 1986 Vince Coleman of the St. Louis Cardinals set the BSR record with 24. This stat recognizes the element of speed, base stealing artistry, and its contribution to offense and run-scoring.

CFF — Career Fielding Factor: originated by baseball researcher David Neft, and is calculated by taking Fielding Range, Putouts, Assists and Games Played into consideration. (A complicated formula enables Neft to make adjustments for shortstops and other individual positions, including provision for such variables as strikeouts.) The product of this equation rates the shortstop on a far more comprehensive basis than does a Fielding Average, which only takes putouts, assists and errors into consideration.

CPI Clutch Pitching Index: a sabermetric measure that calculates the number of runs a pitcher is expected to yield *over* the number of actual runs scored. A league-average pitcher is rated at 100. Expected runs are calculated on the basis of the pitcher's opposing at bats, hits, walks and hit batsmen. The CPI indicates pitching success beyond what might be considered average or normal expectations.

DEF Pitcher's Defense (often abbreviated as PD): a statistic especially designed to measure Fielding Runs (FR) contributed by the pitcher, thereby evaluating his performance as the team's fifth infielder. Ratings above 5 are exceptional.

FA Fielding Average: a statistic computed by dividing the sum of a player's putouts and assists by the total of his putouts, assists and errors.

FR Fielding Runs: the number of runs saved beyond what a league-average player at a given position might have saved. This stat takes into consideration putouts, assists, errors, double plays, all adjusted to league and park factors. Glenn Hubbard's 62 Fielding Runs in 1985 is the all-time standard.

GP Games Played, or Games Pitched, determined by player's indicated position.

HOF, HOFer Hall of Fame, or a Hall of Famer

K/BB Strikeout-to-Walk radio: 40/20 K/BB represents 40 strikeouts and 20 walks, indicating a favorable 2–1 ratio of Ks over BBs.

LL League Leader (e.g., LL, 2BH, indicates the player led the league in 2BH).

OBA Opponents' Batting Average (often codified as OAV): indicates the batting average allowed by the pitcher in a given season or in his career. The record low is held by Luis Tiant of the Red Sox, whose OBA in 1968 was .168. Nolan Ryan holds the career OBA at .204. Tiant's career OBA, .236, ranks 51st all time.

OB% On-Base Percentage (often codified as OOB): indicates the percentage of time batters reached base against the pitcher. Among rookies cited in this book, Christy Mathewson ranks highest, at number 10 all time, with a .273 lifetime mark, and highest for a single season with .225 in 1908, ranking him 12th in that category.

PHI Pitcher's Hitting Index (usually codified as PB [Pitcher as Batter]): indicates the number of runs contributed by the pitcher beyond those of a league-average pitcher (as a hitter). This measure pinpoints the pitcher's contribution to his team's offense. In Guy Hecker's banner 1884 season, his PHI was 28. 20th century pitchers Wes Ferrell (20 PHI in 1935) and Red Ruffing (18 in 1930) recorded unusually high PHIs.

PR Pitching Runs: a statistic indicating the number of runs saved by a pitcher over that of a league-average pitcher (defined as zero). The formula: Innings pitched times the league ERA divided by nine, minus Earned Runs Allowed. Walter Johnson's 79 PR (1912) leads all 20th century pitchers. That factors out to eight Pitching Wins, thus benefitting the Senators an extra eight wins over league-average pitchers in 1912, *or*— an eight-game advantage in the AL's final standings.

PW Pitching Wins: a sabermetric, linear weights measure that calculates the number of wins a pitcher contributes to his team above a league-average pitcher for a given season. All calculations are adjusted to the pitcher's home park.

R Rookie: all players listed as rookies in this book are defined as such by the qualifications set down by the BBWAA in 1980: A player shall be considered a rookie, unless, during a season or seasons, he has (a) exceeded 130 at bats or 50 innings pitched in the major leagues; or (b) accumulated more than 45 days on the active roster of a major league club or clubs during the period of the 25-player limit (excluding time in military service).

RAT Ratio: a statistic for pitchers that measures the number of hits allowed plus walks (BB) allowed and hit batsmen per nine innings pitched. Walter Johnson's 1913 mark of 7.26 is the high for the 20th century and ranks third all-time. An RAT rating under 9.00 is exceptional. This number identifies pitchers who are most successful, per nine innings pitched, at keeping hitters off the bases. The lower the number the more successful the pitcher.

RF Range Factor: indicates how effectively a defensive player such as the fine Phillies' shortstop, Bob Allen, whose profile appeared earlier, covers his position by first of all getting to balls hit in his direction, and then converting possibilities into putouts. Range, a defensive measurement created by Bill James, is calculated by multiplying the number of the defensive player's successful chances (putouts plus assists) times nine and then dividing by the number of defensive innings played.

RP For batters, indicates Runs Produced (runs batted in plus runs scored minus home runs.) For pitchers it is a redesignation standing for Relief Pitcher. (Occasionally RP-RHP, or RP-LHP appears, indicating a relief pitcher is either righthanded or lefthanded.)

RPW Runs Per Win: statistic that states the proportional nature of runs and wins. The more runs per win, the greater the offensive production. Contrariwise, fewer runs per win features the defensive/pitching aspect of the game. RPW is one of the factors considered in the Total Player Rating (TPR) statistic.

RR Relief Ranking: computed by a mathematical formula that factors a relief pitcher's PRs, IPs, Ws, Ls, Ks and Saves, calculating the greater value of the innings pitched by a closing reliever.

RY Rookie of the Year: the Baseball Writers Association of America (BBWAA) Award presented each season to the player elected as the AL or NL Rookie of the Year.

SABR Society for American Baseball Research.

SBR Stolen Base Runs: a sabermetric, linear weights measure that indicates the number of runs a player contributes *beyond* what a league-average base stealer might have gained, based on a two-thirds success rate (league average = zero). Vince Coleman set the record for SBR at 24 in 1986. Ozzie Smith's career high in this category is 12 (1988), tieing him for 47th place all time. Maury Wills (23 in 1962) and Rickey Henderson (21 in 1983) rank second and third.

SH/SV// RBI Shutouts/Saves or Runs Batted In: some of the player listings cite both pitchers and position players in the same statistic columns. The first designation is for pitchers, indicating shutouts and saves for a given season. If the player is a hitter the reader uses the second designation (behind the double-slash indicator) to read the player's RBI mark that year. (Other indicators using double slash marks are similarly read, pitchers first, then hitters.)

TPR Total Player Rating: baseball's official encyclopedia, *Total Baseball*,* lists TPR ratings for position players and TPI (Total Pitcher's Index) for pitchers. The TBR designates a Total Baseball Ranking, used in instances where a player may both pitch and play a position such as left field in the same season. Babe Ruth is such an example. The TPR and TPI are then combined to form a TBR reading for a given season.

In order to simplify terminology and codification for this important designation of the player's overall contribution to his team's success, TPR is used throughout this book to indicate both pitchers and position players even though the ratings use different formulas for each.

Ratings for pitchers and position players may be understood as equalized; that is, a pitcher's 3.0 TPI is of the same value as a position player's 3.0. The example used in the Introduction, citing TPRs for 1953's rookies, lists pitchers Harvey Haddix at 4.7 TPR and Reuben Gomez at 2.3.

In the same list Jim Gilliam, Brooklyn infielder, is cited with a 1.7 TPR. We may infer that Haddix's 4.7 is three better than Gilliam's 1.7, a solid indicator that Haddix was more valuable

---

*Total Baseball, *edited by John Thorn, Pete Palmer, Michael Gershman and David Pietrusza, Viking, New York, 1997 edition. All statistics used in* Rookies Rated *are taken from the 1997 edition of* Total Baseball. *1998 statistics were provided by Pete Palmer.*

to his team in 1953 than was Jim Gilliam.

The TPR has been referred to by sabermetricians as the MVP of baseball statistics. It ranks pitchers and position players by the number of total wins their play has contributed to the team's success during a given year. It is computed, for pitchers, by adding the Pitching Runs to the Fielding Runs and then dividing by the Runs Per Win factor. For batters, it is the sum of the player's Batting Runs, Fielding Runs and Base Stealing Runs (all adjusted), minus his positional adjustment, and then divided by the Runs Per Win factor. This rating represents a thoroughgoing, comprehensive evaluation of a player's total productivity, both at bat and afield. Ratings above 3.00 are superior. A career average of 2.00 to 3.00 over ten years, resulting in a cumulative 20 to 30, rates as credentials for the Hall of Fame. Rogers Hornsby (career TPR 81.1 with a 3.53 average for 23 seasons), Ted Williams (85.7 career and 4.51 average for 19 seasons), and Joe McGinnity (19.5 career and 1.95 average for 10 major league seasons), each one a Hall of Famer, are among the players cited in this book for outstanding rookie seasons.

WP   Winning Pitcher or Wild Pitch, determined by context of the text or box score. Usually the pitcher's record as of the game presented is given to further indicate the meaning of WP.

The Ruthian Rookies

Babe Ruth's 1915 rookie season with the Boston Red Sox was a very good one, earning a 2.8 Total Player Rating. Those ratings soon got better, soaring to stratospheric heights as the years went by. By the time his awesome career ended in 1935 he had left behind so many records, so many "more thans," and so much of everything a player could do—and do better than anyone else—that a new word was coined to describe what it meant to be Olympian in a baseball uniform. The word was *Ruthian*. It's been used for baseball's super deeds ever since, as in Big Mac's 70—simply Ruthian!

The top 20 rookies presented in Part I of *Rookies Rated* fashioned the very best rookie seasons in the game's history. No, the Babe's 2.8 in 1915 isn't among them, but the 20 at the top were indeed Ruthian during their freshman campaigns.

From Curt Davis' 7.8 season in 1934 to Freddie Lynn's banner 1975 campaign, the peerless achievements presented here are studded with the kind of credentials that make for superlative seasons and merit the rewards that go with them. So good were these freshmen whizzes that many of them put together the game's best individual marks during the year they came up as rookies, brushing aside many of the game's established stars.

Hall of Famers? Eventually "Kid" Nichols and "Iron Man" McGinnity, colorful hurlers of a bygone-but-not-forgotten era that featured 30-plus winning seasons, .400-plus BA and 400-plus innings of work, found their way into baseball's Valhalla. Most Valuable Players? How about Fred Lynn's 1975 season, an unprecedented year for first-year honors when his magnificence in every phase of the game left baseball scribes with no choice but to select him as the American League's MVP—as a rookie, no less!

Unknown heroes? Billy Rhines, Jimmy Williams and Vean Gregg, not your typical household baseball hero names, are three great ones to start with. Well-knowns? How about pitcher Wilcy Moore, a Yankee from that 1927 powerhouse? Or Mike Piazza, or "Shoeless Joe," or "The Bird" Mark Fidrych? All of them, as well as the rest of this intriguing top 20, authored sensational seasons their first time around the horn in the Bigs.

Curtis Benton
"Coonskin" Davis

TPR: 7.8

1934, Philadelphia, NL

Born: September 7, 1903, Greenfield, MO. Died: October 10, 1965, Covina, CA
RHP, 6'2" 185 lb. Major League Debut: April 21, 1934
1934: W19, L17; .528 W%; GP 51; 3/5 SH-SV; 54 PR; 2.95 ERA; 9 DEF

Two young pitchers made their professional baseball debut in 1928 with the Salt Lake City Bees of the Utah-Idaho League. One, a 17-year-old portsider with a scorching fastball, led the league in whiffs with 172. The other, a lean, 21-year-old right-hander, tied for the league lead in wins with 16. The lefty was Vernon Gomez, later known as the one and only "El Goofo," who would go on to Yankee and Hall of Fame glory. The other, Curt Davis, was a rangy, breaking-ball pitcher who in 1934 would author the greatest rookie season in the history of the game.

Curt Davis is not a household name even among baseball's more knowledgeable fans. So it would come as no surprise if an arched eyebrow where raised here and there at the mention of his name in connection with all-time records and achievements. But what Curt Davis, who picked up the colorful nickname "Coonskin" in his earlier hunting days, accomplished in

his maiden voyage around the National League cities in 1934 earned him the number one claim to the "Greatest Rookie" title. How that came about will be explored a little further on.

After the 1928 season both Davis and Gomez were moved along to San Francisco of the Pacific Coast League where, in 1929, Gomez was an 18-game winner and Davis, a winner 17 times. Then they parted company, each to l is own baseball destiny.

In contrast to Gomez, whose Yankee career began in 1930, Davis served a full minor league apprenticeship, finally surfacing, at 28, in the City of Brotherly Love after a five-season stint with San Francisco, where, incidentally, Joe DiMaggio became a teammate in 1933. Davis was more than ready for his major league debut. By that time he had logged an impressive PCL record of 90–77. His 1932 mark showcased a league-leading 2.24 ERA, and in 1933, when he added another 20-game season to

15

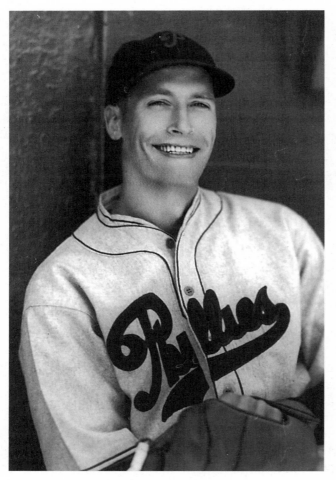

Curt Davis, whose 1934 rookie year was the finest in major league history. (Brace Photo.)

close with 19, Coonskin was fortunate, at that, to put that many notches on his victory belt.

Working in front of a porous defense, Davis soon found that if there was a way to lose a ball game, this team would find it. For example, in his first starting assignment of the season on April 21, the Dodgers beat him, 3–1, when a miscue here and an overrun base there snuffed out any hope of notching his first major league win. That didn't come until May 9, when the Pirates became his first victim. In fact, through mid–May he stood at 1 and 3, and was called on by manager Jimmie Wilson for an additional five relief appearances. Then, on May 20, in one of those rare instances that summer when hitting, pitching, fielding, baserunning — the whole game — came together, the big fellow beat Pittsburgh once again, 16 to 4. He followed up on that one four days later with a three-hit shutout over the Reds to even his record at 3 and 3. Though it would be a struggle each time out, Curt was on his way, and before it was all over, his record sparkled, given circumstances in Philadelphia, with 19 wins — three of them shutouts — and five saves, thus involving him in 24 wins out of the 56 the club managed to scrape together.

One of the more scintillating of those victories came on September 25, at the Polo Grounds, when Davis zapped the front-running Giants, 4 to 0, on a four-hitter, to post his final win of the year. The box score appears on page 5.

Four days later, Davis' name was

his minor league record, the Phillies came calling via the draft.

The quarter century between 1919 and the close of World War II was a long, long stretch of misery for Phillie fans. During that time the Phils wound up dead last 16 times and in 7th place another five seasons. Though 1934 was another one of "those years," the Phils, thanks to Cincinnati, escaped the cellar, though still suffering 93 pastings. The season's bright spots could be counted on a few fingers, and Curt Davis played a part in most of them. Winning 20 games with the '34 Phillies took some doing. And though he came

Box Score

Philadelphia Phillies at the Polo Grounds, New York, September 24, 1934

Philadelphia	AB	R	H	PO	A
G. Davis, cf	4	0	0	2	0
Bartell, ss	4	1	1	1	4
Chiozza, 2b	4	0	3	2	2
John Moore, rf	4	1	2	3	0
Camilli, 1b	4	0	0	12	1
Allen, lf	4	0	2	0	0
Walters, 2b	2	1	0	0	1
Wilson, c	3	1	2	6	0
C. Davis, p	4	0	1	1	3
Totals	33	4	11	27	11

New York	AB	R	H	PO	A
Joe Moore, lf	4	0	0	1	0
Critz, 2b	4	0	1	2	5
Terry, 1b	3	0	1	13	1
Ott, rf	4	0	0	3	1
Jackson, ss-3b	4	0	0	3	2
Watkins, cf	4	0	1	2	0
Mancuso, c	2	0	1	1	2
Weintraub, ph	0	0	0	0	0
Danning, c	1	0	0	1	1
Vergez, 3b	1	0	0	0	0
Ryan, ss	2	0	0	1	5
O'Doul, ph	1	0	0	0	0
Fitzsimmons, p	1	0	0	0	2
Smith, p	1	0	0	0	0
Luque, p	0	0	0	0	2
Totals	32	0	4	27	21

Philadelphia	002	200	000	4-11-1
New York	000	000	000	0-4-1

RBI	Chiozza, Wilson 2
BB	Fitzsimmons 1, Luque 1, Davis 2
K	Fitzsimmons 1, Luque 1, Davis 6
Umpires	Moran, Magerkurth, Stewart

penciled into the Phils' opening lineup for a crack at 20 wins. That attempt against the Braves went well through seven innings, with the Phillies holding a shaky 1–0 lead. But in the eighth stanza the Braves wrote *fini* to the rawboned Missourian's effort, chasing him with a four-run outburst, and handing the Phils a 7–1 scrubbing. That denied Davis a 20-win season and closed out his year-long, uphill effort at 19 and 17. His final ERA reading (2.95) was a full run below the National League average (4.06), fourth lowest in the league behind "King Carl" Hubbell's pace-setting 2.30. But Davis' extraordinary freshman campaign was marked by a good deal more. For one thing, he was the best fielding pitcher in the majors in 1934, and turned out to be one of the very best in the game's history. His 9 reading on the sabermetric Pitcher's Defense rating index is among the top all-time rankings, and his

average over 12 full seasons at 1.8 DEF per season ranks among the all time leaders.

Cat-quick and long-armed, Coonskin covered the middle of the infield like a groundskeeper's tarp. In 1934 he was in on 12 double plays, tieing the major league standard established in 1924 by another Philadelphian, Eddie Rommel of the Athletics. Davis' lifetime Fielding Average, .974, stands as one of the better averages among hurlers with over 2,000 innings pitched. In 429 major league games he committed but 21 errors while chalking up 616 assists.

In 274.1 innings pitched, Davis issued only 60 free passes (he never walked a batter intentionally), averaging only one for every 4.1 innings pitched. His career average was even better, at one per five innings pitched. That suggests far better than average control, and his control came to characterize his pitching. Not possessed of

90+ mph speed, he put the black edges of the plate to work, relying on breaking stuff and his finely tuned control to get him by. And it did.

The premier rookie season in baseball history is not a story about one pitching success piled atop another. To be sure, such seasons are an interesting, if not inspiring, part of the best the game has produced. The Yankees' Russ Ford's 26 and 6 in 1910, Elmer Riddle's 19 and 4 for Cincinnati in 1941, and Ben Sanders' 19 and 10 (including a league-leading eight shutouts for the Phils at the old Huntington Grounds park in 1888) are examples.

Curt Davis, on the other hand, faced a situation in 1934 that would require a massive dose of heroics just to stay even while pitching for the worst fielding team in baseball. Moreover, the team played half its schedule at Philadelphia's Baker Bowl, a veritable graveyard for National League pitchers, what with its cozy, hitter-friendly dimensions.

Despite the handicaps, the gritty and determined Coonskin worked his way into the All-Star break just over the .500 level with a 9 and 7 record, achieved with a typical 11 to 10 Baker Bowl slugfest victory over the Braves that followed two successive relief appearances on July 5 and 6, when the winning tallies read 14 to 11 and 16 to 13. Such was life in Philly, where the exercise was, well, survival rather than the slick artistry of the Giants at the Polo Grounds or the Cubs at the friendly confines of Wrigley Field.

When His Daffiness, Paul Dean, beat the Phils on June 17, it broke Curt's win streak at six. That streak, his best stretch of the season, included his first shutout, a 5–3 hit effort against Cincinnati, and a 2–1 squeaker won by an Ethan Allen homer in the eighth. By the end of July he had surged to a 14 and 8 record and had beaten every team in the league.

While the Cardinals, powered by the St. Louis Gashouse bunch, the Giants of Bill Terry, and the Cubs, under "Jolly Cholly" Grimm, fought for laurels, the Phillies and Reds, along with Pirates and Dodgers from time to time, were waging their own dogfight to escape the league's cellar. That had its effect on the Davis record, as well. By season's end his very respectable 14 and 8 had just about evaporated into thin air under one Phillie misfiring after another. The month of August was particularly disastrous. Curt came up absolutely empty, losing games he started and in relief. For example, the log read 3 to 2, 3 to 1, 6 to 5 in relief, 2 to 1, and 3 to 2 to Carl Hubbell over a disturbing span from August 19 to 28. In at least two of those five games, Davis might have won rather than lost, which would have put him over the magic 20-win mark every pitcher strives for, a plateau he finally achieved, for the only time in his career, as a Cardinal in 1939 with a 22 and 16 record.

Before his final loss of the season, however, Coonskin came through to right a few wrongs with a 4 to 2 win in relief in the 13th inning against Brooklyn and a spiffy 4–0 whitewashing of the Giants, shutting them down on four well-spaced hits. The final reading on his rookie year then read 19 and 17.

How, then, does Davis stack up against the best rookies in 1934? And, for that matter, how does his just-better-than-.500 record rate an awesome 7.8 TPR, the equivalent of some eight victories more than a league-average player, who would be rated an 0.0, might have contributed?

The answers to the first question are provided in the first of our Top Ten lists that accompany each player profile. There, the best rookies of the 1934 season are presented, along with some of the more telling sabermetric numbers, as well as the usual ERA and batting averages, which help to calculate their seasonal TPR. You will not fail to notice the huge gap between Bobo

Newsom's 3.2 (still good enough to get him into the all-time top 100) and Curt Davis' record-setting 7.8.

Two significant numbers brand Davis' achievements as exceptional in 1934. The first, Pitching Runs, at 54, is almost good enough to make the top 100, all time. This calculation, as adjusted to the idiosyncrasies of Baker Bowl, indicates how many runs a pitcher, on the strength of his season-long performance, was able to save his team. Curt Davis started 31 games and appeared in 20 more in other capacities, chiefly relief pitching, for a total of 51 appearances. That 54 rating represents just a little more than a run per game, an outstanding mark. The second, his 9 rating for Pitcher Defense (or DEF), is a rare achievement. Most pitchers never rise above the 2 to 3 level. Davis recorded a 9 and followed that up with one 4 rating, three at 3 and five more at 2. His rookie rating was a career high and ranks as the eighth highest reading ever recorded. That in itself is a remarkable accomplishment, but more importantly, when thrown into the mix of numbers used to calculate a pitcher's TPR, it raises the final season rating — significantly.

Before Davis' last major league pitch had been thrown, there was an All-Star Game appearance in 1934 that immediately followed the stunning Carl Hubbell sequence of strikeouts over the American League sluggers, from Ruth through Joe Cronin, a starting assignment for Brooklyn in the 1941 World Series in which he pitched well at Yankee Stadium but was charged with the Dodgers' 3 to 2 loss, and that 22 and 16 season with the Cardinals in 1939. All of these accomplishments graced a fine, though largely unheralded, career.

Although bypassed by the usual run of postseason all-star teams and honors, he was not forgotten by Bill Deane, the respected sabermetrician and baseball historian who selected Curtis Benton Davis as the Hypothetical Rookie of the Year for 1934. Deane's awards filled in the years between the start of the 20th century and the first year of BBWAA Rookie of the Year selections, which began in 1947 with the selection of Jackie Robinson. Davis' selection is an acknowledgment of the brilliance he brought to an otherwise lackluster Philadelphia scene during those drab Depression years when neither the economy, nor the ballclubs representing the City of the Liberty Bell had much to cheer about. At least as long as he was with the Phillies in 1934 and 1935, Coonskin gave them all reason to believe something good might happen. And more often than not — it did!

1934: Ten Top Rookies

Nm/Pos/TM	GP	W–L/BA	SH/SV/RBI	PR/BR	ERA/FR	TPR
Curt Davis/RHP/Phl-N	51	19–17	3/5	54	2.95	7.8
L. "Bobo" Newsom/RHP/StL-A	47	16–20	5/2	29	4.01	3.2
F. Ostermueller/LHPBos-A	33	10–13	3/0	29	3.49	3.1
Bill DeLancey/c/StL-N	93	.316	40	18	5	2.5
Hal Trosky/1b/Clv-A	154	.330	142	42	0	2.5
John Murphy/RHP (RP)/NY-A	40	14–10	0/4	22	3.12	2.5
Paul Dean/RHP/StL-N	39	19–11	5/2	21	3.43	1.9
Dutch Leonard/RHP/Brk-N	44	14–11	2/5	13	3.28	1.7
Hy. "Zeke" Bonura/1b/Chi-A	127	.302	110	22	5	1.4
Big Bill Lee/RHP/Chi-N	35	13–14	4/1	11	3.40	1.2

Joseph Jefferson
"Shoeless Joe" Jackson

TPR: 6.8

1911, Cleveland, AL

Born: July 16, 1889, Brandon Mills, SC. Died: December 5, 1951, Greenville, SC
OF, 6'1" 200 lb. Major League Debut: August 25, 1908
1911: 147 GP; 226 H; 126 R; 19 3BH; .408 BA; .468 OB%; 70 BR; 41 SB; 8 FR

It took Ty Cobb's whirlwind 1911 campaign to better Shoeless Joe Jackson's rookie year extravaganza. In a season that featured offensive pyrotechnics in both leagues, the Cleveland Indians had their own fireworks with a ballclub that hit .282 (some 38 points higher than its 1910 average), introduced their fans to the outstanding rookie pitcher in the American League (Vean Gregg), improved their standing in the league, and turned loose Joseph Jefferson Jackson on major league pitching. No, Jackson didn't win the batting championship. In fact, he led the league in only one category, On-Base Percentage, at .468. But then, there wasn't much left to go around after Ty Cobb had swept everything in sight, including baseball's very first MVP award. But the 21-year-old rookie wasn't very far behind, and many of the numbers he posted in 1911 are unsurpassed as all-time rookie standards, as well as club records. That will get our undivided attention a bit later.

After a couple nearly disastrous cup-o'-coffee appearances in Philadelphia during the 1908 and 1909 seasons, the Shoeless One was bundled off by Connie Mack to Cleveland, and baseball became fun again for the youngster. Cleveland owner Charley Somers, Mr. E. S. Barnard, the club's front office Secretary, managers Deacon McGuire and George Stovall, and teammate chums Larry Lajoie, Jack Graney, Vean Gregg, and Terry Turner all respected Joe Jackson for what he was, one of the greatest natural ballplayers to wear a major league uniform. There were no pretentions, he wasn't belittled because he was an illiterate country boy, and he was a welcome part of everything the team did. In short, they accepted him, something that was definitely *not* a part of his Philadelphia experience.

Joe thrived in Cleveland. Though he would ultimately wind up with Chicago's 1917 world champions — and as one of the

"Eight Men Out" on Charley Comiskey's 1919 Black Sox — he would always remember his Cleveland days with a special warmth as the best days of his life.

It wasn't as though South Carolina's finest gift to major league baseball snuck up on the Show's blind side. He left calling cards wherever he played, with three successive batting championships: his first coming during his initial season in professional baseball at Greenville, South Carolina; another the very next season, 1909, at Savannah in the South Atlantic League; and a third straight in 1910 in New Orleans, where he was the Big Easy's toast of the town. In each of those three seasons he was brought up to the majors for a look-see, twice with the Athletics and, finally, with Cleveland after a player-purchase deal at $6,000 had been worked out with Ben Shibe's A's in 1910.

It didn't take Jackson long to warm to the task. He played in 20 late-season games, hitting at a .387 clip (this time his calling card had been left for *American League* pitchers), stealing a few bases, throwing out a couple baserunners, and, with one sharp laser shot, crushing a Bob Groom offering against the Senators for his first major league home run on September 17. All of this was prelude, a foretaste of what was in store for fans in the Forest City, who would come to love him as much as they respected their awesome team leader, Nap Lajoie. Neither the Cleveland fans nor their 21-year-old star could wait for another season to come. And when 1911's opener rolled around they were ready.

What Nap's followers were *not* ready for, however, was the numbing news of the death of Addie Joss, who had succumbed to tubercular meningitis on Opening Day, April 14. Team members, making arrangements to attend the funeral, were shocked to learn that the Tigers were not minded to postpone their Opening Day festivities.

Led by their first baseman, George Stovall, who was named the new manager later that season, the players revolted. Ultimately, owner Charles Somers stepped in, the opener *was* postponed, and the players attended the popular hurler's funeral.

The death of their star pitcher had a number of after-effects, including player and managerial changes. Stovall's elevation to manager was but one of them. Another was billed as baseball's first All-Star benefit, staged on July 26 before a supportive throng of 15,270. (Shoeless Joe, at the time involved in a torrid struggle for the batting crown, started in right field for the Naps. Though the Naps lost to the All Stars 6–3, the score mattered little.)

There was still another change that affected Jackson's rookie season — mightily. That was the ball. During the latter stages of the 1910 season, a ball with a cork centerpiece was introduced. It was also used intermittently during the Cubs-Athletics World Series games. The results, though not sustained beyond the 1913 season, were initially, at least, quite dramatic. The real "schlagmeisters" didn't need cork-centered baseballs to help along their batting averages, and Joe Jackson was certainly one of them, callow rookie or not. But it didn't hurt matters either, and from day one of the 1911 season, the hitting spectacular, which lasted all season long, was on. The final results? There were 19 more .300 hitters in 1911 than in 1910, the American League overall batting average jumped 30 points, and the league ERA dropped to 3.34 in 1911 from its lofty 2.53 perch in 1910. There was *some* hittin' goin' on. There were *some* hitters making the rounds, too; and the kid who couldn't read or write, the one with that black-barreled howitzer, was one of them. And so the batting wars raged on, right on down to the last ball game of the season. The fans, of course, were transfixed.

Joe Jackson brought more than sharp

Shoeless Joe Jackson, "The Natural." (Brace Photo.)

Though the Naps lost to Ty Cobb and Co. on May 1, Joe opened up the Merry Month with the first four-hit day of his career. It wasn't the last and further, he added a number of five-hit days to his list of hitting accomplishments. By mid–June his many multiple-hit games began to add up to a serious run on the fabled Cobb for batting honors. At .390 as of June 19, he was within striking distance of the front-running "Georgia Peach" (.428) and Eddie Collins of the A's (.392). There were a few others, like Tris Speaker of the Red Sox, the Senators' Clyde Milan, Homerun Baker and Danny Murphy of the pace-setting Athletics, and Sam Crawford of the Tigers, who were pounding that brand new, cork-centered pellett at a pretty good clip. There were 33, in all, who were over the coveted .300 mark.

Shortly after Independence Day, Joe's personal enemies came to town. If there was any team in the league he wanted to do well against, it was the Athletics of Connie Mack — though not Mack so much as some of those snobs from the college campus Mack seemed to collect on his ballclub. His resentment lingered and festered from his Philadelphia days.

On July 6, Jackson would have one of the many big days he was to enjoy against the Mackmen during his career. Teammate Vean Gregg, the other Cleveland rookie find, snuffed the A's, overpowering them

eyes, that silk-smooth swing and a canon-arm to the game. There was also that unique "Jackson Crack" that exploded across the field when "Black Betsy" made contact with the ball. The very sound sent chills through pitchers, oohs and aahs through the stands, and put knowing smiles on the faces of teammates. Once heard, it was never forgotten. It was, quite simply, the ultimate Jackson trademark.

Box Score

July 6, 1911, Philadelphia at Cleveland

Philadelphia	AB	H	PO	A	E
Lord, lf	4	0	0	3	0
Oldring, cf	3	1	1	0	0
Murphy, rf	3	1	0	0	0
Baker, 3b	4	0	2	3	0
McInnes, 1B	4	1	10	0	0
Barry, ss	4	0	4	1	0
Derrick, 2b	3	1	1	4	1
Thomas, c	3	0	6	2	1
Morgan, p	2	0	0	2	0
Long, p	0	0	0	0	0
Livingston, ph*	1	0	0	0	0
Strunk, pr†	0	0	0	0	0
Totals	31	4	24	15	2

Cleveland	AB	H	PO	A	E
Graney, lf	4	2	2	0	0
Olson, ss	3	1	5	3	1
Jackson, rf	4	3	3	0	0
Stovall, 1b	4	1	10	0	0
Birmingham, cf	3	0	2	0	0
Griggs, 2b	4	3	0	3	0
Mills, 3b	3	1	1	0	0
Fisher, c	3	2	4	1	0
Gregg, p	2	0	0	3	0
Totals	30	13	27	10	1

```
Philadelphia   000   000   000   0-4-2
Cleveland      002   110   000   4-13-1
```

2BH	Graney, Jackson
SB	Griggs
BB	Gregg, 1; Morgan, 2
K	Gregg, 4; Morgan, 3; Long, 1
HPB	Gregg, 1
Umpire	Billy Evans

on a diet of four scratch hits in a 4–0 whitewashing.

Meantime Joe's Black Betsy was busy. There were a couple of singles and a run-producing double that had the sellout Cleveland crowd in an uproar. It was, furthermore, a victory that kept the home-standing Naps in the thick of the hunt with contenders Chicago and Detroit and the pace-setting A's.

As Labor Day began the last furlong of the season, the pennant was all but signed, sealed and delivered to Philadelphia. Not so the various races for individual honors. As of August 25 the table below shows what the Junior Circuit batting race looked like (Top 5, 100 GP or more).

At season's end Cobb (.420), Jackson (.408), and Cree (.348) would be joined by Eddie Collins (.365) and Sam Crawford (.378) among the top five in the American League. Jackson would take home 13 second-place finishes in major hitting categories, lead in one and end up third in triples. His runner-up finishes would have swept almost every major hitting category in all

Nm/Tm	*GP*	*AB*	*H*	*TB*	*SB*	*BA*
Cobb, Det	112	448	189	285	61	.421
Jackson, Clv	111	431	106	257	30	.408
Cree, NY	115	454	157	235	35	.348
Delehanty, Det	112	419	146	203	14	.348
Murphy, Phl	110	395	134	193	19	.339

*Batted for Morgan in 8th
†Ran for Baker in 9th

but five or six major league seasons in the history of the American League to date!

During the course of that wondrous 1911 season, Joe put together a 28-game hitting streak (good for another second place spot, this time on the all-time club list), added 41 stolen bases, and amassed a career high 32 assists. In 1912 he posted another 30 assists, and in 1913, 28. By that time the baserunners around the league finally got the message: Don't try to run on Joe!

Jackson's orbital rookie season left a number of records in its wake, the most significant of which was his 6.8 TPR, which ranks 90th in the game's history, and is the highest single-season rating for rookies among position players. The 6.8 puts him in second place behind pitcher Curt Davis. Among position players he ranks three notches above the Phillies' Dick Allen, at 5.8, in fifth place on the rookie honors list.

Four Cleveland franchise records belong to Shoeless Joe: highest lifetime batting average (.375 over five seasons), highest single-season batting average (.408, which is listed at number 14, all time), most base hits in a single season (233, which is also the all-time standard for rookies), and most triples in a single season (26 in 1912, which ranks at number nine, all time). Jackson's league-leading On-Base Percentage in 1911, .468, ranks a lofty number 72 all time, and the 7.1 Batting Wins he registered in that magnificent rookie year of 1911 puts him in the number 60 spot all-time.

Say what you will about the Black Sox, or his conspicuous absence in the Hall of Fame, no one will ever be able to take away his Cleveland days, when the springtime of his career brought on what might, albeit arguably, be called the game's greatest natural talent, and with it the "Jackson Crack" that made Black Betsy famous. It was during those years that Shoeless Joe Jackson showed them all that the hick from the South Carolina countryside could play nose to nose with the game's greatest.

1911: Ten Top Rookies

Nm/Tm/Pos/ATRR	GP	W–L/BA	SH/SV//RBI	PR/A//BR	ERA/FR	TPR
Joe Jackson, Clv-A, of, 2	147	.408	83	70	8	6.8
Vean Gregg, Clv-A, LHP, 17	34	23–7	5/0	44	1.80	4.7
Gr. Alexander, Phl-N, RHP, 44	48	28–13	7/3	35	2.57	3.6
Thos. O'Brien, Bos-A, RHP, NR	6	5–1	2/0	15	0.38	2.0
James Doyle, Chi-N, 3b, NR	130	.282	62	5	10	1.6
Frank Bodie, Chi-A, of, NR	145	.289	97	7	7	0.9
Sum Caldwell, NY-A, RHP, NR	41	14–14	1/1	7	3.55	0.8
Irish Corhan, Chi-A, ss, NR	43	.214	8	-5	11	0.8
Gus Fisher, Clv-A, c, NR	70	.261	12	-8	8	0.5
Olaf Henricksen, Bos-A, of, NR	27	.366	8	6	0	0.4

Charles Augustus "Kid" Nichols

TPR: 6.7

1890, Boston, NL

Born: September 14, 1869, Madison, WI. Died: April 11, 1953, Kansas City, MO
RHP, 5'11" 175 lb. Major League Debut: April 23, 1890
1890: W27, L19; 47/47, GS/GC; .587 W%; 424 IP; 7/0 SH/SV; 72 PR; 2.23 ERA
Hall of Fame: 1949

The hummer. Gas. Heat. Kid Nichols had it. The boy wonder of the 1890s, whose blinding speed and exceptional control (over his 15-year career he walked but one man per four innings pitched) turned the '90s of another century into his own Boston-based showcase, simply blew away the National League's finest. During that swashbuckling decade he rang up 30-win seasons seven times, posting 20 or more wins from 1890, his awesome rookie year, through 1899. That's the stuff from which Hall of Fame elections are made, and that's precisely what happened in 1949 when baseball's supreme honor was conferred on the fireballing right-hander at Cooperstown.

Kid Nichols, with the third highest Total Player Rating for a single season among first year men, thus becomes the foremost HOFer on the Rookies Honor List, and it brings into focus the performance ratings of the six players who grace the top 50 listing of extraordinary rookie seasons. The listing of HOF luminaries follows (with additional names through the top 100 rookie seasons in baseball history, plus some likely additions in years ahead).

Leading the league in shutouts with seven and Pitching Runs with a titanic 72, which ranked him at 21 on the all time PR listing, Nichols, along with John Clarkson (26–18) and Charlie Getzien (23–17), kept the Boston Beaneaters* in the 1890 pennant race well into the season. True, he had a few things still to learn, but during his initial season in the Bigs, he proved he belonged.

Boston's National League team played under several team names, including Red Stockings, Red Caps, Beaneaters, Nationals, Doves, Rustlers, Bees, and the Braves, their most familiar team name, still used by Atlanta.

Nm/RYr	HOF*	RYTPR†
Kid Nichols, 1890	1949	6.7
Ted Williams, 1939	1966	4.3
Joe Morgan, 1965	1990	4.3
Christy Mathewson, 1901	1936	4.1
Grover Alexander, 1911	1938	3.6
Elmer Flick, 1898	1963	3.5
Rogers Hornsby, 1916	1942	3.5
Paul Waner, 1926	1952	3.1
Kiki Cuyler, 1924	1968	3.0
Joe DiMaggio, 1936	1955	3.0
Billy Herman, 1932	1975	3.0

Top 100 Rookies likely to be elected to the Hall of Fame
Carlton Fisk, 4.4 TPR, 1972
Ozzie Smith, 3.5 TPR, 1978
Mark McGwire, 3.3 TPR, 1987
Kenny Lofton, 3.3 TPR, 1992

Others who might be elected by the HOF Veterans Committee:
Tony Oliva, 4.1 TPR, 1964
Wes Ferrell, 3.4 TPR, 1929
Joe Gordon, 3.2 TPR, 1938
Thurman Munson, 3.0 TPR, 1970

"The Kid," so named because he was not only a mere stripling when he signed his first professional contract with Kansas City of the Western League at 17 in 1887, was, further, blessed with youthful good looks. The handle stuck, but it was about the only boyish thing about him. Kid Nichols, mature beyond his years, was equal to the rough-hewn life of the baseball fraternity, and, with that heater of his, soon had minor league hitters eating out of his hand. Especially impressive was his 1889 showing with Omaha, where his 39 wins and league-leading numbers in whiffs (368) and winning percentage (.830, based on his 39–8 record), overwhelmed the Western Association.

It was Nichols' good fortune to play under the able Frank Selee, who had a justly deserved reputation as a heady manager, good organizer, and, with it all, a nose for exceptional talent. Imagine his de-

light in "finding" the ace of his Omaha staff at his disposal day in, day out! And when the summons came from the Beaneaters late in 1889, you could have bet the farm that he made certain the Kid was on the train with him.

But there is still more. Selee, who built his championship teams in Boston around the strongest pitching staff in the league, started the 1890 campaign with Nichols, Clarkson and Getzien, but soon added Jack Stivetts, and later, Ted Lewis, Freddie Klobedanz and Vic Willis (HOF, 1995). The latter three, with Nichols, won all but one game for the 1898 pennant-winning team. The quartette's total was 101, with Nichols' 31 victories leading the way. They just missed, by one, becoming baseball's first foursome of 20-game winners, as the rookie Klobedanz logged a 19–10 record that year. The pivot point, however, to Boston's glorious run in the '90s was the

HOF = Hall of Fame election year
†RYTPR = Rookie year Total Player Rating

coming of the new skipper, Selee, and his prize find, Kid Nichols, who would start things off with his herculean rookie season and quickly become both staff ace and rallying point.

All of this was initiated in 1890 against a background of seething discontent among owners, leagues (the Player's League and the American Association fielded teams as well as the National League), players, commissions and just about everyone else associated with professional baseball. It was bound to have an effect on the game, and it did. Into that cauldron came the Kid. But the young Mr. Nichols and his Beaneater teammates went about their business despite the swirl of chaos all around them. Frank Selee saw to that. Additionally, it should be kept in mind that pitchers were still doing their hurling from 50' away; the 60'6" measure-

Hall of Famer Kid Nichols, "The Beantown Beauty." (Brace Photo.)

Box Score

At New York, May 12, 1890

Boston	AB	R	H	PO	A
Tucker, 1b	5	0	0	21	0
McGarr, 3b	5	0	0	0	2
Sullivan, lf	3	0	1	0	0
Long, ss	4	0	0	1	9
Brodie, cf	4	0	1	2	0
Hardie, c	4	0	0	10	2
Smith, 2b	3	0	0	5	4
Schellhase, rf	4	0	0	0	0
Nichols, p	4	0	1	0	2
Totals	36	0	3	39	14

New York	AB	R	H	PO	A
Tiernan, cf	6	1	2	2	0
Glasscock, ss	6	0	0	5	2
Esterbrook, 1b	5	0	0	14	0
Bassett, 2b	5	0	0	3	4
Clarke, rf	5	0	0	0	0
Denny, 3b	5	0	1	3	1
Hornung, lf	5	0	0	2	0
Buckley, c	5	0	0	10	2
Rusie, p	5	0	1	0	2
Totals	47	1	4	39	14

Note: New York opted to bat first, though they were the home team at the Polo Grounds.

New York	000	000	000	000	1	1-4-2
Boston	000	000	000	000	0	0-3-5

Home Run, RBI	Tiernan, 13th inning, over center field wall
SB	Tiernan, Glasscock
Sacrifice hits	Glasscock, Tucker, Bassett
LOB	New York 6; Boston 5
BB	Rusie, 2; Nichols, 1
K	Rusie, 11; Nichols, 10
Passed Ball	Hardie
Umpires	Powers and McDermott
Time	2.01
Attendance	1,000 (est.)

ment between home plate and the pitcher's box wasn't introduced until the 1893 season. That tends to color any retrospective look at accomplishments, especially by pitchers, before the 1893 season. Nichols had an answer for that, too. He simply continued to mow batters down, emerging from the 1890s the fastest to 300 wins in a major league career. It clearly proved his freshman year was no fluke.

The most convincing evidence of Nichols' superiority was his ability to prevent opposing teams from running up big innings. The most one could hope for in an inning against the lean right hander was a run or two. Just to emphasize his point, Nichols threw no less than seven shutouts in his banner freshman season, and beyond that, one of his more disheartening losses, a 1–0, 13-inning downer to Amos Rusie (HOF 1977) at New York.

At that point in the season, May 12, Nichols had absorbed five losses against a pair of wins. Four of those five losses might just as easily have been victories, but there were things to learn, hitters to learn, and a pitching "portfolio" to develop. The education of a future Hall of Famer was underway — and the pupil was a willing learner.

Overcoming his early-season woes, Charles Nichols moved on to a 27 and 19 mark, starting — and completing — 47 assignments handed him by manager Selee. As the years rolled on he was to complete 531 of 561 starts, a mind-boggling .9465 percent. To put it simply, he wanted the ball, and he got it. A career 2.95 ERA attests to the fact that it wasn't very often that Selee had to give any thought to taking him out of a game because it was raining runs! There was a mental toughness about kid, furthermore, that kept him in

ball games despite bloop hits, errors, or physical adversities. Many years later, when asked to compare hurlers of the 1940s with those of the '90s, he said, matter of factly, "If I had a kink in the 'ole soupbone, I just kept on pitching until I worked it out. Most of us did. Nowadays they rush the pitcher off to the hospital. These young pitchers try too much fancy stuff and ruin their arms. I pitched with a straight overarm motion and never had much trouble."

Toiling through 424 innings in 1890, Nichols surrendered only 112 free passes while amassing 222 strikeouts, a margin that emphasized his control of the strike zone. His 2.23 ERA was second to Billy Rhines, the author of another superlative rookie season (the Cincinnati twirler follows Kid Nichols on the Honors List in fourth place among the greatest rookie seasons), who logged a stingy 1.95, to rank tops among the three major leagues. And, right: Nichols' 2.23 was the year's second best.

The Beaneaters' ace came through his rookie season with a 6.7 TPR that meant seven wins over the season beyond the league-average pitchers. Had he converted a few of those heartbreakers into victories, the net result might have put a Hall of Famer into the number one slot among rookie kingpins in major league baseball.

Ranking right up there among the five best pitchers of the 19th century — which include John Clarkson, Cy Young, Tim Keefe, and Charley Radbourne — is the pride of Boston, Charles Augustus Nichols. It's no stretch to put him in the number one spot among these fabled Hall of Famers. And in Boston? To this very day the Kid is the standard of excellence against which right-handed pitchers are measured.

Hall of Fame Pitchers: 20 Top Rookie Seasons

Nm/RY/HOF	GP	W–L	SH/SV	PR	DEF	ERA	TPR
Nichols/1890/1949	48	27–19	7/0	72	0	2.23	6.7

Nm/RY/HOF	GP	W–L	SH/SV	PR	DEF	ERA	TPR
Mathewson/1901/1936	40	20–17	5/0	33	8	2.41	4.1
Alexander/1911/1938	48	28–13	7/3	35	1	2.57	3.6
Cummings/1872/1939	55	33–20	3/0	51	–	2.52	3.1
Wilhelm/1952/1985	71	15–3	0/11	23	1	2.43	2.9
Ruth/1915/1936	32	18–8	1/0	8	1	2.44	2.8
Willis/1898/1995	41	25–13	1/0	30	0	2.84	2.5
Keefe/1880/1964	12	6–6	0/0	19	1	0.86	2.2
Joss/1902/1978	32	17–13	5/0	20	6	2.77	2.0
Rixey/1912/1963	23	10–10	3/0	20	-1	2.50	2.0
Clarkson/1884/1963	14	14–3	0/0	13	3	2.14	1.8
Hubbell/1928/1947	20	10–6	1/1	15	2	2.83	1.7
M. Brown/1903/1949	26	9–13	1/0	15	2	2.60	1.6
Drysdale/1956/1984	25	5–5	0/0	15	1	2.64	1.6
Spalding/1871/1939	31	19–10	1/0	23	–	3.36	1.6
E. Ford/1950/1974	20	9–1	2/1	18	0	2.81	1.5
Roberts/1948/1976	20	7–9	0/0	12	-2	3.19	1.5
Lemon/1946/1976	32	4–5	0/1	9	4	2.49	1.3
Vance/1922/1955	36	18–12	5/0	10	0	3.70	1.3
Feller/1936/1962	14	5–3	0/1	12	-1	3.34	1.1
Wynn/1941/1972	5	3–1	0/0	11	0	1.57	1.1

Ties listed alphabetically

Legend:

Nm/RY/HOF	Player's name, Rookie Year, Hall of Fame election year
GP	Games Pitched
SH/SV	Shutouts and Saves in Rookie Year
PR	Pitching Runs (adjusted) in Rookie Year
DEF	Pitcher's defensive rating

William Pearl "Billy" Rhines

TPR: 6.5

1890, Cincinnati, NL

Born: March 14, 1869, Ridgway, PA. Died: January 30, 1922, Ridgway, PA
RHP, 5'11" 168 lb. Major League Debut: April 22, 1890
1890: W28, L17; 6/0 SH/SV; .281 OB%; 72 PR; 1.95 ERA

Dating back to the first season of organized ball in 1871, there have been four years during which three major leagues have vied for the top talent, financial support and facilities necessary to play the game at the professional level. The first such season was in 1884, when the newly formed Union Association joined the American Association, organized in 1882, and the National League in presenting major league ball in some 25 cities from the eastern seaboard to the Mississippi River.

In 1890 the Player's League, like the Union Association before it, operated for its only season in competition with the American Association and the National League. The final, three-league seasons were played out during 1914 and 1915, when the Federal League brought baseball to fans in 12 different cities during its two-year existence. Each time professional baseball broke out into more than two major leagues there have been at least these two similar underlying causes: 1) competition for a place in the baseball sun and 2) player and owner disputes over contractual and legal matters involved in governing the game.

In 1890, the year Kid Nichols, Bob Allen of the Phillies, and Billy Rhines had outstanding rookie seasons in the National League, pro ball at the highest level agonized its way through one of its most chaotic seasons, playing out the year in three leagues that barely made it from April to October. Under those circumstances there were bound to be some bizarre goings-on. There were times when teams were down to the bucketboy after injuries or illness or hangovers or travel problems had depleted the ranks of the able-bodied. Umpires sometimes just didn't get there. Payrolls were delayed or even cancelled. The litany goes on and on.

However, what most affected the

game in that wild, topsy-turvy environment was the thinning of playing talent. That had an immediate effect on the caliber of play in general, and on pitching in particular. Since pitching is our prime concern in the Billy Rhines rookie season profile, it might be well to take a look at what baseball's cognoscenti understand to be 80 percent of the game, that is, pitching.

Let's turn our attention first to how the best pitchers in the three leagues performed. The listing below presents some of the salient numbers that paced the three circuits.

Compared with pitchers' statistics from the past fifty years, these numbers are gargantuan. Won-lost totals, the number of innings pitched and the number of games started and completed seem to present-day baseball buffs surrealistic. The *fewest* number of innings pitched by a member of the 1890's top ten was John Healy's 389, and Bill Hutchison, of Chicago's National League "Orphans" (the Cubs moniker came later), was sent to the hill by manager Cap Anson for a mammoth 603 innings of work. The pitchers in this list *averaged* 53 starts during 1890, *completing* 50 games during the course of the season. Think about that for a moment or two.

There were primarily two circumstances that caused the immense workload the pitchers toiled under in the three leagues. For one thing, the day of larger pitching staffs carried by major league

Billy Rhines, Red Stockings' hurler. (Brace Photo.)

ballclubs had not yet arrived. The starting rotation, if it can even be called that, was usually limited to two and at most three twirlers who were left in the ball game no matter the score or how many innings were played. For another, it was a matter of pride among pitchers to pitch as often and as long as necessary. No one turned to see if the bullpen was stirring. There was no bullpen. Nor was there enough talent around capable of answering big-time pitching demands.

With that little primer on 1890s pitching behind, the focus shifts to the numbers of rookie sensation Billy Rhines, to see how the Cincinnati right hander fared during 1890's season of discontent. To begin with, we note that he fell in line directly behind Boston's prize first year man, Kid Nichols. These two hurlers were the only rookies to break into 1890's top ten pitchers in the three leagues. Both authored superlative seasons. Nichols used his 1890 season as a prelude to dominating NL hitters throughout the '90s, ultimately finding his way to the Hall of Fame.

Nm/Tm-L	W–L	W%	GS/GC	IP	ERA	TPR
Scott Stratton/Lou-AA	34–14	.708	49/44	431.0	2.36	8.9
Charles "Silver" King/Chi-PL	30–22	.577	56/48	461.0	2.69	7.1
Amos Rusie/ NY-NL	29–34	.460	62/56	548.2	2.56	6.9
Charles "Kid" Nichols/Bos-NL	27–19	.587	47/47	424.0	2.23	6.7
Billy Rhines/Cin-NL	28–17	.622	45/45	401.1	1.95	6.5
"Wild Bill" Hutchison/Chi-NL	42–25	.627	66/65	603.0	2.63	5.9
Jack Stivetts/StL-AA	27–21	.563	46/41	419.1	3.52	4.9
Mark Baldwin/Chi/PL	33–24	.579	56/53	492.0	3.35	4.8
John Healy/Toledo-AA	22–21	.512	46/44	389.0	2.89	4.7
William "Kid" Gleason/Phl-NL	38–17	.691	55/54	506.0	2.63	4.6

And where did the Cincinnati Red-legs' relatively unknown freshman whiz, Billy Rhines come from?

The year before cracking the Bigs, Mr. William Pearl Rhines readied himself for the fast-paced action of the majors by pitching in 42 games for Davenport, Iowa, in the Central Interstate League, for manager Robert Allen, the flashy-fielding shortstop who would in 1890 break in with the Phils and enjoy a rookie season of such distinction that it would become the 33rd best of all-time. In 1889 Rhines won 27 and lost 15 before winding up his summer somewhat early when the league's cellar dweller disbanded a few weeks ahead of the season's scheduled closing. Had Davenport lasted through the end of the season,

Rhines might have pitched in as many as 60 ball games, and his victory total might well have been near 40. As it was, his 27 wins represented almost half (47 percent) of the Iowa ballclub's 57 wins that summer.

It was during his 1888 season, Billy's first in pro ball, with Binghamton and Jersey City of the Central League, that he developed the pitch that was to propel him to pitching success. Variously called an "upshoot," a "riseball," or more simply, a curveball, the killer pitch for batters in those days moved toward the plate in a rising, curving motion out of his submarine delivery. By the time the 1888 season had ended Rhines was ready. The next season in Davenport was great fun for Billy even

---

Box Score

Cincinnati at Cleveland, April 30, 1890

Cincinnati	AB	R	H	PO	A
McPhee, 2b	4	2	0	3	2
Marr, 3b	4	0	2	2	3
Holliday, cf	3	1	0	2	0
Beard, ss	4	1	1	0	2
Reilly, 1b	3	0	0	9	0
Knight, lf	3	0	1	2	0
Nicol, ss	3	0	0	1	0
Harrington, c	3	0	0	7	3
Rhines, p	3	0	1	1	3
Totals	30	4	5	27	13

Cleveland	AB	R	H	PO	A
McKean, ss	2	0	0	3	3
Smalley, 3b	4	0	0	2	2
Dailey, rf	4	0	0	0	0
Zimmer, c	3	0	0	4	0
Davis, cf	3	0	2	2	0
Veach, 1b	3	0	0	7	0
Archer, 2b	3	0	0	1	3
Sommers, lf	3	0	1	5	0
Beatin, p	3	0	0	0	1
Totals	28	0	3	24	9

```
Cleveland*    000  000  000   0-3-2
Cincinnati    100  200  01x   4-5-1
```

2BH	Beard
3BH	Davis
SB	Marr, Holliday, Reilly
SH	Sommers, Beard 2, Reilly
DP	Archer, McKean and Veach
LOB	Cleveland 4, Cincinnati 4
BB	Beatin 1, Rhines 2
K	Beatin 3, Rhines 6
WP	Rhines (1–0)
LP	Beatin (2–3)
Umpire	McQuaid
Time	1:50
Att	700

*Cleveland opted to bat first

though his team was, by any standard, lousy. Then, as now, it didn't take long for the word to get around. Cincinnati made the first move, and that was all it took. Rhines was on his way to the Big Show.

After an impressive spring training, manager Tom Loftus brought Rhines along with his 1890 edition of the Redlegs. Loftus put the submarine-baller into a game on April 22 in relief, and then called on Billy to start against Cleveland eight days later. It was Rhines' debut as a starter and it was a rousing success. His three-hit whitewashing at Cleveland was the first of six he would throw that summer.

Little did anyone know that Rhines' conquest of Cleveland's Spiders would be the beginning of an incredible skein of 13 successes in his first 14 decisions. He was off to a blazing start.

The Reds' new ace followed up his 13 and 1 with another five scalps in his next six starts, running his record to 18 and 2. Just when everyone was beginning to wonder if Cincinnati's wunderkind (Billy had turned 21 during spring training in the Southland) was actually the second coming of another Pud Galvin, a few major league realities set in. The hitters around the league began to catch up with Billy's submarine hook, Rhines began to lose confidence in himself, and the Reds ran into one of the tougher sections of their 1890 schedule, a long road trip. The bottom line: Rhines faltered.

After beating Philadelphia on July 7, at which point the Rhines record was a majestic 18 and 2, an arid ten-game stretch, marred by nine losses, quite suddenly lowered his mark to 19 and 11. Though still remarkable for a ballclub struggling around the breakeven point, it was a far cry from his torrid early-season pace.

But the season moved on and so did Rhines, as he finished up with another nine victories in his last 15 decisions for a final 28 and 17 reading in one of the more remarkable rookie seasons in major league history. Though Billy's 28 wins were only fifth in the NL (nine pitchers were credited with 30 or more victories in 1890's three-league season), his glittery 1.95 ERA was the best in major league baseball. Those two marks set franchise marks. And there was another, even more prestigious accomplishment. Rhines' 72 pitching runs put him on the all-time list at number 19, right up there with the likes of Cy Young, Walter Johnson, Lefty Grove and Amos Rusie, whose 126 PR mark in 1894 leads the list.

In 1890 the Cincinnati Redlegs and the Brooklyn Bridegrooms, the latter became the Dodgers, or "Dem Bums," as they were more affectionately called, came into the National League from the American Association. Their debut, while moderately successful, was not nearly as electrifying as that of the Quaker State's Billy Rhines, who started his major league career with the fourth-best rookie season in baseball's history and went on to another five seasons with the Reds, leading the league in ERA once again, in 1896, with a sterling 2.45.

Brooklyn outfielder Thomas "Oyster" Burns, the league's RBI leader (with 128) in 1890 and a mainstay on the NL's pennant-winning team, summed up Billy Rhines' awesome rookie season this way: "He's one of the best pitchers I've ever faced. He is a wonder and his great record this season was *not* a chance record."

Richard Anthony "Rich" Allen

TPR: 5.8

1964, Philadelphia, NL

Born: March 8, 1942, Wampum, PA
3B, 5'1" 190 lb. Major League Debut: September 3, 1963
1964: 162 GP; 632-125-201 AB-R-H; .318 BA; 13 3BH; 91 RBI; 52 BR; 7 FR

Much maligned, oft misunderstood, and, to use Connie Mack's biblical quotation in referring to Shoeless Joe Jackson, more sinned against than sinning, Dick Allen came north with the Phillies in the spring of 1964 as their third baseman — a position he hadn't played before. Somehow that was par for the course for Allen, who, despite Philadelphia's hard-nosed and testy fans, the bizarre twists and turns of an unbelievable pennant race, and the clubhouse warfare that kept the team in turmoil, wrested the Rookie of the Year Award — almost unanimously — from Baseball Writers Association of America voters, who would have gladly rewarded anyone else the honors had it not been for the sensational rookie third baseman's exceptional freshman year.

If ever there was a prototypical mixed-blessings career, it was Dick Allen's. Given his frequent moody spells, his penchant for the controversial, and his seeming indifference to club rules and "training," here was, nonetheless, a player of undeniably immense talent, courage and big-play capability, the kind who could carry a ballclub. Replacing the good-field–no-hit tandem of Don Hoak and Reuben Amaro at the hot corner, Allen fielded acceptably, and provided thunderous, middle-of-the-order hitting with that out-sized 48-ounce bludgeon of his, accounting for 29 four-masters, 13 triples (tied for the league lead), and an all-time NL rookie high of 352 total bases, which led the league. In logging a club-high 162 ball games in 1964, Allen also led National Leaguers in runs scored (125), placed second in runs produced (187), the Cardinals' Ken Boyer led with 195, Batting Runs (52) and finished second high in the majors in TPR with 5.8, good enough to rank him fifth highest on the rookie honors listing.

Allen prepped for the Phillies' varsity with four sterling minor league seasons, culminating his apprenticeship at Little Rock, with the Arkansas Travelers of the International League. There he fashioned league-leading totals in triples, homers and ribbies, and was elected to the league's All-Star team. However rewarding that might have been, 1963 was not a trouble-free season. Controversy and racial tension plagued the budding star, especially in the league's Southern ports of call, and particularly on Allen's home grounds at Little Rock. Ed Roebuck, who had been brought aboard to shore up Philadelphia's relief pitching, contributing a number of outstanding middle-relief jobs in 1964, characterized Allen's plight this way:

> Richie Allen had a hard time in the minors at Little Rock. Ray Culp and a couple of other guys who played with him said the people were merciless to him. But he stuck it out and made the majors. He was an amazing talent. He had poor eyesight, which is why he struck out so much. But he was a great hitter and baserunner, and had a great throwing arm. Richie was a beautiful guy and everyone loved him... [qtd. in Peary, 602].

Roebuck might have felt that way, but Richie Allen was not universally loved. His attitude had a lot to do with that, but it is also true that he was often placed into no-win situations. *Enigma* best describes what he soon became — over a troubled, 15-year career, he remained just that.

Phillies helmsman Dick Mauch got the team off in 1964 to a roaring start with an Opening Day win over the Mets, followed by another six wins their next seven starts to nail down first place as the season got underway. As for Rich, his major league career began with a two-for-three day and just seemed to accelerate from there. Philadelphia scribe Allen Lewis penned a special tribute in *The Sporting News* issue of April 21:

> Richie Allen hit more home runs — nine — than any other player in baseball in the exhibition games this Spring. When the season started, the five-feet 11 inch, 185 pounder kept right on going. His hitting during the first week of the National League season helped the Phillies climb to the top of the National League...
>
> (Said Gene Mauch): "Allen hit three home runs in Chicago, ... and under normal conditions he would have hit five. He tore up two balls in the Saturday game when the wind was blowing in a gale."
>
> Allen finished his first week's play with a batting average of .429, led the Phillies in both home runs with three and runs batted in with seven. As a third baseman he has fully repaid Mauch's confidence in his ability to make the conversion from the outfield."

The Phils' seven and one moved to nine and two, the best April record in the history of the franchise. By the end of May they were still in first place, though in a virtual deadlock with San Francisco. Allen's hitting, which could not be expected to maintain that sizzling start, had cooled to the .300 level, but with increasing emphasis on big hits. And his timely fielding contributed to the Phils' tight defense, which led the league through the first 50 games. With strong rookies like Allen and Danny Cater, steady veterans like Johnny Callison enjoying another fine season, plus a strong, if not spectacular pitching staff headed by Jim Bunning (HOF, 1997) and Chris Short, backed up by reliable relief pitching, it began to look as though there just might be a pennant winner in Quakerland.

But this was 1964. While it might have been Rookie of the Year time for Dick Allen, it would not turn out to be World Series time when October rolled around in Philadelphia, where the printers were already busy turning out ducats for the

Rich Allen, 1964 Rookie of the Year. (Dennis Colgin.)

trips, whiffing every time up for a club record, while the Phils *won*, 5–0, behind the brilliant pitching of Chris Short. There was more than enough in 1964, however, to subdue what should have been an embarrassment. That it no doubt wasn't, where Richard Anthony Allen was concerned, furnishes insight into his complex, but often nonchalant attitude.

Respected baseball historians John Holway and Bob Carroll penned sketches of 400 of the greatest ballplayers for the 1991 edition of *Total Baseball*, including Rich (a.k.a. Dick and Richie, which he hated) Allen. From that résumé here's an insight or two:

Dance with two weeks left to go in the season. That seemed reasonable. The Phils were, after all, six and a half games up on the St. Louis Cardinals and Cincinnati Reds.

Then came "The Great Stretch-Drive Flop," a disastrous coincidence of 10 straight Philly losses combined with winning streaks of nine by the Reds and eight by the Cardinals, eventual winners of the NL prize on the last day of the season. Epitomizing that kind of frustration was a game on September 25, when Rich smoked his 27th home run, along with three other hits, in a four for six day that was still not enough to prevent the Phils from losing to Milwaukee in 12 stanzas.

Contrariwise, in a game at St. Louis on June 28, he went for the collar in five

When his mood was right, he was a one-man offense who could carry a team for a week or a month. When his mood was wrong, he could pout or even disappear for an equal length of time....

In 1970 the Phillies traded him to the Cardinals, who kept him a year and then passed him on to the Dodgers. In both cases, the teams improved their records, but decided Allen would never win the Employee of the Month award. In 1972 he was sent to the White Sox and patient manager Chuck Tanner.... Allen responded with an MVP year, hitting .308 and leading the AL in homers(37) and RBIs (113). After that he got bored or surly or whatever" [303].

Tart, but well stated. Mention of that MVP award brings us to Allen's contributions to the Phillies and baseball's record books. Here are some of the entries:

Box Score

Milwaukee at Philadelphia, September 25, 1964

Milwaukee	AB	R	H	RBI
F. Alou, cf, rf	5	0	2	1
Carty, lf	4	0	1	0
Cline, cf	2	1	1	0
Aaron, rf	4	1	1	0
Kolb, lf	1	1	1	0
Torre, c	6	1	3	3
Oliver, 1b	5	1	0	0
Mathews, 3b	6	0	2	1
x Menke, 2b-ss	2	1	1	0
Alomar, ss	2	0	0	0
de la Hoz, 2b	3	1	2	0
Woodward, 2b	0	0	0	0
Fischer, p	2	0	0	0
Maye, ph	0	0	0	1
Olivo, p	0	0	0	0
Hoeft, p	0	0	0	0
Carroll, p	0	0	0	0
Cloniger, p	0	0	0	0
Klimchock, ph	1	0	0	0
Bailey, ph	1	0	0	0
Totals	44	7	14	6

Philadelphia	AB	R	H	RBI
Gonzalez, cf	6	0	0	0
Allen, 3b	6	2	4	2
Callison, rf	5	2	3	2
Covington, lf	5	0	1	0
Philips, ph-lf	0	0	0	0
Herrnstein, ph	1	0	0	0
Thomas, 1b	4	0	0	0
Dalrymple, c	4	0	0	0
Taylor, 2b	4	0	0	0
Amaro, ss	3	0	0	0
Briggs, ph	1	0	0	0
Johnson, ph	1	0	0	0
Wine, ss	0	0	0	0
Short, p	2	0	0	0
Locke, p	0	0	0	0
Baldschun, p	0	0	0	0
Shantz, p	0	0	0	0
Boozer, p	0	0	0	0
Rojas, ph-ss	3	1	1	0
Totals	45	5	9	4

Milwaukee	000	000	210	202	7-14-3
Philadelphia	000	100	020	200	5-9-0

x	awarded first base on catcher's interference
DP	Philadelphia, 1
LOB	Milwaukee, 10; Philadelphia, 8
2BH	Carty, de la Hoz
HR	Torre (19), Callison (28), Allen (27)
SH	Kolb, de la Hoz, Thomas
SF	Maye
Wild Pitch	Locke
WP	Carroll (1–0)
Save	Cloniger (2nd)
LP	Boozer (3–4)
Time	3:48
Att	30,447

- Elected to the Philadelphia Hall of Fame, 1994
- *Baseball Digest* Player of the Year, 1972
- 8th, all time rookie list, for hits in a single season, 201
- 2nd to Mike Schmidt, extra-inning home runs, career, 6 (club)
- Tie M.L. record with two inside-the-park home runs, one game, July 31, 1972, Chicago

- *Rookie Records*:
  GP, 162 (M.L. and club)
  Runs, 125 (club)
  Hits, 201 (club)
  Ks, single game, 5, June 28, 1964 (club)
  Slugging Average, .557 (club)
- Hit a home run over center field wall and into the second deck with the Dodgers at Veterans Stadium on August 20, 1971

- Had a three–home run, seven–RBI game at Shea Stadium in 1968
- One of six Rookies of the Year to also win MVP awards

Ten Top Rookie Third Basemen

Nm/Yr/Tm	GP	BA	RBI	BR	FR	SB	HR	TPR
Rich Allen, 1964, Phl-N	162	.318	91	52	7	3	29	5.8
Jimmy Williams, 1899, Pit-N	152	.355	116	50	7	26	9	5.2
Billy Grabarkewitz, 1970, LA-N	156	.289	84	30	-1	30	17	3.4
Scott Rolen, 1997, Phl-N	156	.283	92	13	16	16	21	3.4
Al "Flip" Rosen, 1950, Clv-A	156	.287	116	37	1	5	37	3.1
Kevin Seitzer, 1987, KC-A	161	.323	83	27	8	12	15	2.9
Wade Boggs, 1982, Bos-AL	104	.349	44	14	18	1	5	2.8
Andy Carey, 1954, NY-AL	122	.302	65	13	17	5	8	2.7
Jim Ray Hart, 1964, SF-NL	153	.286	81	23	5	5	31	2.7
Chris Sabo, 1988, Cin-NL	137	.271	44	2	19	46	11	2.7

Mark Anthony Eichhorn

TPR: 5.7

1986, Toronto, AL
Born: November 21, 1960, San Jose, CA
RHP (RP), 6'4" 200 lb. Major League Debut: August 30, 1982
1986: W14, L6; .700 W%; GP 69; 10 SV; .191 OBA; .191 OB%; 44 PR; 1.72 ERA

A challenge: name the best rookie relief pitchers in the game's history. Would your list of candidates include Dennis Eckersley, or Hoyt Wilhelm, or Dan Quisenberry, or Mike Marshall, or possibly Goose Gossage? Or how about Lee Smith? Or Bruce Sutter? Or Mariano Rivera?

Sorry, none of these worthies appear at or near the head of the class. The list below is arranged according to Total Pitching Index (TPI, or as we have indicated in the Glossary, TPR, as a designation for all Total Player ratings), with some of the more significant statistics below.

Nm/Tm/Yr	GP	W–L	SV	RPR	RR*	OBA	ERA	TPR
M. Eichhorn/Tor-A/1986	69	14–6	10	44	55.3	.191	1.72	5.7
F. Linzy/SF-N/1965	57	9–3	21	20	37.4	.250	1.43	4.9
W. Moore/NY-A/1927	50	19–7	13	37	*	.234	2.28	4.8
D. Corbett/Minn-A/1980	73	8–6	23	36	46.8	.213	1.98	4.5
T. Worrell/StL-N/1986	74	9–10	36	18	30.5	.229	2.08	4.2
K. Tatum/Cal-A/1969	45	7–2	22	20	30.9	.172	1.36	3.8
R. Radatz/Bos-A/1962	62	9–6	24	26	39.5	.211	2.24	3.7
J. Berry/Phl-A/1944	53	10–8	12	19	32.4	.192	1.94	3.6
C. Acosta/Chi-A/1973	48	10–6	18	19	35.4	.193	2.23	3.6
E. Camacho/Clv-A/1984	69	5–9	23	18	31.6	.229	2.43	3.2
E. Romo/Sea-A/1977	58	8–10	16	16	28.1	.227	2.83	3.0
S. Cliburn/Cal-A/1985	44	9–3	6	22	29.7	.241	2.09	2.9
R. Thigpen/Chi-A/1987	51	7–5	16	18	29.3	.256	2.73	2.8
R. Hernandez/Chi-A/1992	43	7–3	12	17	27.0	.180	1.65	2.8
D. Plesac/Mil-A/1986	51	10–7	14	14	27.2	.240	2.97	2.7
G. Olson/Bal-A/1989	64	5–2	27	20	25.7	.188	1.69	2.7
R. Duren/NY-A/1958	44	6–4	20	13	22.6	.157	2.02	2.5
R. Lee/Cal-A/1964	64	6–5	19	27	27.0	.182	1.51	2.5
R. Perranoski/LA-N/1961	53	7–5	6	17	22.8	.244	2.65	2.3
G. Hernandez/Chi-N/1977	67	8–7	4	17	21.6	.234	3.03	2.3

Wilcy Moore's 1927 statistics account for only his starts, not his relief appearances.

Reliever Mark Eichhorn. (Brace Photo.)

successful of these players is provided in Todd Worrell's 1986 rookie player profile.

Among this talented group, two relievers stood out like mighty sequoias among the pines. One of them was the above-mentioned Todd Worrell, whose number 17(t) season on the rookie honor roll follows shortly. The other, Mark Anthony Eichhorn, dazzled American League hitters with his deliberate pitching rhythm, side-arm delivery and breaking stuff during his career year, especially when he followed Toronto's harder-throwing starting pitchers. Though Jose Canseco, Oakland's colorful power hitter, was voted the league's Rookie of the Year, that still takes absolutely nothing away from the sturdy right-hander's stunning season. It was so good, as a matter of plain fact, that it swept him into the number six spot on the all-time rookie list as the author of the game's finest rookie relief-pitching season. His 5.7 TPR blew Canseco's 0.5 TPR right off the 1986 rookie page, establishing both all-time and Toronto standards that are likely to be around for quite a spell.

Mark Eichhorn and eight others in the fraternity of the relief-pitching brotherhood grace the all-time rookie list. That not only represents a 12 percent slice of the total number of players listed; it's also indicative of the strategic and pivotal role relief pitching has assumed during the latter half of the 20th century. With each passing season, especially since the 1970s, relief pitching has been an ever more refined and sophisticated trade specialty, and when the good ones, like the Eichhorns and the Worrells, take the ball with the game on the line, these high-stakes practitioners roll out nothing but their choice offerings.

Keeping these great rookie relievers in mind, we turn in particular to 1986, when new heights were scaled not only by superb first-year relief men in both leagues, but, further, when a bumper crop of freshies descended on major league baseball, invigorating the grand old game more so than it had been in decades. There was nothing commonplace about the 1986 season, the rookies and the relievers saw to that. With respect to 1986's bumper crop, sportswriter Jon Scher had this to say in *Baseball America*'s 1987 Statistic Report: "The fuzzy-cheeked members of the Class of 1986 collectively were among the greatest group of newcomers ever to hit the sport." No less than 16 from this sensational group received BBWAA Rookie of the Year votes. A rundown on the more

Mark Eichhorn began his career at 21 on August 30, 1982, debuting — and losing, 6–3 — against Baltimore. During the rest of 1982 he was used in six more ball games, working 38 innings and compiling an 0–3 record. It was not an auspicious start, and he spent the next three seasons bouncing around between Knoxville and Syracuse, Toronto's top farm clubs. Though it was obvious that the young Californian was a promising prospect, there wasn't anything decisively compelling to warrant a further look at the big-time level. The strapping young hurler began to wonder whether he would ever make it back to Toronto's Exhibition Stadium.

Enter Al Widmar, Blue Jay pitching coach who, along with Kansas City's John Sullivan (premier reliever Dan Quisenberry's mentor), changed Eichhorn's delivery from a three-quarters motion to throwing from down under à la "the Quis." Mark Eichhorn took to it, and that solved several vexing problems at a single clip. One was a strained shoulder and another was getting command of his changeup, sinkers and sliders, his bread and butter pitches. That was the heart of his repertoire, which featured the slow, soft breaking stuff that so frustrated the big boppers around the league.

The 1986 spring training season at Toronto's Dunedin, Florida, base was Eichhorn's "rise and shine" time. Though he was a non-roster invitee, he impressed manager Jimy Williams enough to make the squad, albeit having been the last player to be named to the Blue Jay contingent that headed north. But that didn't bother Mark Eichhorn in the least!

On April 8 the tall junkballer made his first appearance, against Texas' Rangers, since September 29, 1982, and on April 21 he recorded his first major league win. It had been a long time and a tortuous journey from his first organized baseball debut at Medicine Hat, Alberta, back

there in 1979, but the wheel had come full circle for Mark.

Jimmy Key, the distinguished Toronto lefty who rang up 116 victories for the Blue Jays before moving on to New York's Yankees, was the starting pitcher against the Rangers on April 28. However, this was not to be one of the velvet-smooth southpaw's better days, as he negotiated less than five full innings, and Texas took a 6 to 3 lead into the sixth frame.

Eichhorn came on in the fifth to get the third out of the inning and tacked on three Texas goose eggs before turning the game over to Tom Henke. Big Mark picked up the win and Henke the save. Three of Toronto's better hurlers had appeared in the same game and had managed a four-run conquest with an eighth stanza uprising spearheaded by Cliff Johnson's base-clearing double plus fine relief work from Eichhorn and Henke.

As the season moved on, the rangy right-hander began to attract attention with his success and his slow-slower-slowest pitching style. Darrell Evans, slugging Tiger infielder, commented, "*Nobody* throws *that* slow, not even close!" Orioles' manager Earl Weaver queried, "How slow does he throw that thing? That thing looks like it's going to hit the ground before it gets there." Eichhorn's change-up had them all mumbling and grumbling.

Overcoming an accidental spiking that put him on the shelf between June 16 and July 1, he was just as devastating during the second half of the season as he was the first. By August 10, when he tossed three hitless innings at the Rangers to move his mark up to 9 and 4, he was a single victory shy of the Blue Jay reliever's win record. He would go on to exceed the record by four, as he entered the winner's circle a record 14 times.

In his four seasons as Toronto's skipper, Bobby Cox had brought the Blue Jays from 1982's basement finish to an Eastern Division championship in 1985. Giving

Box Score

Texas at Toronto, Exhibition Stadium, April 21, 1986

Texas	AB	R	H	E
McDowell, cf	5	1	1	0
Fletcher, ss-3b	4	1	1	0
Porter, ph	1	0	0	0
O'Brien, 1b	3	2	1	0
Incaviglia, rf	4	1	1	0
Ward, lf	3	1	1	0
Parrish, dh	3	0	1	0
Slaught, c	3	0	0	0
Paciorek, 3b	3	0	0	1
Wilkerson, ss	1	0	0	1
Buechele, 2b	3	0	0	0
Correa, p	0	0	0	0
Harris, p	0	0	0	0
Totals	33	6	6	2

Toronto	AB	R	H	E
Moseby, cf	4	1	1	0
Fernandez, ss	4	0	0	0
Mulliniks, 3b	3	2	2	0
Upshaw, 1b	3	1	1	0
Bell, lf	4	1	2	0
Gruber, lf	0	1	0	0
Barfield, rf	4	1	1	0
Johnson, dh	4	0	2	0
Garcia, pr	0	0	0	0
Iorg, 2b	4	0	1	0
Martinez, c	2	0	0	0
Leach, ph	1	0	0	0
Hearron, c	0	0	0	0
Key, p	0	0	0	0
Eichhorn, p	0	0	0	0
Henke, p	0	0	0	0
Totals	33	7	10	0

```
Texas     000  330  000   6-6-2
Toronto   000  300  04x   7-10-0
```

2BH	Fletcher, Incaviglia, Ward, Parrish, Johnson
SB	McDowell
DP	Texas, 2
BB	Correa 2, Key 4, Harris 0, Eichhorn 0, Henke 0
K	Correa 6, Key 1, Eichhorn 5, Henke 2
HPB	Eichhorn (Slaught)
WP	Correa, Eichhorn
SV	Henke
Ump	McClelland, Denkinger, Reilly, Coble
Time	2:46
Att	16,219

promise for another crack at a playoff spot were a strong outfield of George Bell, Jesse Barfield and Lloyd Moseby; super infielders Tony Fernandez and Damaso Garcia; a pitching staff sporting the two Jimmies, Clancy and Key; and outstanding relief from the likes of Mark Eichhorn and Tom Henke. When Cox moved on to the Atlanta Braves organization, the Torontonians brought in Jimy Williams, but the ballclub, which was plagued from time to time with racial and temperamental difficulties, didn't get it all together, falling to fourth, while the Boston Red Sox leap-frogged from 1985's fifth-place finish to the divisional championship in 1986. Though winning the entire enchilada is *always* the *only* thing that matters among baseball organizations and players, there were enough goodies to make 1986 worthwhile for the Blue Jays. Here are some of them:

- 2,455,477 turnstile revolutions in Toronto's 10th anniversary season
- Damaso Garcia's four doubles on June 27 against the Yankees
- An 11-game errorless streak
- A nine-game winning streak
- Gold Glove awards for Tony Fernandez and Jesse Barfield
- Tom Henke set a club record with 27 saves

- On July 14 Blue Jay pitchers K'd 14 Seattle hitters, a club record
- On July 14 catcher Ernie Whitt set a club record for putouts at 15
- The Blue Jays hit a club record 46 homers for the month of June
- John Cerutti, one of four Blue Jay rookies, won a two-hitter on May 25
- Jimmy Key beat Chicago on May 22 with a one-hitter
- Hitting streaks of 18 games (Garcia) and 15 games (George Bell)
- Two pinch-hit dingers in a June 14 game with Detroit
- Jesse Barfield's six ribbies against Cleveland on May 18
- An inside-the-park home run by Kelly Gruber on June 12 against Detroit

And then there was Mark Eichhorn, whose super season in 1986 was highlighted by these sparklers:

- 1.72 ERA, a club record for the lowest mark with a minimum of 100 innings pitched
- 14 wins, tieing Roger McDowell (Texas) for most rookie wins in 1986
- Finished 34 games, a club rookie record
- Established a club rookie record with 116 strikeouts

- Held opponents scoreless in 42 of 69 games
- Had at least one whiff in 50 of his 59 appearances
- Struck out eight Seattle Mariners in a July 8 relief appearance
- Set a club mark with 20 relief decisions and 157 relief innings pitched
- Among all-time single-season relief record holders Eichhorn is
    7th in relief ranking, 55.3
    7th(t) in relief games pitched, 89 (1987)
    8th(t) in relief innings pitched, 157.0
    15th(t) in relief wins, 14
- In 1986 Mark Eichhorn was named:
    Sporting News Pitcher of the Year
    Blue Jays Pitcher of the Year (BBWAA Toronto Chapter)
    Labatt's "Blue" Player of the Month for August

Without disparaging Jose Canseco or Wally Joyner, both of whom fashioned fine rookie seasons and out-polled Mark Eichhorn in the 1986 Rookie of the Year balloting, there is abundant evidence on the record to indicate that the BBWAA seems to have slighted the most deserving of the three. That record is set straight here with Mark's lofty number six ranking on the all time rookies honor list.

1986: A Rookie Sampling

April 8   The Giants' new first baseman, Will Clark, homered in his first major league at-bat against Nolan Ryan and the Houston Astros.

April 18   Rookie Bobby Witt, Texas right-hander, no-hit the Milwaukee Brewers for five innings, fanning ten, but walking eight. He was taken out when Texas fell behind, but the Rangers finally won, 7–5.

May 31   Rookie Pirate outfielder Barry Bonds doubled against Rick Honeycutt for his first major league hit.

June 27   Giants' third baseman, rookie Robby Thompson, set a major league record when he was caught stealing four times against Cincinnati. Despite that San Francisco won, 7–6 in 12 innings.

August 6   Freshman Mitch Williams, Texas reliever, got credit for Texas' 13–11 victory over Baltimore in a wild game that had fans in a tizzy over a record three grand slam homers. It was a major league first.

August 11   In an NL record-setting game between the Pirates and Cubs at Wrigley Field, the teams used 17 pitchers to complete a game that had started the previous day. The Pirates won it in the 17th inning, 10–8. Rookies Barry Jones, the winner, and teammate Mike Bielecki pitched for the Pirates, and freshman hurler Chico Walker hurled for the Cubs.

September 29   The brothers Maddux faced each other in a game won by Chicago, 8–3. Loser Mike of the Phils and kid brother Greg were both first year men.

October 8   California rookie first baseman Wally Joyner produced one of California's two runs with a circuit smash in an ALCS game that the Angels lost to Boston, 9–2.

October 11   Red Sox reliever Calvin Schiraldi was tagged with a 4–3 ALCS Game Four loss when he surrendered the winning, 11th-inning run to the California Angels. The Boston rookie pitched 6 innings in the ALCS, and another four in the World Series, and suffered a pair of losses in the first and fatal seventh game against the Mets.

Henry Eugene "Gene" Bearden

TPR: 5.5

1948, Cleveland, AL

Born: September 5, 1920, Lexa, AR
LHP, 6'3" 204 lb. Major League Debut: May 10, 1947
1948: W20, L7; .741 W%; 37 GP; 6/1, SH/SV; 5 PHI; 42 PR; 5 PHI; 2.43 ERA

Part Irish, part Indian, part knuckleballer and part bon vivant, Gene Bearden stormed the Bigs with the greatest rookie season ever authored by a left-handed pitcher. His 5.5 TPR for the world champion 1948 Cleveland Indians is almost a full notch superior to another Cleveland hurler of an earlier day, Vean Gregg (4.7 in 1911). Tops for *all time* is quite an accomplishment in *any* category, and in *anybody's* baseball book!

Had his injuries from military action in the Pacific theater in WWII been any more serious, there might not have been that whirlwind, all-conquering season that thrust the 27-year-old rookie and his Cleveland compadres into the national spotlight. Wounds that crushed his knee and fractured his skull stalled him for a while, but the Indians' first-year star with a dipping, bobbing knuckleball that frustrated top AL hitters like Bobby Dillinger, Barney McCosky, Tommy Henrich, and

the Splinter himself, put all that behind him as he resumed, piece by piece, the professional career that started back in 1941 with the Miami Beach Flamingos of the Class D Florida Eastern Coast League (his 17-7 record that season earned him league All-Star honors) and wound up in Cleveland's cavernous Municipal Stadium.

On his return from the service, Bearden moved on to the Yankees' farm club at Binghamton, where, in 1945, he logged an impressive 15–5 mark with an ERA of 2.41 for the seventh-place Triplets. By the end of 1946, in the much stiffer competition of the Pacific Coast League, he had registered a 15–4 for Casey Stengel's Oakland Oaks, and appeared to be ready for a shot at the Yankee roster. Then, as luck would have it (for Bearden, but not for the Yanks), he was traded to the Indians for Sherm Lollar and Ray Mack, who at that time were Cleveland chattels.

Letting the Arkansan southpaw slip

45

Southpaw Gene Bearden, Cleveland knuckleballer. (Dennis Colgin.)

only single-game playoff for the blue ribbon. And it was precisely that game that set the stage for Bearden in the most important afternoon of a career that crammed a lifetime into a single season.

In tieing the Red Sox for the league championship both teams had just exhausted their pitching staffs. As playoff day approached, just about everyone anticipated a slugfest as the two hard-hitting ball clubs went after each other. Manager Joe McCarthy wrote his somewhat surprising choice of Denny Galehouse into his lineup card, determined to play it out to out and inning by inning with everyone ready to go for an inning or two.

The AL's 1948 MVP, Lou "Boy Manager" Boudreau, after consulting with his wily bench coach, the much-traveled Bill McKechnie, and the even cagier Casey Stengel (who was Bearden's manager in Oakland), decided to check also with his ballclub before naming his pitching choice for the Fenway Park playoff. Joe Gordon, who that summer set a record for home runs by a second basemen at 32, spoke for his teammates in giving Boudreau a green light on any choice he might make.

Something Stengel had told him kept popping back into Boudreau's mind as he mulled over his options: "At Fenway, go with the knuckler." And Boudreau did. Gene Bearden became the man of the hour. It was a choice, though unquestioned by the Indians themselves, that stunned the baseball world.

away ahead of the '48 campaign, though part of "the game," where trades and seasons and the law of averages are many times dangerously slippery, might well have cost the Yankees the '48 pennant. In Bearden they would have possessed the missing link they needed to head off the power-laden Red Sox and the inspired Indians. But that, along with a few other incredible imponderables in baseball's most interesting season since the mid–30s of Gashouse Gang fame in St. Louis, was just not to be. 1948 would come down to a flat-footed tie between Boston and Cleveland, with New York, still shaking its head over the turn of events during the last few games of the season, winding up two and a half games behind the two teams that would play the American League's one and

Box Score

Cleveland at Boston, October 4, 1949

Cleveland	AB	R	H	O	A
Mitchell, lf	5	0	1	1	0
Clark, 1b	2	0	0	5	0
Robinson, 1b	2	1	1	9	0
Boudreau, ss	4	3	4	3	5
Gordon, 2b	4	1	1	2	3
Keltner, 3b	5	1	3	0	6
Doby, cf	5	1	2	1	0
Kennedy, rf	2	0	0	0	0
Hegan, c	3	1	0	6	1
Bearden, p	3	0	1	0	2
Totals	35	8	13	27	17

Boston	AB	R	H	O	A
D. DiMaggio, cf	4	0	0	3	0
Pesky, 3b	4	1	1	3	4
Williams, lf	4	1	1	3	0
Stephens, ss	4	0	1	2	4
Doerr, 2b	4	1	1	5	3
Spence, rf	1	0	0	1	0
a Hitchcock, ph	0	0	0	0	0
b Wright, ph	0	0	0	0	0
Goodman, 1b	3	0	0	7	1
Tebbetts, c	4	0	1	3	1
Galehouse, p	0	0	0	0	0
Kinder, p	2	0	0	0	1
Totals	30	3	5	27	14

a Walked for Spence in ninth
b Ran for Hitchcock in ninth

```
Cleveland    100  410  011    8-13-1
Boston       100  002  000    3-5-1
```

2BH	Doby 2, Keltner, Pesky
Home Runs	Boudreau 2, Keltner, Doerr
SH	Kennedy 2, Robinson
DP	Cleveland 3, Boston 2
LOB	Cleveland 7, Boston 5
BB	Bearden 5, Galehouse 1, Kinder 3
K	Bearden 5, Galehouse 1, Kinder 2
Wild Pitch	Kinder
WP	Bearden
LP	Galehouse
Umpires	McGowan, Summers, Rommel, and Barry
Time	2:24
Attendance	33,957

A packed house of 33,957 saw both teams score a run in the first inning, but while the Indians, particularly Lou Boudreau and Kenny Keltner, soon chased Galehouse and subsequently battered Ellis Kinder for the insurance tallies they needed to win, Gene Bearden settled down after a shakey start to sit down Ted Williams, Vern Stephens and Bobby Doerr and Company, on five hits in a route-going tour de force that put the Indians into the World Series.

Lou Boudreau was the new "Baseball Einstein," wrecking machine, and guiding genius all rolled into one. But it was the gritty Gene Bearden who became the only pitcher in baseball history to become a 20-game winner after the season had ended — and he had won it with only one day of rest, having shut out the Tigers on the last day of the regular season, 8–0, at Cleveland in a game only a shade less meaningful than his playoff victory because it meant that another game would have to be played for all the marbles.

Bearden was clearly on a roll — and Boston was his city. In the World Series, only four days after his win over the Red Sox, he lowered the boom on the Braves at Cleveland, calciming them on a five-hitter in a 2–0 masterpiece that put the Indians up two games to one in the Series. That day Gene also contributed a double in a two-for-three day at the plate. And, just to emphasize his mastery over the Back Bay folks in Massachusetts, he tacked down Bob Lemon's victory at Braves Field with the save that brought the championship banner to Cleveland for the first time in 28 seasons. *It was some kinda season!*

Indeed, 1948 was some kinda season. It was the Year of Veeck, and the Year of Paige, and the Year of the Minor Leagues (46 of them were playing the great American game), and the Year of Boudreau. Let's unpack that suitcase-full.

Under the guiding genius (some would call it tom-foolery) of Bill Veeck, the Indians hustled a record-making 2,620,627 into the seats of Cleveland's Municipal Stadium. That was done, first and foremost, because there was both demand and a red-hot product, those determined Indians. A strong case could be made, though, for the many promotions and explosions that regularly appeared on the Indians' home schedule. The combination had the turnstiles spinning.

And then there was the one and only Leroy "Satchel" Paige. He was another rookie on the ballclub, and what a season he had, winning his first start via the whitewash route against, appropriately, the White Sox, and pitching flawlessly in his World Series relief stint. Making his first appearance in what is known as "organized baseball," he became the oldest rookie in the game's history at forty-something, or maybe even fifty-something. These days he's where he belongs — in the Hall of Fame.

And to bring us back to Gene Bearden and the Indians, it was the Year of Boudreau, whose career year sparked the Indians and merited his MVP Award as the last of the playing managers who won a pennant. Thanks to the portside slants of Bearden, the pitching strength of Bob Lemon and Bob Feller, both of whom rest securely at Cooperstown, and a hustling, solid-hitting team that never let down, kept on plugging, and finally won it all, it was no less the Year of Boudreau.

Gene Bearden's 1948 season, featuring league-leading numbers in ERA (2.43) and Pitching Runs (42), was his only super season, when, at the very top of his game, every call was a welcome challenge he answered with 15 completions in 29 starts, six shutouts and a save. In his first seven starts he was touched for only eight runs, winning six times. He wound up the season with a prodigious September–October effort, winning one clutch ball game after another. In September there were five wins against a single defeat at Chicago, which he avenged later with an 11–0 whitewashing of the Sox on four scattered hits. Additionally, he made two key relief appearances on successive days in St. Louis. Then came October, and that became Indians Hall of Fame history.

1963 was the 15th anniversary year of the '48 championship ballclub, so the team was called back for an Old Timers' Day to celebrate a bit and touch up a few old bases. Prior to the game, Gene Bearden was featured in a Cleveland Press article by Bob Sudyk. In the article Sudyk gets right on down to: what happened after 1948? Bearden couldn't then, and still can't explain exactly what happened. Here's how Sudyk put it:

> Gene had a big league knuckleball and a little league curve and fast ball. After 1948, batters tipped their caps at the knuckler and made love to the curves and straight ones. When Gene couldn't get the knuckler over he may as well have stayed home — which he eventually did!
>
> "It's been a mystery to me.... You tell me what went wrong.... But honestly, long ago I stopped thinking about what

might have happened," said Bearden today.... "Bill McKechnie and Mel Harder had me try everything.... But I couldn't control it like before."

He was offered more home remedies than a guy with hiccoughs. Some suggested liquid potions, throwing right-handed; gals offered to hold his hand, a manufacturer suggested he get a new mattress and fickle fans suggested he get lost.

"I'm not bitter at baseball. I just thank God for being good enough to play in the majors at all. It wasn't a lucky shot, though. I worked seven years in the minors to get there."

When he did, Gene Bearden gave them something to remember.

1948: Ten Top Rookies

Nm/Tm/Pos/	GP	W–L/BA	SH/SV//RBI	PR/BR	ERA/FR	TPR
Gene Bearden, Clv-A, LHP	37	20–7	6/1	42	2.43	5.5
Richie Ashburn, Phl-N, of	117	.333	40	17	18	2.8
Ned Garver, StL-A, RHP	38	7–11	0/5	25	3.41	2.7
Mel Parnell, Bos-A, LHP	35	15–8	1/0	29	3.14	2.7
Bob Chesnes, Pit-N, RHP	25	14–6	0/0	11	3.57	2.1
Roy Campanella, Brk-N, c	83	.258	42	1	10	1.6
Sheldon Jones, NY-N, RP	55	16–8	1/5	13	3.35	1.6
Larry Doby, Clv-A, of	121	.301	66	21	3	1.5
Robin Roberts, Phl-N, RHP	20	7–9	0/0	12	3.19	1.5
Paul Minner, Brk-N, LHP	28	4–3	0/1	11	2.44	1.3

James Thomas
"Jimmy" Williams

TPR: 5.2

1899, Pittsburgh, NL

Born: December 20, 1876, St. Louis, MO. Died: January 16, 1965, St. Petersburg, FL
3B, 5'9" 175 lb. Major League Debut: April 15, 1899
1899: 152 GP; 617-126-219, AB-R-H; .355 BA; 27 3BH; 116 RBI; 26 SB; 50 BR; 7 FR

The National League's 1899 season, its seventh since the great shakedown of 1891–1892, when the demise of the American Association made the NL the sole major professional baseball league, was played out with an unwieldy, twelve-team circuit that was still, years afterward, embroiled in the animosities and backstage bickering that had been so much a part of its shoddy history throughout the waning years of the 19th century. It was loosely banded together without an authorized executive office, a commissioner, or even the desire to weld its franchises together into a disciplined unit. Team moguls preyed on one another, the players were in a constant state of near rebellion, and Joe Fan never quite knew what to expect.

Out in what was at that time the western hustings of a league still dominated by the eastern seaboard, Pittsburgh was the classic example of a franchise football, kicked about by owners and mismanaged by its own front office people. It was, like many other league clubs, an operation tottering at the edge of financial ruin.

As the 1899 season approached, the best the Steel City's ballclub could hope for was to survive the season. There was no pennant talk in Pittsburgh, where it wouldn't be until a new century dawned that stars like Fred Clarke, Chief Zimmer, Deacon Phillippe and, above all, Honus Wagner, would hang their uniforms in a Pirates locker room. All agreed that the team manager Bill Watkins took to spring training in Georgia would hardly threaten the Bostons, Brooklyns or Philadelphias of the NL for the league championship. Nor did they.

What Pittsburgh really needed was an infusion of first-rate talent to replace the has-beens and journeymen players who had seen a better day. New blood, whether in the form of rookies or acquired in trades, was the first order of business, the key to a better ballclub, at least for 1899. And then, quite literally in the nick of time, three rookies came along to help give the Pirates a new look — and new hopes.

Each of the three was instrumental in a Pirate upsurge that pushed the team over the .500 mark at 76 and 73. That was an eight-game turnaround from Pittsburgh's 72 and 76 the previous season, and though they still finished in the seventh slot of the league, it was a notch higher than the year before. Pitcher Sam Leever, who started 39 times, led the league in saves (3), games pitched (51), and innings pitched (379) and posted a 21 and 23 record; Clarence Beaumont, an outer-garden swiftie, stole 31 bases, hit .352, and was promptly dubbed "Ginger" by the Pirate faithful who took immediately to the 22-year-old Wisconsonite; but Jimmy Williams, clearly the stickout, despite the solid seasons turned in by his freshmen teammates. Each of the three would be around for a while: Williams, 11 seasons with four different clubs; Beaumont, 12, chiefly in Pittsburgh; and Leever, 13, as a career Pirate. And in 1899 they were vital cogs in a new look that presented six lineup changes and but one holdover moundsman, Jess Tannehill. The new blood was indeed beginning to arrive.

Jimmy Williams began his pro ball career with Pueblo of the Colorado State League in 1896, subsequently moving up to the Western Association the next year with St. Joseph, where he impressed with his stick work (he hit 31 homers on the season, a huge number in those days) and some eye-catching fielding as the Saints' shortstop. Only 21, he was moved up to the Western League's Kansas City ballclub, where he helped the Blues win the pennant, playing at both short and third while hazing Western League hurlers at a .341 clip. That season's work earned him a shot at the Bigs.

Manager Bill Watkins had determined by the end of the Pirates' spring training camp to move his hard-hitting St. Louisan into the third base spot alongside the veteran William "Bones" Ely, who was entering his fourth season as Pittsburgh's mid-fielder. When the club headed north the

Pirate third-sacker Jimmy Williams. (Brace Photo.)

skipper had penciled Williams into the third slot of the batting order, and Jimmy's rookie teammate, Ginger Beaumont, was Watkins' leadoff man and centerfielder. And that's the way things stayed throughout the season, the two young fledglings justifying the faith Watkins, and his successor, playing-manager Patsy Donovan, had in them.

The third of 1899's exceptional Pirate rookies, Sam Leever, who had served notice regarding his capabilities with a league-leading 179 whiffs for Richmond of the Atlantic League during the 1897 season, was moved into the starting rotation and responded with an over-worked 379 innings pitched in what would turn out to be one of his four 20-win seasons for the Pirates. With Jess Tannehill, the two accounted for 45 of Pittsburgh's 76 victories that season, better than one out of every two.

There actually was another Pirate rookie who debuted in 1899. There were no pre-season rave notices about this chunky, 24-year-old hurler, but he proceeded to make the team, contributing a six and nine record to the Pittsburgh cause. His name was Happy Jack Chesbro, who took a little time in getting on down to the serious business of winning big, but when he did, he packed enough into his 11-year career to merit a niche in baseball's pantheon, the Hall of Fame. By 1902, his last year in Pirate livery, he was already 70 victories deep into his almost 200 major league wins (the record stood at 198–132). In 1899 he started off one of the most interesting series in Pirate history, a five-game set in Pittsburgh with the Philadelphia Phillies. While he wasn't the hero, he was the winning pitcher of the July 21 game that opened the series. The hero? Jimmy Williams, no less. Here's how it happened.

The Phillies visited Pittsburgh at a time when they were very much in the hunt for the pennant, sporting a 48–29 record, in third place. With a line-up that boasted Hall of Famers Nap Lajoie, Elmer Flick and Ed Delahanty, and flanked by a solid ballclub up and down the order, the Phils were expected to be within striking distance of the pennant at season's end. And they were. But not around the 25th of July when the Pirates got through with them!

In the five-game faceoff the Pirates beat them by scores of 6–3 behind Chesbro, 18–4 behind Jess Tannehill, 9–8 and 5–4 in a doubleheader (Sam Leever and Bill Hoffer won those two) and then cooled the Phils off for a fifth-straight time in a 15–12 slugfest won by Tully Sparks in relief of Chesbro. The Phils left town a notch lower in the standings, no doubt wondering where these monsters had been all season. The pumped up Pirates, on the other hand, needed every one of those five wins to get to within a game of .500, at 41 and 42.

The rookie-led assault was headed by Jimmy Williams. In the five games he put 13 base hits into the scorebook, hitting .650 (13 for 20), while smashing five triples and two home runs (he wound up being called "Home Run" that year because of his long-distance hitting). His three-run blast in the ninth won the first game of the doubleheader played on July 24 and resulted in a "coin shower" from grateful Pi-

rate fans. Not to be outdone, incidentally, Ginger Beaumont cracked a 'tweener for a two-run triple that won the second game of the twinbill, resulting in a victory ride on the shoulders of the Pittsburghers, whose cups were filled twice to overflowing on the same day. And to round out the Beaumont contribution to this Pirate onslaught, it must be added that he had a record-breaking six singles in the 18–4 disheveling of the Phillie southpaw, Wiley Piatt. Beaumont's record stands to this day.

It was an awesome series that epitomized the heavy lumber Jimmy Williams carried in 1899. That season he wound up with 219 base hits, the second highest total of all time for a rookie. Another Pirate came along in the twenties to break Williams' record with 223. He was "Big Poison's" little brother, Lloyd Waner. Here are the top 10 rookie hit producers:

1. Lloyd Waner, Pittsburgh, 192, (HOF)   223
2. Jimmy Williams, Pittsburgh, 1899   219
3. Tony Oliva, Minnesota, 1964   217
4. Dale Alexander, Detroit, 1929   215
5. Harvey Kuenn, Detroit, 1953   209
6. Nomar Garciaparra, Boston, 1997   209
7. Kevin Seitzer, Kansas City, 1987 207
8. Johnny Frederick, Brooklyn, 1929   206
9. Hal Trosky, Cleveland, 1934   206
10. Joe DiMaggio, New York, 1936 (HOF)   206

Jimmy Williams' explosive major league start set new standards for the Pittsburgh record book, two of which have endured for a century: 1) his 27-game hitting streak (there was also a 26-game hitting streak during the summer of 1899) and 2)

Box Score

Philadelphia at Pittsburgh, July 25, 1899

Philadelphia	AB	R	H	PO	A		*Pittsburgh*	AB	R	H	PO	A
Cooley, 1b	4	1	1	6	0		Beaumont, cf	5	3	3	0	0
Thomas, cf	1	2	0	2	0		McCarthy, lf	3	2	0	0	0
Delahanty, lf	5	3	2	4	0		Williams, 3b	4	2	4	0	3
Chiles, 2b	6	0	2	3	3		McCreery, rf	5	2	3	4	0
Flick, rf	6	1	4	1	0		Schriver, c	5	0	1	4	0
Lauder, 3b	5	2	2	2	1		Ely, ss	5	2	3	3	3
McFarland, c	5	0	1	3	3		Clarke, 1b	5	1	1	12	0
Cross, ss	6	2	1	4	2		O'Brien, 2b	5	0	0	4	2
Bernhart, p	3	1	0	0	1		Chesbro, p	1	0	0	0	1
Fraser, p	1	0	0	0	0		Sparks, p	2	3	0	0	1
Totals	42	12	13	24	10		Totals	40	15	15	27	10

Philadelphia	320	201	031	12-13-10
Pittsburgh	100	226	31x	15-15-4

2BH	Chiles
3BH	Flick, Williams, McFarland
HR	Williams
SH	McCarthy
SB	Delahanty 2, McCarthy 2, Flick, Cross
K	Chesbro 1, Sparks 2, Fraser 2
BB	Chesbro 5, Sparks 5, Fraser 4
WP	Fraser 2
Winning Pitcher	Sparks
Losing Pitcher	Bernhart
Umpires	Swartwood and Hunt
Att	1,800
Time	2:35

his 27 triples for a single season. Both are rookie records, as well.

After having the pleasure of playing on a completely rejuvenated Pirates ballclub in 1900 with Wagner, Clarke, Phillippe and the others who were moved from Louisville when that franchise was terminated and the swollen National League was pared down to eight teams, Jimmy moved on to the newly organized American League with Baltimore, where he played two more seasons before settling down with New York's Highlanders. There, he became one of the major leagues' better second basemen as a steady, far-ranging infielder and a timely hitter with plenty of pop in that stick of his. And after his major league days were over, he wound up his baseball career in 1915 with a six season stint at Minneapolis.

Jimmy Williams, with plenty to look back on, died at the advanced age of 88. It had been a long and eventful journey, especially that part of it that made its way through his 1899 rookie season.

1899: Ten Top Rookies

Nm/Pos/Tm	GP	W–L/BA	SH/SV//RBI	PR/BR	ERA/FR	TPR
Jimmy Williams, 3b, Pit	15	.355	116	50	7	5.2
Joe McGinnity, RHP, Bal	48	28–16	4/2	52	2.68	5.0

Nm/Pos/Tm	GP	W–L/BA	SH/SV//RBI	PR/BR	ERA/FR	TPR
Sam Leever, RHP, Pit	51	21–23	4/3	27	3.18	3.0
Noodles Hahn, LHP, Cin	38	23–8	4/0	43	2.68	2.8
Roy Thomas, of, Phl	150	.325	35	35	4	2.6
Deacon Phillippe, RHP, Lou	42	21–17	2/1	25	2.17	2.3
Ginger Beaumont, of, Pit	111	.352	38	23	6	1.9
John "Buck" Freeman, of, Was	155	.318	122	38	-12	1.3
Strawberry Bernhard, RHP, Phl	21	6–6	1/0	15	2.65	1.2
Emmet Heidrick, of, StL	146	.328	82	9	4	0.2

Michael Joseph "Mike" Piazza

TPR: 5.1

1993, Los Angeles, NL
Born: September 4, 1968, Norristown, PA
C, 6'3" 200 lb. Major League Debut: September 1, 1992
1993: 149 GP; 81 R; .318 BA; .561 SA; 112 RBI; 35 HR; 41 BR; 5 FR

Some day it will probably be said that Mike Piazza was only drafted by the Dodgers because manager Tommy Lasorda was his godfather. After all, a 62nd-round draft choice only decorates the tail end of the draft list, so someone with clout must have seen to it that Piazza's name was added, and that someone must have been the man who bled Dodger blue. For the record, it wasn't, but the way things turned out, ole Tommy must have been pleased beyond anything even he might have fantasized about.

It *was* the Dodger skipper, however, who was instrumental in converting LA's young draftee into a catcher, thus solving the problem of what to do with a strong young bull who wasn't really an infielder, an outfielder, or a pitcher (he had been tried almost everywhere). In the end, it was godfather Lasorda who came along to suit up their floundering prospect in catching gear. It didn't take long after that for the success story to unfold.

All the Dodgers did in that 1988 draft was to select the player who would become the National League's 1993 Rookie of the Year and the NL's sixth unanimous choice in the award's history. Here's the list:

1. Frank Robinson, Cin, 1956, of, NL All-Star, LL: 122 runs scored, 3.0 TPR, HOF-1982
2. Orlando Cepeda, SF, 1958, 1b, LL: 38 2BH; 0.6 TPR
3. Willie McCovey, SF, 1959, 1b, 52 GP, 2.0 TPR, HOF-1986
4. Vince Coleman, St.L, 1985, of, LL: SB, 110, and SB Runs, 18; 0.9 TPR
5. Benito Santiago, SD, 1987, c, 146 GP, 0.8 TPR
6. Mike Piazza, LA, 1993, c, 149 GP, .561 SA, NL All-Star, 5.1 TPR

Mike's smashing 1993 debut brought about numerous awards and citations. One

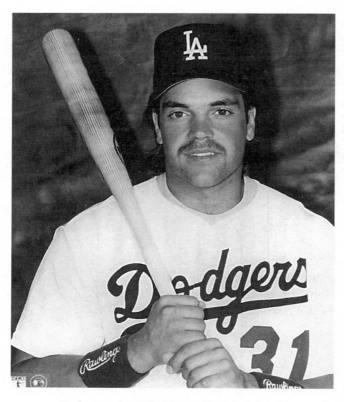

Dodger catcher Mike Piazza. (Dennis Colgin.)

• Named to the UPI and AP Major League All Star Teams
• Named the Dodgers' MVP for 1993

How did the journey to those honors take place? Mark Cresse, the Dodgers' capable bullpen coach with more than twenty years of observing and instructing the club's battery men behind him, was an important part of that journey. His association with the Dodgers' phenom goes back to the days when Mike was a Phillies bat-boy. The one outstanding memory Cresse carries with him about those days was the powerful, sky-high fly balls Mike hit when he had a chance now and then to step in for a few licks at the plate. The young lad exuded power.

The paths of these two erstwhile Philadelphians crossed again in Dodger camps and Spring Training. This time, however, Piazza was no longer a boyish teenager. He was a powerfully built young man, a burly tower of strength in the Los Angeles organization, a success story waiting to happen. And between the tutelage of Lasorda and Cresse, and the fiery determination of their willing pupil, it happened.

There was steady progress not only in hitting but in "the catching arts" through several minor league stops, culminating in a banner 1992 season that convinced the Dodgers to bring Piazza to L.A. Among the more persuasive of his credentials were several postseason honors: selection to Baseball America's Triple A All-Star team, the Pacific Coast League's All-Star and postseason All-Star teams, a .341 batting average and a .564 slugging average. Mike

of these was "Native Son" honors, presented him by the Philadelphia sports writers. Born in the Philadelphia suburb of Norristown, he grew up as an admirer of another Mike, the Phillies' HOFer Schmidt. The Philly award was significant for the young catcher, but it was the national acclaim that vaulted his name into the spotlight. Here is a sampling of the 1993 awards that were showered on Piazza:

• Named Southern California Male Athlete of the Year by the Amateur Athletic Foundation
• Named Baseball America's Rookie of the Year
• Selected as The Sporting News Rookie of the Year
• He was presented a Silver Slugger Award

Piazza was declared Los Angeles' Minor League Player of the Year, and they brought him aboard for a few late season games that same year. They weren't disappointed. On September 1, 1992, just called up from Albuquerque, he pulled on a Dodger uniform for the first time at Wrigley Field, where he doubled his first trip, added two more hits for a three for three day, and threw out Cub speedster Dwight Smith attempting to steal. The Dodgers had themselves a new catcher.

1993 began a string of five straight seasons during which Piazza pummeled National League pitching at the .300 level, averaging a cool .337 between '93 and '97. His power asserted itself early in April of his big freshman campaign, and he moved on to a season's total of 35 circuit smashes, establishing a new record for major league rookie catchers. Those dingers were a big part of the new club record he set in besting Del Bissonette's 1928 standard of 106 RBIs at 112. By the time his fifth season had ended in 1997, he had pumped 167 homers into the seats. That's more than 30 per season. Here's more:

- His 35 homers were the most for a single season since Duke Snider's 40 back in Brooklyn in 1957.
- Piazza had two-homer games five times during the '93 season, his first coming on June 16 at Colorado's Coors Field.
- The all time NL record chart for rookie homers lists Piazza in second place. The list:

Wally Berger, Boston, 1930	38
Frank Robinson, Cincinnati, 1956	38
Mike Piazza, Los Angeles, 1993	35
Earl Williams, Atlanta, 1971	33
Jim Ray Hart, San Francisco, 1964	31

- Piazza's 307 Total Bases ranked third in the NL in 1993 and 8th all time on the Dodger ledger.

And an additional note from behind the plate: Mike threw out seven straight would-be base stealers between April 13 and 18, those repeated attempts no doubt coming at a time when National League basestealers were putting the rookie to the test. During the '93 campaign he was successful in nipping 33 percent of those who tried stealing, running up a total of 58 for a franchise record, *and* the best catcher's mark of the season.

One of Mike's better days during 1993 came at Coors Field in Denver before a jam-packed crowd of 55,772 on June 16, the night he enjoyed his first four-hit, multi-homer ball game. Given the events that unfolded in that wild, 12 to 4 slugfest, the game might more aptly have been called a *brawlgame.* The "Big Cat," Andres Galarraga, who was on the way to a new National League record with nine hits in a row, was involved in a spiking of Jody Reed that resulted in lacerating Reed's arm during a seventh inning Rockies uprising. Though no runs were scored, the thin Denver air became charged with electricity and the stage was set for something more lively than nibbling on crackerjacks. The accidental spiking, which might otherwise have been an unfortunate-but-passing event, was another in a series of incidents that had begun in the sixth inning when pitcher Keith Shepherd hit the Dodgers' Cory Snyder. Two ejections followed some heated exchanges before order was restored. After the Reed spiking, everyone in the ballpark knew the end to the festivities had not yet come. It came in short order.

The very next inning, starting pitcher Ramon Martinez hit Rockies third baseman Charlie Hayes in the chest with a pitch. Hayes charged the mound, the benches cleared, and another of baseball's all-too-frequent free-for-alls was underway. Ten minutes later, and after the irate Hayes had been escorted to the clubhouse, play was resumed.

Mike Piazza not only found himself in the middle of both mêlées, but was busy with his booming howitzer, as well. One of his singles accounted for two Dodger tallies, and his two four-baggers brought home another three. The second, a tape measure blast, cleared the Rockies' centerfield barrier, arching into the seats.

And Andres Galarraga? He tapped a

roller back to the mound and was thrown out by reliever Ricky Trylicek in the ninth inning, thus ending his hitting streak, though entering his name in the NL record book, as a shareholder for first place with his nine consecutive base hits in nine straight at bats. This is the box score of that eventful game:

Would that Team Lasorda had been

Box Score

Los Angeles at Colorado, June 16, 1993

Los Angeles	AB	R	H	BI	E
Butler, cf	6	2	2	1	0
Offerman, ss	5	1	1	1	0
Webster, lf	5	2	3	1	0
Wallach, 3b	4	1	0	0	1
Sharperson, 3b	0	0	0	0	0
Piazza, c	5	3	4	5	0
Snyder, rf	4	1	2	1	0
Karros, 1b	5	0	1	0	0
J. Reed, 2b	3	0	0	0	0
Harris, 2b	1	1	0	0	0
Martinez, p	2	0	0	0	0
McDowell, p	0	0	0	0	0
Hansen§	1	0	1	0	0
Davis**	1	1	1	2	0
Trlicek, p	0	0	0	0	0
Totals	42	12	16	11	1

Colorado	AB	R	H	BI	E
Young, 2b	4	0	2	0	0
Boston, lf	5	1	1	0	1
Bichette, rf	5	1	2	1	0
Galarraga, 1b	5	2	4	0	0
Hayes, 3b	3	0	1	1	0
Castellano, 3b*	1	0	0	0	0
Castilla, ss	5	0	1	0	0
Cole, cf	2	0	0	0	1
Sheaffer, c	3	0	1	1	0
Henry, p	1	0	0	0	0
Tatum†	1	0	0	0	0
Shepherd, p	0	0	0	0	0
S. Reed, p	0	0	0	0	0
Jones††	1	0	0	0	0
Ashby, p	0	0	0	0	0
Wayne, p	0	0	0	0	0
Parrett, p	0	0	0	0	0
Totals	36	4	12	3	2

Los Angeles   000   101   037   12-16-1
Colorado   000   120   001   4-4-2

2BH	Snyder, Davis, Boston, Bichetti, Galarraga
HR	Piazza 2
SH	Martinez
SF	Sheafer
DP	Karros unassisted; Young-Castilla-Galarraga
LOB	Los Angeles, 7: Colorado, 11
BB	Martinez, 4; Parrett, 2
K	Martinez 2, Trlicek 1, Shepherd 1, Parrett 1
HPB	Hayes by Martinez; Snyder by Shepherd
Balk	Martinez
WP	McDowell (3–0)
LP	Shepherd (1–1)

*Castellano ran for Hayes in 7th inning.
†Batted for Henry in 6th inning.
§Batted for McDowell in 9th inning.
**Ran for Hansen in 9th inning.
††Batted for S. Reed in 8th inning.

Umpires   Tata, Davis, Gregg, Bonin
Time   3:22
Att   55,772

---

as productive in 1993 as Mike Piazza was. At the end of the season Lasorda's charges stood at a very middling .500, having won exactly as many as they lost. In the end, the Dodgers went down under the superior hitting and fielding of Atlanta's Braves, and their hated rivals, the Giants. In the last year before a new, two-division setup was to be installed, the Dodgers placed fourth. It might easily have been worse had not Michael Joseph Piazza come along to brighten the long Los Angeles summer with three Player of the Week citations and a Rookie of the Year Award that set him apart on the rookies honor list as the player who put together the all-time greatest rookie season among catchers.

Top 10 Rookie Catchers, All Time

Nm/Yr/Tm	GP	BA	RBI	HR	BR	A	FR	TPR
Mike Piazza, 1993, LA-N	149	.318	112	35	41	98	12	5.1
Carlton Fisk, 1972, Bos-A	131	.293	61	22	33	72	1	4.4
Thurman Munson, 1970, NY-A	132	.302	53	6	19	71	6	3.0
Johnny Bench, 1968, Cin-N	154	.275	82	15	10	102	7	2.6
Bill DeLancey, 1934, StL-N	93	.316	40	13	18	35	5	2.5
Wm. "Buck" Ewing, 1881, Troy-NL	67	.250	25	0	-4	89	25	2.2
Bill Dickey, 1929, NY-A	130	.324	65	10	10	95	1	2.1
Matt Nokes, 1987, Det-A	135	.289	87	32	22	32	-9	1.8
Darrell Porter, 1973, Mil-A	117	.254	67	16	16	47	-4	1.7
Roy Campanella, 1948, Brk-N	83	.258	45	9	1	45	10	1.6

George Barclay "Win" Mercer

TPR: 5.0

1894, Washington, NL

Born: June 20, 1874, Chester, WV. Died: January 12, 1903, San Francisco, CA
RHP, 5'7" 140 lb. Major League Debut: April 21, 1894
1894 as RHP: W17, L23, .425 W%; 39/30 GS/GC; 0/2 SH/SV; 54 PR; 3 PHI; 3.85 ERA
1894 as Batter: 169-29-48, AB-R-H; .291 BA; 5 2BH; 2 HR; 29 RBI; 2 FR; .944 FA

Washington manager Gus Schmelz saw a wiry little fellow (barely 5'7" and 140 pounds dripping wet) pitching for Dover of the New England League in 1893 and decided he would make a good addition to his lackluster pitching staff for the 1894 season. At Dover, Schmelz's prospect, George Mercer, who had picked up the nickname "Win" during his industrial baseball league days, was a 20-game winner with a 2.05 ERA, led the league in strikeouts with 136, and hit a respectable .262.

The Mercer package was appealing. The lean righthander could pitch, play infield or outfield, and was a solid sticker.

But it was the pitching that Schmelz was really after. In 1893 the distance from the mound to home plate had been moved up to 60' 6", and that had upped the ante considerably on good pitching, which he desperately needed. The starting rotation

in 1893 included Duke Esper (12 and 28 with a 4.71 ERA), Smiling Al Maul (12 and 21, 5.30 ERA), Jouett Meekin (10 and 15, 4.96 ERA), and Jesse Duryea (4 and 10, 7.54 ERA). Schmelz no doubt reasoned that it shouldn't be too stiff a challenge to outdo those underachieving numbers. That was before The Great Explosion of 1894, which made a mockery of big league pitching and set the "new and improved" Washington hurling corps on its behind. The National League that summer staggered through its 132 game schedule under the persistent and savage bombardment of hitters gone berserk. The top five batting averages exceeded .400. There were several hitting streaks, capped by Bad Bill Dahlen's 42-game standard (another streak of 28 followed the 42-gamer after a single hitless game); Billy Hamilton scored 196 runs, tallying in 24 straight games; Sam Thompson drove Phillie teammates home at the rate of 1.39 per contest; Hugh Duffy hit .438, had 18 taters and 145 RBIs for what would now be recognized as a Triple Crown; veteran Bobby Lowe hit four consecutive homers against Cincinnati on May 30; and rookie Fred Clarke debuted a month later with a 5 for 5 day.

Sadly, at least for the pitchers, there's more. Between 1892 and 1894, the league batting average had soared from .245 to .309, some 64 percentage points. League-leading Philadelphia hit .349 *as a team!* Washington, nestled down there in 11th place in team batting, averaged a not-too-lightweight .287 BA. League pitchers posted a top-heavy 5.32 ERA, up from the 1893 record of 4.66, and fully two runs per game more than the 1892 ERA of 3.28.

What a time to pick to debut as a major league pitcher! But that was the hand dealt Win Mercer. All too soon he found out that National League hitters in 1894 made few exceptions to their offensive onslaughts. Debuting on April 21, he was summarily roughed up

Versatile Win Mercer. (Brace Photo.)

and suffered his first loss under the Big Tent. The Senators, who were the weakest fielding team in the league, were also pounded frequently in the early going, and entered play on May 4 against Louisville's Colonels in the throes of a 17-game losing streak. But for Win Mercer and the Washington Senators it was the right team on the right day. The Colonels were even weaker than the Senators, finishing last in the league with a 36 and 94 record, as compared to the Senators' 11th place finish at 45 and 87.

On this particular bright spring day Louisville manager Billy Barnie's pitching choice was the veteran George "Old Wax" Figger while Gus Schmelz countered with the 19-year-old Mercer.

Win Mercer's two-hitter was a welcome breath of fresh air. Beating up on the hapless Louisville nine might not have been the most impressive accomplishment of the season, but it *was* a welcome relief from the doldrums 17 straight losses had brought on. And the versatile Mercer came up with quite a day, allowing but two

Box Score

Louisville vs. Washington at Boundary Field, May 4, 1894

Louisville	AB	R	H	PO	A
Brown, cf	2	1	0	2	0
Pfeffer, 2b	3	0	0	5	1
Mitchell, lf	4	0	0	0	0
O'Rourke, 1b	3	0	0	4	2
Weaver, rf	4	0	0	2	0
Richardson, ss	4	0	0	4	1
Denny, 3b	4	0	1	2	0
Hemming, p	3	0	1	2	2
Grim, c	3	1	0	3	5
Totals	30	2	2	24	11

Washington	AB	R	H	PO	A
Ward, 2b	3	2	2	2	1
Joyce, 3b	4	2	2	1	0
Abbey, lf	4	1	3	4	0
McGuire, c	4	2	2	6	0
Hassamaer, rf	4	1	0	4	0
Tebeau, cf	5	2	0	0	0
Cartwright, 1b	4	1	3	8	0
Radford, ss	4	1	2	2	6
Mercer, p	4	0	2	0	2
Totals	36	12	16	27	9

```
Louisville    002  000  000   2-2-5
Washington    305  000  13x   12-16-0
```

2BH	Joyce
3BH	Joyce, Mercer, Abbey
SB	Radford
DP	Richardson, Pfeffer, O'Rourke
BB	Hemming 4, Mercer 3
K	Hemming 3, Mercer 3
HPB	by Hemming (Ward)
Umpire	Hurst
Time	1:55

singles while standing the Colonels' attack on its ear and contributing a triple and a single to the 16-hit barrage that overwhelmed Louisville, 12 to 2. With the victory, the tide began to turn for the diminutive hurler, and although he had to endure a nine-game losing streak during the season, he managed a 17 and 23 record for one of the worst ballclubs in the league during the 1890s.

The National League's Washington franchise was a mess from stem, where owners Earl and George Wagner were far more interested in a quick buck than in producing a winner, to stern, where managers and players struggled along just above the subsistence level. One farcical deal after another kept the ballclub in an unsettled state of confusion. That was hardly the kind of environment that might be conducive to bringing along a young player, and especially one as young as Win Mercer, who approached his 20th birthday as a part of Gus Schmelz' starting rotation.

Inevitably, the results showed in the standings. During its brief tenure in the Senior Circuit (this Senator team lasted only eight seasons) Washington's tail-enders wound up in the second division every time, finishing as high as sixth but once with its best record, an under-.500 61 and 71, in the franchise's brief-but-unfortunate history. Their 1894 record was just good enough to escape the very bottom, occupied by another strife-ridden team, the Louisville Colonels. By 1899 the Wagner brothers, driven by their insatiable appetite for still another profiteering maneuver, arranged for a buyout of the floundering franchise, ultimately pocketing more than $200,000, thus closing out the Washington National League membership.

Win Mercer was one of the many players caught in the middle of the ballclub's misadventures. But he survived — and quite well, at that. During his freshman season he compiled some awe-inspiring numbers, considering the circumstances. His 17 wins in 1894 represented better than a third of the Senators' season total, his 3.85 was minuscule compared to the league's monstrous 5.32 and the Washington staff's even worse 5.51, and his 72 K's were a staff high. Adding three saves to his win total, there were 20 decisions on the plus side of the ledger the handsome twirler had a hand in. Further, he hit .291, played a few games for skipper Schmelz in the outfield, and socked the first home run of his career in a game against the mighty Chicago White Stockings (that must have shocked both Cap Anson and pitcher Addie Gumbert) on June 1.

It all added up to an extraordinary, 5.0 TPR season. Among the league's top hurlers, Mercer's 3.85 was third behind future Hall of Famer Amos Rusie, who was the most dominating pitcher that season and in a hitter's year. The 1894 record shows Rusie with 36 wins and Jouett Meekin, the same 1893 Washington righthander who limped along at a 10–15 pace, and who probably fell to his knees in thankfulness for having escaped to New York, with 33 conquests for a pennant contender. More significantly, Mercer's Clutch Pitching Index was the league's highest at 134, a rating that earned a spot among the top 50 of all time.

Young Mr. Mercer's Washington career was crowned with two 20-win seasons, the second of which was another 5.0 TPR campaign in 1897, during which he led the league in games pitched, shutouts and saves. As long as there was an NL team in the nation's capital, he was there to offer his versatility (he hit .317 during his big 1897 season, and, during 1898 and 1899 he played over 150 games as an infielder and outfielder, plus another 56 in pitching appearances), and after having been bundled off to New York's Giants in 1900, reappeared on the Washington scene for a one-year stint with the newly formed Washington team, this time in the American League.

Win Mercer's last big-time campaign was spent with the 1902 Detroit Tigers, where he resumed his pitching career, winning 15 while losing 18 for the seventh place Detroiters. After the season the Tiger management announced that Mercer would be Detroit's helmsman for the 1903 season. It must have been a rewarding moment in a career that was spent with some of the weakest of 19th century ballclubs.

Not yet 30, Mercer seemingly had a bright future waiting for him. But he was closer to the end than even he might have suspected. Always a lady's man, he enjoyed the bright lights, attractive young damsels, and above all, the races, where he was known to have laid a bill or two on his favorite nags.

In January of 1903 he was in California, playing with National and American League All-Stars in an exhibition series. He also sampled his pet diversions, California's beauties — and the race tracks. It was a deadly combination. And it did him in.

Given charge of the touring teams' funds and receipts during the exhibition series, Win succumbed to the temptation of dipping into the treasury to cover losses he sustained in his extracurricular activities. On January 12, despondent over his wayward misdeeds, he committed suicide in his San Francisco hotel room. It was an untimely, tragic end to an otherwise successful life, one that might well have been filled with future accomplishment. But that was not to be.

As the major leagues closed out the 19th century there was as much turmoil and under-handed deviltry off the field of play as there were stunning successes, superbly talented players, and exceptional ballclubs on it. Leagues, owners, boards of directors, managers and players were in the midst of titanic struggles for the upper hand in controlling pennants and world championships. In the middle of all that, rookie players like Win Mercer kept right on coming. Some of them, like the little West Virginia speed merchant, carved out a rookie niche that merits the honor of top 10 ranking among all freshmen.

1894: Ten Top National League Rookies

Nm/Pos/Tm	GP	W–L/BA	SH/SV//RBI	PR/BR	ÉRA/FR	TPR
Win Mercer/RHP/Was	50	17–23	0/3	54	3.85	5.0
Jim Bannon/of/Bos	128	.336	114	9	18	1.4
Charlie Abbey/of/Was	129	.314	101	9	14	1.0
Bill Hassamaer/of/Was	118	.322	90	6	5	0.5
Fred Tenney/c/Bos	27	.395	21	5	0	0.5
Art Twineham/c/StL	38	.315	16	-2	4	0.4
"Dad" Clarke/RHP/NY	15	3–4	0/1	3	4.93	0.1
Mike Grady/c-1b/Phl	60	.363	40	9	-12	0.1
Joe Sugden/UT/Pit	39	.331	23	3	-5	0.1
Ollie Smith/of/Lou	38	.299	20	5	-2	0.0

Joseph Jerome "Iron Man" McGinnity

TPR: 5.0

1899, Baltimore, NL

Born: March 19, 1871, Rock Island, IL. Died: November 14, 1929, Brooklyn, NY
RHP, 5'11" 206 lb. Major League Debut: April 18, 1899
1899: W28, L16; 48 GP; 38 GC; 343.0 IP; 4/2 SH/SV; .256 OBA; 52 PR; 2.68 ERA
Hall of Fame: 1946

During the 1890s there were very few minor leagues affiliated with organized baseball's National Association. In 1897, for example, there were only six, and by 1898 there were but five. There were, however, 20 nonsignatory leagues, and through baseball's elaborate grapevine, scouts and former players kept a close eye on them.

Peoria, Illinois, fielded a team in one of the nonsignatory leagues, the Western Association, whose 1898 schedule called for a contest between Peoria and the home-standing St. Joseph nine on June 26. Two Irishmen, pitchers McDonald and McGinnity, were slated to go at it that day. And did they!

The game turned out to be far more than one of the summer's many ordinary, everyday bouts, with the two Sons of Erin dueling each other through 20 frames tied at three a piece. In the 21st inning Peoria broke through with a five-spot that finally

decided the contest. The winning pitcher, no less than future Hall of Famer Joseph Jerome McGinnity, opened a few eyes that day with a curveball that absolutely startled St. Joe's hitters.

The word soon traveled eastward to Brooklyn, where the Superbas' owner, Charley Ebbets, made subsequent arrangements to pick up Peoria's breaking ball sensation, a 1C and 3 winner in the Western Association, anticipating an 1899 training camp the following March.

Now it just so happened that in the strange world of multiple ownerships in the National League, which monopolized major league baseball during those bizarre '90s, the league's moguls rearranged team rosters on occasion by swapping ballplayers to teams they owned. In 1898, for example, Charley Ebbets and Ferdinand Abel of Brooklyn and Harry Von der Horst and manager Ned Hanlon of Baltimore forged

Legendary Giants' ace Joe McGinnity. (Brace Photo.)

licked its mortal wounds with a pile of cash for the unsavory player transactions *and* the two wily veterans, named John J. Mc-Graw and Wilbert Robinson, who stayed behind to pick up the pieces. One of those pieces was Joe McGinnity, who had been hidden under the growing pile of un-scrupulous intrigue during the wild, 1898–1899 offseason maneuvering. Consequently, the brilliant right-hander became an Ori-ole for the 1899 season, thus forging a re-lationship with McGraw that would pave the way for future National League domi-nation in the early 1900s, showcasing not only one, but two glittering aces that be-came the toast of the Big Apple on world's championship Giant teams. That other ace? The legendary Christy Mathewson.

By the time Joe McGinnity debuted in the Bigs on April 18, 1899, he was no longer a callow, inexperienced pitcher. He was already 28, had pitched for at least a decade, and had made the rounds of cen-tral Illinois' best semipro clubs, as well as minor league seasons with the Mont-gomery Colts of the Southern League (1893), and Kansas City's Blues of the Western League (1894), before his abbre-viated, 1898 stay in Peoria. During that time he had developed the famous break-ing ball he called "Ole Sal," a swooping, biting curve ball that began less than a foot off the ground with his underhanded de-livery and soared upward as it approached the plate, often breaking three to four feet as it cruised plateward.

McGinnity was famous for more than "Ole Sal." His nickname, indicative of the many games he pitched (there were five oc-casions in which he pitched doubleheaders during his major league career), was coined by Brooklyn scribes who had heard him say, with some pride, that he was an iron man, meaning that he had earned a living during his earlier years as an iron foundry worker. They called him Iron Man McGin-nity and the name stuck.

a syndicate ownership. That enabled them to move most of the Baltimore stars, fu-ture HOFers Wee Willie Keeler, Hughie Jennings and Joe Kelley among them, to Brooklyn, which, as might be expected, proceeded to win the pennant in 1899.

But there were a pair of HOFers left behind in Baltimore, where the franchise

Joe McGinnity's baseball career covered that rough-hewn period of time at the close of the 19th century and early 20th, when rookie-hazing, fighting and an intimidating style of baseball was day-in, day-out *de rigueur*. The Hanlons and McGraws of the day reveled in it and the Iron Man had all the equipment necessary to join the league's battling gladiators. Combative to the core, McGinnity owned the inside of the strike zone, had a reputation for throwing at hitters, and challenged all comers. He wasn't a strikeout pitcher, but specialized in breaking balls that had hitters either grounding his offerings into the dirt, or popping them up. And "Ole Sal" was the enforcer, his out pitch. It was most fortunate that the more genteel and Christianized soul of Christy Mathewson came along two years later to hold in check the contentious McGraw-McGinnity duo. Another one of either might have turned the whole kit and kaboodle into an unmanageable pack of clawing wolves.

The Iron Man wasted little time during his freshman season in getting right on down to the more serious business of winning ball games. His second outing, on April 24, paired him against the capable veteran Jouett Meekin, who had averaged 22 wins per season during his New York years (1894–1898). The powerfully built McGinnity threw the first of his four shutouts that season, beating the Giants 6 to 0. Giving up six well-spaced hits, the new Orioles' pitcher found himself in troubling waters but once, in the ninth stanza, when the Giants put two men on base with none out. At that juncture one of McGinnity's breaking balls caused the Giants' left fielder Tommy O'Brien to lift a little pop up into short center, where George Magoon chased it down and then threw to second baseman Johnny O'Brien doubling Kid Gleason off second base. Magoon then completed a game-ending triple play by relaying the ball to firstsacker

Candy LaChance before the Giants' Parke Wilson could get back to first base. It was a spectacular ending to McGinnity's very first major league win.

As the 1899 season wore on, Baltimore manager Muggsy McGraw more and more went to the tireless McGinnity, who finally piled up 41 starts, completing 38 of them. He appeared in another seven games, earning saves in two more, thus contributing to 30 of the fourth place Orioles' 86 wins. The husky Illinoisan had pocketed 28 victories, tieing him for first in the league with the accomplished Long Tom Hughes of the champion Brooklyn Superbas. Other noteworthy marks for that rookie season included a 2.68 ERA, good for third among NL pitchers (more than a full run under the league ERA at 3.85); and thirds in Pitching Runs (51) and Total Pitching Index (5.0). His Herculean efforts put him among the top ten rookies on our honors listing.

Beyond McGinnity and McGraw (who turned in a career year, hitting .391, stealing 73 bases and running up an astounding .547 On-Base Percentage), there was another outstanding rookie, Harry Howell, who won 13 while losing eight and showed flashes of the fielding brilliance that was to characterize his play as one of the game's finest fielding pitchers, later to become the all-time leader in chances per game for a pitcher with 5.42 for the 1905 St. Louis Browns. However, there was far from enough pitching and offense to overtake Philadelphia, Boston or Ned Hanlon's Brooklyn nine that finished atop the league, so the Orioles wound up a solid fourth just ahead of the Cy Young-led St. Louis team, which during the season had switched from its traditional brown stockings to a cardinal red and, after a little time, became known as the Cardinals.

Iron Man McGinnity is one of the very few short-term major leaguers who was voted into the Hall of Fame. On the

Box Score

Baltimore at the Polo Grounds, New York, April 24, 1899

Baltimore	AB	R	H	PO	A		New York	AB	R	H	PO	A
McGraw, 3b	2	2	0	1	2		Van Haltren, cf	4	0	1	1	0
Holmes, lf	4	2	3	2	1		Grady, 1b	4	0	0	7	0
Brodie, cf	4	0	1	0	0		Gleason, 2b	4	0	2	7	3
Scheckard, rf	2	1	1	4	1		Wilson, c	3	0	1	5	0
J. O'Brien, 2b	5	0	0	3	4		T. O'Brien, lf	3	0	0	1	0
LaChance, 1b	4	1	1	11	0		Hartman, 3b	3	0	0	3	0
Magoon, ss	5	0	1	3	5		Foster, rf	3	0	0	3	1
Robinson, c	3	0	1	2	1		I. Davis, ss	3	0	1	2	6
McGinnity, p	4	0	1	0	3		Meekin, p	3	0	1	0	0
Totals	33	6	9	27	17		Totals	30	0	6	27	10

```
Baltimore    100   001   112    6-9-1
New York     000   000   000    0-6-4
```

2BH	Magoon, Gleason
HR	Holmes
SB	McGraw, Holmes 2, Brodie, Sheckard, J. O'Brien
DP	I. Davis, Gleason and Grady; Gleason, I. Davis and Grady; Foster and Wilson
TP	Magoon to J. O'Brien to LaChance
LOB	Baltimore, 10; New York 5
BB	McGinnity 1, Meekin 6
K	McGinnity 1, Meekin 3
WP	Meekin
PB	Wilson
HBP	By Meekin, McGraw and Holmes
Umps	Gaffney and Andrews
Time	1:58
Att	1,501

basis of his ten-year career, which is the minimum career length considered for eligibility, he was elected in 1946. A career of such duration would had to have been extraordinary in order for the Hall's electors to cast a sufficient number of votes. It certainly was.

McGinnity's name will be found in the major league record books in a number of significant categories: he's 29th in authoring shutouts in a single season (nine in 1904); 42nd in single-season winning percentage (.814 in 1904); 59th with 35 wins in 1904; 47th with a 133.9 Clutch Pitching Index in 1908; and 68th in the Wins Above Team category, with 9.3 in 1904. Beyond that, his illustrious career as a part of John McGraw's Giant powerhouses of the early 1900s, which featured

one of the most dynamic duos in pitching history, that of New York's other "M and M Boys," Mathewson and McGinnity, struck an awesome winning chord with an overall 246–142 record. That amounts to ten straight seasons at just under 25 wins each year. McGinnity was one of the reasons John McGraw looked in contempt (he would pay dearly for that arrogance in years to come) on the then-fledgling World Series, contending that no American League team was worthy of stepping onto the diamond with his Giants in 1904, the year that his aces, Matty and the Iron Man, were right next to untouchable. (Mathewson won 34 and Joe added 35 more in that wondrous Giants' year of 1904.)

Nor was his last major league season in 1908 the end of the line. From 1909 through 1918, and again from 1922 to 1925 he added another 15 seasons before finally calling it a day at age 54. During that post–big time span he added at least 188 more pitching conquests to his lifetime record (the exact number will never be known since he also pitched here and there for other teams on semipro levels). That's almost beyond believability, or at least beyond the pale of mere mortal durability *and* career longevity.

Quite a man was the Iron Man from Rock Island, Illinois!

The 1890s: The Best of the Baltimore Oriole Rookies

Nm/Pos/Yr	GP	W–L/BA	SH/SV//RBI	PR/BR	ERA/FR	TPR
Joe McGinnity/RHP/1899	48	28–16	4/2	52	2.68	5.0
Bill Hoffer/RHP/1895	41	31–6	4/0	54	3.21	4.3
Jay Hughes/RHP/1898	38	23–12	5/0	13	3.20	1.9
Arlie Pond/RHP/1896	28	16–8	0/2	19	3.49	1.5
Edgar McNabb/RHP/1893	21	8–7	0/0	10	4.12	0.6
Joe Corbett/RHP/1896	8	3–0	0/1	9	2.20	0.3
Heinie Reitz/2B/1893	130	.286	76	1	-1	0.3
John McGraw/UT/1892	79	.269	26	3	1	0.2
Harry Howell/RHP/1899	28	13–8	0/1	1	3.91	-0.2
Charlie Harris/UT/1899	30	.279	1	-3	-5	-0.7

Mark Steven "The Bird" Fidrych

TPR: 5.0

1976, Detroit, AL

Born: August 14, 1954, Worcester, MA
RHP, 6'3" 175 lb. Major League Debut: April 20, 1976
1976: W19, L9, .679; 29/24 GS/GC; 97/53 K/BB; 9.8 Ratio; 38 PR; 5 DEF; 2.3 ERA

"The Bird Is the Word." That slogan was plastered across store windows, bedroom walls, bumpers — seemingly everywhere — and not only in Detroit, when the Bird himself, Mark Fidrych, had captivated the baseball world. Mention of his name caused people to stop in the streets to talk about him. It also caused SRO crowds to show up at the Motor City's ancient baseball emporium when he was scheduled to take the mound. Yes sir, he was Mr. Phenom of 1976, groundskeeper extraordinaire, an offbeat hero in a single, high-voltage package — a Hollywood script waiting to be written.

Mark Fidrych had spent two very ordinary minor league seasons bumping around at stopovers like Bristol, CT, Lakeland, FL, Montgomery, AL, and Evansville, IN — and all of that in two short seasons. When manager Ralph Houk took his charges to spring training the tall, blond righthander with those curly, attractive long tresses wasn't even listed on the roster. Though he had logged a fine 1.58 ERA in 40 innings at Evansville, his minor league prep work was something far less than a convincing A.

But that mattered little once the 21-year-old addressed the task of making Sarge Houk's varsity. With each outing he took huge steps forward. His lightning-like fast one and that sneaky slider, a pitch that become more deadly each time he used it, soon got the brass' attention. When Houk prepared his pitching staff list, which included veteran twirlers Dave Roberts, Vern Ruhle, Jim Crawford and Ray Bare, he was painfully aware of its inadequacies. There was room to spare for the Bird.

To handle the Fidrych slants, Houk determined to bring catcher Bruce Kimm along not only to spell Tiger great Bill Freehan, entering his last season, but to become the young fireballer's personal battery mate. As things turned out, the decision was a stroke of Houkian genius. The Bird debuted on April 20, and his 24-year-old catcher, also a first-year man, debuted two weeks later, on May 4. Both had inaugurated their best major league seasons in what proved to be short-lived careers. But who was to know about that, or even give it a second thought in 1976, when the sweet smell of success was in the air!

Mark Fidrych recorded the finest rookie season in Tiger history, besting four other hurlers for the honor.* His 5.0 TPR puts him into the number 10 spot on the all-time honors list. But that really isn't the story as far as the Bird is concerned, as critical as those numbers are to ranking the rookies' brightest and best. No, the story is the Bird himself. Call him eccentric, flaky, a space cadet — whatever — but here was a refreshing, immensely talented young pitching phenomenon (in the proper sense and meaning of the word) who captured the hearts of baseball fans everywhere with his style, antics and offbeat approach to a game steeped in ritual and convention. None of that mattered to Bird. He was his own man doing it his own way.

Stories, many of them apocryphal, poured from the pens of sports scribes and feature writers. The Bird provided one and all with material galore. And TV captured one improbable "happening" after another. However, it was a late June telecast showcasing the Yankees, 1976s AL pennant winners, that catapulted Fidrych into the national spotlight as he set down Billy Martin's resurgent New Yorkers with one of his better outings of the season. That would mean not only smart pitching, keeping his snapping heater low and staying ahead of the hitters, but even more spectacularly, chasing down teammates who had turned in fielding gems, landscaping the pitching mound (his personal

workshop), and, above all, conversing with the ball between pitches. The routine kept his national audience riveted. In Detroit the effect was at once mesmerizing and inspiring for a blue collar citizenry that was in the midst of angst and tough times over the downswing in the automobile industry's mid–'70s woes. This is the way Joe Falls, the very capable Motor City sports writer, described it in his *The Detroit Tigers: An Illustrated History*:

> He talked to the baseball and they all loved him. They loved him beyond belief. No player in Detroit history has been responsible for drawing more people into the ballpark in one season than Mark Fidrych in 1976. He came out of nowhere and from June 1 on, he won 19 games, losing only nine. But more than that, he was a fresh face on the scene — a free spirit who turned the whole town on with his almost unbelievable enthusiasm.... Four months — June, July, August, and September of 1976 — he flashed across the sky of Detroit. That was all. But he touched people in ways they had never been touched before. (p. 156)

That observation about drawing fans to the park deserves additional comment. Let the record show that on those days when Mark Fidrych got the ball from manager Ralph Houk, over 60 percent of the seasons' attendance showed up. That amounted to 605,677 turnstile rotations. And Tiger revenues soared over the million dollar mark on the shoulders of the Bird alone. Those numbers tell it all.

Good copy? In one interview after another, which, incidentally, he was always willing to give, he furnished enough choice tid-bits to go around for all the writers who clustered around him. For instance, in explaining why he had asked an umpire for a new ball, he explained, "Well, the ball

---

The top five in Tiger history: Fidrych, Roscoe Miller (1901), 3.5 TPR; Herm Pillette (1922), 3.2; Dave Rozema (1977), 2.8; and Reliever Terry Fox (1961), 2.8.

Mark "The Bird" Fidrych. (Dennis Colgin.)

real thing. And, indeed, he was. He won the starting assignment for AL manager Darrell Johnson's All-Stars, and though tagged with the 7–1 loss to the National League, the man and the mystique moved into the second half of the season with a full head of steam.

On July 16 the Tigers were scheduled to play the Oakland A's in a night game at Tiger Stadium. Predictably, there was a full house on hand, 45,905 jamming the rafters at Michigan and Trumbull avenues, because the Bird, by that time nine and two, was scheduled to pitch.

The "happening" that night turned out to be one of Fidrych's four 1976 whitewashings, as he doled out seven scattered singles in a taut, 11-inning, 1–0 victory, pushing his soaring record to

had a hit in it, so I wanted it to get back in the ball bag and goof round with the other balls in there. Maybe it'll learn some sense and come out as a pop-up next time" (Dickson, *Baseball's Greatest Quotations*, 133). And here's one the writers, especially, just loved: "I'm supposed to be writing a book, and I can hardly read" (Glenn Liebman, *Baseball Shorts*, 29).

The Bird's first 1976 appearance was in April — in relief. There followed several more relief appearances before Houk was willing to put his prodigy into a starting role. That finally came a month into the season when, on May 15, he won a 2–1 squeaker from Cleveland. By the end of June, with a six-game winning streak under tow, the word had spread through the league: the screwball in Detroit's the

10 and 2. The action climaxed in the 11th when the Athletics threatened to bring an end to all of the goose eggs on the scoreboard with a bunt single by Billy North and a stolen base by pinch runner Matt Alexander. John Wockenfuss, who had subbed for the Bird's number one catcher, Bruce Kimm, threw the ball into centerfield attempting to nail Alexander, who moved on into third with one out.

But after walking Ken McCullen, Fidrych settled down, dusting his 90+ MPH heater past dangerous Don Baylor and then inducing a Joe Rudi fly ball that Rusty Staub pocketed to retire the side. The Bird followed the out with a hand-to-the-forehead "phew!" and did the usual sprint from the mound to the dugout as the Detroit faithful cheered wildly. In the

Box Score

At Tiger Stadium, July 16, 1976, Oakland vs. Detroit

Oakland	AB	R	H	RBI
North, cf	5	0	3	0
Alexander, pr	0	0	0	0
Haney, c	0	0	0	0
Williams, dh	1	0	0	0
Lintz, ph	0	0	0	0
McMullen, dh	1	0	0	0
Baylor, rf	5	0	0	0
Rudi, lf	5	0	2	0
Bando, 3b	4	0	0	0
Tenace, 1b	4	0	0	0
Washington, cf	4	0	1	0
Garner, 2b	4	0	1	0
Sandt, ss	3	0	0	0
Torrez, p	0	0	0	0
Fingers, p	0	0	0	0
Totals	36	0	7	0

Detroit	AB	R	H	RBI
LeFlore, cf	5	1	2	0
Veryzer, ss	3	0	0	0
Staub, rf	3	0	1	0
Horton, dh	5	0	1	1
Thompson, 1b	4	0	0	0
Johnson, lf	3	0	1	0
Rodriguez, 3b	4	0	1	0
Garcia, 2b	3	0	1	0
Ogilvie, ph	1	0	0	0
Krimm, c	3	0	0	0
Wockenfuss, c	0	0	0	0
Meyer, ph	1	0	0	0
Scrivener, 2b	0	0	0	0
Fidrych, p	0	0	0	0
Totals	35	1	7	1

```
Oakland    000  000  000  00   0-7-1
Detroit    000  000  000  01   1-7-1
```

2BH	Rodriguez
3BH	Staub
LOB	Oakland, 7; Detroit, 8
BB	Fingers 2, Fidrych 4
K	Torres 3, Fingers 1, Fidrych 5
HPB	Johnson by Torrez
WP	Fidrych (10–2)
LP	Fingers (5–6)
Time	2:25
Att	45,905

bottom of the 11th, Willie Horton came through with a clothesline shot off Hall of Fame reliever Rollie Fingers that scored the nimble-footed Ron Leflore with the winning run. Mark Fidrych was the first out of the dugout to congratulate both Leflore and Horton. It had happened again! Now the Bird stood at a league-leading 10 and 2.

Fidrych rounded out his fairytale season with nine more wins and a 19 and 9 record. He iced his bicentennial cake with league-leading figures in games completed (24 in 29 starts), earned run average (2.34), and Pitching Runs (36). In a league that averaged 8.7 hits per game, the Fidrych average was an even seven, and he issued a mere 53 free passes, an average of one per 4.2 innings pitched. Further, he went through the entire season without an error, earning an outstanding 5 rating in pitcher's defense. He had done about everything except hit .300 — which, of course, he couldn't since Rusty Staub usually took care of the designated hitting in Detroit — while serving as groundskeeper, public relations "manager," *and* the club's leading pitcher.

In Mark Fidrych we have a thoroughly American folk-hero who quite ably rounds out the top dozen among the rookie titans who gave America's baseball fans a golden season in the sun. Among them, the charmer *non pareil* was the Bird.

1976: Ten Top Rookies

Nm/Pos/Tm	GP	W–L/BA	SH/SV//RBI	BR/PR	ERA/FR	TPR
Mark Fidrych, RHP, Det-A	31	19–9	4/0	38	2.34	5.0
Willie Randolph, 2b, NY-A	125	.267	40	4	15	3.2
Pat Zachry, RHP, Cin-N	38	14–7	1/0	17	2.74	1.4
Paul Hartzell, RHP, Cal-A	37	7–4	2/2	10	2.77	1.3
Bruce Sutter, RHP(RP), Chi-N	52	6-3	0/10	11	2.70	1.3
Clarence Metzger, RHP(RP), SD-N	77	11–4	0/16	5	2.95	0.7
Rick Jones, LHP, Bos-A	24	5–3	0/0	6	3.36	0.4
Bruce Kimm, c, Det-A	63	.263	6	-1	4	0.4
Gary Templeton, ss, StL-N	53	.291	17	-3	1	0.4
Jerry Augustine, LHP, Mil-A	39	9–12	3/0	4	3.30	0.3

Frank Alfred Linzy

TPR: 4.9

1965, San Francisco, NL

Born: September 15, 1940, Fort Gibson, OK
RHP (RP), 6'1" 190 lb. Major League Debut: August 14, 1963
1965: W9, L3, .750 W%; 57 GP; 0/21 SH/SV; 20 PR; 5 DEF; 1.43 ERA

On the heels of a 1964 season marred by the racial insensitivities of manager Alvin Dark and the internal unrest that went with it, the Giants turned to Herman Franks, a grizzled veteran of the baseball wars, to lead the ballclub in 1965. A more fatherly, patient figure, he took the team to spring training with a short list of goals: 1) to execute the fundamentals and play together as a team; 2) to concentrate on playing out the season a game at a time; 3) to straighten out the bullpen; and 4) to beat the contenders, especially the Giants' arch-rivals in Los Angeles.

The '65 club got most of it right, but not quite right enough to win the pennant, falling two games short at the hands of the Dodgers.

There were three rookies who reported to the Giants' Phoenix training base whose talents didn't escape the eyes of Herm Franks. All three ultimately accompanied the team to Pittsburgh for the season opener. The three were Jim Ray Hart, a stocky third baseman with punch in his stick, reliever Masanori Murakami, Japan's first export to major league baseball, and a sinkerballer by the name of Frank Linzy, a rawboned Oklahoman who quietly but very definitely impressed skipper Franks with his command of the strike zone. Hart wound up holding down the hot corner all season long in a fine rookie campaign, Murakami contributed eight saves to the Giants' cause in 45 appearances of rather solid relief work, and Linzy was one of the National League Rookie of the Year contenders on the basis of a magnificent season that sparkled with numbers like 1.43 (ERA), 9 and 3 (W–L), 21 (saves), and 23 (the number of walks [8 of those intentional] in 82 innings pitched).

But let's get back to the start of the Linzy story. When Frank was playing semi-pro ball in 1959 for Muskogee he was spotted by the Giants' Oklahoma scout Billy McLean. The bespectacled right-hander so impressed McLean that he immediately sat down to write "the home office." Against club regulations he had signed Linzy and

Relief pitcher Frank Linzy. (Dennis Colgin.)

in the deal. Right or wrong, the deed was done and Frank Linzy was ready to get on with it.

An implacable sort, Linzy had a way of persisting, of keeping after it, until the job was done. That was just what Herman Franks needed in the bullpen, where "the inmates" often won ball games as much on mind-games as they did with out pitches. After some minor league seasoning Linzy appeared to be about ready as the 1965 season got under-way, and the Giants' major domo determined to give it a try. It was one of his better decisions in 1965, that is, once his new reliever got un-tracked. And by mid–May, particularly after a game-ending strikeout that sent Ernie Banks and the Cubs packing, sealing a 3–0 shut-out at "The Stick," Linzy was definitely untracked. Just a couple of weeks earlier his ERA had been sitting at a hefty 3.83, but by early June it had been trimmed down to a svelte 2.20, the result of six solid appearances that put his save count at 5.

wrote to explain: "I've just signed something, but I don't know what it is, outfielder or pitcher. The one thing I'm sure about is that it's a big league prospect at either position! I didn't sleep a wink last night for fear that Frank would get away so I signed him today without your authorization, since no bonus was involved." Three things stand out here beyond bird-dog McClean's anxiety. He had an athlete par excellence on his hands, he had signed an 18-year-old youngster who didn't mind taking the responsibility for signing, and the big bonus money was simply no factor

For some discerning eyes in the Giants' organization, it was evident that Linzy was just about ready by mid–1964, when he began tearing up the Eastern League with San Francisco's farm club at Springfield, MA. By season's end he was elected to the league's All-Star Team, having put together a league-leading 16 wins and a microscopic 1.55 ERA. A year later, by September of 1965, big Frank and his ERA, hovering around the 2.00 mark, were well on the way to Rookie of the Year candidacy. While not elected the BBWAA's Rookie of the Year, Linzy *was* honored with *The Sporting News*' rookie honors when the post-season laurels were handed out. That merits closer attention a bit further on.

On July 28 the St. Louis Cardinals visited Candlestick Park with the Cards' Tracy Stallard going against Ron Herbel. It was a game Frank will never forget, if for no other reason than that he had a perfect day at the plate, two for two, and sent his one career home run into the seats as the Giants won 8–5. The victory went to Herbel and Linzy picked up the save, number 10, coming on to retire the third out in the

sixth inning, following Murakami, and finishing out the final two frames.

The win put the Giants a half game behind Milwaukee, two behind second place Cincinnati, and four away from the Dodgers, in first. As the race moved into its final two weeks, the Giants and the Dodgers, led by the powerful Koufax-Drysdale pitching tandem, had the pennant hunt down to themselves. Most of Herm Franks' goals were on the verge of being accomplished.

But the big fish got away. Leading the league as late as September 25, the Giants stumbled into a tie with the Dodgers the very next day, finally succumbing after a three-game deadlock when Los Angeles

---

Box Score

St. Louis at Candlestick Park, San Francisco, July 28, 1965

St. Louis	AB	R	H	RBI
Brock, lf	5	1	1	0
Groat, ss	4	1	0	0
Flood, cf	3	1	1	2
Boyer, 3b	4	1	2	1
White, 1b	3	0	1	0
Gagliano, 2b	4	0	1	2
Francona, rf	3	0	1	0
Skinner, ph	1	0	0	0
McCarver, c	4	0	0	0
Stallard, p	1	0	0	0
Shannon, ph-rf	2	1	0	0
Totals	34	5	7	5

San Francisco	AB	R	H	RBI
Schofield, ss	5	2	3	2
Davenport, 3b	3	0	1	2
Mays, cf	3	0	0	0
McCovey, 1b	4	1	2	0
Hart, lf	3	1	2	1
M. Alou, pr-lf	0	0	0	0
J. Alou, ph-rf	1	0	1	1
Gabrielson, rf	3	0	0	0
Peterson, ph	1	0	0	0
Henderson, lf	0	0	0	0
Lanier, 2b	3	1	0	0
Bertell, c	3	1	0	0
Herbel, p	1	1	0	1
Linzy, p	2	1	2	1
Totals	32	8	11	8

St. Louis   000 003 200   5-7-0
San Francisco 050 001 20x   8-11-2

DP	St. Louis 1, San Francisco 2
LOB	St. Louis 6, San Francisco 5
2BH	McCovey, Flood, White
3BH	Davenport
HR	Linzy (first major league hit)
SB	Hart
SH	Davenport
WP	Herbel (7–5)
LP	Stallard (7–4)
SV	Linzy (10)
Time	2:37
Att	12,711

beat Cincinnati, 2–1, in 12 innings and the Cardinals drubbed the homestanding Giants nine to one on September 28. The World Series would open at Minnesota with Don Drysdale working against Mudcat Grant a little more than a week later. Though Frank Linzy's last appearance of the season, on October 2, resulted in save number 14 and a 3–2 victory over Cincinnati, it was a meaningless win inasmuch as the Dodgers won over the pesky Braves, 3–1. Herman Franks' boys had no alternative but to watch the World Series.

One other 1965 incident colored the pennant race a bright red, and that involved the prime antagonists, the Dodgers and — who else — the Giants. That was the slugfest that involved Giant ace Juan Marichal and Dodger catcher Johnny Roseboro in an ugly scene at home plate when words between the two led to Marichal's turning in the batter's box to slug Roseboro in the head with his bat. The benches cleared, the teams went at it, and finally Marichal was not only ejected but suspended long enough so that he would be unable to appear in the next scheduled series, which was in Los Angeles on September 6. Linzy didn't pitch in the August 22 game, but appeared in the Los Angeles tilt on September 6, picking up the victory, number seven on the season, as the Giants won seven to six in the twelfth inning before 53,581 screaming Angelinos in a scenario made to order for the tight-lipped, relentless reliever.

Despite his impressive debut season, Frank Linzy didn't win the 1965 Rookie of the Year Award. Jim Lefebvre, Dodger (of all things) second baseman, did. Big Frank didn't even make it to a runnerup slot. The three vote-getters were Lefebvre (13), Joe Morgan (4), and Linzy (3). By contrast, a more searching look at the record, along with puzzling through what the players actually meant to their teams' pennant chances, points in a different direction.

The numbers present a more realistic picture.

Rookie of the Year Award winners Jim Lefebvre of Los Angeles and Curt Blefary of Baltimore in the American League were decisive winners in their leagues. Both, by sabermetric analysis, were eclipsed by equally decisive margins, Lefebvre by Joe Morgan (4.2 to 0.5 TPR ratings) and Blefary by Linzy (4.9 to 2.3). Note that Lefebvre's -5 rating in Fielding Runs is below Joe Morgan's -2, and that both are several sub-standard notches below the league-average fielders.

Note, also, that both Frank Linzy of the National League and Marcelino Lopez, Angels lefty, had outstanding fielding ratings, Linzy with a superior 5 DEF rating and Lopez, a 4 rating. Linzy fulfilled the fifth infielder role in perfect form with no errors for a 1.000 Fielding Average (the league average was .956), while participating in two double plays and recording 39 assists.

The mystery remains: why were both Morgan and Linzy passed over for National League honors? Their clearcut superiority stands in sharp contrast to the BBWAA pick, Jim Lefebvre.

Frank Linzy went on to record his name in the Giants' record book in career saves (fourth with 77) and appearances (tenth with 308). He was the Giants' team leader in saves five consecutive seasons.

Frank Linzy's 4.9 makes him the Giants' number one rookie in franchise history, a history replete with Christy Mathewson, Carl Hubbell and Juan Marichal among its hurlers, and Bill Terry, Willie Mays and Bobby Bonds among many, many other distinguished players. His number 13 position on the honors list with a solid, workmanlike contribution is, much like its author, a sturdy addition to the upper echelon that should stand the test of future challenges.

1965: Ten Top Rookies

Nm/Pos/Tm	GP	W–L/BA	SH/SV//RBI	PR/BR	DEF/FR	ERA/OB%	TPR
Frank Linzy, RHP (RP), SF-N	57	9-3	0/21	20	5	1.43	4.9
Joe Morgan, 2b, Cin-N	157	.271	40	28	-2	.375	4.2
Curt Blefary, of, Bal-A	144	.260	71	25	2	.382	2.3
Marcelino Lopez, LHP, Cal-A	35	14–13	1/1	11	4	2.93	2.3
Willie Horton, of, Det-A	143	.273	104	21	5	.326	1.6
Sandy Alomar, Sr, inf, Mil-N	67	.241	8	-7	14	.245	1.0
Gary Wagner, RHP (RP), Phl-N	59	7–7	0/7	5	1	3.00	0.8
Ray Barker, 1b, Clv/NY-A	109	.246	31	1	6	.326	0.7
Dave Boswell, RHP, Minn	27	6–5	0/0	2	-1	3.40	0.5
Jim Lefebvre, 2b, LA-N	157	.250	69	5	-5	.339	0.5

Mitchell Otis "Mitch" or "The Rage" Page

TPR: 4.9

1977, Oakland, AL

Born: October 15, 1951, Compton, CA

OF, 6'2" 205 lb. Major League Debut: April 9, 1977

1977: 145 GP; 85 R; 21 HR; .307 BA; .407 OB%; 42 SB; 10 SBR; 39 BR; 7 FR

As a junior majoring in physical education at California Polytechnic University in Pomona, outfield speedster Mitch Page hit .304 and led the baseball team in RBI's with 33. That spring he was listed as an Honorable Mention selection on The Sporting News' College All-American Team. That he was a promising prospect had already been established during his senior high school year, when the Oakland A's liked what they saw of the rangy lad and selected him as a fourth-round choice in the 1970 free agent draft. But Page didn't sign, opting to go on to college.

Three years and many drafts later, the Pirates made him their third 1973 selection. This time he signed and was promptly sent to Pittsburgh's Charleston, South Carolina, farm club, where he spent parts of the 1973 and '74 seasons. Moving up to the Pirates' Class AA affiliate in the Texas League at Shreveport, he hit .291 in 1975 and led the league in RBI's (90). Boosted yet another notch by Pittsburgh's front office, the fellow they called "The Rage" checked into Triple A ball with the Pirates' top farm club at Charleston, West Virginia. Playing first base, he hit International League pitching at a strong .294 clip, driving home 83, stealing 23 bases and smashing 22 round-trippers.

Though Mitch Page had proven that he was ready for a shot at the big time, there was a problem. Back in Pittsburgh the Pirates had been in the midst of several pennant-contending seasons with strength at the very places he played. Future Hall of Famer Willie Stargell led his "Pirate Family" from first base, and a rock 'em–sock 'em outfield of Dave Parker and Al Oliver, with the swift Omar Moreno between them, were primed for a divisional championship.

The Page dilemma was finally resolved during the 1977 spring training season, when the Corsairs decided to part with six of their players in order to shore up their infield. They picked up Phil Garner and Tommy Helms from Oakland's A's for four pitchers plus young outfield hopefuls Tony Armas and "The Rage" Mitchell Page.

So the Rage packed his bags and headed for Arizona where he promptly nailed down a starting outfield berth. Manager Jack McKeon started both Armas and Page in his Opening Day lineup, hitting his new leftfielder, Page, in the third spot just ahead of the recently acquired Rich Allen. Tony Armas started the season in right field, batting seventh. And by April 13, in a game against the Angels, Mr. Page had found the range, blasting his first major league four-bagger against California's Wayne Simpson.

Unfortunately, his right hand wasn't. But despite a nagging soreness on the left side of his throwing hand, Page's debut month of April was a huge success. Up there among the league's leading hitters, he finished the first month of the season around the .350 mark, fielding adequately, if not spectacularly, and causing increasing concern around the league with his baserunning. Nonetheless, by mid–May, after a few incidents of bat-tossing caused by his weakened grip, it was evident that stop-gap measures like ice and the peeling of callus that had formed on his tender paw weren't going to be enough to get him by.

Consequently, in the midst of an early–June series in Detroit, the budding star boarded a plane for Oakland to see a hand specialist. Earlier in his career at

A's swiftie Mitch Page. (Colgin Photo.)

Shreveport a correction of a different kind had to be made. During the 1974 season at Salem in the Carolina League, while caught in the throes of an anemic .200 average, he had gone to an eye doctor, who told him he needed glasses. Just how badly he needed them was evident the next time he stepped into the batting cage. The correction transformed his sight —*and* his batting average. Hopeful that specialist Dr. Jack Tupper of Oakland could bring his hand around, as glasses had previously done for his eyes, Mitch made his way back to Oakland. To make a painful, long story (the source of his problem was a deep-seated growth caused by a wart) short, Dr. Tupper's ministrations were indeed helpful, and once again Page's BA showed it, soaring back over the .300 mark after a season's nadir point at the .270 mark. Thereafter, a daily callus-trimming kept Page in the lineup. Although he would have to wait until after the season for an operation that would get at the core of the deeply embedded callus, at least he was able to do battle on a daily basis.

There was another equally helpful source of assistance in Oakland. His name was Robert Ricardo, owner of Ricky's Restaurant in nearby San Leandro, with whom Page had struck up an alliance. By furnishing Mitch videotaping equipment, the slumping rookie was able to study his hitting style at a time when his ailing hand had also interfered with his bat speed. What followed his doctoring and film analysis was a Player-of-the-Week tear that raised his average back over the .300 standard with a smoking .478 over a seven-day stretch just before the All-Star break.

Page's manager the first 100 games of the season before his replacement, Bobby Winkles, took over, was Jack McKeon, who was instrumental in bringing Mitch to Oakland in the spring training swap with Pittsburgh. McKeon liked the lithe outfielder's speed and encouraged him to study pitchers and outfielders and to pick his spots, adding the baserunning dimension to his offensive arsenal. Page listened, and he studied. By the time the rest of the league caught on, he had swiped 26 bases — consecutively. His 27th came against the same Wayne Simpson who had offered up his first dinger in the Bigs. That one was a record-setter, both for the American League and Rookie record books.

He was once again the beneficiary of help, this time from another basepath swiftie, Matt Alexander, who stole 26 bases in part-time duty for the A's. The two watched pitchers together and compared notes on hurlers' moves, habits and inclinations. That paid off. At season's end, the Rage had swiped 42 of Oakland's league-leading 176 total. The A's 176 thefts, by the way, was the only such accomplishment, unless their league-lowest Fielding Average, a pitiful .970, might be listed as a "first."

There might have been a shortcoming or two in Mitch Page's game (although he had 11 outfield assists and 279 putouts, there were also 14 league-leading errors in the scorebook), but a lack of self-confidence was not one of them. A boisterous sort, he came straight out with what was on his mind, and he played no favorites. No matter how tough the summer of 1977 was for the ballclub, the one they called "the Rage" either *was* one, was getting into one, or was just getting over one. But it's well to remember that brash, outspoken rookies have been part of the major league scene since Abner Doubleday's time, so why should 1977 be any different? There was no chance for the season to be ordinary with young Mr. Page around.

Of the several exceptional days Mitch put together (like his game against the Tigers' rookie sensation, Dave Rozema, when he touched up one of his prime rivals for Rookie of the Year honors with a pair of long distance shots that saddled the Detroit sensation with his sixth loss), his Fenway Park extravaganza on August 29, which enabled the A's to edge the Bosox 8 to 7, was the gem of them all.

Though Jim Rice slugged three homers, driving in four Boston tallies, it wasn't good enough, as the Rage combed Red Sox pitching with a pair of homers and a triple, countering Rice's productivity with four ribbies of his own. His second tater of the evening came in the top of the

Box Score

Oakland Athletics at Boston Red Sox, August 29, 1977

Oakland	AB	R	H	RBI	E		Boston	AB	R	H	RBI	E
North, cf	4	1	1	0	0		Burleson, ss	6	1	1	1	0
Murray, cf	0	0	0	0	0		Helms, dh	4	0	2	0	0
Perez, 2b	1	0	0	0	0		Dillard, pr	0	0	0	0	0
R. Scott, 2b-ss	5	0	0	1	0		Carbo, dh	1	0	0	0	0
Page, lf	5	2	3	4	0		Hobson, 3b	5	0	0	0	0
Tabb, 1b	4	0	0	0	0		Yastrzemski, lf	5	1	1	1	0
B. Williams, dh	4	0	2	0	0		Rice, rf	5	3	4	4	0
Alexander, pr	0	0	0	0	0		G. Scott, 1b	4	1	1	0	0
McKinney, dh	1	0	1	0	0		Lynn, cf	5	0	3	0	0
Sanguillen, c	3	0	1	0	0		Fisk, c	4	0	2	1	0
Mallory, pr-cf	1	1	0	0	0		Doyle, 2b	5	1	1	0	0
Gross, 3b	2	2	1	0	0		Wise, p	0	0	0	0	0
Tyrone, rf	4	1	3	2	0		Willoughby, p	0	0	0	0	0
Picciolo, ss	2	1	1	1	1		Campbell, p	0	0	0	0	0
Crawford, ph	0	0	0	0	0		Stanley, p	0	0	0	0	0
Newman, c	0	0	0	0	0							
Coleman, p	0	0	0	0	1							
Torrealba, p	0	0	0	0	0							
Bair, p	0	0	0	0	0							
Totals	36	8	13	8	2		Totals	44	7	15	7	0

```
Oakland    001   041   011    8-13-2
Boston     021   202   000    7-15-0
```

2BH	Sanguillen, Gross, Tyrone, Burleson
3BH	Page
HR	Rice 3, Page 2, Picciolo
SB	North, Dillard, Mallory
SH	Picciolo
DP	Boston 2
LOB	Oakland 6, Boston 13
BB	Coleman 1, Torrealba 2, Bair 3, Wise 2, Willoughby 0, Campbell 3
K	Coleman 1, Torrealba 2, Bair 3, Wise 4, Willoughby 3, Campbell 1
HBP	By Wise (North)
WP	Bair (3–2)
LP	Campbell (12–9)
Time	3:24
Att	29,750

ninth and proved to be the game-winning blast.

When the season was over Kansas City and New York had won divisional titles and Oakland finished in the next county, some 38.5 games out of sight. Though snubbed by the BBWAA scribes for Rookie of the Year laurels, he was informed on October 22 that American League players had voted him Rookie of the Year in *The Sporting News* balloting, an honor that earned him *TSN*'s engraved Bulova Accuquartz wrist watch. Leading his teammates in every offensive category except home runs (third-baseman Wayne Gross beat him by one, 22 to 21), he had endured the hardships of his freshman season to forge a stellar 4.9 TPR rating, the best rookie season in the Athletics' long and legendary history.

1977: Ten Top Rookies

Nm/Pos/Tm	GP	W–L/BA	SH/SV//RBI	PR/BR	ERA/FR	TPR
Page/of/Oak-A	154	.307	75	39	7	4.9
Romo/RHP/Sea-A	58	8–10	0/16	12	2.83	3.0
Rozema/RHP/Det-A	28	15–7	1/0	29	3.09	2.8
Guidry/LHP/NY-A	31	16–7	5/1	26	2.82	2.6
W. Hernandez/LHP/Chi-N	67	8–7	0/4	17	3.03	2.3
E. Wills/2b/Tex-A	152	.287	62	8	3	2.3
R. Jones/of/Sea-A	160	.263	76	8	22	2.2
Lacey/RHP-RP/Oak-A	64	6–8	0/7	13	3.03	2.0
S. Henderson/of/NY-N	99	.297	65	17	6	1.9
Richards/of/SD	146	.290	32	11	1	1.6

Edward Marvin "Big Ed" Reulbach

TPR: 4.8

1905, Chicago, NL

Born: December 1, 1882, Detroit, MI. Died: July 17, 1961, Glens Falls, NY
RHP, 6'1" 190 lb. Major League Debut: May 16, 1905
1905: W18, L14; 28 CG; 5/1 SH/SV; .201 OBA; 29/28 GS/GP; 51 PR; 1.42 ERA

The very creative Arch Ward, *Chicago Tribune* sportswriter who regaled *Tribune* readers for many years with his "In the Wake of the News" column, interviewed Ed Reulbach shortly after the former Cub's 50th birthday. Ward started the story, based on his January 7, 1936, interview, like this:

> The old Cubs, whose deeds will linger long around the places where baseball yarns are spun, had their Frank Chance, their Johnny Evers, their Mordecai Brown, their Joe Tinker, and their Frank Schulte. They also had their Edward M. Reulbach, who leaped the barrier between college and major league baseball, to launch a career which involved him in four successful pennant struggles with the old west side machine.

It's those "four successful pennant struggles with the old west side machine" that most readily capture the hearts of Cubbie fans. But often there is a genuine star who is relegated to the second tier of heroes by some of the more colorful players. "Big Ed," as he was known, was one of those. That certainly doesn't mean his accomplishments were second tier, for his entries into the Cubs' record book — some quite remarkable — are still there.

The hurler who came to the Colts, as the Cubs were then known, arrived off the college campus in 1905 after having been tracked down by scout George Huff, who had chased all over the countryside for the right-hander, an engineering major, first at Notre Dame and then at Vermont University. Reulbach had been playing under assumed names on several teams, and his most recent baseball adventures had taken place at the little university town of Burlington, Vermont. Huff finally caught up with his man there, brought Ed back to the Midwest, and saw to it that his name wound up on a Cubs pact, which, by the

Big Ed Reulbach of the Cubs. (Brace Photo.)

that the Giants used their five bingles to good advantage, producing four tallies against a punchless Cub "attack," which could muster but two safeties and nary a run. So the college phenom went down to the first defeat of his major league career. There would be more, of course, but before he had thrown his last pitch under the Big Tent, the ratio of wins to losses was two to one for a career record of 161 victories against 96 losses in the National League. Reulbach added 21 more wins and 10 more losses for the 1915 Newark Peppers of the Federal League, for a grand total of 182–106.

By the time the Cubs got to Philadelphia they found their hitting shoes. In a game started by Carl Lundgren on May 25, they picked up a few early-inning runs, but fell behind as the Phillies cuffed around the Cub veteran to take the lead in the fifth frame. That brought on Reulbach, who soon put an end to the Phils' attack and went on to blank them the rest of the way in his four-inning relief job, his first big league win. That prompted skipper Selee to put Reulbach into the starting rotation, and on May 30 the big fellow recorded his first shutout over the Cincinnati Reds at the Palace of the Fans in a spine-tingling ball game in which Frank Chance singled home Frank Schulte with the winning run in the top of the fourth. That's all Reulbach

way, was the youngster's first professional baseball contract.

It was mid–May before manager Frank Selee started Reulbach, and when he did start him, it wasn't against one of the league's patsies. Selee started Ed against the arch-rival Giants on May 16, and Ed responded with a workmanlike five-hitter against the New Yorkers. The trouble was needed in his 1 to 0 win as he nudged the Chicagoans over the .500 mark at 20 and 19. That was the first of his five shutouts for the season, a still-standing rookie record.

During the 1905 season New York beat Reulbach three times by one-run margins, Philadelphia and St. Louis once each, Brooklyn twice (by 2–1 and 2–0 scores), and he lost to Pittsburgh by a 6–4 margin. That amounts to eight of the 14 losses he suffered. A run here or there might easily have turned his final 18–14 record into a 21- or 22-victory season. As it turned out, it was all a part of the rookie's big league education. Both Reulbach and the Cubs were building toward a climax: the World Series. That would come the very next season and remain as part of standard Chicago fare right on through the 1910 season — a part of those "four successful pennant struggles with the old west side machine." Through that glorious skein of National League supremacy Ed Reulbach followed closely on the heels of the legendary "Three-Finger" Brown as one of the two big cogs in the Cubs' magnificent pitching staff. During a three-year span from 1906 to 1908 he won 60 while losing only 15, leading the league in winning percentage each season. That, too, found its way into the record books.

Equally remarkable was Reulbach's performance in two exceptional extra-inning games in 1905. In these two mid-summer games he outlasted the Phillies 2 to 1 in 20 innings, and in the stifling heat of St. Louis, beat the Cardinals, again by a 2 to 1 count, in 18 innings. The tally on those two games includes 38 innings (four games plus two frames) played to get the two decisions, and a yield of only four runs. That's right: he's the only one, ever, to have turned that trick!

Big Ed's rookie year ERA, a scintillating 1.42, was a career low, second best in the majors to Christy Mathewson's 1.28 (Rube Waddell's 1.48 led the AL) in a year of ultra low-scoring games. Reulbach led the league in opponents' batting average (OBA) at .201, good enough to rank him in the top 100, all-time, in this category. His other all-time marks, also established in his freshman campaign, include single-season ERA, good for the number 29 spot, and 6.42 hits given up per game, which puts him in the number 78 slot. In 1906 Ed narrowed down his hits per inning pitched to a miserly 5.33, and that puts him in the number three position in baseball history — quite an accomplishment!

Ed Reulbach moved on from his remarkable rookie season to a number of noteworthy achievements, the most widely heralded of which occurred on September 26 of the 1908 season, when he went the route in a doubleheader at Brooklyn, winning both games by shutout scores, 5 to 0 and 3 to 0, before 15,000, cheering Washington Park fans who knew they were in on something very special. That day he completed his 30th consecutive scoreless inning, and added another whitewashing his next time out to run the streak to 41 (that included the last two innings of a game in Boston that preceded the Brooklyn twinbill) before yielding his next run.

A pitcher so much involved in low-scoring games is bound to have a game or two that stand out as personal favorites. One most certainly occurred in the World Series of 1906, when he shut down the Series winner, the White Sox, on one hit, 7 to 1, in the second game of the Fall Classic. While that Series loss might have galled most of the Cubs and all of their fans, it didn't bend Reulbach too badly out of shape. He had the satisfaction of throwing the first one-hitter in World Series history, and anyway, his steady-as-she-goes attitude took him beyond things he couldn't immediately control.

There *was* one shutout, almost as gratifying, if not on a par with his World Series masterpiece. That was his rookie season conquest of the one and only Joe McGinnity, great Giants' Hall of Famer, on a bright Chicago afternoon, the 11th of June, at West Side Park.

Beginning on May 30, Reulbach had run up impressive shutouts against the Reds, 1 to 0 and Pittsburgh, 4 to 0. Then he sat down Boston's Beaneaters, 10 to 2, before being matched against the World Series' ace, McGinnity, who that season logged 21 wins and a World Series shutout against the Philadelphia Athletics. Those three wins brought him to his brilliant five-hit calcimining on June 11 at the Polo Grounds. A week later his winning streak stretched to seven, a string that ran to nine before Deacon Phillippe and the Pirates snapped it on July 6.

But on June 11 Reulbach was the boss man, helping his own cause along by initiating two Reulbach-to-Tinker-to-Chance twin-killings, walking only one batter and causing the Giants to ground into infield outs most of the afternoon. A crowd of more than 24,000 enjoyed it immensely, especially since the proud New Yorkers were the victims.

Frank Linzy and Mitchell Page, tied at 4.9 TPR's to rank 13 and 14 on the rookies honor list, presented us with the first of a number of ties among our rookie honorees. Each of those ties, including the two involving Wilcy Moore and Ed Reulbach, both of whom are rated at 4.8 TPR, would have called for a subjective selection to arrange these tightly bunched player ratings. Instead, all ties are arranged chronologically. While that might appear at first

---

Box Score

The Chicago Cubs at the Polo Grounds, New York, June 11, 1905

Chicago	AB	R	H	PO	A		New York	AB	R	H	PO	A
Slagle, cf	4	0	1	1	0		Donlin, cf	4	0	1	0	0
Schulte, lf	4	1	1	2	0		Browne, rf	4	0	1	2	0
Maloney, rf	4	2	2	2	0		McGann, 1b	4	0	0	10	2
Chance, 1b	3	1	2	11	0		Bresnahan, c	4	0	0	6	2
Tinker, ss	3	0	1	4	4		Mertes, lf	2	0	1	2	0
Evers, 2b	3	0	1	4	4		Dahlen, ss	5	0	0	1	1
Casey, 3b	2	0	0	1	1		Devlin, 3b	3	0	0	1	3
O'Neill, c	3	0	0	2	1		Gilbert, 2b	3	0	2	2	5
Reulbach, p	3	0	0	0	4		McGinnity, p	2	0	0	0	2
Wiltse, p	0	0	0	0	0		Strang, ph	1	0	1	0	0
Totals	29	4	8	27	14		Totals	29	0	6	27	13

New York*   000   000   000   0-6-1
Chicago   100   120   00x   4-8-1

2BH	Chance
LOB	Chicago 3, New York 4
SH	Tinker
SB	Schulte, Maloney 2, Mertes
DP	Reulbach, Tiner and Chance 2, Evers and Chance
K	Reulbach 1, McGinnity 4, Wiltse 2
BB	Reulbach 1, McGinnity 2
HPB	Devlin by Reulbach
Umpires	Emsle and Bausewine
Time	1:28
Att	24,000

*New York opted to bat first

blush like getting on base with a bloop hit rather than a line drive, it does get these "dead heat" seasons arranged in a more objectively ordered selection process. Concerning Big Ed and Wilcy, Moore's combination of timely starting roles and brilliant relief pitching might easily be interpreted as reason enough to shade, by the thinnest of margins, the fine hurling of Ed Reul-bach, which featured those five shutouts, extra-inning victories and the many low-scoring games that went into his 18 and 14 record, causing a personal (and subjective) reading to place the Yankee great ahead of Reulbach. Nonetheless, both were eminently qualified for their lofty perch among the top 20 rookies of all time.

1905: Ten Top Rookies

Nm/Pos/Tm	GP	W–L/BA	SH/SV//RBI	PR/BR	ERA/FR	TPR
Ed Reulbach, RHP, Chi-N*	34	18–14	5/1	51	1.42	4.8
George Stone, of, StL-A*	154	.296	52	32	2	2.9
Orv Overall, RHP, Cin-N	42	18–23	2/0	16	2.86	1.5
Charlie Chech, RHP, Cin-N	39	14–14	1/0	12	2.89	1.2
Eddie Hahn, of, NY-A	43	.319	11	7	2	0.8
Irv Young, LHP, Bos-N	43	20–21	7/0	8	2.90	0.4
John Hummel, of, Brk-N	30	.266	7	2	0	0.2
Gabby Street, c, Cin-N	34	.238	8	-4	2	0.1
Buster Brown, RHP, StL-N	23	8–11	3/0	0	2.97	0.0
George Gibson, c, Pit-N	46	.178	14	-7	3	0.0

*Awarded the Deane Hypothetical Rookie of the Year

William Wilcy "Cy" Moore

TPR: 4.8

1927, New York, AL

Born: May 20, 1897, Bonita, TX. Died: Hollis, OK, March 29, 1963
LHP (RP), 6'0" 195 lb. Major League Debut: April 14, 1927
1927: W19, L7, .731 W%; 1/13 SH/SV; .234 OBA; 10.4 RAT; 37 PR; 8 DEF; 2.28 ERA

You would be an odds-on favorite to win a trivia contest by naming the player who had the greatest Yankee rookie season in the fabled history of New York's all-everything franchise. The clues: 1) He played in the '20s (No, not Lou Gehrig or Tony Lazzeri); 2) He was a New York favorite (No, not Waite Hoyt or Earle Combs); 3) He was a right handed pitcher (No, not Spud Chandler or Mel Stottlemyre).

The answer? William Wilcy Moore, better known to his teammates as "Cy," or just plain Wilcy. His 4.8 TPR is far and away the best rookie single-season mark, bettering the next highest Yankee rating (Russ Ford's 4.0 masterpiece), by a full season victory, and five wins better than league-average players were able to contribute to their teams' victory totals in 1927. Neither of these players makes the Yankees' glamor list, but, strictly on a performance basis, as first year men they ran up some impressive numbers that not only

top the Yankee honor roll, but rate very high on the all-time honors list. The Yankee top 10 rookie list follows:

1. Wilcy Moore, 4.8, 1927
2. Russ Ford, 4.0, 1910
3. Joe Gordon, 3.2, 1938
4. Willie Randolph, 3.2, 1976
5. Joe DiMaggio, 3.0, 1936
6. Thurman Munson, 3.0, 1970
7. George McConnell, 2.9, 1912
8. Andy Carey, 2.7, 1954
9. Ron Guidry, 2.6, 1977
10. Mel Stottlemyre, 2.5, 1964

Several interesting entries are part of Wilcy Moore's career dossier, including his dual role as starter and reliever for Team Huggins' 1927 juggernaut, the pivotal role he played in the Yanks' overwhelming success in the World Series, and the many years he spent getting ready for the Show. The latter is really a story in itself, putting his 1927 season into perspective, and makes for a good starting point.

Like many players during the first 50 years of organized baseball, Wilcy Moore started his career right near home (born in Texas, he was brought up on a farm in Oklahoma) in one of the many semipro leagues, making his way with a wicked fastball and a breaking pitch that sat down the rough-hewn semipros and interested a scout or two. He was ultimately signed to a contract with Fort Worth of the Texas-Oklahoma League at the advanced baseball age of 24 — a little late to get started, especially if making the majors was to be the end object of a ball-playing career. But none of that mattered too much to Wilcy, a fun-loving Oklahoma rancher who was more at home plowing up the north 40 than with the boys in the big city. Still, the game had a grip on him.

As the next few seasons progressed, so did Moore. He was moved from league to league, winning more than losing. Finally, in 1925, he began to put a few things together in the Southern Association at Greenville, South Carolina, where he was assembling some league-leading numbers when suddenly his season was put on hold as he suffered a shattering blow to his pitching arm. He came back toward the end of the season but found that throwing was a painful chore. Although he was next to finished for the season, his career wasn't. What happened made his injury a blessing in disguise. The "new and improved" Moore delivery was sidearmed, pain-free and effective beyond imagination. Throwing sidearm gave the right-hander's sinker a far different spin and movement as it headed to the plate, and while his sinker had always been a good breaking pitch for him, now it was absolutely devastating.

The first great Yankee reliever, Wilcy Moore. (Colgin Photo.)

Moore came back to Greenville in 1926 and promptly tore up the league, reeling off 17 straight en route to a 27 and 2 record before losing his third of the season and finishing up at 30 and 4. His team demolished the South Atlantic Association, winning the pennant by 17 games, and then won the Southern Championship playoffs, beating Richmond, of the Virginia League, four games to one. Moore was the prime mover.

In the Big Apple there was a wily fellow in the front office of the New York Yankees named Ed Barrow, a veritable genius in matters baseball, who didn't let Wilcy Moore's 1926 exploits pass him by unnoticed. He had sent one of his top scouts, Bob Gilk, on down to South Carolina to find out about Greenville's free-wheeling sinkerballer. Gilk came back with a message: "He can't pitch, and anyway he says he's thirty but he must be forty." Business manager Barrow, former manager and veteran Mr. Everything in the Yankee office, didn't let that fool him one moment, countermanding his scout and — on a hunch — purchasing the crafty veteran from Greenville for a paltry $3,500. It was the deal of the year though few knew it, and no one cared much outside the Yankee inner sanctum.

The balding, weathered Oklahoma rancher became Yankee property, and before the 1927 season began, Wilcy Moore inked a Yankee contract. The numbers on the contract read $1,800 — not for a week, or as a bonus, but for the entire season. Even by 1927 standards that was an embarrassment. But not to Wilcy Moore. Those things would not bother him. The country bumpkin would make out anyway.

The Yankees opened up the 1927 season at home on April 12 with an eight to three victory over the Athletics behind Waite Hoyt. Just two days later Wilcy Moore faced his first major league batter in relief of starter Bob Shawkey. There he was, the rube from Okieland, pitching in a ball game in the House That Ruth Built. It was a long, long way from the Texas-Oklahoma League.

The diminutive Yankee skipper, Miller Huggins, saw to it that his new reliever would get a lot of work. April and May were the months to get the preliminaries out of the way. On April 21, a week and three appearances after his first game, Wilcy hurled 4.2 innings in picking up his first win of the season, this time at Philadelphia, in relief once again of Hoyt.

By the end of May, Moore had made 15 appearances, had been involved in 9 decisions, and sported a 5–4 record. It was enough to warrant keeping him, but he knew better than anyone that there was a long way to go. This was *not* the Sally League.

Between June 1 and October 1, his last warmup start before the World Series (Moore started and pitched only five innings, just enough to get credit for his 19th victory), the savvy reliever and his bewitching sinker settled into a championship groove that rocketed him into the glare of New York's klieg lights. He had made the improbable leap from the bushes to the World Series in a blaze of glory, chalking up 13 saves, a 19 and 7 record. He finished with six complete games, a shutout, 38 relief appearances, a league-leading 2.26 ERA and an extraordinary defensive sabermetric rating of eight, which ranks as the 32nd highest, all time. And the world's championship was still to come!

In the month of June there were nine appearances and four winning decisions (three in relief and a complete game 7 to 3 victory). Between mid–August and the end of the season Moore raised an already red-hot tempo to a still higher level, posting an eight and two record, mostly in starting assignments. Everyone from Babe Ruth to batboy Eddie Bennett knew that Cy was the real deal, and, on his own terms, he was everyone's pal. His friendship was as genuine as his achievements were authentic.

The World Series of 1927, a quick, four game bloodletting that paired the Pittsburgh Pirates and "The Window-breakers," as the New Yorkers were often called, proved to be a microcosm of Cy Moore's season. He simply did the same things he had done all summer long: win a game as a starter and save a game as a reliever. Why should anything change now?!

Huggins wasted no time calling on Moore, sending him in to relieve for Waite Hoyt in the first game of the Series at Pittsburgh, just as he had done four times in regular season play. Called in to protect a razor-thin, five to four lead, he gave up a harmless single in an inning and a third as he shut down the Pirates, and the Yanks took the opener, five to four.

When it came time to administer the *coup de grace* at Yankee Stadium Wilcy Moore was Huggins' moundsman, and in a route-going performance he toughed-out a tight, Series-ending game, surviving the Pirates' last-ditch attempt to win it in the ninth and push the Series at least into one more game. That was not to be, not at Mr. Moore's expense. The Yankees took it, 4 to 3.

The *New York Times'* Richard Vidmer captured Moore's contribution to the Yan-

kees' 1927 success: "There has been no more valuable player than Mr. Wilcy Moore. Without him the Yanks would not have made a joke of the American League race. Moore has come to the rescue of many a game that was about to die on the Yanks' hands."

With a top-flight pitching staff and a defense, albeit unheralded, that was among the best in the major leagues, the Yankees came together in 1927 to avenge the last vestige of remorse over the 1926 World Series loss to St. Louis (they would wreak havoc the very next year with a four-

---

Box Score

New York at Pittsburgh, World Series Game 4, October 8, 1927

New York	AB	R	H	PO	A
Combs, cf	4	3	2	2	0
Koenig, ss	5	0	3	0	3
Ruth, rf	4	1	2	1	0
Gehrig, 1b	5	0	0	14	2
Meusel, lf	5	0	0	2	0
Lazzeri, 2b	3	0	0	5	4
Dugan, 3b	4	0	1	1	4
Collins, c	3	0	3	2	1
Moore, p	4	0	1	0	3
Totals	37	4	12	27	17

Pittsburgh	AB	R	H	PO	A
L. Waner, cf	4	1	3	0	0
Barnhart, lf	5	0	1	2	0
P. Waner, rf	4	0	1	0	0
Wright, ss	4	0	1	1	6
Traynor, 3b	4	0	0	1	4
Grantham, 2b	4	0	2	0	2
Harris, 1b	4	0	2	13	0
Smith, c	3	0	0	6	0
Yde, pr	0	1	0	0	0
Gooch, c	0	0	0	3	0
Hill, p	1	0	0	0	0
Brickell, ph	1	0	0	0	0
Miljus, p	1	0	0	0	0
Totals	35	3	10	26*	12

Pittsburgh 100 000 200 3-10-1
New York   100 020 001 4-12-2

2BH	Collins
HR	Ruth
SH	L, Waner, P. Waner
SB	Ruth
DP	Lazzeri and Gehrig; Dugan, Lazzeri and Gehrig
	Traynor, Wright and Harris
LOB	Pittsburgh, 9; New York, 11
K	Hill 6, Miljus 3, Moore, 2
BB	Hill 1, Miljus 3, Moore, 2
Wild P	Miljus
Losing P	Miljus
Umpires	Ormsby (AL), Quigley (NL)
	Nallin (AL), Moran (NL)
Time	2:15
Att	57,909

Two out when winning run scored

games-to-none humiliation of the 1928 Cardinals). But redemption would hardly have been possible without the country bumpkin from Oklahoma, Wilcy Moore.

1927: The Top Ten Rookies

Nm/Pos/Tm	GP	W–L/BA	SH/SV//RBI	PR/BR	FR/ERA	TPR
Wilcy Moore, RHP (RP), NY-A*	50	19–7	1/13	37	2.28	4.8
Irving "Bump" Hadley, RHP, Was-A	30	14–6	0/0	27	2.85	2.6
Johnny Schulte, c, StL-N	64	.288	32	16	3	2.1
Clyde Beck, 2b, Chi-N	117	.258	44	-9	22	1.7
Wm. "Watty" Clark, LHP, Brk-N	27	7–2	0/2	13	2.32	1.5
Earl Webb, of, Chi-N	102	.301	52	18	2	1.4
Willis Hudlin, RHP, Clv-A	43	18–12	1/0	6	4.01	1.1
Foster "Babe" Ganzel, of, Was-A	13	.438	13	8	0	0.7
George Smith, RHP, Det-A	29	4–1	0/0	2	3.91	0.4
Ownie Carroll, RHP, Det-A	31	10–6	3/4	4	3.98	0.3

*Wilcy Moore was cited by Bill Deane as the AL Hypothetical Rookie of the Year and the winner of the Hypothetical Cy Young Award for the 1927 season. These "awards" were made to bridge the gap between 1900 and the 1950s, when the first BBWAA awards were initiated for MVPs, Cy Young and Rookie of the Year selections.

Sylveanus Augustus "Vean" Gregg

TPR: 4.7

1911, Cleveland, AL

Born: April 13, 1885, Chehalis, WA. Died: July 29, 1964, Aberdeen, WA
LHP, 6'2" 185 lb. Major League Debut: April 12, 1911
1911: W23, L7, .767 W%; 22/5 CG/SH; 9.9 RAT; .205 OBA; 44 PR; 1.80 ERA

There were a number of outstanding players in 1911s rookie class, and the best among them would have stocked a ballclub capable of holding its own under the Big Tent. How about an outfield of Ping Bodie, Max Carey and Shoeless Joe Jackson? Around the infield we would find Jim Esmond, Stuffy McInnis, Irish Corhan and Jimmy Doyle, and a catching corps of Art Wilson and Gus Fisher. The pitching staff? How about Pete Alexander, Ray "Sum" Caldwell, George Chalmers, Buck O'Brien and Vean Gregg? Reserves might well include Del Gainer, Swede Henriksen and George Jackson. Here are some of their 1911 numbers:

Nm/Tm-L/Pos	GP	BA/W–L	RBI//CG/SF⁻	BR/PR	FR/ERA	TPR
J. Jackson/Clv-A/of	147	.408	83	70	8	6.8
V. Gregg/Clv-A/LHP*	34	23–7	22/5	44	1.80	4.7
G. Alexander/Phl-N/RHP†	48	28–13	31/7	35	2.57	3.6
Buck O'Brien/Bos-A/RHP	6	5–1	5/2	15	0.38	2.0
J. Doyle/NY-N/3b	130	.282	62	5	10	1.6
Ping Bodie/Chi-A/of	145	.289	97	9	7	0.9
Sum Caldwell/NY-A/RHP	41	14–14	19/1	7	3.35	0.8
Irish Corhan/Chi-A/ss	43	.214	8	-5	11	0.8
G. Chalmers/Phl-N/RHP	38	13–10	11/3	7	3.11	0.6
Gus Fisher/Clv-A/c	70	.261	12	-8	8	0.5
Swede Henriksen/Bos-A/of	27	.366	8	6	0	0.4
Art Wilson, NY-N/c	66	.303	17	5	-6	0.3
Jim Esmond/Cin-N/1b	73	.273	11	-1	1	0.2

Designated AL Rookie of the Year, Bill Deane Hypothetical RY Awards
†*Designated NL Rookie of the Year, Bill Deane Hypothetical RY Awards*

Nm/Tm-L/Pos	GP	BA/W–L	RBI//CG/SH	BR/PR	FR/ERA	TPR
George Jackson/Bos-N/of	39	.347	25	5	-2	0.1
Del Gainer/Det-AL/1b	70	.302	25	3	-4	-0.1
Stuffy McInnis/Phl-A/UT	126	.321	77	12	-15	-0.1
Max Carey/Pit-N/of	129	.258	43	-3	7	-0.3

True, many of these players are something less than household names among baseball fans, and some of them — Art Corhan (two seasons), George Jackson and Buck O'Brien (three seasons each), and Jimmy Esmond (two years with Cincinnati and two years with Federal League teams),

Indians lefty Vean Gregg. (Brace Photo.)

for example — weren't around long enough to warrant more than a line or two in baseball's statistic books. But at the top of the 1911 list are three stellar figures, players of justifiably enduring fame. One is a Hall of Famer and another belongs there. Their names? Pete Alexander and Shoeless Joe Jackson. (The 1911 list above also includes HOFer Max Carey, whose debut season was not as electrifying as the those of Jackson and Alexander, but whose career did merit Cooperstown honors.)

The third of this towering triumvirate is Sylveanus Gregg, better known as "Vean" among teammates and close friends like Joe Jackson, Nap Lajoie, George Stovall and Terry Turner. Despite his very impressive numbers, Gregg is another one of those whose name, because of his brief stay among the American League's pitching elite, is relatively unfamiliar except around Cleveland, and perhaps a wider circle of hardcore baseball knowledgeables. Nonetheless, there he is, perched at a lofty number 17 spot, all-time, among the rookie elite, one of three Cleveland Indians who hold down top 20 positions on our honors list.

The Vean Gregg story begins in the Pacific Northwest where, in and around the tiny community of Clarkston, Washington, he developed strong, sinewy arms as a plasterer. That was ideal for pitching, and the lean southpaw with the whiplash arm didn't fail to notice how fast his quick one covered the distance from the mound to the plate. Soon he was starring for semi-pro teams around the state. It took only one look-see for a veteran ballplayer like Walter McCredie, who managed the Portland team in the Pacific Coast League, to conclude that the Spokane Indians' star was ready for a step or three upward to the P.C.L. With Portland's Beavers during the 1910 season, the young southpaw tore the league apart with a record-setting 14 shutouts, a September 2 no-hitter against Los Angeles, and a staggering total of 368 strikeouts in 387 innings. He worked in 52 games in the P.C.L.'s elongated season of 220 games, winning 32 of them. Along the way he managed an almost unbelievable stretch of flame-throwing efficiency. Here is the way Eddie Hughes explained it in the March 26, 1933 San Francisco Chronicle:

> One day when he [Gregg] was feeling particularly good he whiffed eight Los Angeles batsmen in a row, and only one of them, George Wheeler, got as much as a foul off him. For years Wheeler bragged about that foul. He was the only one of the eight who got as much as a piece of the ball. The others either swung at empty space or ducked away from the plate while the umpire barked, "strike."

The Naps, named after Cleveland's hero Nap Lajoie, acquired the Portland swiftie after the 1910 season, hoping that he would add some punch to a rather anemic pitching staff that was slated for a much needed overhaul. The revamping was not to be merely cosmetic. Only one twirler, Willie Mitchell, would return for a starting berth. Further, everyone had high hopes for Nap ace Addie Joss, who was expected to return to form after experiencing a troubling season marred by a sore arm. That was a vain hope, however, when the ballclub and fans around the country lost the future Hall of Famer to tubercular meningitis just before the season opened. All things considered, Cleveland would need a superhuman effort to make much of a dent on the front-running contenders in the chase for pennant gold in 1911.

The season opener at Cleveland's League Park was delayed because of the Joss funeral, and when it finally did open on April 12, the last day of Gregg's 25th year, the St. Louis Browns clubbed the homestanding Naps, 12 to 3. In what was his major league debut, Gregg got into the game as a relief pitcher, and while the opener for the Naps was a disaster, manager James "Deacon" McGuire's reliever stifled the Browns and cracked a double in his first at-bat.

So far so good. But the lanky left-hander was not destined for immediate or stunning success. Vean got off to an uncertain start, relieving for an inning or two now and then, and losing the first decision of his career to Detroit two weeks after his debut. And it wasn't until May 3 that he notched his first win, an 8 to 7, route-going squeaker that went down to the bottom of the ninth when the Naps scored three to beat Chicago. It wasn't pretty, but it was a W, and Vean Gregg was on his way. Unfortunately, the Naps weren't.

By mid–May Gregg began to hit his stride, posting a five-hit shutout — his career first — beating New York, 2 to 1, and then quieting Washington bats in an 8 to 1 whipping. Meanwhile, Cleveland wallowed in the second division on into June, and as summer came on they were still mired in a sixth-place rut.

During this time Cleveland's popular first baseman, George Stovall, who was Gregg's roommate, kept passing along the know-how that made promising rookies big league professionals. Years later Vean Gregg would point to those early months under the tutelage of Stovall as the time when those tips and pointers set him on his way to success in the Big Show.

It took the Naps until September to work their way out of the AL's lower ranks. But shortly after Labor Day they found themselves in third place, vying with Boston and Detroit for second. Winning the pennant was out of the question. Even John McGraw, in one of his few complimentary moments, had congratulated Connie Mack on his Athletics' powerhouse ballclub.

Vean Gregg was very much a part of the Cleveland upsurge. He fashioned five shutouts during the 1911 season and was involved in a number of one-run victories (and defeats) en route to a 23–7 record. His .767 winning percentage was the second highest registered in the American League, and his 1.80 ERA was the best in the majors. Though American League teams averaged a salty .273 (up 30 points over 1910, before the 1911 ball with its cork and rubber center was introduced), Vean led his league with an awesome .205 opponents' batting average. It isn't surprising, then, that he also led both leagues in hits per game with a miserly 6.33, three less than the major league average.

On August 27, at a time when Cleveland began to move upward from its second division surroundings, Washington visited the Forest City. The pivotal game of the series was one of those deadball era classics, featuring the smothering slants of the Senators' Carl Cashion and Dolly Gray, and the Naps' Gregg, who had blanked the Senators and Long Tom Hughes on August 2 in a white-knuckle special by a 1–0 count. Was more of the same on tap this time?

Scoreless through seven stanzas, the Naps finally pushed across the winning run in the bottom of the eighth. Gregg mastered the Senators in the ninth to nail down the victory, pushing toward the 20-game mark and pulling the Naps along in their late–August surge. In the space of one week following Labor Day, Boston, with a momentary hold on the league's top spot, fell from first to fifth and Cleveland had put a claw into the third spot, where they finally ended the season behind Detroit and Mack's Quaker City champions. Before

Box Score

Washington at Cleveland, August 27, 1911

Washington	AB	H	PO	A	E
Milan, cf	4	0	6	0	0
Morgan, 3b	3	0	1	3	0
Henry, 1b	4	1	6	0	0
Gessler, rf	2	1	1	0	0
C. Walker, lf	3	1	2	0	0
McBride, ss	3	1	3	6	0
Cunningham, 2b	3	0	4	0	0
Street, c	3	0	1	1	0
Ainsmith, c	0	0	0	0	0
Cashion, p	1	0	0	0	0
Gray, p	2	0	0	0	0
Johnson, ph	1	0	0	0	0
Totals	29	4	24	10	0

Cleveland	AB	H	PO	A	E
Graney, lf	4	1	0	0	0
Olson, ss	4	0	2	5	0
Jackson, rf	4	0	0	0	0
Lajoie, 1b	4	2	15	0	0
Brimingham, cf	4	2	1	0	0
Ball, 2b	4	1	1	6	0
Turner, 3b	3	1	2	1	0
Smith, c	2	1	6	3	1
Gregg, p	3	0	0	2	0
Totals	32	8	27	17	1

Washington	000	000	000	0-4-0
Cleveland	000	000	01x	0-8-1

SB	Ball, Graney, Gessler
DP	Ball and Lajoie
K	Cashion 1, Gray 1, Gregg 5
BB	Cashion and Gray 0, Gregg 2
WP	Gregg
LP	Gray
Umpires	Connally and Sheridan

it was all over Vean Gregg had pushed to three beyond the coveted 20 mark, teammate Joe Jackson had pummeled AL pitching at a .408 clip, and the Naps, who finished out the season under George Stovall, had pulled off an 18-game turnaround from the 1910 season, winning 81 as opposed to their 71-win total the previous season.

Two rookies were the toast of Cleveland, Shoeless Joe and the hard-throwing portsider from the Pacific Northwest, Vean Gregg. Philadelphia might have had a pennant winner and Grover Alexander, but Forest City fans had their own heroes. The old "wait till next year" mantra had some steam in it this time around!

Vean Gregg went on to a pair of follow-up, 20-win seasons, cruising along with a 2.59 ERA in 1912 and a 2.23 ERA for the third place Cleveland ballclub of 1913. The road to Cooperstown had been staked out. Alas, that old pitcher's nemesis, a sore arm (probably pulled tendons that never actually healed and robbed him of the electricity his fastball was famous for), felled him during the Spring of 1914. Though he pitched many more years (with Boston and Philadelphia before his one-season swan song for Washington in 1925) on a major league level, and well into his 40s in the Pacific Coast League and for semipro teams, the famous Gregg hummer that

struck terror in the hearts of hitters during his first years in the Bigs was no more than a cherished memory.

During Vean Gregg's time, salary and contract disputes had risen to a level that once again threatened to raise havoc with organized baseball, just as it had done in the late 1880s. At that time one of the consequences was the Player's League, which rose and fell in one season's play in 1890. This time around, it was to be The Federal League, and following Gregg's third consecutive 20-game season in 1913, he was one of the new league's hottest prospects. It helped him to negotiate a lucrative, three-year Boston contract, thus keeping him out of the new league. But that was the selfsame Spring that arm troubles laid him low, and though he finished out his Red Sox contract just as another bright young lefty on that team — Babe Ruth — was making his first major league rounds the Boston club decided that it had gone as far as it could go with Vean Gregg.

But Gregg, a substantially level-headed citizen, moved on. However nice it would have been to scale transcendent heights, there was reward enough for him in those halcyon Portland and Cleveland years to sustain him. His death at 79 occurred in his beloved Northwest, at Aberdeen, Washington, in 1964.

1914 and 1915: Ten Top Federal League Rookies

Nm/Pos/Tm/Yr	GP	BA/W–L	RBI//SH/SV	BR/PR	FR/ERA	TPR
Bill Kenworthy, 2b, KC, 1914	146	.317	91	38	21	4.5
Benny Kauff, of, Ind, 1914	154	.370	95	52	16	4.4
Dutch Zwilling, of, Chi, 1914	154	.313	95	33	2	1.4
Art Kores, 3b, StL, 1915	60	.234	22	-6	19	1.2
Chas. Watson, LHP, Chi-StL, 1914	35	12–12	5/1	26	2.01	1.1
Tex Johnson, RHP, Chi, 1915	16	9–5	2/0	14	1.58	1.1
Erv Lange, RHP, Chi, 1914	36	12–11	2/2	15	2.23	0.9
Ernie Johnson, ss, StL, 1915	152	.240	67	-8	18	0.9
Jim Kelly, of, Pit, 1915	148	.294	50	11	14	0.5
Clint Rogge, RHP, Pit, 1915	37	17–11	5/0	13	2.55	0.5

Darrell Elijah "Cy" Blanton

TPR: 4.7

1935, Pittsburgh, NL

Born: July 6, 1908, Waurika, OK. Died: September 13, 1945, Norman OK
RHP, 6'0" 180 lb. Major League Debut: September 23, 1934
1935: 35 GP; W18, L13; 4/1 SH/SV; .229 OBA; .272 OB%; 9.8 RAT; 43 PR; 2.58 ERA

In answer to Giants' manager Bill Terry's question "Is Brooklyn still in the league?" the lowly Dodgers replied with two victories over the New Yorkers the last weekend of regular season play in 1934 that sent the boys from Coogan's Bluff home for the winter. So much for "Giants' Pride," another World Series in the Big Apple and the acerbic "Memphis Bill."

Only a week before the pennant chase in the Senior Circuit had come down to the Cardinals and the Cubs, closing fast with a furious, late September rush in a winning streak that got the baseball world's attention. While that was going on the other teams in the league were busy with late season call-ups, already attending to the business of the 1935 season. In Pittsburgh, for example, the Pirates put one of their most promising young pitchers on display, starting him in a Sunday game on September 23. The solidly built right-hander's name was Darrell Blanton, better known as "Cy." His skipper, Pie Traynor, long-time Pirate favorite, and just that summer elevated to managerial status, wanted to see how Blanton would respond to big-league hitting. Although Cy Blanton was tagged with a loss that day, he had turned in eight decent innings, giving up five hits while fanning five. As Traynor thought ahead to the 1935 campaign, he knew right then and there that Cy would be a part of his plans. Here is the way that came about.

Although he was born at Waurika, Oklahoma, which is on the old Chisholm Trail, Cy Blanton was raised in Fort Worth, where baseball, along with the cattle business, was a consuming Texan passion. Cy found his way to the ballpark and soon attracted attention with a curveball that blew away the locals in the Fort Worth City League. An impressive string of victories in 1928 and '29, which included three no-hitters, persuaded the Shawnee club of the

Western Association to sign Blanton to a professional contract, and in 1930 the young right-hander, with his assortment of bedevilling breaking pitches, was on his way. That first season he didn't break even, finishing up with a 12 and 16 mark, but he did strike out 177 batters in the 222 innings he worked.

During the next four seasons the auburn-haired hurler fine-tuned the variety of hooks and speeds he used, mastering the strike zone while adding some zip to his fastball as he matured. In 1933 Blanton, by then 24 and playing for St. Joseph of the Western Association, led manager Dutch Zwilling's team to the league championship with a 21 and 7 record, fanning a league high 284 and throwing a no-hitter against Joplin. Another league-leading mark in whiffs the next season with Albany, featuring a 20-K game against Syracuse, convinced the Pirates that the "Whiffmeister" was ready for the Big Show. Pittsburgh bought his contract and Cy debuted on September 23, 1934. The next March, Blanton reported with the battery men to Pittsburgh's spring training base in San Bernardino, California.

During the 1930s the Pirates fielded good, but not great, ballclubs. Always good enough to raise pennant hopes, they never quite made it all the way to the top. And 1935 was a typical season during that era.

The Waner brothers, Paul and Lloyd, veteran holdovers from the 1927 championship team, and Floyd "Arky" Vaughan, who would lead the league in 1935 with a record-setting batting average of .385, were the headliners. Waite Hoyt, ace of the

The Pirates' breaking ball pitcher Darrell "Cy" Blanton. (Brace Photo.)

Yankee dreadnaught that whipped the Pirates in the 1927 World Series, was back for the third of his five seasons with the Corsairs after a fine 15 and 6 season in 1934, presumably to lead the pitching staff once again. Bill Swift and Red Lucas, one of baseball's all-time great hitting pitchers, also returned to Pie Traynor's staff. The newcomers to the hurling corps included a 6'6", 220 pounder who threw aspirin-like heaters, Jim Weaver, and two rookies, Mace Brown, a reliever, and the K king, Cy Blanton.

Two months into the season several things became quite clear. The Pirates would be a middle-of-the-road team, though dangerous, hard-hitting, and strong enough not to be taken lightly. A .300-hitting outfield, added to the punch provided by Arky Vaughan, who was powdering the ball at the .400 level, would furnish a solid offensive attack. And finally, Cy Blanton would step to the fore as Pittsburgh's ace. His staff-leadleading wins, complete games, ERA and strikeouts, (at a 2-to-1 ratio over walks), soon made him Pie Traynor's go-to guy. Alas, despite a sensational rookie season by Blanton, Arky Vaughan's batting crown (his .385 set a National League record for shortstops), and occasional flashes of championship form, they were not a strong enough ballclub to win the pennant. When World Series time rolled around the Pirates finished in fourth, a solid fourth to be sure, but nonetheless out of contention.

Chicago's Cubbies won the National League pennant in 1935, brushing aside the Cardinals and the Giants, but not without a struggle. In fact, it took a bruising, 21-game winning streak in September to salt away the pennant — and in St. Louis — where Cub aces Lonnie Warneke and Big Bill Lee turned aside the Dean brothers to capture the flag.

They were particularly tough on the fourth-place Pirates, beating them 9 out of 11 meetings at Mr. Wrigley's "Friendly Confines." One of the two times they didn't was on August 6, when Cy Blanton set them down on nine scattered hits, blanking them, 6–0. Then in second place, Charlie Grimm's charges needed every win they could muster. But while they would yet prevail in the Senior Circuit, they would not overcome the Corsair ambush on this bright, mid-summer day.

With 13 conquests behind him, Blanton fanned four, walked a pair of Bruin hitters and gave up only one extra base blow, a double, to Larry French, the wily Cub lefty, who was banished by umpire

Dolly Stark in a two run, Pirate fifth, and was tagged with the loss.

The whitewashing was one of Blanton's four in 1935, tieing him for league leadership with teammate Jumbo Jim Weaver. Bill Swift added another three shutouts to help the staff, which recorded 15, take the league's leadership in that department. Weaver, at 14, Swift, with 15, and Blanton, with another 18, were credited with 47 of the Pirates' 86 wins.

Cy Blanton's sturdy 18 and 13 record, fashioned in 254.1 innings (there were 23 complete games and one save), led the Pirate staff in 1935s pitching stats. He also paced both leagues with a glittering 2.58 ERA. At 5.02 per game, his breaking pitches were sufficiently deceptive to chalk up 142 strikeouts, fifth best in the National League, and he led both circuits in fewest hits per game, with 7.79. And more. Cy starved opposing NL offenses on a meagre diet of .229 hitting and a .272 on-base percentage. Those numbers were also the best recorded in either league. To cap it off, Blanton's 43 PRs and a Total Player Rating of 4.7 topped NL pitchers.

Cy Blanton's steady, workmanlike performance earned him Bill Deane's Honorary Rookie of the Year Award for 1935. Teammate Arky Vaughan, the NL batting champ at .385, was accorded National League MVP honors by *The Sporting News*. The two remained as Pirate mainstays throughout the remainder of the 1930s.

Between his sparkling rookie season and the close of the '30s, Cy Blanton notched 56 Pirate victories, in double figures each season. There were the usual highlights, and along with them one rather bizarre play that must rank as a baseball one-and-only. The play occurred as he delivered one of his sharply breaking curves. The ball he delivered on a two strike count completely fooled the hitter, causing him to swing at a pitch that actually struck home plate and bounced back to Blanton,

Box Score

Pittsburgh at Wrigley Field, Chicago, August 7, 1935

Pittsburgh	AB	R	H	PO	A		*Chicago*	AB	R	H	PO	A
Jensen, lf	5	3	3	1	0		Galan, lf	4	0	1	1	0
P. Waner, rf	3	0	1	2	0		W. Herman, 2b	4	0	0	4	3
Vaughan, ss	4	2	2	2	2		Klein, rf	4	0	2	1	0
B. Hafey, cf	5	0	1	4	0		O'Dea, c	4	0	0	7	3
Lavagetto, 2b	5	0	3	2	4		Demaree, cf	3	0	0	1	0
Thevenow, 3b	4	0	0	0	3		Cavarretta, 1b	4	0	2	9	0
Suhr, 1b	4	0	1	11	0		Hack, 3b	4	0	2	2	2
Padden, c	4	1	2	5	1		Jurges, ss	4	0	0	2	3
Blanton, p	4	0	1	0	1		French, p	1	0	1	0	1
							Kowalik, p	1	0	1	0	0
							Shoun, p	0	0	0	0	0
							Lindstrom, ph	1	0	0	0	0
Totals	38	6	14	27	11		Totals	34	0	9	27	12

Pittsburgh   200   022   000   6-14-0
Chicago   000   000   000   0-9-3

2BH	French
SH	P. Waner 2
SB	Demaree, Cavarretta
WP	Blanton
Balk	French
DP	Pitssburgh 2
K	Blanton 4, French 2, Kowalik 2, Shoun 2
BB	Blanton 2, French 1
LP	French

who fielded the ball and threw to first base, giving him an assist on the putout — and a strikeout!

Among his highlights surely must have been his All-Star Game appearance at Griffith Stadium in 1937, when National League manager Bill Terry brought him in to relieve Carl Hubbell in the fourth inning. With two out he faced the unpleasant prospect of pitching to Joe DiMaggio with Charlie Gehringer aboard. The K king proceeded to do what he did best: strike out the hitter. Yankee Clipper or no, the result was another K in the scorebook. That ended the American League inning. Lifted in the next frame for pinch-hitter Mel Ott, who doubled for him, Cy didn't get to continue in the game. And worse yet, from a National Leaguer's standpoint, the Americans beat the Senior Circuit that day, 8 to 3. But Cy had done his job.

On Easter Sunday of 1939, during the Pirates' pre-season workouts in the sunny South at New Orleans, Cy was called on to pitch against the Indians. Not only was he in rare form, he breezed through the first five frames without allowing so much as a baserunner. Traynor had scheduled him to go about six to seven innings. In the sixth inning Earl Averill finally worked him for a walk, but the inning ended with a no-hitter still in the making. Here's how Boss-man Traynor saw it that day: "I had intended to allow Blanton to go about six or seven innings that day in New Orleans against the Indians. I never saw Cy look as good as he did that spring. He was in great shape and his arm was loose and strong that year.... When Blanton went out for the seventh I could see him bearing down all the harder. He actually forced himself in those late innings [Blanton went the route to no-hit the Indians], and that isn't good for a pitcher in the spring…. That no-hitter took so much out of Blanton's right arm that he was a total loss to us that season."

Les Biederman's report to *The Sporting News* some ten years later was written in response to an oft-asked question: What ever happened to Cy Blanton and the Pirates in 1939, a season during which they fell from the ranks of the contenders with a thud—all the way into sixth place, almost 30 games off Cincinnati's winning pace?

For Cy Blanton it was not merely the beginning of the end of his baseball career, though he hung on, as ballplayers usually do, into the Second World War years, winding up his career in the Pacific Coast League with Hollywood in 1943. There were other, and much more troubling problems, with depression more and more taking command of his life. Finally committed to a mental institution at Norman, Oklahoma, he passed away on September 13, 1945, in a tragic, saddening ending at 37, just a little more than a decade after the beginning of a most promising major league career.

Cy Blanton's 4.7 for 1935 stands as the Pittsburgh franchise's best season for a rookie pitcher, ranking him among the top 20, all time. With third baseman Jimmy Williams of the 1899 Pirates, he adds to the luster of Pirate history, placing both a position player and a pitcher among the higher echelons of rookiedom. Only three franchises are represented thusly in the top 20: Cleveland with three, Joe Jackson, Gene Bearden and Vean Gregg; Philadelphia's Phillies with two, Curt Davis and Dick Allen; and Pittsburgh's terrific twosome, Jimmy Williams and Darrell Elijah "Cy" Blanton.

1935: Ten Top Rookies

Nm/Pos/Tm	GP	W–L/BA	SH/SV//RBI	PR/BR	ERA/FR	TPR
Cy Blanton/RHP/Pit-N	35	18–13	4/0	43	2.58	4.7
John Whitehead/RHP/Chi-A	28	13–13	1/0	22	3.72	2.0
Vern Kennedy/RHP/Chi/A	31	11–11	2/1	17	3.91	1.8
Bucky Walters/RHP/Phl-N	24	9–9	2/0	6	4.17	1.1
Roy Henshaw/LHP/Chi-N	31	13–5	3/1	10	3.28	1.0
Ed Heusser/RHP/StL-N	33	5–5	0/2	16	2.92	1.0
Lew Riggs/3b/Cin-N	142	.278	46	-3	8	1.0
Jack Wilson/RHP/Bos-A	23	3–4	0/1	13	4.22	0.7
Mace Brown/RHP(RP)/Pit-N	18	4–1	0/0	4	3.59	0.4
Gilly Campbell/c/Cin-N	88	.257	30	1	0	0.3

Harvey "The Kitten" Haddix

TPR: 4.7

1953, St. Louis NL

Born: September 18, 1925; Medway, OH. Died: January 8, 1994; Springfield, OH
LHP, 5'9.5" 170 lb. Major League Debut: August 20, 1952
1953: W20, L9; .690 W%; 6/1 SH/SV; 163/69 K/BB; 10 PHI; 34 PR; 3.06 ERA

Harvey Haddix was no exception to the rule of service in the Armed Forces. Like so many young Americans, he put on Uncle Sam's uniform during the Korean conflict era, returning in August of 1952 to debut with the Cardinals. That left just enough of the '52 season for a few starts, a 2 and 2 record with a respectable 2.79 ERA, and a very persuasive showing to solidify his hold on a staff position for 1953.

Haddix joined Cardinal rookies Rip Repulski and Ray "Jabbo" Jablonski in the '53 St. Louis lineup, helping the ballclub finish in the National League's third spot a third consecutive year. All three wound up contending for Rookie of the Year laurels, but it was the little lefty, Haddix, who, though denied NL rookie honors, fashioned not only the most productive season of his career, but the premier rookie campaign in the Cardinals' distinguished history.

Ten years and two wars after Walter Shannon and Tony Kaufman, two of the Cardinals' scouting corps had seen him at an August 1943 tryout camp in Columbus, Ohio, the diminutive Buckeye farmboy was ready for the Bigs. It had been an eventful decade, starting out with his 1943 signing with the Red Birds after what must have been the fastest tryout and signing in the franchise's history.

Here's how Harvey himself explained it:

> I saw Shannon, who died recently, in 1979 in the World Series against Baltimore. I was with the Pirates and I asked him, "Look, you didn't see me throw more than 18 pitches in two days time. What the heck did you see in me? He said, "The first day I saw your fastball, and the second day, as soon as I saw your curveball, I wanted you." That's how simple it was; he didn't see me throw more than 18 pitches altogether in two days time! (Hines, 202).

105

Walt Shannon knew a good thing when he saw it. On that August day in the very depths of World War II he knew Haddix's breaking slants were the stuff of big league pitching and wasted no time in putting a St. Louis investment in the future on the dotted line. Deferred from military service because of his farming exemption, Harvey's professional baseball debut was delayed until 1947, but he made up for lost time in a hurry, storming through the Carolina League with a sparkling 19 and 5 record that included a seven-inning no-hitter for Winston-Salem against Danville. His .792 winning percentage and 1.90 ERA led the league, and he was named to the Class C circuit's All-Star team.

During the prime time of the St. Louis organization's farm club days, when players were moved on up the system's ladder a step at a time, and sometimes spending two to three seasons in the same classification (from C to B to A and on up to AAA ball), Harvey was moved directly from Winston-Salem to the top Cardinal affiliate at Columbus for the next three years until his departure for military duty from 1950 to 1952. His 1950 record at Columbus was 18 and 6, featuring league-leading numbers in wins, whiffs (160), and ERA (2.70). Once again, he was an All-Star selection, this time with the American Association League. Had he not been drafted into the military, Haddix would have been in the starting rotation for the 1951 Cards. That would have to wait. After one appearance in the Junior World Series between Columbus and Baltimore of the International League, Harvey traded uniforms, and from September of 1950 until his August 1952 return to the Cardinals, his career was put on hold.

Cardinal ballplayers dubbed Haddix "The Kitten." In almost every respect he was a smaller-sized Harry Brecheen, nicknamed "The Cat," who was one of St. Louis' better-fielding hurlers. Brecheen

spent eleven strong seasons in Cardinal togs, and during his last Red Bird season in 1952 the Cat and the Kitten were teammates, if only for the last six weeks of that campaign.

The two southpaws specialized in breaking pitches, were superb fielders, possessed exceptional control (Bob Skinner, who later in Haddix's career was a teammate, once said that the tiny portsider could have knocked a gnat off a hitter's nose) and later both became pitching coaches. Further, the two were not your typical automatic outs in the batter's box. In this category Haddix had a slight edge on Brecheen, as he did with controlling the strike zone. And, as if those similarities were not enough, they bore a striking resemblance to one another, and both, above all, were gutsy competitors.

Long before the first ball had been thrown in 1953, there was big news coming out of Cardinal headquarters. Fred Saigh, a wealthy attorney who had purchased controlling interest in the St. Louis franchise in 1947, was convicted on February 20, 1953, of income tax evasion and was sentenced to 15 months in prison. That occasioned the team's purchase by August A. Busch, and a new era was born with the completion of the 3.75 million dollar deal.

Eddie Stanky, one of the last of baseball's playing managers, who had replaced popular Marty Marion, was retained for 1953, back for a second season as the team's skipper. It was Stanky who had insisted on bringing Harvey Haddix directly to the varsity at the end of the '52 season rather than having him report to one of the top Cardinal farm clubs at Houston, Rochester or Columbus. That was one Stanky decision that was a good one. The embattled and confrontational helmsman was not the most popular fellow on the banks of the Mississippi, and his aggressive, scrapping style of play, harking back to the old Gas House days, was equally unpopular around the league. But he did know his baseball fundamentals and saw to it that his charges executed — or else.

Stanky and the Kitten got along — at least decently. Just how far Stanky could take the ballclub with a pitching staff that included Vinegar Bend Mizell, Gerry Staley, Joe Presko and Al Brazle was a tad iffy. The field general, and he was that in every sense of the word, needed a front rank storm trooper to make the difference. In 1953 Harvey Haddix was that difference, responding with a 20 and 9 effort that kept the Cardinals in the first division. If the Cardinals were not actually a pennant contender, neither were the Phils, whom they tied for the third spot, or the runnerup Braves, who finished a distant 13 games behind the Dodgers, winners of their second straight pennant, this time with a handsome 102–49 record.

Southpaw Harvey Haddix, the best of the Cardinal rookies. (Brace Photo.)

Although future Hall of Famers Stan "The Man" Musial hit .337, Red Schoendienst .342 and Enos Slaughter, who hit .291 in his last Cards' season, were in the lineup, and rookies Repulski and Jablonski broke in with good freshman years, there wasn't enough consistency to sustain the offensive punch needed to beat the Dodgers and Braves. Aside from Haddix, Gerry Staley, who would enjoy one of his finest seasons as a starter, was about all the Cards could come up with in those important late season series when the blue chips were on the line. And it didn't happen.

But the Kitten rolled along. During the course of the season he turned in six shutouts to lead the league in calciminings. One of them flattened the Phillies, 2 to 0, on the evening of August 6.

Haddix was touched for two safeties — but not until the ninth inning, when Richie Ashburn and Del Ennis singled. The game ended on a Granny Hamner grounder that was converted into a twin-killing to preserve the shutout. That brush with fame more or less presaged an even more famous May evening in 1959 when the Kitten brushed aside the Braves in Milwaukee, only to lose his perfect 12-inning masterpiece on an error that opened the 13th, and subsequently, a Joe Adcock home run that resulted in a heart-rending 1–0 loss to Milwaukee hurler Lou Burdette. That 1–0 loss to Milwaukee turned out to be the lead story from the Haddix major league scrapbook. That's a shame. The very able craftsman enjoyed a fine, 14-year career that reached its peak in the famous

Box Score

Philadelphia at Sportsman's Park, St. Louis, August 6, 1953

Philadelphia	AB	R	H	PO	A
Kazanski, ss	4	0	0	2	2
Ashburn, cf	3	0	1	2	0
Torgeson, 1b	4	0	0	8	0
C. Ryan, pr	0	0	0	0	0
Ennis, lf	3	0	1	0	0
Hamner, 2b	4	0	0	1	4
Lopata, c	2	0	0	4	0
Wyrostek, rf	3	0	0	4	0
Jones, 3b	2	0	0	3	0
Simmons, p	3	0	0	0	0
Totals	28	0	2	24	6

St. Louis	AB	R	H	PO	A
Hemus, ss	4	0	0	3	3
Schoendienst, 2b	2	2	1	1	8
Musial, lf	3	0	1	2	0
Jablonski, 3b	3	0	1	0	2
Castiglione, 3b	0	0	0	0	1
Slaughter, rf	4	0	1	2	0
Bilko, 1b	3	0	0	15	0
Rice, c	4	0	1	3	0
Repulski, cf	4	0	1	1	0
Haddix, p	4	0	1	0	1
Totals	31	2	7	27	15

Philadelphia	000	000	000	0-2-0
St. Louis	101	000	000	2-7-0

RBI	Jablonski, Slaughter
2BH	Repulski
DP	Hemus, Schoendienst, Bilko
LOB	Philadelphia 5, St. Louis 11
K	Simmons 3, Haddix 2
BB	Simmons 6, Haddix 4
WP	Haddix (14 and 4)
LP	Simmons (9 and 9)
Umpires	Boggess, Engeln, Stewart and Pinelli
Time	2:06
Att	9,073

1960 World Series when the Pirates beat the Yankees at Forbes Field in the dramatic finish that featured Bill Mazeroski's bottom-of-the-ninth "mother of all World Series homers." Harvey Haddix was the pitcher who shut down the Yanks in his one-inning relief stint, gaining credit for the series-winning victory. As a matter of fact, he finished that Series with a glittery 2–0 mark, having won the fifth game to put the Corsairs ahead in the Series, 3 games to 2.

Harvey Haddix's 4.7 TPR for 1953 was light-years removed from the 1.7 recorded by Jim Gilliam, the fine rookie second baseman of the Dodgers who was the BBWAA's 1953 National League Rookie of the Year. The 3.0 difference between the two represents a six-game swing in victories over the season. That's one of the largest discrepancies on record between the election results and the actual sabermetric calculation on the basis of the total record.

With six shutouts and 20 victories for a ballclub that ended the season only 12 games over the .500 standard, a superb hitting season that resulted in a huge, 10 rating in the Pitcher's Hitting Index, and a ratio of almost three to one in strikeouts over walks, there just isn't much quibbling room over the superiority of the Kitten's 1953 effort. (Compare Haddix's and Gilliam's records in the top 10 1953 rookie listing.)

There is only one Haddix entry on the Cardinal record lists: Rookie Shutouts, 6. It's likely to stand for quite a while, just as the Kitten's 1953 seasonal 4.7 TPR, a sturdy, number 13(t) on the all-time honors list of rookie seasons.

1953: The Top Ten Rookies

Nm/Pos/Tm	GP	W–L/BA	SH/SV//RBI	PR/BR	ERA/FR	TPR
Harvey Haddix, LHP, StL-NL	36	20–9	6/1	34	3.06	4.7
Ruben Gomez, RHP, NY-NL	29	13–11	3/0	20	3.40	2.3
Bob Keegan, RHP, Chi-AL	22	7–5	2/1	14	2.74	1.9
Bob Buhl, RHP, Mil-NL	30	13–8	3/0	16	2.97	1.8
Jim Gilliam, 2b, Brk-NL	151	.278	63	8	3	1.7
Jack Collum, LHP, Stl/Cin-NL	37	7–11	1/3	6	3.97	1.5
F. Baczewski, LHP, Chi/Cin-NL	33	11–4	1/1	12	3.64	1.1
Don Larsen, RHP, StL-AL	38	7–12	2/2	1	4.16	0.8
"Red" Wilson, c, Chi-AL	71	.250	10	-5	10	0.6
Jim Greengrass, of, Cin-NL	154	.285	100	1	8	0.2

Fredric Michael "Freddie" Lynn

TPR: 4.7

1975, Boston, AL

Born: February 3, 1952, Chicago, IL
OF, 6'1" 190 lb. Major League Debut: September 4, 1974
1975: 145 GP; 528-103-175, AB-R-H; .331 BA; 105 RBI; 47, 2BH; 40 BR; 13 FR

While there was every indication from Freddie Lynn's call up to the Red Sox in 1974 that their acrobatic outfielder would become a star, it was no foregone conclusion. First year men off to a hot start have been a dime a dozen over the seasons. The reality check would come with the grind of a 162-game schedule.

To say that Freddie Lynn was up to it would be the understatement not only of 1974's late-season's pondering, but of 1975 and all the other seasons that have found their way into the history books. To come to the point forthwith: not everyone is crowned with Rookie of the Year and MVP honors his first crack out of the box. In fact, Lynn's is the *only* such occurrence — ever. Such was the Boston Red Sox' greatest rookie season, and one of the more remarkable achievements of the latter part of 20th century baseball.

While Lynn was in the midst of his 1974 warm-up, there was another Boston rookie, fresh from the International League, where his Triple Crown and MVP honors prompted the Red Sox front office to bring him to Boston earlier than originally planned. His name was Jim Rice, soon to become the "Samson" in the heart of the Beantown batting order. Though Rice's late season debut, and, for that matter, his 1975 rookie season, were not as arresting as Lynn's, the ox-strong outfielder quickly became a fixture in the Red Sox lineup.

Jim Rice's teammate at Boston's Pawtucket farm club, the 22-year-old Chicagoan, Lynn, had toured the International League with enough elan to win league All-Star honors. Further, his 21 four-baggers, only four shy of Rice's total, demonstrated his long-range power capabilities. No one, however, and certainly not Freddie, was quite prepared for Lynn's September of 1974. Lynn got right on with it, playing in 15 games, hitting at a torrid .419, clip (with a .698 SA), throwing out a pair of baserunners and lowering the boom on a Jim Slaton offering for his first major league tater just ten days after his September 5 debut.

Lynn was teamed with Rice and Dwight "Dewey" Evans in the outfield. The latter, a slick-fielding, strong-armed right fielder, was in the third full season of his distinguished 19-year career with the Carmine when Lynn and Rice came along. The three formed an outer-garden trio that was, if not the superior to, at least the equal of the legendary Duffy Lewis–Tris Speaker–Harry Hooper combo of the 1910s. They were two of the Red Sox' best outfield units in franchise history.

The national pastime enjoyed a banner year in 1975. Among innumerable highlights packed into the season were these: the Cleveland franchise, with more than a few firsts in its history, came up with another when Frank Robinson was named the first black manager (the future Hall of Famer opened the season with a home run his first time up to lead the Tribe to a 5 to 3 win over New York); Nolan Ryan threw another no-hitter, his fourth; the millionth run in major league history was scored; Hank Aaron smashed an *American* League four-bagger in Milwaukee, his 734th; Dennis Eckersley started his big league career with a rookie-record 28.2 consecutive scoreless innings; and the millionth Dodger fan made his way through the turnstiles on Los Angeles' 27th home date. And that was all entered into the 1975 ledger by mid–June.

With three more eventful months on tap plus baseball's "second season"— the playoffs and the World Series (Fenway and the Sox would host four games in the 1975 Fall Classic)— there was every reason to believe that baseball would get even better as the season unfolded. And, sure enough, it did.

But during the first half of the 1975

Freddie Lynn, 1975 MVP and Rookie of the Year. (Dennis Colgin.)

campaign there was no more sensational display of fireworks than those set off by Freddie Lynn on a late-spring evening in June at Tiger Stadium. In that record-setting extravaganza, Lynn tore into Tiger pitching like a man possessed.

Here is the tab on that Lynn-Bosox orgy: on the strength of their 15 to 1 annihilation of the Tigers, Darrell Johnson's ballclub moved 2.5 games up on the Yanks in the American League East. At the end of the evening Fred Lynn was at the front of the league hitting parade with a spiffy .352 and a league-leading 50 RBIs, and that only begins to tell the story. His 16 total bases, three homers and 10 ribbies that evening established or tied club and major league records and were also rookie records. He added a triple and a single to round out his five-hit game. By the time three frames had gone by, the score stood at 12 to 1, Boston's one-man demolition machine had jacked a pair of dingers into the seats and added a three-bagger, El Tiante had his ninth win locked up, and Detroiters

Box Score

Boston at Tiger Stadium, Detroit, June 18, 1975

Boston	AB	R	H	RBI		*Detroit*	AB	R	H	RBI
Beniquez, lf	5	1	1	1		LeFlore, cf	4	0	2	0
Burleson, ss	3	3	2	0		Sutherland, 2b	2	1	1	0
Griffin, 2b	2	1	1	0		Knox, 2b	2	0	0	0
Yastrzemski, 1b	3	3	3	2		Meyer, lf	4	0	1	1
Cooper, 1b	3	1	1	0		Horton, dh	4	0	1	0
Lynn, cf	6	4	5	10		Ogilvie, dh	0	0	0	0
Rice, dh	4	1	2	0		Roberts, rf	4	0	0	0
Evans, dh	2	0	0	0		Pierce, 1b	4	0	0	0
Carbo, rf	3	0	0	0		Rodriguez, 3b	4	0	1	0
Miller, rf	3	0	1	0		Wockenfuss, c	2	0	0	0
Petrocelli, 3b	3	1	3	1		Veryzer, ss	3	0	0	0
Doyle, 2b	4	0	0	0		Coleman, p	0	0	0	0
Blackwell, c	4	0	1	0		LaGrow, p	0	0	0	0
Tiant, p	0	0	0	0		Reynolds, p	0	0	0	0
Cleveland, p	0	0	0	0		Walker, p	0	0	0	0
						Moret, p	0	0	0	0
						Segui, p	0	0	0	0
Totals	46	15	20	14		Totals	33	1	6	1

```
Boston    435  000  003   15-20-0
Detroit   100  000  000    1-6-2
```

2BH	Yastrzemski, Rice
3BH	Burleson, Sutherland, Lynn
HR	Lynn 3
SB	Rice
DP	Detroit 2
LOB	Boston 9, Detroit 6
BB	Tiant 1, LaBrow 2, Reynolds 2, Walker 1
K	Tiant 4, Coleman 1, Reynolds 3, Walker 1
WP	Coleman, Cleveland
PB	Wockenfuss
Win. P	Tiant (9–6)
Los. P	Coleman (3–10)
Time	2:26
Att	13,029

undoubtedly had seen all they wanted to see of anything with Boston written on it.

The other half of the terrific Bosox rookie tandem, Jim Rice, meanwhile, was also producing Rookie of the Year numbers, and as June moved on into July, Rice and Lynn spearheaded a Boston drive that, with just enough pitching help from the crafty Cuban, Luis Tiant, Rick Wise and "The Spaceman," Bob Lee, turned Boston hearts aglow with the growing awareness that this outfit might just get it done.

Rice, the muscular left fielder, began

to connect for some eye-popping long distance blows that prompted his "Samson" monicker. One, in particular, had Beantowners agog over a cannon shot that cleared the center field wall, on July 18, one of the longest ever hit at Fenway.

With the ever-reliable Carl Yaztrzemski, Boston's beloved Yaz, still around, and with a sound supporting cast led by Rick Burleson, Carlton Fisk — playing when possible in an injury-marred season (he had missed a month earlier in April and May) — and Bernie Carbo, the Red Sox headed on into September under full sail. Fred Lynn sparred with Rod Carew, Thurman Munson, Rico Carty, George Brett and teammate Rice for hitting laurels, and the pitching staff was able enough to ward off Earl Weaver's challenging Orioles and the injury-riddled Yankees.

The first harbinger of possible disaster ahead surfaced on September 21, when an errant Vern Ruhle pitch fractured Jim Rice's hand in Detroit. That sidelined the productive rookie for the remainder of the season. In Boston the groaning began: "Here we go again. The curse of Ruth is alive and well!" Rice's big stick, responsible for 102 runs driven in over the 144 games he played, would be missed.

But the Carmine closed ranks, finally beating out the Orioles by 4.5 games and winning the American League East. Freddie Lynn finished the year second to Rod Carew's .359 with his .331 effort, and league-leading figures in slugging average (.566), doubles (47), and runs scored (103). Further, his breakneck, dashing outfield play rounded out his game to persuade the BBWAA, almost unanimously, to vote him Rookie of the Year honors. Of 24 votes cast, he poled 23.5. The other .5? Jim Rice's.

And what was this about disaster ahead? Bostonians, always on the edge of panic when it comes to playoff and World Series games, have come to expect the black hood of doom where their Red Sox are concerned. Although there are many theories about the ballclub's rather perverse insistence on lousing up championship engagements — particularly since the 1920 departure of Babe Ruth — and though reams of sports writing have been expended on it, the team does have a way with its doomsday fate. Few have captured that scenario better than Ed Linn:

> It is no secret that the Red Sox are the team with the fatal flaw.... There is a Hand, to paraphrase a local poet named James Russell Lowell, that bends the Red Sox to mightier misfortunes than should be rightfully borne [*The Great Rivalry*, xx].

In 1975 the Red Sox thrashed the American League West's champion Oakland Athletics three games to none to get off to a start on the world championship trail that raised expectations and at least forestalled the inevitable, inasmuch as Sparky Anderson's Big Red Machine was heavily favored to win it all. In the ALCS, however, Freddie Lynn drove home Carlton Fisk with a crucial, fourth inning hit in the pivotal second game of the best-three-of-five series to stake the Bosox to its never-relinquished lead. They moved on from there to Oakland in need of but one more to wrap up the series. They did the next time out, 5 to 3, and flew back to Boston to prepare for the Dance. The Sox, led by Lynn (.364), Fisk (.417), Yaz (.455), and Burleson (.444), had clubbed the A's into submission with a .316 team BA. Who was to say that beating the Reds was impossible, especially when the Series was to start in Boston?

But in Boston? To quote Mr. Linn once more, "Boston's own Seventh Commandment decrees: Thou Shalt Not Win the Seventh Game" (xx). It was the sixth game of that famous TV celebration that kept most of America up and on the edge of their seats. Again, it was Freddie Lynn who got the Red Sox off and running with a towering blast that brought home three in the first inning. Then, after watching the Reds storm back to take a 6 to 3 lead, Bernie Carbo sent one into the center-field seats that tied it up at 6 and 6. The end came in the Boston 12th with one of the most famous home runs in baseball history, Carlton Fisk's game-winning blast, just fair, into the left-field crowd. Boston was delirious. But not for long.

The Fisk blast brought it down to

"Boston's Seventh Commandment"— which proved to be unbreakable. Misfortune struck again with a grubby pop single that scored the fourth and Series-winning run (of course, the Red Sox had three by virtue of a three-run third inning) in the top of the ninth.

Boston went down in order in the bottom of the ninth. Fred Lynn had found out both what it was like to play in a championship series *and* that the old ghosts in Boston meant business. For him there would be no second chance in Red Sox livery. After another five seasons he took up residence in California wearing an Angels uniform.

Freddie Lynn's freshman season in the Bigs was one of titanic achievements. When the last hit had been made and the last out recorded for his 1975 Rookie of the Year season, it went down as the greatest rookie season in Red Sox history — and there have been some exceptionally good ones, including those, among the rookie honors list, of Carlton Fisk (number 24), Ted Williams (26), Johnny Pesky (33), Dick Radatz (47), Dave Ferriss (68), Nomar Garciaparra (73) and Fritz Ostermueller (81), all in the game's top 100.

1975: Ten Top Rookies

Nm/Pos/Tm	GP	W–L/BA	SH/SV//RBI	PR/BR	ERA/FR	TPR
Fred Lynn/of/Bos-A	145	.331	105	40	13	4.7
Dennis Eckersley/RHP/Clv-A	34	13–7	2/2	24	2.60	2.3
John Montefusco/RHP/SF-N	35	19–9	4/0	25	2.88	2.0
Mike Vail/of/NY-N	38	.302	17	3	11	1.3
Jim Rice/of/Bos-A	144	.309	102	17	–1	1.2
Rawly Eastwick/RHP-RP/Cin-N	58	5–3	0/22	10	2.60	1.1
Doug Flynn/UT/Cin-N	89	.268	20	–3	10	1.0
Will McEnaney/LHP-RP/Mon-N	70	5–2	0/15	11	2.47	1.0
Dan Warthen/LHP-RP/Mon-N	40	8–6	0/3	13	3.11	0.9
Rick Manning/of/Clv-A	120	.285	35	1	13	0.8

PART II

The Cum Laudes

"The Milkman," Jim Turner, of Boston's Braves, leads off the second tier of our rookie honorees. In this outstanding group, 15 of the 22 players presented are starting pitchers, two are superb rookie relievers (Doug Corbett and Todd Worrell), and the remainder include catcher Carlton Fisk, outfielders Vada Pinson, Tony Oliva, and Ted Williams, and infielders Joe Morgan, Bob Allen of the Phillies' 1890 ballclub, and Johnny Pesky.

Among them, these "Cum Laudes" average a four-game difference in their teams' victories during their rookie seasons. That's a full victory less (the Ruthian Rookies averaged a 5.3 TPR; our Cum Laudes, a 4.2) than our first contingent of premier rookies produced, but it nonetheless represents a considerable achievement.

Hall of Famers Christy Mathewson, Ted Williams, Joe Morgan, and Carlton Fisk add a classy touch to this group. Fur-

ther, Tony Oliva might well be called on to make the symbolic trip to Cooperstown. All of these stalwarts used great rookie seasons as a springboard to long and distinguished careers.

Who were Jocko Flynn, Bill Hoffer, Reb Russell and Scott Perry? These four relatively unknown pitchers, all active before 1920, are interesting studies in the pitching arts. Flynn, one of the champion 1886 Chicago White Stockings, came to the Windy City for one, and one only, season of glory. His story is one of the more intriguing among our rookie heroes. The others are equally captivating.

From Jim Turner, then, to Vada Pinson, we have another 22 notable rookie seasons, bringing to 42 the number of rookie greats reviewed. Their TPRs range from 4.5 to 3.9, representing the 14th on through the 20th rank of our honors list.

James Riley
"The Milkman" Turner

TPR: 4.5

1937, Boston, NL

Born: August 6, 1903, Antioch, TN. Died: November 29, 1998, Nashville, TN
RHP, 6' 185 lb. Major League Debut: April 30, 1937
1937: W20, L11; .645 W%; 24 CG; 5/1 SH-SV; 34 PR; .274 OOB%; 4 PHI 2.38 ERA

The 1937 season was Bill McKechnie's eighth and last with the Boston Bees. Who was McKechnie and who were the Bees? "The Deacon," church-going William Boyd McKechnie, was one of two major league managers to have won pennants with three different ballclubs (Pittsburgh, St. Louis and Cincinnati, all of the National League). He was elected to the Hall of Fame in 1962 on the basis of his managing credentials, primarily those involving the development of sound defensive teams and capable pitching staffs. In Boston those were dire necessities.

As to the Bees, they were really the Braves; but when Bob Quinn, who had been elected the club's president after the franchises restructuring following the 1936 season, took over, he decided a Pilgrim-town contest to rename the team was in order. It was done, and the Braves were rechristened the Bees. If only the new name, which didn't last very long anyway,

could have carried with it a transformation on the field of play as easily and inexpensively as the team had taken on its new moniker! Of course, around the Back Bay everyone knew better.

It had been an eon since Boston's dwindling coterie of Braves — now Bees — fans had experienced the thrill of a champion. That miracle had taken place back in 1914 when George Stallings' Miraclemen beat the mighty Mackmen of Philadelphia in an electrifying World Series after having risen from the ashes of their more familiar, second-division surroundings.

But there was another miracle, of sorts, on the way. It came in the form of two grizzled minor league veterans named Lou Fette and Jim Turner. Fette and Turner had rumbled around enough minor league cities to learn what pitching was all about. The former had been in the American Association long enough to win almost a hundred games there, and the latter, a

117

21-game winner with Hollywood as early as 1930, had already turned 30 as an 18-game winner with Indianapolis in 1936. It's this latter pitcher, a right-hander named "The Milkman" in his still-later years, that attracts our attention in this profile. His name is James Riley Turner, a husky Tennesseean who combined with Lou Fette to chalk up 40 (20 a piece) of the Bees' 79 victories in 1937.

The one thing that Jim Turner learned, above all others, was that good pitchers have outstanding control. It was his number one priority, the *sine qua non* he stressed in his later years as a well-respected pitching coach with the Yankees, and it was, for him, the difference between toiling endlessly in the minors and getting a shot at the Bigs. When it came, after his purchase from Indianapolis for the 1937 season, he made the most of his opportunity.

There is still another 1937 rookie phenom, a somewhat younger, 25-year old chap from the hills of North Carolina they called "The Mountain Man," Cliff Melton, who is linked with Fette and Turner in one of those rather special, once-only coincidences. All three were 20-game winners in exceptional freshman years, and all three beat the Phillies in garnering their 20th victory. Melton's 3.9 TPR in the 1937 season ties him with pitchers George McQuillan and George Scott and outfielder Vada Pinson for the number 20 spot on the honors list.

Moundsman Jim Turner, whose outstanding rookie season was recognized with his selection as the National League's Rookie of the Year in Bill Deane's hypothetical listing of pre–1947 award winners, was a well-traveled craftsman when he reported to manager Bill McKechnie at Boston's training camp at St. Petersburg, Florida, in 1937. But he still hadn't had his big chance. "The Deacon" changed all that. Interviewed by Paul Shannon of the

Boston Globe during a lull in his second Boston year after his sterling freshman campaign, Jim Turner was unstinting in his praise of McKechnie, who by 1938 had moved on to Cincinnati.

> I want to give Bill McKechnie plenty of credit for allowing me to compile the record I made.... I had a change of pace, a fairly effective slow one, and everything I figured was in the pitching repertoire when I joined the Bees last spring. And yet I was only a gamble in spite of a rich hurling experience. This is where I became infinitely obligated to Bill McKechnie.... McKechnie gave me my chance. In spite of a rather dubious start and an early pounding by the St. Louis Cardinals, he seemed to have acquired a lot of confidence in me and I wanted to show my appreciation. So I bore down from the start and before I realized it myself, I was going along very nicely.

How nicely soon became evident. Jim Turner's 1937 season was a strong statement about intensity of focus in a winning pitcher. Always thinking, and with super concentrating abilities, Turner made his way on brains as well as on good speed mixed with change-ups and breaking balls. And his entire game came down to a matter of control — of his pitches, the edges of the strike zone and of himself. That combination, on display in almost all of his 30 starts, produced league-leading figures in complete games (24), shutouts (5), ratio (9.8), opponents' batting average (.274), the lowest ERA in the league (2.38) and the highest TPR for pitchers at 4.5.

As October rolled around he could look back at a winning log against the two chief pennant contenders, 1937's Giants and Cubs. He beat the Giants three times, losing only one, and bested the Wrigleymen two times out of three. Against Cincinnati's Redlegs he was a winner four times, while losing the two times the Bees were shut out by Cincy pitching. And as far as that control factor is concerned, Boston's late-blossoming sensation issued only one free pass for every five innings he pitched, walking a scarcely visible total of 52 over the season.

All these wonders were achieved in front of a punchless ballclub (at best) that had nary a .300 hitter, stole but 45 bases all season and registered eighth place finishes in team batting average, runs and hits, slugging average, and on-base percentage, and fanned more (707 times) than any other team besides Detroit in either league. They were, in fact, better suited to the glory days of 1914, when a crack defense, strong arms, good catching, near-obsessive desire and, above all, superior pitching were the order of the day. And so it was that when Lou Fette, Danny MacFayden or Jim Turner was out there with Al Lopez behind the plate, and the rest of the boys on their toes defensively, the Bees looked like those better Braves teams, winning 54 games among the top three hurlers, while losing only 35, a .606

The Braves' Milkman Jim Turner. (Colgin Photo.)

winning percentage that would have put them right behind the pennant-winning Giants. Alas, there were those other days. So the ballclub had to settle for a 79–73 mark, which landed them just out of the first division.

As the leaves began to turn in Boston and the season entered its last weekend, both Lou Fette and Jim Turner had still not crossed the 20-game threshold. Gentleman Jim got his chance first in a game at Braves Field against the Phillies' Bob "The Thin

Man" Allen. In another of the game's strange twists and turns, Bob Allen's loss to Jim Turner that day was the Phils' rookie's only major league start in his only major league season.

Driving in the first Bees run with a sharp single, spacing nine hits, and otherwise handcuffing the Philadelphians, Jim Turner picked up his 20th conquest of the season. His victory had followed Cliff Melton's 20th by four days and preceded Lou Fette's 20th win by 24 hours, which

Box Score

Philadelphia at Braves Field, Boston, October 2, 1937

Philadelphia	AB	R	H	PO	A		Boston	AB	R	H	PO	A
Norris, 2b	4	0	2	1	5		R. Johnson,	3	1	1	2	0
Browne, 1b	3	0	1	1	0		English, 3b	4	0	1	0	1
Klein, rf	3	0	0	1	0		Garms, rf	5	0	2	1	0
J. Moore, cf	4	0	1	2	0		Cuccinello, 2b	3	1	1	3	2
Arnovich, lf	4	0	1	3	0		Fletcher, 1b	5	1	2	14	1
Walters, 3b	4	0	2	0	1		V. DiMaggio, cf	5	0	1	4	1
Atwood, c	4	0	1	6	0		Warstler, ss	5	1	1	3	7
Scharein, ss	4	0	0	3	4		Mueller, c	4	1	1	0	0
R. Allen, p	2	1	1	0	0		Turner, p	4	2	2	0	2
Mulcahy, p	0	0	0	0	0							
Wilson, ph	1	0	0	0	0							
Burkart, p	0	0	0	0	0							
Grace, ph	1	0	0	0	0							
Totals	35	1	9	24	10		Totals	38	7	12	27	14

```
Philadelphia    000   010   000    1-9-5
Boston          030   004   00x    7-12-0
```

2BH	Norris, Browne, Arnovich, Garms
DP	Scharein, Norris and Browne; Norris, Scharein and Browne; DiMaggio and Fletcher
LOB	Philadelphia 8, Boston 13
BB	Allen 6, Turner 1, Mulcahy and Burkart 0
K	Allen 4, Burkart 1, Turner and Mulcahy 1
WP	Turner (20–11)
LP	Allen (0–1)
Umpires	Stewart, Barr and Klem
Time	1:50

also came at the expense of the Phillies, who seem to have spread late season joy around in both New York *and* Boston.

Jim Turner pitched into his 41st calendar year, ending with the New York Yankees as a relief pitcher and his age earned him his "Milkman Jim" tag. He got into two World Series, one each with Cincinnati and the Yankees, and wound up with a .535 pitching log over nine seasons under the Big Tent. That was followed by distinguished hitches as both a minor league manager and a major league pitching coach. Predictably, his number one coaching emphasis was: "Control, boys, Control with a capital *C*."

1937: Eleven Top Rookies

Nm/Pos/Tm	GP	W–L/BA	SH/SV//RBI	PR/BR	ERA/FR	TPR
J. Turner/RHP/Bos-N	33	20–11	5/1	34	2.38	4.9
C. Melton/RHP/NY-N	46	20–9	2/7	35	2.61	3.9
L. Fette/RHP/Bos-N	35	20–10	5/0	20	2.88	2.5
R. Bauers/RHP/Pit-N	34	13–6	2/1	21	2.88	2.3
S. Chandler/RHP/NY-A	12	7–4	2/0	15	2.84	1.7
E. Smith/LHP/Phl-A	38	4–17	1/5	17	3.94	1.7
J. Tobin/RHP/Pit-N	20	6–3	0/1	8	3.00	1.4
R. York/c/Det-A	104	.307	103	25	-19	0.9
T. Henrich/of/NY-A	67	.320	42	14	-4	0.8
M. Arnovich/of/Phl-N	117	.290	60	3	7	0.7
J. Krakauskas/LHP/Was-A	5	4–1	0/0	8	2.70	0.7

Gary Charles Peters

4.5 TPR

1963, Chicago, AL
Born: April 21, 1937, Grove City, PA
LHP, 6'2" 200 lb. Major League Debut: September 10, 1959
1963: 41 GP; W19, L8, .704 WP%; 4/1 SH/SV; .216 OBA; 9 PHI; 32 PR; 2.33 ERA

Just ahead of cutdown day, a day that raises the dreaded specter of trade, demotion, release, or some other fearful fate for rookies, Gary Peters was written into Al Lopez' White Sox lineup as the starting pitcher. The Sox' respected skipper, known far and wide as a pitcher's manager, had originally written another lefty into his lineup, Juan Pizarro, for the May 6, 1963, game with Kansas City's Athletics, but the Puerto Rican was not up to par, so Peters got the nod. It came at a time when the 26-year-old southpaw had just about made up his mind that if he were sent down — again — or traded, he would pack it in, leave the game, and move on with his life.

Many a rookie before Gary Peters had made that very decision under similar circumstances. Those who made that choice number in the thousands. And were the information made available, an encyclopedia could be compiled about the legions of talented young ballplayers who went back home and literally started over.

May 6, then, was not to be one of those plebian work days in the mind of the number one son of Oak Grove, Pennsylvania. Though the White Sox organization might not have looked at it the way Peters did, for Gary the moment had come.

As it turned out, however, May 6 was a decisive turning point in Peters' career, for on that day he squelched the Athletics in a convincing 5 to 1 win. And it wasn't only his first major league victory. It was, further, the occasion for that very special delight among pitchers, a dinger-day, when Gary ripped into a Ted Bowsfield offering and crushed it for the first of his three round-trippers that season.

At the end of May, Lopez' five-man starting rotation included veterans Ray Herbert and Johnny Buzhardt and younger hurlers Joel Horlen and the aforementioned Juan Pizarro, plus the lefty with the silky-smooth delivery, Gary Peters. They had spurred the team to 20 wins that month, as many as any Sox club had ever mustered. Though serious contenders for the league's top spot at that point, it was

The White Sox' slick lefty Gary Peters. (Brace Photo.)

compensation, but it wasn't enough, not nearly enough to dislodge Ralph Houk's Yankees from a pennant berth at season's end. The distance of 10 games between the New Yorkers and Chicago's second-place Pale Hose might just as well have been 10 miles. The Yanks' success, especially against the White Sox, was a source of no little frustration around the Windy City. Peters himself maintained that the South Siders never played well against New York, and recalled, further, that all Whitey Ford had to do was to warm up and the Sox could already see a long afternoon ahead. It usually was.

But there came a time when that changed — at least for a day. In an August 17 matchup with the Bronx Bombers, Lopez started Peters at Comiskey Park, hoping, with the White Sox faithful, that the willowy southpaw could at least salvage one game out of their four-game set. With a seven-game winning streak in tow, Gary faced off against Al Downing (8–3) before 29,719 of the more optimistic among Chicago's fandom. What they were treated to was a four-hit masterpiece that brought the victorious Sox to within eight and a half games of first place, which was about as close as anybody got that summer. And the leader of the band was the lanky Pennsylvanian, Gary Peters.

Edward Prell, whose long sportswriting tenure with the *Chicago Tribune* was distinguished by many a fine article on both the Sox and the Cubs, covered that game, and in his droll style recounted the

already evident that whatever plusses were inherent in an outstanding pitching corps might be nullified by an under-achieving offense.

Dick Linberg, the sage White Sox historian, sized it up this way: "The younger pitchers who came along — Gary Peters, Juan Pizarro, Joel Horlen — and a fine bullpen anchored by Eddie Fisher, Hoyt Wilhelm, and Bob Locker, compensated for a wobbly, weak-kneed offense that conjured up distant memories of the Hitless Wonder era" (*Stealing First in a Two-Team Town*, 150).

Superior pitching might have been a

Box Score

New York Yankees at Comiskey Park, Chicago, August 16, 1963

New York	AB	R	H	RBI	PO	A	Chicago	AB	R	H	RBI	PO	A
Linz, ss	4	0	0	0	0	3	Hershberger, rf	4	1	2	0	3	0
Richardson, 2b	4	0	0	0	4	5	Fox, 2b	3	0	0	0	3	3
Tresh, cf	4	0	2	0	1	0	Lemon, 1b	4	1	1	0	6	0
Howard, c	3	0	1	0	6	0	McCraw, 1b	0	0	0	0	1	0
Bright, 1b	4	0	0	0	7	0	Nicholson, lf	2	0	0	0	1	0
Lopez, lf	2	0	0	0	3	1	Ward, 3b	3	0	3	2	0	2
Pepitone, rf	3	0	0	0	3	0	Landis, cf	4	0	1	0	3	0
Boyer, 3b	3	0	0	0	0	2	Hansen, ss	2	0	0	0	5	5
Downing, p	2	0	1	0	0	0	Carreon, c	4	0	0	0	5	0
Mantle, ph	0	0	0	0	0	0	Peters, p	2	0	1	0	0	1
Reed, pr	0	0	0	0	0	0							
Metcalf, p	0	0	0	0	0	0							
Totals	29	0	4	0	24	11	Totals	28	2	8	2	27	11

```
New York   000   000   000   0-4-1
Chicago    100   010   00x   2-8-0
```

2BH	Tresh
SH	Peters
SF	Ward
DP	Richardson, Bright; Hansen, Lemon; Ward, Fox, Lemon; Linz, Richardson, Bright
LOB	New York 6, Chicago 9
WP	Peters (13–5)
LP	Downing (8–4)
Time	2:08
Umpires	Carigan, McKinley, Chylak, Haller
Att	29,719

Yankee embarrassment, a four-hit whitewashing: "The ninth inning held no terrors for Gary Peters of the White Sox yesterday. Baseball's most spectacular rookie pitcher of the year went into the final round in Comiskey Park leading the New York Yankees 2 to 0. A few minutes later he walked off the mound, winner by that score, and the White Sox could hold their heads high again…. His fourth shutout brought his earned run average down to 1.88, the best among American League starters. Closest to him is the Cubs' Dick Ellsworth at 1.93" (*Chicago Tribune*).

The win was Peters' eighth in a string that would reach 11 and raise his record at that mid–August point in the schedule to a gaudy 16 and 5, before leveling off to a final 19 and 8 reading in a lustrous season that earned the BBWAA's Rookie of the Year Award. The ghost of minor league seasons past had been exorcised, and a sparkling 14-year career had begun.

Artistic as his conquest of Mantle, Boyer, Howard and Company was, it was surpassed by an even better effort earlier in the season when, on July 15, he whiffed 13 Baltimore Orioles in a sterling one-hitter, 4 to 0, one of his four 1963 shutouts. Robin Roberts, almost as good a hitting pitcher as Peters, solved one of the lefty's slants for a line-drive single to spoil an otherwise perfect game. On that day he fashioned the finest American League pitching effort of 1963.

When it came time to tally up the numbers on Peters' freshman campaign, he was up there among the league's best, finishing first with a superb 2.33 ERA, fourth in winning percentage at .704 and strikeouts with 189, and fifth in both opponents' batting average (.216) and opponents' on-base percentage (.278). He headed a fine White Sox staff, perhaps the best in the league. These numbers tend to substantiate that claim.

Nm	W–L	SH	ERA	TPR
Peters	19–8	4	2.33*	4.5
Pizarro	16–8	3	2.39	3.0
Wilhelm	12–9	27 SV	2.64	1.6
Herbert	13–10	7*	3.24	1.5
Buzhardt	9–4	3	2.42	1.4
Horlen	11–7	0	3.27	0.7

*indicates league leader

On a weak-hitting ballclub a hitting pitcher is always more than welcome. Gary filled that role with such vigor that he was often used as a pinch hitter (his career record was 16 for 66 with four pinch homers, one of which won an extra-inning game for the Sox), and in 1968 he was used in the sixth spot in the batting order. The 1963 log showed appearances in 50 games, in which he hit .259 (21 for 81) with 12 RBIs and a .444 slugging average. It goes without saying that the hitting-starved Pale Hose needed every last one of Peters' contributions to their sputtering offense.

Gary followed up his roaring start in 1963 with an equally good 1964. It was a season marked by an authentic bid for the American League bunting, as the Sox chased the Yankees once again, this time right on down to the final wire. The Señor, Al Lopez, whose pitching staff was the envy of the league, had but one addition, reliever Eddie Fisher, to his outstanding, Peters-led staff. This time around the slider-sinkerball smoothie was a 20-game winner whose 2.50 ERA wasn't good enough to lead the staff! Joel Horlen and Hoyt Wilhelm, both of whom had sub–2.00 ERAs, took the honors on a staff that averaged 2.77 to lead the league with a few earned runs to spare. But when the last of 1964's outs had been made, the results were still the same: Yanks (99–63, 1st) and then the White Sox, one game in arrears (98–64, 2nd).

After seven strong seasons in Chicago, not including the tiny bits and pieces of the four trial runs that preceded his rookie season, the White Sox saw fit to move their accomplished southpaw on to Boston, where Gary spent the last three years of his career, totaling another 33 wins before retiring.

Although Gary Peters' career, with its lengthy minor league apprenticeship, is an oft-repeated story, the southpaw's journey was more successful than most, and his rookie season, usually a bumpy ride for any first-year man, was an extraordinarily good one. So good, in fact, that it merits top-billing among the Chicago franchise's rookies with a gold-plated 4.5 TPR. That's also a strong enough credential to place him on an even keel with pitchers Jim Turner and the Minnesota Twins' Doug Corbett at the very top of the second tier of rookie honorees.

1963: Eleven Top Rookies

Nm/Pos/Tm	GP	W–L/BA	SH/SV//RBI	PR/BR	ERA/FR	TPR
G. Peters/LHP/Chi-A	41	19–8	4/1	32	2.33	4.5
R. Hunt/2b/NY-N	143	.272	42	6	2	2.3
P. Ward/3b/Chi-A	157	.295	84	27	–5	2.1
R. Veale/LHP/Pit-N	34	5–2	2/3	19	1.04	1.9
A. Weis/UT/Chi-A	99	.271	18	–4	14	1.9
V. Davalillo/of/Clv-A	90	.292	36	3	17	1.5
R. Tracewski/ss/LA-N	104	.226	10	–10	19	1.3
R. Brand/c/Pit-N	46	.288	7	2	9	1.2

Nm/Pos/Tm	GP	W–L/BA	SH/SV//RBI	PR/BR	ERA/FR	TPR
R. Culp/RHP/Phl-N	34	14–11	5/0	6	2.27	0.7
M. Alvis/3b/Clv-A	158	.274	67	13	-5	0.7
P. Rose*/2b/Cin-N	157	.273	41	1	-23	-1.3

*Voted NL Rookie of the Year

Douglas Michael "Doug" Corbett

TPR: 4.5

1980, Minnesota, AL

Born: November 4, 1952, Sarasota, FL
RHP (RP) 6'1" 185 lb. Major League Debut: April 10, 1980
1980: W8, L6; .571 W%; 73 GP; 23 SV; 9.6 Ratio; 36 PR; 3 DEF; 1.98 ERA; 4.5 TPR

In 1980 the Twin Cities chapter of the BBWAA voted Relief Pitcher Doug Corbett the Minnesota franchise's Bill Bone (Outstanding Rookie) and Joseph Haynes (Pitcher of the Year) awards. The Floridian right-hander, whose wicked sinker had baffled American League hitters en route to a record-breaking 23 saves, had put together the kind of numbers that convinced both writers and fans in Minneapolis and St. Paul that there wasn't a better reliever in either league. That took in the likes of New York's Goose Gossage, Boston's Tom Burgmeier, Atlanta's Rick Camp and Joe Sambito of Houston, all of whom enjoyed strong years out of the bullpen.

While he had impressed the local partisans, there apparently weren't enough scribes around the league's cities to garner Corbett the necessary votes for Rookie of the Year honors. Instead, the BBWAA honored Cleveland first sacker Joe Charboneau 1980's laurels, with Boston infielder Dave Stapleton selected as the 1980 runner-up. The American League BBWAA honorees stack up as shown below. The numbers reveal that White Sox portsider Britt Burns and the Twins' Doug Corbett both fashioned

Nm/Tm	RY Votes	W–L/BA	ERA/RBI	PR/FR	TPR
Charboneau/Clv	102	.289	87	1	1.3
Stapleton/Bos	40	.321	45	10	2.1
Corbett/Min	38	8–6	1.98	36	4.5 (23 Sv)
Garcia/Tor	35	.278	46	16	0.5
Burns/Chi	33	15–13	2.84	31	3.5
Peters/Det	3	.291	42	0	-0.2
Dotson/Chi	1	12–10	4.27	-5	-0.4

better seasons than the BBWAA's first- and second-place winners according to 1980's TPR ratings. The difference in the ratings between Charboneau and Stapleton and the two rookie hurlers, Burns and Corbett, further, is striking. Corbett and Burns both tower over Joe Charboneau (4.5 and 3.5 to 1.3) and Dave Stapleton (2.1).

Corbett's 4.5 represents upwards of five wins beyond an average pitcher's contribution over a full season's play. It's the premier Minnesota rookie season, and completes the three-way tie for the number 14 position on our list of all-time rookie honorees. What made it such a hit will be explored shortly.

Corbett added still more luster to his 1980 achievements by out-distancing an absolutely outstanding corps of relievers. Dan Quisenberry of Kansas City, the Dodgers' Steve Howe, Jeff Reardon of the New York Mets, Houston's Dave Smith, and the Giants' Al Holland, each and every one a reliever, all crashed the Show with solid freshman marks.

Among the 74 players cited for banner rookie seasons with TPR ratings of 3.3 through Curt Davis' number one rating at 7.8, 10 are relief pitchers. All save Wilcey Moore (1927) and Joe Berry (1944) have been active since the 1960s, illustrating the important and strategic place relief pitching has assumed these past 35 years. The role is not new to the game, however.

Because the tap root goes back to the nation's capital, Washington, D.C., the original home of the Minnesota franchise (Washington was granted a franchise in 1901 as a charter member of the American League), it might be well to trace, if only briefly, the development of relief pitching

since it was the brainchild of Calvin Griffith, former White Stockings (NL) and New York Highlanders (AL) pitcher.

Griffith came to Washington in 1912 as both manager and 10 percent shareholder in the Senators' fortunes — such as they were in those days. He had been a fair-country twirler on his own for Cap Anson and his Chicago National Leaguers. The two had talked over late-inning strategies, and bringing in a fresh arm was part of that strategy. Within a season or two, the "Old Fox," as he was known, had designated a pitcher here and there for those late inning appearances. By 1914 Harry Harper had become Griffith's first reliever. Another ten years later the job began to take on the marks of a pitching specialty, and in 1924, when the Senators won their first pennant, Fred Marberry led a number of American League relievers with league-leading totals in appearances (50) and 15 saves.* Marberry's contribution to the Senators' success was not lost on the rest of the league. A significant milestone had been reached, and from that point on major league ballclubs began to use relievers like the Yankees' Wilcey Moore (1927), Dolph Luque (NY-N, 1933), Clint Brown (Chi-A, 1937), Joe Berry (Phl-A, 1944), Hoyt Wilhelm (NY-N, 1953), Elroy Face (Pit-N, 1959) and Dick Radatz (Bos-A, 1962). All, plus many more, nudged the art ever farther. Managers were keeping tabs and specialized pitching coaches were introduced.

Relief pitching was a Washington-Minnesota original, however, and the franchise had some great relievers: Jack Russell in the '30s, followed by Al Carrasquel and Pedro Ramos, Al Worthington,

---

The save designation was originated by Jerome Holtzman, distinguished Chicago sports writer, who suggested prior to the 1969 season that a relief pitcher who enters a game and holds his team's lead the remainder of the game should be credited with a save, provided he is not named the winner. Since that time the save rule has been refined, and the 1975 ruling has remained in effect to indicate not only when the save is awarded a pitcher, but a hold, as well.

Saves listed for pitchers prior to 1969 are calculated on the basis of the original 1969 save ruling.

Doug Corbett, Twins rookie record-setter. (Brace Photo.)

Ron Perranoski and Mike Marshall. And then came Doug Corbett. His rookie season was rated higher than any other franchise reliever's except Mike Marshall's, whose monster 1979 season was rated at an orbital 5.7 (1979 was Marshall's 12th ML season), ranking him as the organization's number one, single season reliever.

Douglas Mitchell Corbett was originally signed by the Kansas City Royals in 1974, and then knocked around the Cincinnati organization for the next four seasons before being drafted by the Twinkies on December 3, 1979. The next spring he reported to the Twins' training base at Orlando, and by Opening Day was ready to go to work in Gene Mauch's bullpen.

It didn't take long for the first call to come. Opening at Oakland, the Twins managed to pull out their first win of the season by a 9 to 7 score. The winning pitcher was Doug Corbett, who tucked away the first of his eight 1980 wins in his first major league appearance. If this was to be a harbinger of things to come, it was a very good one.

Later during the same month, once again involved with Oakland, which ultimately wound up just ahead of Minnesota's third place finish in the AL West, the Twins mauled the A's in a game that set several club records, 20 to 11. Again the reliever — and winner — was Corbett. Just days before their bombardment of the A's, the Minnesotans barely avoided being no-hit by California's Bruce Kison, when Ken Landreaux's ninth inning two-bagger spoiled the rangy Angels right-hander's masterpiece. But that's one of the things major league baseball, over its grinding, marathon schedule, is all about.

Despite a subpar season, there were a few frills and thrills along the way: Ken Landreaux strung together a club record 30-game hitting streak beginning in April and ending on May 30 (the Twins' left fielder also went 25 straight at-bats without a hit in 1980); starting lefty Geoff Zahn experienced the very good, the bad and the ugly in winning one of his five shutouts via the one-hitter route (he beat Toronto,

5 to 0), giving up a club record 14 hits in that 20–11 slugfest with Oakland, and coughing up 10 earned runs against Baltimore, another record. Then too, the 1980 Twinkie ace, Jerry Koosman, whiffed 15 Royals on June 23 and second baseman Rob Wilfong set a fielding record with a stellar .995 fielding average, forged on only three miscues in 120 games.

Doug Corbett also had a hand in 1980's festivities. His 1.98 ERA, 79 appearances and 23 saves were, and remain, club rookie records. On October 2 he saved his 23rd game, which was the 11th straight in a string of 12 the Twins put together for their longest winning streak of the season.

Nonetheless, 1980 marked the begin-

Box Score

Minnesota at Kansas City, October 3, 1980

Minnesota	AB	R	H	BI
Ward, lf	4	1	4	1
Castino, 3b	5	1	1	2
Landreaux, cf	5	1	1	0
Morales, dh	5	1	4	0
Jackson, 1b	4	0	2	1
Wynegar, c	3	0	0	1
Mackanin, ss	5	0	1	0
Rivera, rf	4	0	0	0
Wilfong, 2b	4	1	1	0
Koosman, p	0	0	0	0
Corbett, p	0	0	0	0
Totals	39	5	14	5

Kansas City	AB	R	H	BI
Wilson, lf	4	1	1	0
Washington, ss	3	0	1	0
Brett, 3b	3	0	1	1
McRae, dh	4	1	2	1
Otis, cf	4	0	0	0
Aikens, 1b	4	0	1	0
Concepcion, pr	0	0	0	0
Porter, c	2	1	0	0
Wathan, ph	1	0	0	0
Cardenal, rf	3	0	0	0
LaCock, ph	1	0	0	0
White, 2b	3	0	2	1
Gura, p	0	0	0	0
Totals	32	3	8	3

Minnesota	120	001	001	5-14-0
Kansas City	010	001	100	3-8-0

2BH	Jackson 2, Ward 2, White, Mackanin
3BH	Wilfong, White, Morales
HR	Castino, McRae
SH	Wynegar
SF	Ward, Brett
DP	Minnesota 2
LOB	Minnesota 11, Kansas City 5
BB	Koosman 2, Corbett 0, Gura 2
K	Koosman 4, Corbett 0, Gura 0
WP	Koosman (16–13)
SV	Corbett (23, club rookie record)
LP	Gura (18–10)
Time	2:29
Att	20,714

ning of a stretch of several seasons during which Twins fans were subjected to a string of losers. The 1979 club, which almost took the West Division's title, thanks to some timely hitting, Jerry Koosman's 20 wins and super relief pitching from Mike Marshall, drew over a million. But 1980's losing, rather uninteresting ballclub, drew 300,000 less, and was characterized rather scathingly as "not only inept, (but) indeed altogether boring," by Dave Mona and David Jarz in *25 Seasons: The First Quarter Century of the Minnesota Twins*.

True or not, one thing stands out: Doug Corbett's efforts lifted Twinkie hopes each time he took to the hill. Johnny Goryl, who succeeded manager Gene Mauch and assumed the reins of the club late in August, put it this way for Twins correspon-

dent Pat Reusse: "I know all about Joe Charboneau at Cleveland and Damaso Garcia at Toronto, but I have to believe the most valuable rookie to his team this season has been Corbett. Without Corbett, the Twins would be so far back we would be in a different league…. I can't believe there has been a more consistent reliever this season. I can recall only two or three games where he blew a lead. That's amazing, in as many appearances as Corbett has had."

Doug Corbett signed a lucrative contract for the 1981 season, providing 17 more saves, an All-Star Game appearance, 73 more relief appearances and a 2.95 ERA. With a tailender (the Twins won only 41 and lost 68 in 1981's strike-abbreviated season), he was worth every last dime.

1980: Ten Top Rookies

Nm/Pos/Tm	GP	W–L/BA	SH/SV//RBI	PR/BR	ERA/FR	TPR
Corbett/RP-RHP/Min-A	73	8–6	0/23	36	1.98	4.5
Burns/LHP/Chi-A	34	15–13	1/0	31	2.84	3.5
Quisenberry/RP-RHP/KC-A	75	12–7	0/33	14	3.09	2.9
Stapleton/UT/Bos-A	106	.321	45	6	10	2.1
Holland/RP-LHP/SF-N	54	5–3	0/7	16	1.75	2.0
Howe/RP-LHP/LA-N*	59	7–9	0/17	8	2.66	1.8
D. Smith/RP-RHP/Hou-N	57	7–5	0/10	15	1.93	1.8
Tudor/LHP/Bos-A	16	8–5	0/0	12	3.02	1.4
Charboneau/1b/Clv-A*	131	.289	87	18	1	1.3
Reardon/RP-RHP/NY-N	61	8–7	0/6	12	2.61	1.3

*Voted Rookie of the Year

Carlton Ernest "Pudge" Fisk

TPR: 4.4

1972, Boston, AL

Born: December 26, 1947, Bellows Falls, VT
c, 6'2" 220 lb. Major League Debut: September 18, 1969
1972: 131 GP; 457-74-134, AB-R-H; .293 BA; 9, 3BH;
61 RBI; .538 SA; 33 BR; 1 FR; .984 FA

It's going to cost you if you're a perfectionist, especially if you're a baseball perfectionist who is a catcher. Carlton Fisk was both. Outspoken, proud of his iron-willed Puritan work ethic, he was unrelenting in his approach to Doing It Right. It was the driving force in a major league career of catching virtuosity. Granite-tough, he asked no quarter and certainly gave none. Just ask the Yankees. He was demanding of those around him and even more demanding of himself. But above all he was a pro's pro. And he was that way right from the start.

Selected first by Baltimore in the June 1965 free agent draft, he remained a free agent because he refused to sign on with any other organization than the Red Sox. Those rugged "upstaters," after all, are die-hard Red Sox fans, and Carlton Fisk was one of them. The Boston signing was, therefore, a foregone conclusion, and was accomplished two years later after the January 1967 free agent draft.

Fisk's professional debut was made with the Waterloo Hawks of the Class A Midwest League, where, in 1968, he hit .338 and handled the catching responsibilities with an impressive verve and command that registered in the front office. Subsequently, two trial runs with the varsity in 1969 and 1971 preceded the 1972 training camp at Winter Haven, Florida. The Carmine headed north for their April opener with the rookie Fisk on the roster as one of three Bosox receivers. Only two games into the season Duane Josephson was hurt, and then Bob Montgomery was used behind the plate. When baserunners began to steal almost at will on Montgomery, Fisk got his chance — and he made the most of it. It took him no time at all to nail down the job, and there he remained.

A lean, 6'2", 200 pounder, which

Unanimous Rookie of the Year selection, Carlton Fisk, 1972. (Dennis Colgin.)

had the Bosox taken the season-ending series in Detroit, but after losing the first two games to Al Kaline, Mickey Lolich and Company, it was all over and the champagne had to be stored for another year. Fisk's 1972 experience with championships would serve as a harsh introduction to the bizarre twists and turns of Boston's utterly frustrating chase for championship gold, dating all the way back to 1918, when the last world championship was tucked away in the Fenway Park treasure house.

The All-Star Game, traditional half-way mark of the baseball season, was played in Atlanta in 1972. At that point in the American League race it was a four-way dogfight for the top spot, and it would remain that way well into September when Baltimore and New York finally dropped off the sizzling championship pace, leaving the Red Sox and Tigers to fight it out. The race went right on down to the final series in Detroit, in which Boston was able to salvage only the last game of the three-game series.

Shortly before the All-Star Game break there were a number of ball games that would warm the cockles of any rookie's heart. One was on July 11, when Marty Pattin, 17–13 on the season, one-hit the Oakland Athletics, the American League's eventual pennant winners. The only hit in that contest came with one out in the ninth on a Reggie Jackson single. Pattin went on to retire the side, winning 4 to 0.

Earlier, on June 21, Bosox shortstop Rico Petrocelli drove in six runs in one official bat, a baseball oddity if ever there was one. His grand slammer chased home four, and two sacrifice flies, the other two.

belied his nickname "Pudge," Fisk went on to do battle and persevere through 24 big-time seasons in baseball's most exacting position. Although he missed parts of no less than seven seasons, winding up on the disabled list enough to cut severely into the longevity marks he set, he still managed to catch a record 2,226 games in the fourth-longest career on record.

The first of that record 2,226 games dates back to a season that didn't make it to the starting gate on time. Baseball's first general strike, called on April 6, 1972, washed a total of 86 games down the drain before a settlement was reached a week later. That was to prove disastrous for the Red Sox six months later when they lost the division title by a half game to Detroit because they played one game less than the Tigers as a result of games lost to the strike. That might still have been overcome

And as far as Beantown's sensational freshman was concerned, he had already knocked home several game-winning runs, eventually running his total of game-winning RBIs to a team-high 10 for the season.

It was Fisk's first All-Star Game, however, that provided the American League's top rookie with his biggest thrill of the year. What was it? Just being there, to say nothing of getting into the game and singling in two trips. Larry Claflin, Boston correspondent to *The Sporting News*, reported Fisk's reaction: "I think I'd have to say that [the All-Star Game] was the biggest thrill yet for me. And getting into the game was just that much extra. Just to be there was honor enough, but when you get to catch a few innings, it's really too much."

Shortly after Fisk's Atlanta visit he moved into the upper echelon of the American League's hitters, raising his batting average over .300 and his slugging average over the .600 mark going into the final weeks of July. He was especially rough on the California Angels' pitching staff, although he soon came to realize that in Boston, hitting and playing well against the archrival Yankees was about the only thing that really mattered.

Neither Fisk nor the other hitters in the league chasing Rod Carew for batting honors, could maintain much of an edge on the .300 mark, however, in a year that was a bummer for AL swatsmiths. When the final averages were posted, the league batting average turned out to be a puny .239. Shades of the '60s! That's when major league hitting was so anemic that the powers that be ordered a new and lower pitching mound level of ten inches above home plate, reasoning that it would bring some sock back into the ball game. It would seem the hitters didn't get the message. Rod Carew's .318 won the batting title and Carlton Fisk's .293 wasn't all that far behind.

As the second half of the season wore on the youngster behind the plate began more and more to take charge and step up the level of intensity that his personal standard of excellence demanded. Though only a rookie, it didn't prevent Fisk from getting on veterans Carl Yastrzemski and Reggie Smith in an August 7 confrontation that raised a fuss in Boston and was characterized as "flap time in the Country Club." Carlton Fisk could not have cared less. After the ruckus settled down, Boston did, indeed, elevate its game, staying in contention for the pennant with a hustling, more concentrated attack. They were beginning to find out, both in the dugout and around Beantown, that young Mr. Fisk had come to play. He might not have been loved by everybody, but the huge respect factor that accompanied him throughout his career had its inception in those August dog days of 1972.

By August 15 the Yawkeymen had moved on to Arlington, Texas, where another rookie, southpaw John Curtis, was scheduled to face yet another newcomer to the major league scene, right-hander Don Stanhouse. The rookies went at it, and in one of the better pitching performances of the season, the 24-year-old Curtis sat down the Rangers on a glossy three-hit shutout, working his way through the Texas order without yielding a hit until Stanhouse himself singled in the sixth frame. Reggie Smith provided all the punch Curtis needed to post the seventh of his 11 1972 victories with a solo shot in the fifth inning. Batterymate Pudge Fisk chipped in a perfect day at the plate with three singles.

Although the Red Sox didn't win their division in 1972, they finally had themselves a catcher after eons of waiting and a bushel basketfull of wannabes had tried on the pads at Fenway Park. If his first season was any indication of what was ahead, at least the uncertainties of filling the catching

Box Score

Boston Red Sox at Arlington Stadium, vs. the Texas Rangers, August 15, 1972

Boston	AB	R	H	BI
Harper, cf	4	0	1	0
Aparicio, ss	5	0	1	0
Yastrzemski, lf	4	1	2	0
R. Smith, rf	4	2	3	3
Petrocelli, 3b	4	0	0	0
Fisk, c	4	0	3	0
Cater, 1b	3	0	0	0
J. Kennedy, 2b	4	0	0	0
Curtis, p	4	0	0	0
Totals	36	3	10	3

Texas	AB	R	H	BI
Maddox, cf	3	0	0	0
Nelson, 3b	4	0	0	0
Bittner, lf	3	0	0	0
Billings, c	4	0	1	0
F. Howard, 1b	4	0	0	0
Ford, rf	1	0	0	0
Grieve, rf	2	0	0	0
Mason, ss	3	0	1	0
Harris, 2b	1	0	0	0
Stanhouse, p	2	0	1	0
Cox, p	0	0	0	0
Lovitto, ph	1	0	0	0
Lindblad, p	0	0	0	0
Totals	28	0	3	0

```
Boston   000  010  020   3-10-0
Texas    000  000  000   0-3-1
```

HR	R. Smith 2
SB	Harris, Maddox
DP	Boston 2, Texas 2
LOB	Boston 10, Texas 5
BB	Curtis 4. Stanhouse 4, Cox 0, Lindblad 0
K	Curtis 5, Stanhouse 4, Cox 1, Lindblad 1
WP	Curtis (7–6)
LP	Stanhouse (2–3)
Time	2:15
Att	6,822

spot could be put aside. Fisk's freshman season included:

- American League Rookie of the Year honors
- *The Sporting News* Rookie of the Year award
- A Gold Glove Award
- A spot on *The Sporting News* American League All-Star Team
- A spot on *The Sporting News* AL All-Star Fielding Team
- American League leadership in total chances (933), putouts (846), and assists (72)
- American League leadership in triples

- Man of the Year honors awarded by the Boston chapter of the BBWAA
- A team-high batting average (.293)

The start was, by any standard, impressive. What followed in the years to come was no less considerable, indeed imposing enough to command more than enough Hall of Fame votes to assure his election soon after his eligibility. That would round out the Hall's catching corps with an even dozen. The 12th of that dozen, Mr. Fisk, in the select company of fellow Northeasterners Gabby Hartnett and Mickey Cochrane, is a natural for a position among those who donned the "tools of ignorance" with great distinction.

1972: Nine Top Rookies

Nm/Pos/Tm	GP	W–L/BA	SH/SV//RBI	PR/BR	ERA/FR	TPR
Fisk/c/Bos-A*	131	.293	61	33	1	4.4
Matlack/LHP/NY-N*	34	15–10	4/0	28	2.32	2.9
Hooten/RHP/Chi-N†	33	11–14	3/0	24	2.80	2.8
Forster/RP-LHP/Chi-A	62	6–5	0/29	10	2.25	2.5
Baker/of/Atl-N	127	.321	76	23	2	1.7
R. Reuschel/RHP/Chi-N	21	10–8	4/0	13	2.93	1.6
Barr/RP-RHP/SF-N	44	8–10	2/2	12	2.87	1.4
Willoughby/RHP/SF-N	11	6–4	0/0	11	2.36	1.4
Duffy/ss/Clv-A	130	.239	27	-8	3	1.2

*Voted BBWAA Rookie of the Year
† Pitched a 4–0 no-hitter on April 16 against Philadelphia

William Leopold "Wizard" or "Chick" Hoffer

TPR: 4.3

1895, Baltimore, NL

Born: November 8, 1870, Cedar Rapids, IA. Died; July 21, 1959, Cedar Rapids, IA
RHP, 5'9" 155 lb. Major League Debut: April 26, 1895
1895: GP 41; W31, L6; .838 W%; 4/0 SH/SV; .245 OBA; 54 PR; 3.21 ERA

By 1895 the 12 National League franchise owners had things pretty much their own way. The NL schedule literally provided the only game in town, and without competition or interference from other leagues — or the law — they ruled with an iron fist. Entrenched, these magnates fought a panicky 1890s economy, any intrusion on *their* game, *their* players and *their* managers, and finally, one another.

The national pastime careened toward the 20th century somewhat like a runaway freight train headed for derailment. Gambling scandals, brawling ballplayers whose drinking habits were as shameful as the owners' salary caps and other illegalities that scarred the game, and a choking grip on the movement of franchises and players all contributed to a rough-house, chaotic world of professional baseball.

Into that wild and woolly orbit, headed straight for the big cities of the Senior Circuit, came a wiry 24-year-old from the Hawkeye State, the land of tall corn and other wholesome products. His name was Bill Hoffer, and he was the property of the Baltimore Orioles. It's hard to imagine a more incongruous match, pairing an apparently frail Midwesterner, "saddled" with smalltown virtues and values, with those bickering, battling, off-kilter Orioles of the 1890s who played — and quite successfully — *outside* the rules and conventions of the game as often as possible. Bill Hoffer would soon find out what that was all about, and though he didn't like everything his hinterland eyes beheld, he did come to appreciate the incisive and creative baseball mind of the Orioles' indomitable Hanlons and McGraws.

"The Wizard," as Hoffer was called, started his pay-for-play career right in his own backyard with Cedar Rapids of the Illinois-Iowa League, a nonsignatory affiliate of the National Association. During the 1890s there were few minor leagues in organized baseball. Times were tough and there were only 12 teams at the major league level. Few rookies crashed the well-established rosters of the existing ball clubs in the Bigs, so many of the young players turned to what became known as semipro ball.

Bill Hoffer was one of those young, aspiring ballplayers who put his name on the dotted line right in his own backyard with the Cedar Rapids nine. The year was 1890 and the pay was 40 bucks a month. Two seasons later he was signed by the Joliet, Illinois, team, which folded; he moved on to Grand Island, Nebraska, a team that also folded; and then on to Toledo of the Western League, and this time the whole league folded. Since it was still only mid–July, he picked up his spikes and headed north to finish out the season with Marinette of the Wisconsin State League. Was there a message here? If there

was, it certainly didn't indicate that there would be no baseball for the Wizard in 1893.

In 1893 the Hawkeye pitcher-outfielder made his way to Buffalo, where, finally, he wound up in the hands of a knowledgeable baseball man. It was here, under Johnny Chapman, his manager, that Bill Hoffer blossomed into a .321 hitter as an outfielder and a pitcher possessed of a sneaky-fast hummer responsible for a 28 and 17 record that had the Baltimore club more than mildly interested. To make certain they would know exactly what they were dealing with in this slightly built workhorse (the workhorse part was always of special interest during an era of four- to five-man pitching staffs) the Orioles brought him to their training camp for a look-see. They liked what they saw, signed him up, and put him to work. Hoffer debuted on April 26 of the 1895 season, and

Box Score

Baltimore	AB	R	H	PO	A		Brooklyn	AB	R	H	PO	A
McGraw, 3b	4	3	0	1	0		Griffin, cf	3	0	0	2	0
Keeler, rf	6	2	5	0	0		LaChance, 1b	3	0	0	12	1
Jennings, ss	6	2	4	6	4		Corcoran, ss	1	0	0	0	1
Kelley, lf	5	1	2	4	1		Shoch, ss	3	0	1	2	2
Carey, 1b	6	0	2	6	0		Daly, 2b	3	0	1	1	5
Brodie, cf	6	2	4	3	0		Burns, lf	4	0	0	3	0
Reitz, 2b	4	1	1	1	0		Anderson, rf	4	0	0	1	0
Robinson, c	5	0	1	6	0		Mulvey, 3b	3	0	1	2	7
Hoffer, p	4	0	0	0	3		Grim, c	4	0	1	2	3
							Stein, p	4	0	1	2	3
Totals	46	11	19	27	8		Totals	32	0	5	27	22

Baltimore   212 010 032   11-19-1
Brooklyn   000 000 000   0-5-2

2BH	Grim, Keeler, Jennings, Brodie 2
3BH	Keeler
SB	Jennings, Brodie
SH	Robinson
LOB	Baltimore 13, Brooklyn 9
BB	Hoffer 2, Stein 5
K	Hoffer 2, Stein 2
WP	Stein 2
Umpires	Murray and Long
Time	1:55
Att	10,010

just a week later, on May 4, he recorded his first major league shutout with an 11 to 0 whitewashing of the Brooklyn Bridegrooms.

An interesting feature in this game was the appearance of five future Hall of Famers, all of whom wore Baltimore uniforms, including the top four in the batting order, leadoff man Muggsy McGraw, Wee Willie Keeler, Hughie Jennings, and Joe Kelley. The fifth, and not least, was the catcher who steadied Bill Hoffer and guided him through his sensational rookie season, a chunky backstop by the name of Wilbert Robinson, who later became the "Uncle Wilbert" of Brooklyn fame. They all lent a hand in the demolition of the Bridegrooms, 11 to 0.

Billy Hoffer, a.k.a. "Chick," or just plain "Bill" (and don't forget his "Wizard" sobriquet), picked exactly the right time to cast his baseball lot with the Baltimore Orioles. In 1894, with the wily and hard-driving Ned Hanlon at the helm, the O's had become the scourge of the National League, at least until Temple Cup time, when they stumbled, tarnishing their first place finish with an embarrassing loss of four straight games to New York's Giants, the NL's second-place finishers, in the postseason championship playoffs.

Baltimore was steamed and the town's hotshots were sent back into the fray in 1895 with but one mission: Bring Home The Cup! Enter a rebuilt pitching staff, more trick plays and innovations, a new second baseman, converted pitcher Kid Gleason, and a new first sacker in the person of George "Scoops" Carey, who, with young Mr. Hoffer, was to make his maiden voyage around the Senior Circuit in 1895. The whole bundle came together in another first-place finish, this time by three games over the Cleveland Spiders. The most colorful band of swaggering, scratching, and bellicose ballplayers the game had to offer in the 1890s had won with a team

that had hitting (the team hit .324), air-tight defense with league-leading figures in fewest errors and fielding average, and a staff ERA of 3.80 (the NL ERA was a swollen 4.28).

They also had Bill Hoffer, who became baseball's first rookie 30-game winner. His 31 wins in 1895 were second only to Cy Young's 35 for Cleveland. With those 31 wins, as against but seven losses, went four shutouts, which tied for the lead league (teammate John "Sadie" McMahon, 10 and 5, also had, amazingly, four shutouts among his 10 wins; others with four included Amos Rusie, Cy Young and Emerson "Pink" Hawley, who also won 31 games in 1895). Hoffer's 314 innings pitched, 3.21 ERA, 8.48 hits per game total, and miserly (for 1895) opponents batting average of .246 were all leading staff figures for the Orioles and placed in the top five of the league. It's no stretch at all to say that Chick's rookie year would have won Rookie of the Year laurels in a walk had there been one. His 4.3 TPR was two full points above Roddy Wallace, who, in 1895, broke in as a pitcher, and later won Hall of Fame honors as one of the great shortstops in the early years of the 20th century. Jimmy Collins, another future HOFer who won his Cooperstown laurels on the strength of his outstanding play and pioneering work around the hot corner with Boston, also made his debut in 1895, rating a 1.3 TPR. By any yardstick, however, Bill Hoffer's contribution to Baltimore's success in his freshman campaign made him the pick of a weak 1895 rookie litter. They are shown on the next page.

Much to the chagrin and total frustration of the Baltimoreans, their Orioles went south in the championship series, falling this time to Cy Young (three times in the series, one of which was a victory over Hoffer) and to George "Nig" Cuppy. In the fifth and final game Hoffer was victimized by a three-run outburst in the

Nm/Pos/Tm	GP	W–L/BA	SH/SV/RBI	PR/BR	ERA/FR	TPR
W. Hoffer/RHP/Bal	41	31–6	4/0	54	3.21	4.3
R. Wallace/RHP/	30	12–14	1/1	23	4.09	2.0
J. Collins/3b/Bos-Lou	107	.273	57	-2	19	1.3
A. Orth/RHP/Phl	11	8–1	0/1	9	3.89	0.9
H. Truby/2b/Chi	33	.336	16	-1	0	0.1
W. Everitt/3b/Chi	133	.358	88	6	-8	0.0

seventh inning after having blanked Cleveland's Spiders the first six frames. It was all manager Patsy Tebeau's men needed to win the cup four games to one.

But there would be another year, and this time both Hoffer and his Oriole teammates finally crushed the Spiders when it counted, and, paced by their ace right-hander's two wins in the 1896 series, they left no doubt about who was cock of the walk. They simply stomped Cleveland's defending champs in four straight.

In 1896 and 1897 Bill Hoffer produced two more outstanding seasons with 47 more victories, raising his three year total to 78. He followed up the 1896 campaign with two more Temple Cup conquests against Boston's fine ballclub as the O's took home the cup at the expense of the pennant-winning Beaneaters. Another pair of Temple Cup wins in 1897 raised his overall series mark to 6 and 2 over the three-year span.

The 1895–1897 stretch turned out to be the top years of his meteoric career. But the meteor faded as quickly as it had arisen, and by the turn of the century it was twilight time.

During 1901, the inaugural season of the American League, a self-proclaimed major league consisting of eight ball-clubs — many of which were purposefully and spitefully placed in National League cities — there was suddenly room for twice as many ballplayers. Many of the new roster spots were filled by former National Leaguers in the bidding wars that followed, depleting the ranks of Senior Circuit clubs by nearly 100 players. Bill Hoffer was one of them, and as the 1901 season began he was decked out in a Cleveland Blues uniform.

The Blues, who became, in turn, the Naps, and then the Indians, debuted on April 24, 1901, playing the first game in the history of the American League. The Opening Day pitcher was Bill Hoffer, who, with the first pitch of the season, became one of history's footnotes. He was also the AL's first pitcher to lose a ball game by virtue of the Blues' loss to Chicago by an 8 to 2 margin, the first to record a strike-out and a base on balls. That season he won only three games, but did manage to become the AL's first league-leader in saves with three.

Many years later, seven years shy of his 88th and final birthday, he joined others in celebrating the 50th anniversary of the American League. He made the trip from Cedar Rapids, the town in which he was born, began his baseball career, and ended it. For Bill Hoffer the baseball cycle had come full circle.

Theodore Samuel "Ted" Williams

TPR: 4.3

1939, Boston, AL
Born: August 30, 1918, San Diego, CA
OF; 6'3" 205 lb. Major League Debut: April 20, 1939
1939: 149 GP; 131 R; .327 BA; 31 HR; 145 RBI; 107 BB; .609 SA; 51 BR; 2FR; .945 FA
Hall of Fame: 1966

Eddie Collins, Connie Mack's second baseman of $100,000 infield fame and a Hall of Famer, Class of 1939, was Red Sox' owner Tom Yawkey's right-hand Bauer in the front office after his playing career. In 1937 Yawkey dispatched him to San Diego to check on a promising infielder by the name of Bobby Doerr. The Californian impressed him to the extent that he was signed for delivery to manager Joe Cronin's 1938 ballclub.

What *really* impressed Collins, however, was a skinny kid who was taking batting practice before a game at the Padres ballpark. He didn't know the fuzzy-cheeked kid's name, but there was no denying the eyepopping ropes he was hitting all over the place, and he knew right then and there that the spindly teenager, silk-smooth stroke and all, was going to have to be signed to a Red Sox contract. Collins saw to it — pronto.

The young fellow's name was Ted Williams, and most every baseball buff can tell you all about him. He was Teddy Ballgame. The Splendid Splinter. The Thumper. Baseball's *enfante terrible* one day and delightful charmer the next.

It was somehow inevitable that Williams' greatness would evidence itself from the very beginning with a rookie season that found its way onto still another list of baseball bests. And there he is, the 26th name on our roll of rookie honorees with a glittering 4.3 TPR, fashioned in baseball's centennial year, 1939, the very year the Hall of Fame was dedicated in Cooperstown. The link between the two was established on April 20 when "The Kid," as he was also known, stepped up to the plate for his first major league at-bat in the House That Ruth Built, Yankee Stadium.

The Yankees' season opener, delayed two days by rain, was part of the opening festivities of the World's Fair exposition held in the nation's number one metropolis, and as far as the 30,278 Yankee fans and New York dignitaries were concerned, it was a huge success, as Red Ruffing turned back the Bosox and Williams in a strong Opening Day performance with a 2–0 calcimining. But the game also marked the 20-year-old's debut, as he lined a scorcher, his first major league hit, between Joe DiMaggio and Joe Gallagher into right-center field for a two-bagger that day.

Rarely, if ever, were more Hall of Fame names involved than those gracing the box score of that April 20, 1939, game. Four Yankees and five of the Red Sox in that game eventually received Hall of Fame plaques. A composite infield might have Jimmy Foxx at third, a position he played from time to time, with Joe Cronin at short, Bobby Doerr at second and Lou Gehrig at first base. The outfield might see Red Ruffing or Lefty Grove filling in for a right fielder, with Joe DiMaggio in center and Williams in left, and Bill Dickey behind the plate. You might win a game or two with a lineup like that!

After the first game of the season for both teams, the Yankees were perched atop the American League standings and the Red Sox found themselves looking up. That was precisely the way things ended in 1938, with the New Yorkers winning the pennant and the Bosox taking home the second-place money. And, when 1939's final out of the regular season had been made, it was exactly the same way, or as a noted Yankee catcher some years later would say, "It was *deja vu* all over again."

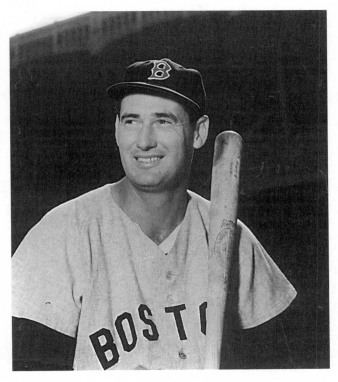

Ted Williams, "The Splendid Splinter." (Colgin Photo.)

After their opening game setback, the Carmine moved on to Philadelphia where, despite a 12 to 8 loss, young Mr. Williams turned a few heads with his first big day in the big time.

It hadn't taken him long to find the range, sending one of Bud Thomas' deliveries on a searing line into Shibe Park's right-field seats for his first major league dinger. There were more to come, of course — 31 in that freshman year — and another 490 after that for a grand total of 521 career round-trippers. But, somehow, there is nothing quite like number one. In Williams' case, however, the very last one was one of the three or four most stunning of his career, coming as dramatically as it did in his last major league at bat, and at Fenway Park on September 20, 1960, as the Yawkeymen beat Baltimore, 5 to 4, enabling him to leave the game on a winning note.

Box Score #1

Red Sox vs. Yankees at Yankee Stadium, April 20, 1939

Boston	AB	H	PO	A
Cramer, cf	4	1	2	0
Vosmik, lf	4	2	3	0
Foxx, 1b	4	0	5	0
Cronin, ss	4	0	2	1
Tabor, 3b	4	1	0	1
Williams, rf	4	1	3	0
Doerr, 2b	4	1	4	3
Desautels, c	3	0	5	1
Nonnenkamp, ph	1	0	0	0
Grove, p	2	1	0	1
Peacock, ph	1	0	0	0
Totals	35	7	24	7

New York	AB	R	PO	A
Crosetti, ss	4	0	0	0
Rolfe, 3b	4	0	0	2
Posell, lf	4	3	4	0
DiMaggio, cf	2	1	3	0
Gehrig, 1b	4	0	6	0
Dickey, c	3	2	7	0
Gallagher, rf	3	0	3	0
Gordon, 2b	3	1	4	3
Ruffing, p	3	0	0	3
Totals	30	7	27	8

```
Boston       000  000  000   0-7-2
New York     010  010  00x   2-7-1
```

2BH	Williams, Tabor, Dickey, Vosmik
3BH	Powell
HR	Dickey
DP	Doerr, Cronin, Foxx; Doerr and Foxx
BB	Grove 2, Ruffing 1
K	Grove 5, Ruffing 5
Umpires	Ormsby, Summers, Basil and Pipgras
Att	30,278

The 1939 Red Sox were essentially an offensive machine without much of a pitching staff, even though "Ole Mose," Lefty Grove, fashioned a super 15 and 4 record with league-leading figures in winning percentage (.789) and ERA (2.54). But did they hit! The offense was led by Jimmy Foxx, whose 4.9 TPR trailed only Bob Feller and MVP winner Joltin' Joe DiMaggio (Foxx was runner-up in the MVP derby and Bill Deane's Hypothetical Rookie of the Year, Williams, garnered 126, fourth place votes), but sophomore Bobby Doerr, manager Joe Cronin, veteran outfielders Doc Cramer and Lou Finney and rookies Jim Tabor and the Splendid Slinter *each hit .300.* The Sox, in fact, thundered through their schedule with the highest team batting average (.291), the most base hits (1543) and a slugging average of .436 (second to New York). But Foxx, Williams, et al., aside, New York was better — 19 games better — and went on to beat Cincinnati four straight in the World Series.

Teddy Ballgame's season marked the beginning of an era in Boston baseball history that didn't end until some 45 years later, when Carl Yastrzemski's brilliant career as the heir apparent and successor to Williams as guardian of Fenway's monster — and Red Sox fortunes — came to an end in 1983. And Williams saw to it that the era got off to a resounding start. Here are some of those 1939 numbers:

- Total Bases   344   Number 1 in the AL
- Runs Scored   131   Number 2
- Two Base Hits   44   Number 2
- Bases on Balls 107   Number 2
- Batting Runs   56   Number 2
- Runs Produced* 245   Number 1

*This sabermetric measure is calculated by adding the player's runs batted in and runs scored, and subtracting from that sum his home runs. In 1939 Williams had 145 runs, 131 runs scored (total of 276), and 31 home runs (subtract 31 from 276).

Box Score #2

Red Sox vs. Athletics at Shibe Park, Philadelphia, April 22, 1939

Boston	AB	R	H	PO	A		Philadelphia	AB	R	H	PO	A
Cramer, cf	4	1	0	4	0		Moses, rf	5	1	2	1	0
Vosmik, lf	4	1	1	0	0		Gantenbein, 2b	4	1	0	2	0
Foxx, 1b	5	2	2	8	1		Nagel, ph	0	0	0	0	0
Cronin, ss	3	0	0	4	0		Dean, ph	1	0	1	0	0
Tabor, 3b	4	1	1	2	1		Ambler, 2b	1	0	0	0	0
Williams, rf	5	2	4	1	0		Chapman, cf	5	2	1	5	0
Doerr, 2b	5	1	3	2	2		R. Johnson, lf	4	1	0	2	0
Desautels, c	4	0	1	6	0		Hayes, c	3	2	2	4	1
Auker, p	0	0	0	0	0		Lodigiani, 3b	4	1	2	0	1
Galehouse, p	2	0	0	0	0		Etten, 1b	4	2	2	10	1
Ostermueller, p	0	0	0	0	0		Newsome, ss	4	0	2	3	4
Heving, p	0	0	0	0	0		Thomas, p	1	0	0	0	0
Dickman, p	0	0	0	0	0		D, Smith, p	0	0	0	0	0
							Pippen, p	2	0	0	0	1
							E. Smith, p	0	0	0	0	0
							Finney, ph	1	1	0	0	0
							Parmelee, p	0	0	0	0	0
Totals	36	8	12	27	4		Totals	39	12	11	27	7

Boston	402	002	000	8-12-1
Philadelphia	320	010	060	12-11-2

2BH	Lodigiani, Etten, Newsome, Williams, Doerr, Desautels
HR	Williams (a 420 foot line drive into the right center bleachers)
SB	Tabor
SH	Tabor
DP	Pippen, Gantenbein, Etten; Gantenbein, Newsome, Etten
LOB	Boston, 9; Philadelphia 10
BB	Thomas 1, D. Smith 2, Pippen 1, E. Smith 2, Parmelee 1
	Auker 5, Galehouse 4, Dickman 1, Ostermueller and Heving 0
SO	Pippen 3, E. Smith 1, Parmelee 1, D. Smith and Thomas 0
	Galehouse 3, Dickman 2, Auker, Ostermueller and Heving 0
WP	Eddie Smith
LP	Joe Heving
Umpires	Ormsby, Summers and Basil
Time	2:55

Nine games into the season Boston's rookie phenom was belting the ball at a .350 clip, but one month later some of the sheen had worn off and he was down a hundred points, swinging at far more pitches than even the Splinter himself thought wise. In a career fanatically devoted to swinging only — and the definitive word here is only — at those strikes in *his* strike zone, he was learning that those fellows out there on the mound meant business, and would soon find what the lean young slasher was all about in the batter's box.

In a doubleheader split with Detroit on Memorial Day, the early season slump was broken with a light-fixture blast over the right-field wall, and by June 8 Williams was up from his .250 doldrums to the .285 level — and climbing. At that point New York already sat on a 15½ game lead over Boston's 35 and 25 record. From then on, the hunt, for all practical purposes, was over, and the race for second had begun.

But then new hope was rekindled that there might still be a race when, shortly before the All Star Game break, Boston and New York went head to head in two series. Lo and behold, the Bosox rose to the occasion by decking the Yankees seven out of eight games.

Just before the American League victory over the Nationals, 3 to 1, the Bosox' other rookie find, Jim Tabor, paced the team to a doubleheader sweep of the Athletics by 17 to 7 and 18 to 12 scores on July 4 — the day of Lou Gehrig's farewell at Yankee Stadium — pounding Connie Mack's pitchers for four circuit smashes and 11 RBI. Williams joined Tabor with a dinger of his own in the 18 to 12 nightcap.

As the season moved on into August, with Foxx in the .350 to .360 range and Williams, now hitting third in Cronin's batting order, up into the .320s, the team kept on shelling opposition pitching but yielding far too many runs to cut into the substantial Yankee lead. The staff ERA, worse off than any ballclub other than cellar dwellers Philadelphia and St. Louis, was well over the 4.00 mark and headed for a final 4.46, a full run-plus over New York's league-leading 3.31.

Here are some of the Williams August-September benchmarks:

- August 4 — 3 for 3 with a home run and a triple
- August 19 — A grand slam to notch his #95 RBI
- September 1 — 3 for 3 at Detroit
- September 2 — 3 for 5 as Boston beats Ruffing (NY), 12 to 7
- September 7 — 127th RBI leads the American League
- September 14 — Up to .327 with 133 RBI
- September 23 — 30th homer in a 3 for 4 game at Philadelphia

There was an unusually high number of American League icons during the pre-

and post–World War II era. There were pitchers Bob Feller, Lefty Gomez, Red Ruffing and Hal Newhouser, Hall of Famers all. There were Foxx, Greenberg, Bill Dickey and Luke Appling. Over in the National League, Warren Spahn, Bill Terry, Stan Musial, Carl Hubbell and Mel Ott were all headed for Cooperstown. But among them all, none were as towering as were the two arch rivals of the day representing teams perennially involved in baseball's most bitter, hotly contested rivalry. The names were Joseph Paul DiMaggio and Theodore Samuel Williams.

At opposite poles in temperament, purpose and personality, their teams rose and fell on their shoulders. The one was as graceful as a Yankee Clipper asea, and the other, as tempestuously aflail as a Boston Tea Party. The two of them, the Clipper and the Splinter, dominated their era as majestically as the Babe and Lou did 20 years earlier.

Nor was there a season quite like 1941, when the two went at it, each with his own claim to fame in seasons best characterized by their TPRs: Williams at 7.9 and DiMaggio at 6.4, with DiMaggio winning the MVP Award over Williams by a vote of 291 to 254. That was the year, as one and all recall, that the legendary Yankee hit safely in 56 straight games. It was also the year that Ted Williams became the last .400 hitter, and, among other notable things, hit one to Kingdom Come to pull the American League through to a 7 to 5 win over the National League in the bottom of the ninth with Joe "D" and Joe Gordon aboard.

A sportswriter covering the game had this to say: "Williams' ball taveled a good 450 feet before it hit the third tier (at Briggs, now Tiger Stadium), but unobstructed I'm sure it would have gone over 500 feet. I've never seen a ball hit harder not even by Babe Ruth…. When it comes to hitting, Ted has the most perfect coordination of any batter in baseball. He puts

Box Score #3

The All Star Game, Briggs Stadium, Detroit, July 8, 1941

Nationals	AB	R	H	PO	A	Americans	AB	R	H	PO	A
Hack, Chi, 3b	2	0	1	3	0	Doerr, Bos, 2b	3	0	0	0	0
Lavagetto, Brk, 3b	1	0	0	0	0	Gordon, NY, 2b	2	1	1	2	0
T. Moore, lf	5	0	0	0	0	Travis, Was, 3b	4	1	1	1	2
Reiser, Brk, cf	4	0	0	6	0	J. DiMaggio, NY, cf	4	3	1	1	0
Mize, StL, 1b	4	1	1	5	0	Williams, Bos, lf	4	1	2	3	0
F. McCormick, Cin, 1b	0	0	0	0	0	Heath, Clv, rf	2	0	0	1	0
Nicholson, Chi, rf	1	0	0	1	0	D. DiMaggio, Bos, rf	1	0	1	1	0
Elliot, Pit, rf	1	0	0	0	0	Cronin, Bos, ss	2	0	0	3	0
Slaughter, StL, rf	2	1	1	0	0	Boudreau, Clv, ss	2	0	2	0	1
Vaughan, Pit, ss	4	2	3	1	2	York, Det, 1b	3	0	1	6	2
Miller, Bos, ss	0	0	0	0	1	Foxx, Bos, 1b	1	0	0	2	2
Frey, Cin, 2b	1	0	1	1	3	Dickey, NY, c	3	0	1	4	2
Herman, Brk, 2b	3	0	2	3	0	Hayes, Phl, c	1	0	0	2	0
Owen, Brk, c	1	0	0	0	0	Feller, Clv, p	0	0	0	0	1
Lopez, Pit, c	1	0	0	3	0	Cullenbine, StL, ph	1	0	0	0	0
Danning, NY, c	1	0	0	3	0	Lee, Chi, p	1	0	0	0	1
Wyatt, Brk, p	0	0	0	0	0	Hudson, Was, p	0	0	0	0	0
Ott, NY, ph	1	0	0	0	0	Keller, NY, ph	1	0	0	0	0
Derringer, Cin, p	0	0	0	0	1	E. Smith, Chi, p	0	0	0	1	0
Walters, Cin, p	1	1	1	0	0	Keltner, Clv, ph	1	1	1	0	0
Medwick, Brk, ph	1	0	0	0	0						
Passeau, Chi, p	1	0	0	0	0						
Totals	35	5	10	26	7	Totals	36	7	11	27	11

```
Nationals   000   001   220   5-10-2
Americans   000   101   014   7-11-3
```

2BH	Travis, Williams, Walters, Herman, Mize, J. DiMaggio
HR	Vaughan 2, Williams
SH	Hack, Lopez
DP	Frey, Vaughan, Mize; York and Cronin
LOB	Nationals 6, Americans 7
Managers	Nationals, Bill McKechnie (Cin); Americans, Del Baker (Det)
Umpires	Summers and Grieve (AL); Jorda and Pinelli (NL)
Time	2:23
Att	54,674

absolutely his whole body into the swing, including his ass."

Teddy Ballgame was some kinda ballplayer. His election to the Hall of Fame in 1966 in his first year of eligibility, an honor that somehow escaped his distinguished Yankee rival, DiMaggio, was the culmination of a career like none other, singular in its achievements, and hewn in the image of its creator. Baseball's centennial year, and those to follow, for that matter, would have been far the poorer without Ted Williams.

Hall of Famers: Eleven Top Rookie Hitters

Nm/Tm/Yr	GP	BA	RBI	BR	FR	TPR
Williams/Bos-A/1939	149	.327	145	51	2	4.3
J. Morgan/Hou-N/1965	157	.271	40	28	-2	4.3

Nm/Tm/Yr	GP	BA	RBI	BR	FR	TPR
Flick/Phl-N/1898	134	.302	81	40	7	3.5
Hornsby/StL-N/1916	139	.313	65	29	-2	3.5
P. Waner/Pit/1926	144	.336	79	34	8	3.1
Cuyler, Pit-N/1924	153	.354	85	30	5	3.0
W. Herman/Chi-N/1932	154	.314	51	6	17	3.0
J. DiMaggio/NY-A/1936	138	.323	125	23	15	3.0
F. Robinson/Cin-N/1956	152	.290	83	32	6	3.0
Ashburn/Phl-N/1948	117	.333	40	17	18	2.8
R. Jackson/Oak-A/1968	154	.250	74	23	8	2.8

Joe Leonard Morgan

TPR: 4.3

1965, Houston, NL
Born: September 19, 1943, Bonham, TX
2b, 5'7" 160 lb. Major League Debut: September 21, 1963
1965: 157 GP; 601-100-163, AB-R-H; .271 BA; 12 3BH;
97 BB; 20 SB; 28 BR; 1 FR; .969 FA
Hall of Fame: 1990

Nellie Fox, Chicago White Sox second sacker supreme for so many years, finished his Hall of Fame career with the Houston Astros (so named in 1965; the new name, succeeding the original Colt .45's team name, was a salute to Houston's prominent position in the nation's space program). At the end of the 1964 season Fox was retained as a coach for the 1965 season, with the proviso that he would play if necessary. The "if necessary" hinged on Joe Morgan, a promising young keystoner who had burned up the Texas League in an MVP, 1964 season that had earned him a shot at the Astro's nagging second base problem. The position had been as much of a plague as the mosquitoes that pestered Houston's fans and players at the team's original playing field, Colt Stadium.

The diminutive Morgan made it. Big. Houston now had two second basemen. One, Fox, played in only 21 games, retiring to his coaching job, while the other, Morgan, took over at second, playing with a baseball instinct and know-how that belied his youthful 21 years.

1965 ushered in new hopes for the fledgling expansion franchise with baseball's first major league indoor playing facility,* an artificial playing surface promptly dubbed Astroturf, and a very able, intense infielder whose confidence presaged a lengthy and distinguished career.

Joe Morgan had come to play. That meant, as ably put by the astute baseball observer Roger Angell, that Morgan "had the conviction that he should affect the outcome of every game he played, everytime

*The first indoor ball diamond was built in 1939 under Manhattan's 59th Street Bridge for use by the New York Cubans of the Negro National League.

Astro second baseman and Hall of Famer, Joe Morgan (Dennis Colgin.)

paign showcasing 492 assists, 20 steals in 29 attempts, 100 runs scored, and a league-leading 97 bases on balls. As time moved on, Li'l Joe would improve on every one of his rookie numbers, a dead certain indication that a great career was in the making.

A confident sort, Joe Morgan had a flair about him marked by his distinctive batting style, featuring that trademark pumping of his left arm just before a pitch was thrown. That usually came just ahead of the solid contact that made him a tough out (for a hard-swinging hitter, his strikeout ratio of one in ten-plus at-bats was low) and often resulted in extra bases. In fact, his 268 career homers rewrote Rogers Hornsby's record for second basemen. Fourteen of those four-baggers were hit in his rookie season, the first of which came against Lindy McDaniel of the Cubs on May 8.

The 1964 campaign brought an end, mercifully, to a season that began under Houston's first manager, Harry Craft, and then ended with the Astros in ninth place under Lum Harris, who was appointed the new manager with two weeks left in the season. They wound up — almost in the Gulf of Mexico — 27 games behind the front-running Cardinals. General manager Paul Richards, a canny Texan who had survived almost two score years of professional baseball before taking on the Houston front office challenge, had been the brains behind the Astros' player moves from the beginning, and recognized the club's weaknesses. But he stuck with the younger ballplayers and, in fact, showcased a starting lineup of them as early in the team's brief history as September 27,

he came up to bat, and every time he got on base." Now that's a tall order for a little fellow, but Joe Morgan's Cooperstown career verified his payment in full.

Positioned up there with the best of the rookies in the number 16 spot, Morgan is tied with Ted Williams and that 19th century pitching whiz of the Baltimore Orioles, Bill Hoffer, at a 4.3 TPR, earned on the strength of a superb rookie cam-

1963, when he had Harry Craft start a rookie at each position in a game against the Mets. The second baseman was Joe Morgan, and one of the outfielders was Morgan's 1965 roomie, Jimmy Wynn, Houston's Toy Cannon.

After 1964, 1965 had to be better. It wasn't — at least insofar as the final season's record was concerned. Houston had once again wound up in ninth place, this time losing one more game than in 1964. The 1965 squad, however, was a full cut better than the previous year, with better hitting, a better defense, and with pitching at least on a par with the 1964 ballclub. There was indeed some progress.

It all began on April 9, when the Yankees came to town to inaugurate the brand new Harris County Domed Stadium, which soon became known as the Astrodome. A crowd of 46,876 more-than-mildly curious baseball aficianados turned out to watch the hometown nine subdue the proud New Yorkers, 2 to 1, in the last exhibition of the 1965 spring training season. Even though Mickey Mantle put one of his signature blasts into the seats, thus producing the first major league dinger in an indoor baseball facility, the Astros beat the Yanks in a 12-inning thriller, 2 to 1.

The season opened shortly thereafter when the Phils came to town to rain on the Houston parade with a 2 to 0 win over Bob Bruce, Houston's 1964 ace (15–9), who gave up another enemy homer, this time to the 1964 Rookie of the Year, Dick Allen. Still another 48,546 were on hand, including baseball commissioner Ford Frick and National League prexy Warren Giles. Young Joe Morgan, who bagged two of Houston's four hits, was keeping some pretty high-stepping company.

After struggling in the opening two weeks of the season, during which the Astros played second-division baseball, the team came to life in Quaker Town, where they drubbed the Phillies with a late-inning surge that produced an 11 to 4 victory. The team's pint-sized rookie second baseman turned in his first three-hit day. The date was April 21, and it marked the beginning of Houston's best stretch of games the entire 1965 season.

By the end of April the surprising Astros had put together the longest winning streak in their brief history. The number was eight, and smack in the middle of that 4 to 3 victory was Joe Morgan, who knocked out the Chicago Cubs' Bob Buhl with a gapper that went for three bases and then scored on Al Spangler's sacrifice fly to bring home the winning tally. A crowd of 27,491 Houstonians tore the place apart. The next day another 37,255 turned out to see their favorites extend their streak to ten with a twin killing that sent the Cubs home winless in the series. As they soared to within a half game of the league lead, unbelieveable as that was in and about the environs of NASA town, so did Joe Morgan's batting average. Casting aside some early-season hitting woes, he moved on up to the .275 range, a pace that he maintained throughout the season, finally settling for his rookie season average of .271. Equally important were the strides he was making as a pivot man around the keystone sack. Gobs of practice and timely coaching from Nellie Fox gradually brought his defensive game around. Morgan never, ever, short-changed practice time, a move that paid off handsomely in five straight Gold Gloves during his celebrated Cincinnati years.

There was another part of Joe Morgan's game that was beginning to make itself felt in the Houston scheme of things, his baserunning. Studying pitchers, fielders and catchers, he began to steal, take extra bases, and otherwise make his speed count. His career 81 percent success rate in stealing ranks 11th of all time, one of his more persuasive Hall of Fame credentials. Houston's other mighty mite, Jimmy

Wynn, was successful 91.5 percent (43 for 47, factoring out to 11 base stealing runs) of the time in 1965, giving the ballclub the speed it needed to offset an otherwise feeble offense. Roommates Morgan and Wynn constituted a solid foundation that, with another stick or two, might easily have made a huge difference in the final standings of the Senior Circuit.

During a span of three weeks just ahead of the All-Star Game break Joe Morgan went on a tear that evidenced his growing familiarity with the major league scenario—and his sensational rise as an Astro star. It came to a head in Milwaukee, where the Braves played host to Houston on July 8. By that time the Astros had settled back into their more accustomed ways, losing enough to move on down to an eighth place level, just ahead of the Cubs and Mets, teams they had manhandled for 14 of their 37 victories to that date. Though the Astros were headed downward, Joe was heading in the opposite direction, and on July 8 number eight helped himself to quite a plateful.

Joe's six hits in that heart-breaking, 12-inning loss, might have taken an overtime to get the job done, but it was, and remains, the only time in Astro history that a player has had a six-hit game. He missed hitting for the cycle by a three bagger, pacing the club with three ribbies.

In the first game of a day-night twin-bill on July 24, Don Nottebart beat the Cincinnati Reds on three hits. But he was outdone by a salty, 15-year veteran, Joe Nuxhall, in the evening tilt when the Redleg lefty sat down the Astros on two hits, winning 2 to 0, over Turk Farrell (11–11 on the season), who also pitched well, but apparently not well enough. The day-nighter attracted 73,333, a still-standing record. The total was a part of the ballclub's first 3 million season draw, a record that stood until 1979, when 3,488,726 fans made their way through Astro turnstiles.

The Labor Day weekend provided Astro fans with one of the better attractions of the 1965 season, a game highlighted by the prospect of a pitching duel between Robin Roberts and Sandy Koufax. The Sunday headliner drew the fourth largest crowd in Houston's history, a throng of 49,442. Roberts, picked up by Paul Richards after the Hall of Fame-bound pitcher was released by the Orioles, had won four straight as an Astro, and Koufax, en route to a 26 and 8 slate and a Cy Young Award for the 1965 world champion Dodgers, dueled head to head through eight innings, Roberts himself contributing a run batted in as the Astros moved ahead of the Dodgers, 2 to 1, in the seventh. But the Astros went down under a pinch-hit triple by Jim Gilliam in the ninth, losing 4 to 2. While Koufax wasn't the winner, Roberts was tagged with his first loss as an Astro.

Hopelessly out of the race, Houston played out the string, finally bedding down in a ninth-place finish, 12 games behind the eighth-place Cubs, but still 15 games ahead of the cellar-dwelling Mets. Before bidding the season farewell, the Texans visited St. Louis for their final series of the year. On October 3, Bob Gibson faced rookie Carroll Sembera, in search of his 20th victory. Gibby won it by a 5 to 2 count, reaching the magic 20-game winner's circle for the first time in his sparkling career. But not before he gave up a perfect day to Joe Morgan. Battling to the very end, Joe's 4-for-4, garnished by a pair of fine fielding plays, wound up a season that was capped by *The Sporting News'* announcement that he had been selected the National League's Rookie of the Year.

Except for Joe Morgan's rookie award, the Houston cupboard was bare. That cost both Paul Richards and manager Lum Harris their jobs. On the other hand, Joe Morgan had made an auspicious beginning to a career that would wind its way

Box Score

Houston at County Stadium, Milwaukee, Wisconsin, July 8, 1965

Houston	AB	R	H	BI		Milwaukee	AB	R	H	BI
Morgan, 2b	6	4	6	3		F. Alou, cf-3b	5	2	2	2
L, Maye, lf	5	1	1	1		Bolling, 2b	6	0	1	1
Gentile, 1b	5	0	3	2		H. Aaron, rf	5	1	2	1
W. Bond, rf	1	0	0	0		J. Torre, 1b	4	0	0	0
Staub, pr-rf	3	1	1	1		Mathews, 3b	2	0	0	0
Aspromonte, 3b	6	0	1	0		Kolb, pr-cf	1	1	0	0
Wynn, cf	4	0	2	1		Oliver, c	5	0	0	0
Brand, c	5	0	0	0		Menke, ss	2	0	0	0
Lillis, ss	6	0	0	0		Cline, ph	1	0	0	0
Nottebart, p	2	1	0	0		Jones, ph	1	1	1	0
Giusti, p	2	1	1	0		Blasingame, p	1	0	0	0
MacKenzie, p	1	0	1	0		Carty, lf	5	2	2	3
Gaines, pr	0	0	0	0		Cloninger, p	1	0	0	0
						Woodward, ss	1	0	0	0
						de la Hoz, ph-ss	3	2	3	2
Totals	46	8	16	8		Totals	43	9	11	9

```
Houston      300  020  102  000   8-16-0
Milwaukee    102  010  013  001*  9-11-1
```

*One out when winning run scored

E	Oliver
2BH	Morgan, Jones, Carty, Aaron
3BH	Maye
HR	Morgan 2, Aaron, Carty, Alou, de la Hoz 2
SB	Wynn 2, Morgan
LOB	Houston 9, Milwaukee 4
DP	Milwaukee 4
SH	Brand, Alou
SF	Maye
BB	Nottebart 1, Giusti 1, Cuellar 0, Owens 1, MacKenzie 0, Taylor 0
	Cloninger 1, Kelley 1, Osinski 0, Sadowski 0, O'Dell 0, P. Niekro 2, Blasingame 1
K	Nottebart, Cuellar, Owens 0; Giusti, MacKenzie, Taylor 1
	Cloninger 4; Osinski, O'Dell 1; Kelley, Sadowski, Niekro, Blasingame 0
WP	Blasingame (9–6)
LP	Taylor (2–3)
Att	2,522

through championship seasons in Cincinnati and Philadelphia, MVP awards, and the ultimate honor, a Hall of Fame plaque at Cooperstown.

Rookie Second Basemen: The Top Twenty

Nm/Tm/Yr	GP	BA	RBI	BR	FR	TPR
Morgan/Hou-NL/1965	157	.271	40	28	1	4.3
Hornsby/StL-N/1916	139	.313	65	28	-2	3.5
Gordon/NY-A/1938	127	.255	97	3	24	3.2
Randolph/NY-A/1976	125	.267	40	4	15	3.2
R. Alomar/SD-N/1988	143	.266	41	3	17	3.1
W. Herman/Chi-N/1932	154	.314	51	6	17	3.0

Nm/Tm/Yr	GP	BA	RBI	BR	FR	TPR
Pratt/StL-A/1912	152	.302	69	16	14	2.8
Knoop/Cal-A/1964	162	.216	38	-20	37	2.8
Stringer/Chi-N/1941	145	.246	53	-4	20	2.6
Schlafly/Was-A/1906	123	.246	30	8	14	2.5
Zientra/Cin-N/1946	78	.289	16	-4	24	2.4
Hunt/NY-N/1963	143	.272	42	7	2	2.3
Whitaker/Det-A/1978	139	.285	58	3	12	2.3
R. Adams/Cin-N/1946	94	.244	24	-8	24	2.2
Veras/Fla-N/1995	124	.261	32	4	7	2.2
Doran/Hou-N/1983	154	.271	39	11	5	2.0
Weis/Chi-A/1963	99	.271	18	-4	14	1.9
Stanky/Chi-N/1943	142	.245	47	-3	12	1.8
Blattner/NY-N/1946	126	.255	49	8	1	1.8
Herzog/NY-N/1908	64	.300	11	13	1	1.6

Alexander Bennett "Big Ben" Sanders

TPR: 4.2

1888, Philadelphia, NL

Born: February 16, 1865, Catharpin, VA
Died: August 29, 1930, Memphis, Tennessee
RHP, 6' 210 lb. Major League Debut: June 6, 1888
1888: 31 GP; W19, L10, .655 W%; 8/0 SH/SV; 5 PHI; 33 PR; 4 DEF; 1.90 ERA

He was a big, handsome young lad of 23, an intelligent, independent thinker, not the kind who would drift aimlessly, playing games and whiling away his time at the local pubs. Known as "Big Ben," Alexander Sanders was not the typical, garden variety baseball player of the 1880s and 1890s, and his ambitions, tastes and aims, as well as the demands he made in negotiating his contracts, were clearly beyond the norm of what was considered appropriate — or even thinkable, for that matter. That figured prominently in what turned out to be a very brief professional baseball career. Consequently, he wasn't around long enough to make as much as a dent in Philadelphia's record books, but the two years he spent in a Phillies uniform were enough to convince the locals that he was quite a ballplayer.

The first of these two seasons, a gem of a freshman campaign so solid that it would ultimately be positioned among the top 30 rookie seasons of all time, was achieved for the 1888 Phils, a third-place finisher behind the champion New York Mutuals and Chicago's White Stockings. Although Sanders didn't get into a ball game until June, he wound up leading the team in hitting while running up a glistening 19 and 10 pitching log. He appeared in 57 games, including 25 as an outfielder, one as a third baseman, and the remainder as a flame-throwing right-hander.

Bearing in mind that Big Ben was added to Harry Wright's pitching staff following a highly successful 1887 season when the Phils had battled the talented Detroit Wolverines all the way to the last days of the season for the pennant, and that the Wrightmen had accomplished their first second-place finish in franchise history on the strong arms of Dan Casey (28 and 13), Charlie Buffinton (in a career year 28 and

Phillies rookie Big Ben Sanders. (Brace Photo.)

17), and the accomplished Charles Ferguson, who had finished out the 1887 season with eight straight en route to a 22 and 10 record, it was rather plain that the Phils' pitching staff, with its stars set to return in '88, would hardly have room for a rookie — at least not in a day and time when two to three starters were the rule.

Then, disaster struck in the City of Brotherly Love. "Fergy," the "Philadelphia Prince," contracted typhoid fever and died on April 29, shortly after the start of the 1888 season opener. The team, as well as the community, was plunged into mourning for their fallen star. Furthermore, without Ferguson, the Philadelphians would be hard put to make another strong run for the 1888 blue ribbon. And they were indeed hard put, tumbling into a more mediocre season just above the .500 level that dropped them into third place at season's end, barely a heartbeat above Boston's Beaneaters.

Who would stand in the Ferguson breach? Certainly not Alexander Sanders, whose spotty Spring Training season and even weaker performance in the final exhibition games ahead of regular season's play had not at all endeared him to Philadelphia's fandom. In fact, Quaker City scribes were quite critical of manager Harry Wright for not releasing Sanders and picking up a better pitching replacement. But the sage old veteran Wright stuck by his young find, held on to San-

ders, and picked a spot here and there to bring him up to scratch in the Big Show. Wright was right. By June, with the team hovering at the break-even mark, the time had come to get Big Ben on the firing line.

The skeptical Philadelphia sportswriters scrutinized Sanders' first several outings, which, though nothing to rave about, were admittedly workmanlike. Then, on July 14, "Big Ben's" finesse and power began to make their presence felt. Batting fourth, he pitched his first shutout at Pittsburgh, winning 4 to 0. Note his position in the batting order. The only run he needed was one he drove home himself as he shut down the Pirates on four singles. Mr. Wright had himself a pitcher, and the scribes began to quiet down; in fact, before long they were calling Sanders the reincarnation of Charlie Ferguson.

As the season wore on the Sanders log brightened considerably. Though involved in six extra-inning games (he won three of them, tieing another in a white-knuckler at New York, where he matched goose eggs with the great Mickey Welch for 11 innings), he beat every team in the league save the champion Mutuals of New York, and helped spark Philadelphia's late-season rush to third place as the team won eight of their last nine games. These were some of Sanders' better games during his banner rookie season:

- July 28 — Lost to 35-game-winner Tim Keefe, 4 to 2; Sanders had 10 assists
- July 31 — Beat HOFer John Clarkson at Boston in 11 innings, 6 to 5
- August 4 — Won a 7–0, 4-hitter at Washington, striking out six
- August 8 — Won at Chicago, batted sixth, and tripled in a 16–5 game
- September 1 — At home Sanders won over Washington's Widner in 11 innings, 2 — 0

- September 22 — Beat Indianapolis' Healy in 11 innings, 6–5
- October 14 — Closed out the season with his 19th win, defeating Cleveland, completing Philadelphia's 1888 record at 69–61

One other game begs mention. That occurred on a sunny, late summer day in the Windy City, when, on September 18, Big Ben one-hit Cap Anson's Chicago White Stockings, 5 to 0. His game-of-the-year performance that day drew rave notices from the *Chicago Inter-Ocean*. In that quaint, late–19th century style of sports writing, here is the way coverage of Sanders' brilliant one-hitter began:

> One of the most remarkable games of the season was that played by Philadelphia and Chicago yesterday. It was remarkable for several things. First for Sanders' pitching, which was simply perfection itself. He held the Chicago batsmen down for eight innings without a hit and without a man reaching first base. There was no hope to be gained by errors — the battery made none. The fielding of the visitors was perfection, not an error being made of a chance accepted…. The Philadelphias began their work in the first inning. Wood flew out to Ryan. Andrews retired on a foul fly that Burns captured. Farrar made a base hit to left field. Sanders (note that Sanders batted in the cleanup spot; ed.) hit the ball over Van Haltren's head in left field, and before it was fielded home Sanders had made the circuit and scored a home run bringing Farrar in with him.

That was about all Big Ben needed, but the Phils added another four runs, nibbling away at Chicago's prize rookie, Gus Krock, as the game progressed. The account of the final 6 to 0 *Chicagoing* (a term that meant "a whitewashing") of the White Stockings also took due note of the Sanders blast. It was his first major league round-tripper. In "Notes of the Game," which followed

the box score, it was further stated that "Sanders is now the king pitcher of the National League." Perhaps a bit much, especially by New York Standards (Famers Keefe and Welch, after all, were on the way to 35- [Keefe] and 26- [Welch] game seasons), but the few who showed up to see Sanders on this remarkable afternoon were no doubt as impressed as the press corps. The box score follows on page 156.

The recap on Ben Sanders' outstanding rookie season reveals what a complete ballplayer he was. Manager Wright used him in almost every spot in the batting order, moved him into the starting rotation and took as much advantage of his versatility as possible. Though his unorthodox delivery left him vulnerable to the bunts and dribblers that plague most pitchers, he was a cat-quick, slick-fielding player who registered a superior 4 rating in the Pitcher as Fielder (DEF) sabermetric category for 1888.

And he hit. On a punchless Philly nine, he was better with a stick in his hands than his teammates who played every day. The team batting average was hardly there at all, the Phillies mustering an anemic .225. Except for Deacon McGuire, who caught a few games and totaled only 51 bats, hitting .333, Sanders led the ballclub with a .246, stole 13 bases, whiffed only 12 times in 248 plate appearances, and beyond that, fielded his position, or one should say positions, as well as anyone on the team. Add to that his 19 victories, including *eight* shutouts, which tied New York's Keefe for the league lead, and you have what today would be called a Rookie of the Year season.

Big Ben added another 19 conquests to his Phillies win totals in 1889, but the restive young man with a good deal more on his mind than baseball, became more and more demanding of his time and career direction, insisting on time off to complete his degree work in engineering.

Box Score

Philadelphia at West Side Park, Chicago, Illinois, September 18, 1888

Philadelphia	AB	R	H	PO	A		Chicago	AB	R	H	PO	A
Wood, lf	4	1	2	2	2		Ryan, cf	4	0	0	4	0
Andrews, cf	4	1	2	4	0		Van Haltren, lf	3	0	0	0	0
Farrar, 1b	3	1	2	14	1		Duffy, rf	3	0	0	2	1
Sanders, p	4	1	1	2	3		Anson, 1b	3	0	0	7	0
Fogarty, rf	4	0	1	0	0		Pfeffer, 2b	3	0	0	1	2
Mulvey, 3b	4	0	1	0	4		Williamson, ss	3	0	0	3	4
Clements, c	4	1	1	4	0		Burns, 3b	3	0	0	3	3
Irwin, ss	3	1	1	0	4		Krock, p	3	0	1	0	5
Bastian, 2b	4	0	0	1	2		Farrell, c	2	0	0	6	2
Totals	34	6	11	27	16		Totals	28	0	1	24	17

```
Philadelphia   201   002   100    6-11-0
Chicago        000   000   000    0-1-5
```

3 BH	Wood, Andrews
HR	Sanders
LOB	Philadelphia 5, Chicago 1
DP	Farrell and Anson
K	Sanders 2, Krock 4
BB	Sanders 0, Krock 1
Time	1:10
Umpires	Powell and Daniels
Att	1,008

His talent was of the caliber that could force Philadelphia's entry in the Player's League and later Philadelphia's American Association team to acquiesce to his demands, though one cannot help but wonder how this young Virginian got away with it.

Finally, after the 1892 season, played out with lowly Louisville, Ben Sanders had fired his last hummer. He signed on with a different team, the engineering firm that was building the famed Chicago Elevated Railway system.

During the five seasons he was around to make the grand tour of organized baseball's major league circuits, he had put together an 80–70 record, had hit at a very respectable .271 average, and had managed to keep his independence in tact as he pursued what were for him those more important things in life. That, too, is as noteworthy as it is commendable.

1888: Ten of the National League's Top Rookies

Nm/Pos/Tm	GP	W–L/BA	SH/SV//RBI	PR/BR	ERA/FR	TPR
Sanders/RHP/Phl	31	19–10	8/0	33	1.90	4.2
Hoy/of/Was	136	.274	29	25	7	2.7
Sowders/RHP/Bos	36	19–15	2/0	27	2.07	2.3
Krock/LHP/Chi	39	25–14	4/0	22	2.44	1.6
Duffy/of/Chi	71	.282	41	5	5	0.8
Sutcliffe/UT/Det	49	.257	23	-3	7	0.6
Beatin/LHP/Det	12	5–7	1/0	-1	2.86	0.4
John TenerRHP/Chi	12	7–5	1/0	3	2.74	0.4
Wilmot/of/Was	119	.224	43	-5	11	0.3
G. Keefe/LHP/Was	13	6–7	1/0	0	2.84	0.2

Ewell Albert "Reb" Russell

TPR: 4.2

1913, Chicago, AL

Born: April 12, 1889, Jackson, MS; Died: September 30, 1973, Indianapolis, IN
LHP, 5'11" 185 lb. Major League Debut: April 18, 1913
1913: 52 GP; W22, L16; .579 W%; 8/4 SH/SV;
9.5 Ratio; .219 OBA; 3 PHI; 36 PR; 1.90 ERA

Pitching has been a White Sox long suit from the earliest days of Chicago's Southside franchise. Given the generous proportions of the Comiskey ballparks, a long-standing tradition of strong pitching, a sturdy, fleet-footed defense and a "hit 'em where they ain't," station-to-station offensive seems to have been a sensible game plan. That strategy was characteristic of the first quarter century of baseball in Chicago, where both the Cubs and the Pale Hose paraded great pitchers like Mordecai Brown, Ed Walsh, Doc White, Big Ed Reulbach and Death Valley Jim Scott in front of major league hitters.

Charley Comiskey, White Sox founder and major domo, came up with one master moundsman after another, and in 1913 brought Reb Russell to town to take up the slack left by Ed Walsh, who, after an eight-year span of 315 innings per season on the firing line, had simply worn the old soup-

bone down to a nub. (Hall of Famer Walsh's 1913 mark of 8 and 3 was but a pale reflection of his glory years.) It was evident already at the Sox' Paso Robles, California, training base that the Ed Walsh magic had disappeared and that someone was going to have to step up to account at least in part for the 20-plus victories he was capable of adding to the Chicago win column. The 23-year-old southpaw, whose meager minor league record gave little promise of a 20-game winner in the making, was the one who stepped up to fill the void. His name was Ewell Russell, of the Jackson, Mississippi, Russells, proud Southern folk who hadn't really counted on having a professional ballplayer in the family, much less one who would ply his trade in the northland.

For rather obvious reasons they called him "Reb." His repertoire included a variety of pitches, and the youngster was in the habit of changing speeds and letting rip an occasional "quickie" that moved just enough to sneak past the big boppers in the league. A little on the pudgy side, Russell had enough punch in both his arm and bat to get the job done. Hitting, especially, was a most welcome bonus among his punch-and-judy-hitting teammates, who managed only a puny .236 team batting average during an especially weak summer of few hits and fewer runs. That was only six percentage points better than the "Hitless Wonders" of 1906 fame, improbable winners of the first single-city World Series. So pitching for a ballclub like the 1913 White Sox had its obvious occupational hazards.

Bill "Kid" Gleason, who was to become the Sox' manager in 1919, only to have the bottom drop out of the awesomely talented machine that became known as the Black Sox, was manager Nixey Callahan's top coach, one who knew a thing or two about pitching. Gleason lost no time at all sizing up Reb Russell's potential and completed the portsider's pitching portfolio with a curveball that complemented his assortment of breaking pitches. As the season opened Kid Gleason, a veteran of more than a score of years as a pitcher and an infielder in big-league play, was confident that by mid season his rookie protegé would be ready to contribute a decently pitched ball game here and there. Russell, however, was more than ready.

As the Sox completed their first few weeks of the 1913 season, it became evident to the White Sox brass that the pitching corps would need more than Jim Scott and Eddie Cicotte to carry the burden of the starting rotation. Though it might have been a bit early, there weren't many alternatives. Reb Russell was available.

On May 17, Chicago celebrated "Frank Chance Day" at Comiskey Park. It was the day Callahan chose to use Russell in a starting role for the first time in his major league career. Matched against the newly renamed New York Yankees (they started out in 1903 as the Highlanders), Russell's southpaw slants made the day a Chicago success, winning 6 to 3 in front of more than 35,000 fans. The Reb was on the march.

At the mid-season mark in 1913 the White Sox were a better-than-.500 ballclub, but found themselves behind Washington, Cleveland and Philadelphia in the standings. Unable to muster much of an offensive attack, it was already painfully clear that manager Nixey Callahan's charges weren't going to move upward; in fact, they finished the season in fifth place, a notch lower than their mid–July perch. All things considered, their 78 and 74 finish was somewhat of a minor miracle.

The new ballpark on Chicago's Southside, opened in 1910 and grandly christened "Comiskey's Baseball Palace," was a pitcher's haven, and the new "Reb" in town, Ewell Russell, made the most of it as he paced the pitching staff with 22 wins. Jim "Death Valley" Scott, a cagey veteran into his fifth campaign, won 20, but also lost that many. His 1.91 ERA, which equalled Russell's, is a sure sign of one- and two-run losses. The third of the Chisox' Big Three was 18-game-winner Eddie Cicotte, whose moistened, scuffed and otherwise doctored offerings bobbed and weaved all over the strike zone, but never quite settled down long enough for American League hitters to catch up with. The rest of the staff contributed another 18 wins here and there, some of them saved by the ace himself, as Russell accounted for four saves, thus involving himself in 26 of Chicago's 78 wins. The final accounting for the season revealed a highly commendable staff ERA of 2.33, which actually led both leagues, and, with the exception of the Cardinals' superb 2.38 ERA in the National League, led the major leagues by plenty.

Hitting was not a problem in Boston, not with the legendary outfield patrol of Duffy Lewis, Tris Speaker and Harry Hooper, ably supported by infielders Clyde Engel and Larry Gardner. The Red Sox were the defending world champs, and though they encountered rough going in the first half of the campaign, no one had given up on getting back into the pennant race.

Shortly after the halfway mark of the 1913 season, these same Red Sox rolled into Chicago for a four-game set, and on July 14 scheduled rookie Rube Foster, fresh from a successful season in the Texas League with the pennant winning Houston Buffalos, to pitch against the Pale Hose. Foster, who had thrown a one-hitter against the St. Louis Browns (the lone Brownie hit was a triple) his last outing, took on Russell, who had hurled for the seventh-place Fort Worth Panthers in 1912, and Russell proceeded to beat him with the finest game of his career.

Record-setting White Sox rookie portsider Reb Russell, 1913 (Brace Photo.)

On this day Foster, 24-game winner with Houston the year before, w o u l d find out about the new Ewell Russell and his White Sox compadres, as he absorbed one of his four losses (he won three in spot assignments during the 1913 season) and yielded a triple to Russell that proved decisive in Chicago's 8–0 victory. Between the two of them, Foster and Russell had given up two hits in 16 innings of pitching, and both were triples. Russell's, however, was the telling blow in one of those strange twists that often mark career turning points.

Reb Russell's 1913 season was his career pinnacle. Though hampered by an ailing arm later in his career, when carefully spotted with enough rest, he continued to come through for the Comiskeymen, turning in an American League–leading winning percentage on a fine 15 and 5 record for the 1917 World Champions.

Russell's 1913 log featured 52 appearances, which led the AL, and eight shutouts, five of which, remarkably, were 1 to 0 victories. Both set rookie and club marks for the Pale Hose. His 22 wins that season also established a club mark for

Box Score

Boston at Comiskey Park, Chicago, Illinois, July 14, 1913

Boston	AB	R	H	PO	A		Chicago	AB	R	H	PO	A
Hooper, rf	3	0	1	2	0		Rath, 2b	5	1	1	1	2
Yerkes, 2b	3	0	0	2	3		Lord, 3b	4	1	2	0	0
Speaker, cf	4	0	0	3	0		Chase, 1b	4	2	2	9	1
Lewis, lf	3	0	0	1	0		J. Collins, rf	3	1	1	2	0
Gardner, 3b	2	0	0	1	2		Schalk, c	4	1	2	5	1
Engle, 1b	3	0	0	7	1		Bodie, rf	4	1	3	3	0
C. Wagner, ss	3	0	0	2	0		Mattick, cf	4	0	1	2	0
Carrigan, c	3	0	0	6	3		Weaver, ss	3	1	0	4	4
Foster, p	2	0	0	0	4		Russell, p	4	0	2	1	3
Wood, ph	1	0	0	0	0		Moseley, p	0	0	0	0	0
Totals	26	0	1	24	13		Totals	35	8	14	27	11

```
Boston    000  000  000   0-1-2
Chicago   000  012  50x   8-14-1
```

2BH	Bodie, Collins
3BH	Russell
LOB	Boston 3, Chicago 6
DP	Carrigan, Yerkes; Weaver, Rath, Chase
HPB	By Russell, Hooper, Gardner
BB	Foster, 1; Moseley, 0; Russell, 0
K	Foster, 4; Moseley, 1; Russell, 0
WP	Foster
Win. P	Russell
LP	Foster
Time	1:44
Umpires	Evans and Sheridan

rookies. Russell is one of ten lefties in the history of the Sox to post 20-game seasons:

1. Nick Altrock: 21, 1904; 21, 1905; 20, 1906
2. Guy "Doc" White: 27, 1907
3. Reb Russell: 22, 1913
4. Claude "Lefty" Williams: 23, 1919; 22, 1920
5. "Dickie" Kerr: 21, 1920
6. Thornton Lee: 22, 1941
7. Billy Pierce: 20, 1956; 20, 1957
8. Gary Peters: 20, 1964
9. Wilbur Wood: 22, 1971; 24, 1972; 24, 1973; 20, 1974
10. Jim Kaat: 21, 1974; 21, 1975

In addition to his pitching, there was also the matter of Russell's hitting, so good that when his failing arm no longer got the job done, his shillelagh did. After a three-year "sabbatical" he returned to the Bigs in 1922 as an outfielder with the Pittsburgh Pirates, hitting a robust .368. Reb spent the last seven years of his professional baseball career as an outfielder–first baseman, chiefly with Minneapolis and Indianapolis of the American Association, where, in 1927, he led the league with a hefty .385 average.

In 1930, at age 41, he was released by Chattanooga of the Southern Association, and moved on to Quincy, Illinois, where he finished out his career with the second-place Indians as a first baseman. Hitting well, as always, he ended the season at .310, enabling him to wind up his minor league career with a .330 average (in the major leagues he hit at a creditable .268 lifetime average).

Russell settled down in Indianapolis, where he lived for many years among his many Hoosier friends, who respected him as a solid citizen. It was a long way from Jackson, Mississippi, and his Texas boyhood years, but the Rebel had earned his spurs. He died in Indy at 84 telling baseball stories to the very end.

1913: Ten Top Rookies

Nm/Pos/Tm-L	GP	W–L/BA	SH/SV//RBI	PR/BR	ERA/FR	TPR
E. Russell/LHP/Chi-A*	52	22–16	8/4	36	1.91	4.2
J. Boehling/LHP/Was-A	38	17–7	3/4	21	2.14	2.6
R. Rudolph/RHP/Bos-N	33	14–13	2/0	10	2.92	1.9
H. Leonard/LHP/Bos-A	42	14–16	3/1	16	2.39	1.7
G. Dauss/RHP/Det-A	33	13–12	2/1	11	2.48	1.5
W. Schang/c/Phl-A	79	.266	30	12	-5	1.4
H. Groh/3b/Cin-N	121	.281	48	4	10	1.3
G. Pearce/LHP/Chi-N	25	13–5	3/0	16	2.31	1.3
W. James/RHP/Bos-N	24	6–10	1/0	8	2.79	1.0
A. Demaree/RHP/NY-N	31	13–4	2/2	20	2.21	0.9

*Reb Russell was named Hypothetical Rookie of the Year for 1913

Todd Roland Worrell

TPR: 4.2

1986, St. Louis, NL
Born: September 28, 1959, Arcadia, CA
RP-LHP; 6'5" 215 lb. Major League Debut: August 28, 1985
1986: 74 GP; W9, L10; .474 W%; 36 SV; .229 OBA; .307 OB%, 18 PR; 2.08 ERA

It was 1985. Ozzie Smith, the Cardinals' "Wizard of Oz," proclaimed it a special year. The Cards had captured the National League East, beating out Dwight Gooden and the New York Mets in a dogfight for the division's title, brandishing some top flight pitching of their own plus a blistering running game that specialized in thievery and taking extra bases. Mercurial Vince Coleman, a talented rookie, was in the vanguard of the attack. The Wizard himself and Willie McGee weren't far behind, as the St. Louis swifties pilfered a club record 314 bases, 132 more than their closest rival, the Chicago Cubs. That is an absolutely staggering bulge.

There was, however, a problem, and that was in the bull pen. Bruce Sutter, with his 45 saves, had moved on to Atlanta. Could relievers like Jeff Lahti or Ken Dayley pick up that kind of slack? That seemed unlikely.

Operating on a committee-of-the-whole plan most of the season, manager Whitey Herzog had called on most of his available hands to fill the brilliant Sutter's role. Sometimes it worked — and sometimes it didn't.

But there was a flamethrower down on the farm who was blazing a hot trail through the American Association, that more than mildly piqued Herzog's interest. His name was Todd Worrell, a strapping, 6'5" right-hander who had already been selected the Pitcher of the Week twice in July. So the call was sent to Louisville to bring him to St. Louis. It was the Cardinals' best call-up of the season. By far.

Appearing in his first game on August 28, he picked up where he left off in the American Association. In the brief span of the 21.2 innings he hurled before the season was over, he won three times in relief and added five saves as the Cardinals surged to the division championship. And it didn't end there. Helmsman Herzog called on his recruit four times during the National League Championship Series with the Los Angeles Dodgers and the rookie responded with six innings of spotless relief, holding the Dodgers while adding a playoff victory in Game 7 to put St. Louis into the World Series. Although the World Series encore was not quite as impressive (he was charged with the loss in Game 6 against cross-state rival Kansas City, which emerged victorious in the 1985 Series) his pitching in baseball's most volatile pressure cooker was once again imposing as he emerged from the championship series with three appearances and a save to go with his loss.

But three wins, five saves and 21-plus innings do not a rookie season make. A full season of baseball warfare under the Big Tent would put the test to the Cardinal phenom, showing in due time whether he was the real deal. It did—and he was.

In 1986 Todd Worrell followed Wally Moon (1954), Bill Virdon (1955), Bake McBride (1974) and Vince Coleman (1985) as Cardinal winners of the BBWAA's prestigious Rookie of the Year Award. That was but one among a number of awards presented him, including the NL Player of the Week, July 21–27; NL Pitcher of the Month for July; Rolaids Relief Man Award for 1986; and the Relief Pitcher slot on the UPI Postseason NL Team. In addition he established a major league rookie record for saves (36), recording at least two against every other NL team; he was the first Rookie of the Year to lead the league in saves; he became the first rookie to win the Rolaids Relief Man Award; and finally, was named the St. Louis BBWAA chapter's Man of the Year. That plateful was negotiated against the accomplished competition of relievers like Lee Smith (Chicago: 33 saves, 2.4 TPR), Kent Tekulve (Philadelphia: 73 appearances, 2.4 TPR), and Jesse Orosco (New York: 21 saves, 2.3 TPR).

Although the Cards' ace closer was the National League's premier reliever, his 9 and 10 record is more indicative of the miseries the team encountered in 1986. Slipping from their championship rung in

Star Cardinal reliever Todd Worrell. (Dennis Colgin.)

1985 to third in 1986, the St. Louisans found repeating an impossibility with another subpar (.236) team batting average and middling starters who came up with only 17 complete games and a major league low of four shutouts. That made for frequent relief work. Two of the middle, or long, relievers included Ricky Horton, who appeared in 49 games, and Pat Perry (46 games and 68.2 IP). Workhorse Worrell accounted for a career high 103.2 innings in relief, posting a 2.08 ERA and a league-leading 4.2 TPR for pitchers.

Over the years the Giants had always been tough for the Cardinals to beat at Candlestick Park. "The Stick," with its raw, cool weather and tricky winds, presents problems quite unlike any other major league ballpark. 1986 was no different. Whitey Herzog's boys were hard-pressed for a win in San Francisco. But on July 6, 1986, they managed to push the Giants into extra innings and beat them with a three-run outburst in the top of the tenth.

Despite their usual modest hitting,

Box Score

St. Louis at Candlestick Park, San Francisco, July 6, 1986

St. Louis	AB	R	H	BI
Coleman, lf	3	1	1	1
McGee, cf	4	1	1	0
Herr, 2b	3	0	0	0
A. Knicely, 1b	1	1	0	1
C. Ford, rf	0	1	0	0
Landrum, rf	2	1	0	0
Van Slyke, rf	0	0	0	0
Heath, c	4	1	1	3
Worrell, p	0	0	0	0
Oquendo, ph	1	1	0	1
Dayley, p	0	0	0	0
O. Smith, ss	5	0	2	2
Pendleton, 3b	4	0	1	0
Lawless, 3b	1	0	0	0
Tudor, p	2	0	0	0
LaValliere, c	1	0	0	0
Totals	31	7	6	7

San Francisco	AB	R	H	BI
Kutcher, cf	3	3	1	0
R. Thompson, 2b	3	1	1	0
Maldonado, lf	3	0	1	2
C. Davis, rf	3	0	2	0
C. Brown, 3b	4	0	1	2
Brenly, 1b	4	0	0	0
Melvin, c	3	0	0	0
Uribe, ss	2	0	0	0
J. Leonard	1	0	0	0
F. Williams, p	0	0	0	0
Spahn, ph	1	0	0	0
Berenguer, p	0	0	0	0
J. Robinson, p	0	0	0	0
Blue, p	1	0	0	0
L. Quinones, ph	1	0	0	0
M. Davis, p	0	0	0	0
Youngblood, rf	2	0	0	0
Totals	31	4	6	4

St. Louis	100	003	000	3	7-6-0
San Francisco	100	002	010	0	4-6-1

2BH	Pendleton, Kutcher
3BH	O. Smith
HR	Heath
LOB	St. Louis 7, San Francisco 4
SB	Coleman 2; Kutcher
SH	Tudor, R. Thompson, Herr
SF	Knicely, Maldanado
DP	St. Louis 2
BB	Tudor 4, Worrell 1, Blue 6, Williams 1, Berenguer 3
K	Tudor 3, Worrell 1, Blue 7, M. Davis 1, Williams 1
WP	Worrell (6–8)
LP	Berenguer (1–1)
Balk	Berenguer
Umpires	Hallion, Runge, Pallone, Engel
Time	3:27
Att	20,747

coming up with only six hits in the game, they managed to dispose of Vida Blue after six frames, and took a lead going into the eighth inning. Then John Tudor faltered and Herzog summoned Todd Worrell from the bullpen. Worrell prevented any fatal damage, escaping the inning with a 4–4 score, the tieing run having been charged to Tudor. Jose Oquendo batted for Worrell in the tenth inning, got on and scored, and then reliever Ken Dayley, who picked up his fifth and final save of the season, sat down the Giants to preserve the win. But the real hero that day was Worrell, whose mixture of well-spotted pitches, sliders and heaters quelled a big San Francisco inning in the making, as he came on with the bases dripping with Giants and only one away. Picking his way through the meat end of the 'Frisco batting order, Worrell put an end to the uprising and received credit for his sixth win of the year.

In a year that produced a bumper crop of outstanding rookies, two stood out spectacularly among the rest. These two, both relievers, were Todd Worrell and Mark Eichhorn, already cited in these pages for his 5.7 TPR in 1986, in the sixth position on our all-time rookie list. And, though not accorded BBWAA honors as the Rookie of the Year, Eichhorn nonetheless heads up the top 10 listing following the Todd Worrell profile. Other outstanding freshmen are shown below.

Worrell followed up his award-winning rookie year with one that was almost as good as his debut season. In 1987 the Cardinals regained the division championship they surrendered to the 1986 New York Mets and went on to beat the NL West champions, San Francisco, besting them in a taut, seven-game series that was won in Brewtown by Danny Cox with a 6 to 0 win that matched the Giants' Dave Dravecky's 5–0 calcimining in Game 2. In the Series,

the Cards' Mr. Rescue appeared in three games, saving one and posting a 2.08 ERA. At the "Big Dance," as the World Series is sometimes called, there was another seven game set-to that once again slipped through the hands of the Cardinals, this time to the Minnesota Twins. This time around Worrell made seven nearly perfect appearances, saving two games while shutting down the Twins on a 1.29 ERA that permitted them but one earned run in seven innings of crunch-time work.

Todd Worrell knew how to keep things in perspective, including two world championship losses, the inevitable down times that come with injuries, trades and, finally, baseball's pink slip, the release. A strong set of Christian values has been a part of the Worrell persona, providing the guidance and direction that have made of his exemplary life as a professional athlete the kind of role model parents point to.

Nm/Pos/Tm	RY Votes	GP	W–L/BA	ML Yrs	TPR
D. Mohorcic/RP-RPH/Tx-A	0	58	2–3	5	1.4
W. Joyner*/1b/Cal-A	98	154	.290	*	1.4
D. Tartabul/of/Sea-A	4	137	.270	13	1.2
M. Williams/RP-RHP/Tx-A	0	80	8–6	12	1.0
J. Canseco†/of/Oak-A	110	157	.240	*	0.5
J. Kruk/of/SD-N	1	122	.309	10	0.5
B. Larkin*/ss/Cin-N	1	41	.283	*	0.4
E. Correa/RHP/Tx	0	32	12–14	3	0.3
J. Deshaies/LHP/Hou-N	1	26	12–5	12	0.3
W. Clark*/1b/SF-N	5	111	.287	*	0.0
K. Mitchell/of/NY-N	22	108	.277	12	-0.1
R. Palmeiro*/1b/Chi-N	0	22	.247	*	-0.1
C. Snyder/of/Clv-A	16	103	.272	9	-0.2
R. Thompson/2b/SF-N	22	149	.271	12	-0.2
P. Incaviglia/of/Tx-A	0	153	.250	*	-1.0
R. Sierra/of/Tx-A	1	113	.264	12	-1.4

*Still Active
†1986 BBWAA selection as AL Rookie of the Year (Canseco is still active)

1986: The Top Ten Rookies

Nm/Pos/Tm-L	GP	W–L/BA	SH/SV//RBI	PR/BR	ERA/FR	TPR
Eichhorn/RP-RHP/Tor-N	69	14–6	0/10	44	1.72	5.7
Worrell/RP-RHP/StL-N	74	9–10	0/36	18	2.08	4.2
Plesac/RP-RHP/Mil-A	51	10–7	0/14	14	2.97	2.7
Schiraldi/RP-RHP/Bos-A	25	4–2	0/9	16	1.41	2.2
R. Murphy/RP-LHP/Cin-N	34	6–0	0/1	18	0.72	2.1
Bonds/of/Pit-N	113	.223	48	2	15	2.0
McCullers/RP-RHP/SD-N	70	10–10	0/5	13	2.31	1.9
A. Thomas/ss/Atl-N	102	.251	32	-14	26	1.8
Karkovice/c/Chi-A	37	.247	13	0	14	1.6
Kerfeld/RP-RHP/Hou-N	61	11–2	0/7	10	2.59	1.5
Ruffin/LHP/Phl-N	21	9–4	0/0	23	2.46	1.5

John "Jocko" Flynn

TPR: 4.1

1886, Chicago, NL

Born: June 30, 1864, Lawrence, MA; Died: December 30, 1907, Lawrence, MA
RHP; 5'6" 143 lb. Major League Debut: May 1, 1886
1886: 32 GP; W23, L6; .793 W%; 2/1 SH/SV; 146/63 K/BB; .210 OBA; 40 PR; 2.24 ERA

The Sporting News, that venerable St. Louis sports weekly dating back to 1886, came out with issue number one on March 17 of its inaugural year. Included among other front page items about the St. Louis Roadsters (a trotting club) and an interview with a Japanese wrestler was a fetching article about the Chicago White Stockings and their plans for the 1886 season. Brimful with optimism, *TSN*'s correspondent Hugh Keough mentioned manager Cap Anson's preparations for defending the "Whites'" hard won pennant in 1885. Chief among them was a trip to Hot Springs, Arkansas, to "boil out the beer and booze the boys swilled over the winter." That was typical Cap Anson: blunt and hard-nosed about handling whatever might confront him (usually beer, booze and umpires), because he was, verily, the team's absolutely fearless leader.

The Hot Springs training trip wasn't the first of its kind. Trips to Southern climes had been made prior to season openers before, but when the Chicagos made the trip under the aegus of Al Spalding, that was front page news. Spalding, retired from a highly successful pitching career of his own, and subsequently a successful sporting goods entrepreneur, was used to winning, putting a touch of class on everything he attempted. So when the team's stars headed south, they made the trip in style.

Two recruits who made that trip were former teammates with their local Lawrence, Massachusetts, ballclub. Their names were George "Prunes" Moolic, a catcher, and his batterymate John "Jocko" Flynn, a flamboyant pitcher who was known to have frequented the local and outlying watering holes. They signed on for a look-see as a pair.

The two made their way to Chicago to join the training brigade and discovered, gleefully, that their new teammates, fellows like Mike Kelly, Ned Williamson and Silver King were not only great shakes at the game of baseball, but equally adept at the local saloons. That, of course, made

Anson's concerns about his men an urgency of the first order. Jocko Flynn, his abilities aside, soon became a *real* concern.

When the ballclub headed north, Moolic and Flynn went with it. Having made the team, they were about to find out what baseball life was like in the Philadelphias and Bostons and New Yorks of the big leagues. That, and more.

Of the two, Flynn was the more gifted ballplayer. He was not only a fine pitcher whose fast one had good movement, but he could play the outfield as well and knew what to do with a bat in his hands.

Spalding and Anson knew talent when they saw it, and Flynn definitely had it. Consequently, it wasn't long before Jocko was written into the White Stockings' lineup either as an outfielder, where he played in 28 games during the 1886 season, or as a pitcher in the starting rotation behind two other fine hurlers, ace John Clarkson (53 and 16 in 1885) and Jim McCormick (20 and 4 with Chicago in 1885 after coming to the Windy City from Providence). Anson figured to use Flynn as a third starter, replacing the departed Ted Kennedy, to help relieve the logjam created by rain-outs and those stretches of back-to-back ball games that placed undue stress on the "Big Two."

It didn't quite work out that way. Flynn was just too good. During another championship season Clarkson led the staff with 55 starts, followed by McCormick's 42, both of which were down from the previous season, and the rookie right-hander started 29 times. Jocko had proven so reliable that Anson slated him on an every-three-to-four game basis, and without losing a step in a heated pennant race that the Whites were hard pressed to win. Clarkson piled up 36 wins, 27 less than in 1885, and McCormick added 31, but it was Flynn who had pulled up the slack by adding a lustrous 23 and 6 record to the Chicago title. What was now the "Big Three" had

accounted for every one of the team's 90 victories. And Jocko Flynn's .793 winning percentage topped the league. His 23 conquests, further, represented the most victories ever recorded by a major league one-year-career man.

One-year-career man? How could that be?! As a matter of fact, Jocko Flynn's meteoric pitching career vanished into the distant blue yonder as suddenly as it had appeared. One year of extraordinary mound work — and carousing — was about all the frail right-hander was up to. There is only one game to account for in the rest of his major league career, a cameo appearance as an outfielder the next season, 1887, and in that game (undated), just long enough to get in one at-bat.

Dave Nemec, whose delightful history of 19th century baseball fills in a host of missing details from the misty past of baseball's earliest days, devotes a few lines to Flynn and the 1886 Chicago White Stockings:

> Flynn, a native of Lawrence, Massachusetts, arrived in Chicago in the spring of 1886 as a twenty-two year old rookie pitcher outfielder…. Over the next five months Flynn won 23 games so quickly that it was said of him: "On the street he looks like one of your lawn-tennis dudes. On the field he is, to quote everybody, a perfect terror." The words had hardly appeared in print than Flynn blew out his arm. Not a great one for caring for himself, he never pitched again in the majors (*Encyclopedia*, 290).

That last bit of information — about his not caring for himself — seems to be the telltale clue here, substantiated by a July 22, 1886, report in the Chicago papers that A. G. Spalding had hired detectives to keep him informed about the after-hour activities of those ballplayers whose thirst seemed to be insatiable. Jocko's name was on the list. Right near the top.

But there were at least 23 times during that season of championship glory that Mr. John A. Flynn was lord and master of everything on a baseball diamond that he surveyed. Among his 23 wins that summer, none was as brilliantly pitched as a contest in St. Louis in which he was matched against "The Egyptian," John Healy, a second-year man even younger, at 20, than Flynn himself.

The only run in the game came in the third inning when Jocko led off with a grounder that the usually reliable Jack Glasscock fumbled, putting Flynn on first. Jimmy Ryan flew out to right fielder Patsy Cahill. On the next pitch, in what must have been a delayed steal, Jocko broke for second base. Attempting to flag down the swift-moving Flynn, catcher George Myers overthrew the base, and Flynn, who never hesitated, moved on to third. He scored moments later on a single by the Whites' hard-hitting outfielder, George Gore. That was all it took. Flynn had mastered the St. Louis Maroons on a four-hitter, chalking up his second major league shutout by a 1 to 0 score.

Prior to his calciming of the Maroons there was one other shutout as Flynn moved on to the 23 victory mark against only six losses. And, all things considered, it was even more remarkable that 14 of those victories were reeled off in succession.

Among the league's pitchers, his 7.25 hits per game was third in the "fewest hits" category. He also managed better than five whiffs per game (fifth among league hurlers), tied for second in opponents' batting average (.210), and placed third in opponents' on-base percentage (.257). His 2.24 ERA, which tied for second, was 1.05, or a full run under the league average (3.29) and better than both John Clarkson's (2.41) and Jim McCormick's (2.82), Anson's aces. The numbers factored into a lofty 4.1 TPR, strong enough to merit a number 18(t) on

John "Jocko" Flynn, White Stockings rookie, 1886. (Brace Photo.)

the all time rookie honors list. Spalding and Anson had come up with quite a find in the young rookie from Massachusetts. Unfortunately, however, this young luminary was as fast-burning as he was bright.

Jocko Flynn was an important 1887 roster listing. But the record shows that he played in only one game, and thereafter simply faded from view. An interesting sidenote, however, gives some indication about A. G. Spalding's estimation of Flynn's capabilities. It turns out that, rather than risk losing him to someone else, "A. G." refused to release him from roster status in 1887, preferring to keep him under Chicago contract even though he knew the young pitcher's career was all but over. What happened here?

A few clues may help. The prodigy was signed by the Omaha club in January of 1888, probably reasoning that he had to

Box Score

Chicago at the Union Baseball Grounds, St. Louis, Mo., September 13, 1886

Chicago	AB	R	H	PO	A
Gore, cf	3	0	1	2	0
Kelly, rf	4	0	1	1	0
Anson, 1b	4	0	0	9	0
Pfeffer, 2b	3	0	0	5	2
Williamson, ss	3	0	0	2	2
Burns, 3b	3	0	1	1	1
Hardie, c	3	0	0	4	1
Flynn, p	3	1	0	2	2
Ryan, lf	2	0	0	3	0
Totals	28	1	3	27	8

St. Louis	AB	R	H	PO	A
Glasscock, ss	3	0	0	1	2
McKinnon, 1b	4	0	0	11	1
Denny, 3b	4	0	1	1	3
Myers, c	4	0	0	1	5
McGeachy, cf	3	0	2	4	0
Seery, lf	3	0	0	3	0
Cahill, rf	3	0	0	2	1
Crane, 2b	3	0	1	4	5
Healy, p	3	0	0	0	1
Totals	30	0	4	27	18

```
Chicago     001  000  000   1-3-2
St. Louis   000  000  000   0-4-8
```

2BH	Denny, Crane, Burns, Kelly
LOB	Chicago 2, St. Louis 6
DP	Pfeffer and Anson
BB	Healy 2, Gore 1
K	Healy 2, Gore 1
Time	1:30
Umpire	Quest

have something left in that young arm. But shortly after Independence Day, Flynn found himself unemployed once again. The trail leads back to his native Northeast where he probably played a season or two before finally going into business in Lawrence, his home town, where, at 43 he died in 1907.

Though the details are as vague as the record books of those early years, of this much we can be certain: John Flynn, the rocket-armed rookie of the Chicago White Stockings who disarmed the National League in 1886, would surely have made Bill Deane's Hypothetical Rookie of the Year list — booze or no booze — had baseball historian Deane chosen to go back into the 1800s with his provocative list. Flynn was truly a one and only, and his major league career, if indeed it can be called a career, was a bittersweet affair, filled with the exuberance and superior achievement of a gifted youth, and the sadness of its untimely demise.

Top Rookies in the Union Association and in the Player's League

During the 1880s and into the 1890 season a number of leagues vied for the top baseball players of the day. The American Association, which remained competitive for ten seasons, was the National League's number one rival. The Union Association and the Player's League each lasted only one year. In these three leagues there were some prominent players, many of whom wound up in the National League after the leagues were disbanded. These are the top five rookie seasons in each.

The Top 5 Rookies in the Union Association, 1884

William "Buster" Hoover, 1.5 TPR, Philadelphia   of   .364 BA   -1 FR

Henry Boyle, 0.8 TPR, St. Louis	of	.260 BA	0 FR
William "Yank" Robinson, 0.7 TPR, Baltimore	3b	.267 BA	16 FR
Bill Krieg, 0.4 TPR, Chicago-Pittsburgh	c	.247 BA	15 FR
Perry Werden, 0.2 TPR, St. Louis	RHP	W12–L1	1.97 ERA

The Top 5 Rookies in the Player's League, 1890

Bill Dayley, 1.1 TPR, Boston	LHP	W18–L7	3.60 ERA
Phil Knell, 1.1 TPR, Philadelphia	LHP	W22–L11	3.83 ERA
Tom Kinslow, 0.7 TPR, Brooklyn	c	.264	11 FR
Charlie Bartson, 0.6 TPR, Chicago	RHP	W9–L10	4.11 ERA
Willie McGill, 0.1 TPR, Cleveland	LHP	W11–L9	4.12 ERA

The Top 5 Rookies in the American Association, 1886, Jocko Flynn's Rookie Year

Joseph Mack, 1.5 TPR, Louisville	2b	.244	6 FR
Nat Hudson, 0.9 TPR, St. Louis	RHP	W16–L10	3.03 ERA
Matt Kilroy, 0.4 TPR, Baltimore	LHP	W29–L34	3.37 ERA
Chip McGarr, 0.0 TPR, Philadelphia	ss–1b	.266	1 FR
Joe Werrick, -0.3, Louisville	3b	.250	-1 FR

Christopher "The Big Six" or "Matty" Mathewson

TPR: 4.1

1901, New York, NL

Born: August 12, 1880, Factoryville, PA; Died: October 7, 1925, Saranac Lake, NY
RHP, 6'1.5" 205 lb. Major League Debut: July 17, 1900
1901: 40 GP; 38/36 GS/GC; W20, L17; .541 W%; 221/97 K/BB; 33 PR; 8 PD; 2.41 ERA
Hall of Fame: 1936

There was big baseball news as the century turned. In 1901 a new league appeared on the baseball horizon, and a new personality hit New York, as well as the National League, with the full force of peerless talent and spotless character. The new league was named the American, and Christy Mathewson was the name of New York's latest sensation. The two would soon be matched in a 1905 World Series that all but cinched the young Pennsylvanian's ultimate resting place at Cooperstown among the game's hallowed titans. Although that gets us a little ahead of our story, it's altogether proper in the case of Mr. Christopher Mathewson to set the record straight right from the top. This is no "ordinary" Hall of Famer, and even though his first major league season was a few light years removed from his career apex, a zenith that stretched across an electrifying decade, that Mathewson name —

and a precious few like it — is what makes the Hall of Fame not merely the national pastime's repository of plaques, stats and memorabilia — but of the myth that makes it baseball's treasurehouse.

But back to 1901. On February 12 of that year Ban Johnson, the president of the newly organized American League, announced that if the league were to have waited for the older and well-established National League to acknowledge its major league status (or that it was even around), it would have remained a minor league forever.

"The American League will be the principal organization of the country within a very short time. Mark my prediction!" said the new circuit's leader. Those were, of course, the fightin' words that set the stage for a seriously unhealthy and acrimonious relationship. But the die had been cast, and by mid–March the new league announced its rosters. The American

172

League had contracted 185 men to fill out its rosters; no less than 111 of them were former National Leaguers. The war was on. But not for Christy Mathewson.

Few could have forecast at the time that the young man who was entering his rookie season (there had been three starts and just over 30 innings of major league pitching in 1901 as an introduction to the Bigs with the Giants) was on the cusp of the kind of career that was, after all the years of brawling, course vulgarities and gambling associated with the game, worth emulating. A new force was about to make itself felt, a force that would be morally circumspect in every respect, *and* dominating in its grip on National League hitters, teams, and, yes, even the owners. But Matty's loyalty to his team and to his contractual obligation was unswerving. Now that was refreshing.

Matty's career didn't begin in a blaze of glory. Baseball history's elite seldom hit it big right off the bat. Truly great leaders and heroes usually come through adversity to the rewards of superior achievement. That was the Mathewson prescription. There was a mediocre beginning (at least by later Matty standards), a brief struggle with one of his managers, Horace Fogal, about whether he might be better off at first base than pitching, and a taste of eighth place dregs in the first three years of his career.

His debut, on July 17, 1900, was made in a game against Brooklyn at the old Washington Park Grounds (below). The lineups that day showcased four future Hall of Famers: Joe McGinnity (the winning pitcher), Joe Kelley, George Davis and Mathewson, the only Giant HOFer.

Other than its noteworthiness just

Box Score #1

New York Giants at Washington Park, Brooklyn, July 17, 1900

New York	AB	R	H	PO	A
Van Haltren, cf	5	2	3	6	0
Selbach, lf	5	0	1	2	0
Doyle, 1b	5	1	2	10	0
Smith, rf	3	1	2	1	0
Davis, ss	3	1	0	1	0
Grady, 2b	4	1	1	2	0
Hickman, 3b	4	1	0	0	5
Bowerman, c	4	0	2	2	1
Doheny, p	2	0	0	0	0
Mathewson, p	2	0	0	0	2
Totals	37	7	11	24	8

Brooklyn	AB	R	H	PO	A
F. Jones, cf	4	2	1	2	0
Sheckard, rf	2	3	0	2	0
Demont, 2b	3	2	2	1	2
Kelley, lf	3	2	2	4	0
Dahlen, ss	4	0	0	3	2
Cross, 3b	4	1	1	3	1
Daly, 1b	4	1	0	6	1
Farrell, c	4	0	0	5	1
McGinnity, p	5	2	3	1	1
Totals	33	13	9	27	8

New York   200   301   001   7-11-5
Brooklyn   001   155   10x   13-9-4

2BH	Smith 2, Doyle, Demont, Van Haltren
SH	Demont 2
SB	Selbach, Grady, Bowerman, Cross, Kelley, Demont
DP	Dahlen and Daly
BB	Doheny 4, Mathewson 2, McGinnity 2
K	Doheny 0, Mathewson 1, McGinnity 4
HBP	Doheny 1, Mathewson 3, McGinnity 1
WP	Doheny
PB	Bowerman 2
Umpire	Swartwood
Time	2:31

"The Big Six," Christy Mathewson. (Colgin Photo.)

Matty was on the mound. Manager George Davis, in his ninth year with the club and first full season as its skipper, had but one pitcher who won more than he lost. That was Mathewson. The rest, fourteen of them, all had losing records that contributed, finally, to an abysmal 52 and 85 record. In 1902 helmsman Davis found solace in the American League, and Mathewson found himself surrounded by different teammates at every last position, so thorough was the housecleaning! Mathewson lost 17 times in 1901 to run his record to 20 losses as a big leaguer. But he also won 20 in 1901. On the next page is a rundown on the first 20 of Matty's 373 big time conquests.

The no-hitter against the Cardinals came on July 15 in St. Louis, the first of two major league no-hitters. The second was thrown in Chicago on June 13, 1905. In that game the score was 1 to 0. The 1901 no-hitter box score follows on the next page.

Matty's no-no came just beyond the mid-point of his freshman campaign. By that time he was already at the 15 and 7 mark while his team was under .500 and heading farther south. Still a month away from his 21st birthday, the young whiz was well on his way to 20 wins. During the final six to seven weeks of the season, however, the trip was a good deal bumpier, as he finished out the season with another 10 losses against only 5 victories. The final tally read 20 and 17. There were obviously a few things left to learn.

By the time his magnificent, three-shutout stunner in the 1905 World Series was over, it was manifestly evident that a few things, indeed, *had* been learned. From that point on, his Hall of Fame career was

because it was Christy's first major league game, it might further be noted that John McGraw's most famous pitching duo was linked, as Joe McGinnity pitched for the Superbas. It wouldn't take long to have McGraw, then at St. Louis in the midst of a .337 year, and the two legendary right-handers, McGinnity and Mathewson, all united in what was baseball's most prominent "Three Ms." They were to run rough-shod over both leagues at one time or another during the first decade of the new century.

There were enough evidences of Mathewson's brilliance already in his first full season for all to see that a career of immense achievement was about to set sail. Let's begin with a season-opening, eight straight victories that provided one of the Giants' weaker, early 1900s entries with a modicum of respectability, at least when

Win#/Tm/Score   Comment

1.	Brk	5–3	4-hitter; April 26; 8 K's; beat Wild Bill Donovan
2.	Phl	3–2	At Baker Bowl; 3-hitter; beat Al Orth
3.	Bos	2–1	At South End Grounds; 3-hitter; beat Kid Nichols
4.	Phl	4–0	First ML shutout; K'd 7; beat Red Donahue
5.	Brk	7–0	At Washington Park; 2-hitter; beat Bill Kennedy
6.	Chi	3–0	Gave up nine hits; beat Jack Taylor
7.	Pit	2–1	K'd 3; beat Deacon Phillippe
8.	Cin	1–0	3-hitter; beat Bill Phillips
9.	Bos	2–1	K'd 10; beat Kid Nichols
10.	StL	3–2	K'd 7; 6-hitter; beat Willie Sudhoff
11.	Cin	6–2	Allowed 9 hits; K'd 6; beat Dick Scott
12.	Chi	14–1	4-hitter; beat Rube Waddell
13.	Pit	5–3	12-inning game at Exposition Park; beat Jack Chesbro
14.	Cin	9–3	At League Park; 6-hitter; beat Dick Scott
15.	StL	5–0	At Robison Park; *no-hitter*; beat Willie Sudhoff
16.	Bos	9–8	At South End Grounds; gave up 9 hits; beat Kid Nichols
17.	Brk	4–1	Gave up 9 hits; K'd 9; beat Jim Hughes
18.	Phl	3–1	At Baker Bowl; 5 BB; 7 K's; beat Red Donahue
19.	StL	5–1	5-hitter, 8 K's; beat Ed Murphy
20.	Cin	5–1	At League Park, September 21; beat Bill Phillips

on automatic pilot, and shortly afterward, when he began to be called "The Big Six," it was just a matter of summing up the final numbers to send on to Cooperstown, where he was inducted with the Class of '36, the first group to be enshrined in the pantheon of baseball's greats.

What made that all possible from a

Box Score #2

New York at Robison Field, St. Louis, July 15, 1901

New York	AB	R	H	PO	A
Van Haltren, cf	5	1	2	1	0
Selbach, lf	4	1	2	1	0
McBride, rf	3	1	1	1	0
Davis, 3b	3	0	1	0	3
Ganzel, 1b	4	0	0	14	1
Hickman, ss	4	1	2	2	6
Strang, 2b	4	1	2	1	2
Warner, c	3	0	0	5	1
Mathewson, p	4	0	0	2	3
Totals	34	5	10	27	16

St. Louis	AB	R	H	PO	A
Burkett, lf	3	0	0	0	0
Donovan, rf	4	0	0	2	0
Schriver, 1b	3	0	0	10	3
Padden, 2b	2	0	0	3	5
Wallace, ss	3	0	0	4	3
Krueger, 3b	3	0	0	2	2
Ryan, c	3	0	0	4	1
Nichols, cf	3	0	0	0	0
Sudhoff, p	3	0	0	2	3
Totals	27	0	0	27	17

New York   220   000   001   5-10-1
St. Louis   000   000   000   0-0-1

SB	Van Haltren
SH	Davis, Warner
LOB	New York 5, St. Louis 3
BB	Mathewson 4, Sudhoff 2
K	Mathewson 4, Sudhoff 3
WP	Mathewson (15–7)
LP	Sudhoff (7–5)
Umpire	Dwyer
Time	1:35
Att	5,008

pitching standpoint was a razor-sharp curve, that much ballyhooed "fadeaway" (a pitch that would later become known as a screwball, breaking in on right-handed batters and falling away from the lefties), a spitter (legal until the 1920s), and a fastball which, if clocked today, would range into the 90s. A number of these pitches were thrown at varying speeds, which in the hands of a master craftsman made for a devastating mix.

But there was still another dimension that topped off the Mathewson arsenal, fitting all the pieces together. That was intelligence. In a little piece entitled "My Thoughts On Pitching," written late in his career, here is what Mathewson himself had to say about "pitching with your head as well as your arm: I have found that a pitcher, in order to make the grade in the major leagues, must be able to use his intelligence. Every individual batsman represents a new problem. A pitcher must make a study of each of his opponents. He must be clever enough to recognize their weak spots, and his memory must be strong enough to catalogue these weaknesses for future reference."

The whole package, as we are prone to label it today, took a little time to develop, and it was, quite obviously, not entirely in place during Matty's rookie season, but even then, it was a year of more than middling accomplishment. To begin with,

there were 38 starts and 36 complete games. There were 5 shutouts (including the July 15 no-hitter), 20 victories, and an earned run average of 2.41, which was almost a full run below the league average. Additionally, he ranked among the top five pitchers in the following categories:

- Appearances   40 (5th)
- Innings Pitched   336.0 (5th)
- Pitching Runs   33 (4th)
- TPR   4.1 (4th)
- Ks per Game   5.92 (3rd)
- Complete Games   36 (3rd)
- Opponents' BA   .230 (2nd)
- Hits per Game   7.71 (2nd)

Beyond all the superlatives lavished on the many talents Christy Mathewson possessed, there is yet another that begs mention. The statistic line for Matty's 1901 season also bears a notation on PD, that is, the pitcher as a fielder, or pitcher defense. The rating is 8, the highest rating recorded for 1901 (Nixey Callahan, Chicago righthander rated a 6 for second place). And what does this mean? "The Big Six" fielded his position as well as he pitched, and that was a considerable achievement. Brought into the mix in calculating a pitcher's TPR, this variable weighs in with real punch in the overall rating, thus enabling recognition for this vital part of a pitcher's game. Here again, Mathewson had it.

1901: Ten Top Rookies

Nm/Pos/Tm	GP	W–L/BA	SH/SV//RBI	PR/BR	ERA/FR	TPR
Mathewson/RHP/NY-N	38	20–17	5/0	33	2.41	4.1
R. Miller/RHP/Det-A	38	23–13	3/1	33	2.95	3.5
Parent/ss/Bos-A	138	.306	59	12	0	2.1
Conroy/ss/Mil-A	131	.256	64	-7	19	1.9
Winter/RHP/Bos-A	28	16–12	1/0	20	2.80	1.5
J. Farrell/UT/Was-A	135	.272	63	1	17	1.4
Siever/LHP/Det-A	38	18–15	2/0	19	3.24	1.3
G. White/LHP/Phl-N	31	14–13	0/0	5	3.19	1.3
Maloney/c/Mil-A	86	.293	22	-5	9	0.9
A. Davis/of/Brk-Pit-N	112	.291	40	26	2	0.7
Harvey/of-p/Chi-Clv-A	62	.333	27	9	3	0.7

John Michael (Paveskovich) Pesky

TPR: 4.1

1942, Boston, AL

Born: September 27, 1919, Portland, OR
ss, 5'9" 168 lb. Major League Debut: April 14, 1942
1942: 147 GP; 620-105-205, AB-R-H; .331 BA; 29 2BH; 14 BR; 18 FR; .375 OB%

For all the good days Johnny Pesky enjoyed in St. Louis at Sportsman's Park, and there are many good ones to pick from, one day tends to overshadow them all. That would be October 15, 1946, when Enos Slaughter scored from first base in the seventh game of the World Series to win the Classic for the Cardinals. Strange how one play can color a career. Strange, but true. It's happened many times before and since.

There are a number of versions about Slaughter's dash and the little Red Sox pepperpot's relay throw to catcher Roy Partee. None ever changed the outcome. And as for John Michael Pesky, he moved on, looking back rarely while putting together an otherwise scintillating major league career of ten seasons, the first eight of which were spent with the team he served as player, coach, manager, scout, front-office executive, TV color man, instructor-at-large, and personnel evaluator.

If there were any other positions not mentioned above, rest assured that he filled those as well in a carmine colored career that covered a half-century of distinguished service. For all of that — and more — the Oregonian was awarded Boston's "Good Guy" award in 1982. And rightly so.

But our interest is in the beginnings, and though it is comforting to know that the Pesky story would have a pleasant ending, the years before 1946 are the ones that command our attention. Those are the years during which Johnny Pesky prepared for, and then broke into, the major leagues.

Any time a rookie breaks in with a 200-hit season, something very special has been achieved. The list of those who have accomplished that particular feat is very short, including just 13 names since 1900. Pesky's 206 bingos in 1942 ties him for seventh on that list. Further, he has the rare

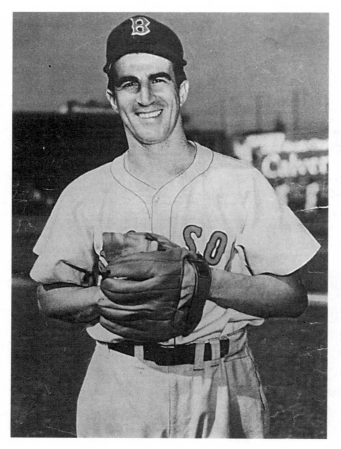

Johnny Pesky, hustling Bosox shortstop. (Colgin Photo.)

a pesky little fellow who came up with balls around the infield he had no right getting at, as well as making a general nuisance of himself as a hitter. That kind of play will eventually attract the bird-dogs, and it did. A Lincoln High School star in Portland, he was wooed by Red Sox, Yankee, Dodger, Cardinal, Brownie and Tiger scouts before finally settling on the Red Sox, even though the Yankees' bid was better.

That brings us to 1940 and Rocky Mount, North Carolina, where, in his first year of organized baseball, he led the Piedmont League in base hits, 187 of them, and captured a berth on the league's All-Star team. The Pesky style was already in place and the numbers told the story: 435 assists in 136 games, 95 double plays, a .325 BA (third in the league), and 16 triples (league high). A promotion was in order.

The Bosox moved their hustling midfielder along to Louisville for the 1941 season. It was a sizeable leap from the Piedmont League to the American Association. If he could make the move without falling on his backside, perhaps a season or two in Louisville would get him ready for the Big Show. Joe Cronin, the incumbent shortstop whose Hall of Fame career was winding down, would be available for another year or two in any case, so if the rising young star could just hold his own, the plan for his future at Fenway might have enough leeway in it to make it work.

Johnny Pesky didn't quite see it that way. His plan had very little, if any, leeway in it. He would take the challenge head-on and make it work, and by the end of the

distinction of being the only player who amassed 200 or more hits each of his first three seasons with 205 in 1942, 208 in 1946 (on his return from military service), and 207 in 1947. That 1942 achievement was one of the many reasons he was named Hypothetical Rookie of the Year on the Bill Deane list.

Pesky, whose original family name was Paveskovich, inherited a name that didn't fit into the box scores of Portland's or any other town's newspaper. Johnny simply changed it to make it possible to fit the new name in there with all the other players.

So the Paveskovich solution was Pesky, a name that was also descriptive of his play on a ball diamond. He was indeed

1941 season his play at Louisville was so convincing that in the front office at Boston there was no room left for conjecture. He certainly had the American Association sportswriters convinced. Another .325 season, infield play that demonstrated his baseball smarts, and, above all, his poise, persuaded them to select Pesky for the league's MVP Award. Back at Fenway the decision was made: move Mr. Pesky up to the varsity roster. At the Sarasota, Florida, spring training base the Red Sox would sort out just what that would mean for the team's 1942 lineup. Pesky was ready.

During Johnny's award-winning season at Louisville, New York's Yanks had stormed the American League, and though the Red Sox finished the season in second place, they were a distant 17 games off the New Yorkers' scorching pace. Yet, the Back Bay ballclub went south with realistic hopes of winning the pennant in 1942. There was, however, one unknown that was about to play havoc with every team's plans.

The war clouds that gathered in 1940 and 1941 broke loose to unleash their full fury on America, the full effect already felt in 1942. Literally everything was affected — including baseball. Under the prevailing circumstances everyone concerned would have to make do, rolling with one punch after another, while the major effort of the nation was directed at providing the all-consuming necessities of wartime. Some of the big names in baseball were already gone. More would follow.

The 1942 season, then, was the last that bore any resemblance to prewar baseball, and even then, players like Bobby Feller and Hank Greenberg had already left huge holes in their teams' rosters with early departures for the military. But as the teams gathered for spring training the wholesale movement of players had not yet begun. Joe DiMaggio and Joe Gordon of New York's defending World Champions, Stan Musial, Johnny Mize, and John VanderMeer, among many others, would be on hand to see the season through before leaving for Army, Navy, Marine, or Air Force duty. And before 1942 was over Johnny Pesky would be one of them.

There was still another force at work helping to shape the 1942 season. It served, at least somewhat, to counter-balance the effect of the war on baseball manpower.

By the late 1930s and early 1940s, the farm systems developed by major league franchises began to pay huge dividends. Promising ballplayers, many of them veterans by the time they reached the Bigs, began to arrive in numbers with each new season. All of them, the younger and older players alike, made for a highly competitive situation as spring training season rolled around. And 1942 produced a bumper crop filled with Beazleys and Borowys — and Peskys.

Although they trimmed the Yankees' sails to a certain extent in 1942, the Bosox ended that season in the same spot, second, as in 1941. The pennant-winning Bronx Bombers had enough hitting from Joe DiMaggio and their MVP second baseman Joe Gordon to go along with enough pitching and defense to win the blue ribbon by nine games over Boston's hard-hitting Carmine. But Boston's boys did hit. They were led by Navy-bound Triple Crown Winner Ted Williams, who was supported by Pesky's .331, Bobby Doerr and Dom DiMaggio. Their team batting average paced both leagues at .276. So, too, did their on-base percentage at .352 and team slugging average, .403.

The Red Sox' big right-hander, Tex Hughson, had a monster season with a superb 22 and 6 record. But beyond their ace there wasn't enough top-level pitching to go around. The results were predictable, epitomized early on, when a May 2 game went down to the bottom of the ninth before a Williams cruncher won it, 11 to 10.

The message: either score a ton or lose. The Yankeemen scored enough to win 93 games. The Yankees won 103. The Bosox settled for second-place money.

On July 24 the Red Sox played a doubleheader at Sportsman's Park in St. Louis. They split with the third-place Brownies, winning the opener, 5 to 3, behind a two-run, Johnny Pesky four-bagger. There weren't that many Pesky homers (17 in his entire career, to be exact), but he caught up with one of Al Hollingsworth's deliveries and put it in the seats. You might well imagine that the Pesky home run trot was developed in a hurry that day, not having had any prior occasion to practice it!

So the singles hitter enjoyed his first major league tater. And that brings up one of those clubhouse stories ballplayers are forever telling. Before a mid-summer game in Chicago a number of players were standing around the batting cage, including Luke Appling and Williams, who was the next hitter. Appling, who was watching Johnny Pesky take his cuts, said to Williams, "So this is the guy who's hittin' .340? How does he get his hits?" Williams replied, "See those dribblers and loopers?

Box Score

Boston Red Sox at Sportsman's Park, St. Louis, July 24, 1942

Boston	AB	R	H	PO	A
D. DiMaggio, cf	5	0	0	3	0
Pesky, ss	4	2	2	3	5
Lupien, 1b	3	1	0	8	0
Williams, lf	4	0	1	5	1
Doerr, 2b	3	0	1	3	3
Cronin, 3b	4	0	2	1	2
Tabor, 3b	0	0	0	0	0
Fox, rf	4	1	2	0	0
Conroy, c	3	0	0	4	0
Chase, p	3	1	0	0	0
Hughson, p	1	0	0	0	1
Totals	34	5	8	27	12

St. Louis	AB	R	H	PO	A
Gutteridge, 2b	5	0	1	2	3
Clift, 3b	5	0	2	1	2
McQuinn, 1b	5	0	1	11	1
Judnich, cf	3	0	0	1	0
Berardino, ph	1	0	0	0	0
Criscola, rf	1	0	1	1	0
Stephens, ss	4	1	1	2	2
Laabs, rf	4	1	2	1	0
McQuillen, lf	4	1	2	2	0
R. Ferrell, c	4	0	2	6	2
Muncrief, p	1	0	1	0	2
Heffner, ph	1	0	0	0	0
Hollingsworth, p	0	0	0	0	1
Sundra, p	2	0	1	0	3
Totals	40	3	14	27	16

Boston	002	002	001	5-8-1
St. Louis	011	000	100	3-14-3

2BH	Laabs, Clift
HR	Pesky, Stephens, Fox
SH	Lupien
LOB	Boston 5, St. Louis 12
DP	Cronin and Conroy; Clift, Gutteridge, McQuinn; Sundra, Ferrell, McQuinn
BB	Chase 2; Muncrief 1; Sundra, Hollingsworth, Hughson 0
K	Chase 3; Muncrief 3; Sundra 2; Hughson, Hollingsworth 0
HBP	Hollingsworth (Doerr)
Balk	Chase
WP	Chase
Win. P	Chase
Sv	Hughson
LP	Hollingsworth
Time	2:12
Umpires	Hubbard, McGowan and Stewart
Att	20,812

Those are his hits. All I know is, almost every time I look up, he's out there dancing around on first."

Johnny Pesky finished his Boston career in 1952 when a huge swap brought George Kell, among others, to Boston. During his seven-plus seasons with the Carmine (he lost three years of playing time to military service), he hit .313, played superlative ball at both short and third, and beyond his considerable baseball abilities was a consummate professional, a credit to baseball in general and to the Red Sox in particular.

1942: Ten Top Rookies

Nm/Pos/Tm	GP	W–L/BA	SH/SV//RBI	PR/BR	ERA/FR	TPR
Pesky/ss/Bos-A	147	.331	51	14	18	4.1
Beazley/RHP/StL-N	43	21–6	3/3	31	2.13	4.0
H. White/RHP/Det-A	34	12–12	4/1	25	2.91	2.6
Musial/of/StL-N	140	.315	72	28	1	2.4
Trucks/RHP/Det-A	28	14–8	2/0	23	2.74	2.3
Borowy/RHP/NY-A	25	15–4	4/1	18	2.52	1.9
Fleming/1b/Clv-A	156	.292	82	38	-9	1.7
Holmes/of/Bos-N	141	.278	41	8	15	1.7
Kurowski/3b/StL-N	115	.254	42	0	9	1.1
Butland/LHP/Bos-A	23	7–1	2/1	15	2.51	1.0

Pedro "Tony" Oliva

TPR: 4.1

1964, Minnesota, AL

Born: July 20, 1940, Pinar Del Rio, Cuba
of; 6'2" 190 lb. Major League Debut: September 9, 1962
1964: 672-109-217 AB-R-H; .323 BA; 43 2BH; 94 RBI; .557 SA; 42 BR; 5 FR; .981 FA

How does a person named Pedro become Tony? Well, it's easy if you have a brother by that name and need a passport. You just use his name and then make the trip from Cuba to play ball in the U.S.A.

To make what was a long story much shorter, let's simply say that the all-important passport was the link "Tony O," as he would soon be called, needed to get to the U.S.A. to play major league baseball some day. That's what his goal was, and that's what it all came down to.

We're talking about Tony Oliva, the gifted Latino who could hit falling out of bed. He's the one who became the first rookie in the American League's history to win a batting crown. In itself, that was quite an accomplishment, something which, incidentally, was achieved before in the National League back there a baseball eon ago, in 1882, by Pete Browning, and before that by Abner Dalrymple in 1878. Three times in almost 125 years makes such a rarity more than notable.

The Oliva odyssey began in 1961, the

year the transplanted Twins finished in no-man's land in the American League standings. During their first season in the Twin Cities the team moved Sam Mele into the manager's slot, replacing skipper Cookie Lavagetto. The Twins bounced up to a second-place finish behind New York with a 91–71 record in 1962, and then slipped a notch to third in 1963 while drawing another million-plus, wildly supportive Minnesotans. Having raised expectations to a straining point, Cal Griffith, the front office link between the original franchise home in Washington and the brave new baseball world "out there" in Minnesota, had his new following primed for a championship in 1964. It didn't happen, but what did happen was the arrival of the 1964 Rookie of the Year, Tony Oliva.

During Minnesota's first three seasons in the Twin Cities, Tony O was groomed for the Bigs "down on the farm," which, in the sparse Twins' system meant slim pickin's from among seven spots on the baseball map. At the bottom of the list was Wytheville, Virginia, the Twins' rookie league entry in the Appalachian League. That was OK with Tony. His appreciation showed up in the form of a blistering, league leading batting average of .410. Sweeping the boards in most of the league's hitting departments, he was selected to the All-Star team and voted the league's MVP. When the full story was told at headquarters in the Twin Cities, there were more than a few raised eyebrows. The consensus: move the Cuban phenom onward and upward to the Class A Sally League to see if he could come reasonably close to his 1961 numbers in faster company.

With a last place ballclub at Charlotte, Tony spent another summer knocking the seams off the horsehide with a sizzling .350. He was rewarded with another all-star team selection. In the front office the decision was made to bring him to Metropolitan Stadium for an at-bat or two against major league pitching. A strong 4-for-9 day was Tony's response. Those raised eyebrows of a year ago turned into knowing grins this time around. The consensus for 1963: one more year of seasoning, this time in the Pacific Coast League at the Twins' top farm club in Dallas–Ft. Worth. This time around the fast Triple A company did slow the Latin-American slasher down a little, but his batting average hung up there over .300, not all that far behind the league's leader, Chico Salmon, at .325. One final, season-ending trip to Paul Bunyanland resulted in a little more spot-duty, and a 3-for-7 record at the plate. That moved his two-year log in Twins' livery to a snazzy 7 for 16 (.438). There was nothing left to prove. Oliva would go to the Orlando spring training base in 1964 as a Twin outfielder. Tony's lifelong ambition had been fulfilled. Now it remained for him to make good on his golden opportunity.

The Twins opened up at Cleveland in

1964 with a 7 to 6 victory won by Jim Perry in relief of the Hispanic curveballer, Camilo Pascual, a 20-game winner in 1963. Manager Sam Mele had Oliva in the second spot of the batting order, playing right field. That's where Tony O was to be found on the last day of the season, as well. He had played in every game on the schedule. And while the Twins opened the season in first place at least for a day, they found enough ways to mismanage their chances for one of the top rungs on the league's ladder, settling for sixth place in the ten-team Junior Circuit.

There was an icon in the '64 Twins lineup. His name was Harmon Killibrew, one of the franchises all-time greats, a home run hitter of rare distinction, and one of the very few to blast more than 500 career round-trippers into American League grandstands. "Killer," as he was called, began wondering a few seasons earlier just what it would take to win all the marbles — if only once. More than one established star had, of course, been frustrated in search of pennant gold. Having come close in 1962 and 1963, Killebrew hoped that with an addition here or there to a power-laden nucleus of returning veterans, the Twins might just get it done.

Killibrew, Jimmie Hall and Bob Allison formed the Twins' outfield in 1963. To make room for Oliva, Mele moved Allison to first base. Putting Oliva, a strong-throwing right fielder into the mix, tightened the outfield defense and jacked up the quality of the entire ballclub perceptibly. It was the pitching, however, that faltered. Two mid-season trades brought reliever Al Worthington and Mudcat Grant to Minnesota's pitching corps, but neither could pull the staff out of the mud. That would take another year. Only Jim Kaat improved on his 1963 record, moving from a 10 and 10 mark to 17 and 11 in 1964. Nor was there much help from a so-so defense. The net result, as far as both the team and another

Minnesota's hit machine, Tony Oliva. (Dennis Colgin.)

Vern Handrahan, whose job was to put an end to the blood-letting. That was a tough assignment considering who the next hitter was. Standing at the plate to greet him was "The Killer," Harmon Killibrew. A few pitches later the Twins had their fourth straight run on four straight four-baggers — Oliva, Allison, Hall and Killibrew all having homered. That was more than enough. The Twins won it 7 to 3.

There aren't many secrets in the Bigs. Word got around about as fast as one of Tony's ropes made it to the outfield. The Cuban was a player. So the pitchers did what pitchers usually do. That meant loosening up the hitter with a calling card or two. A number of those calling cards put Oliva in real jeopardy, just too close for comfort as far as Twins owner Cal Griffith was concerned. He ordered production of a special, beaning-proof batting helmet for Oliva and sent down the order to make certain his budding star wore it.

That was an important adjustment but not the only one Tony had to make as he made his way around the league. Hitting as well as he did — right from the start — didn't make things any easier, and there was a great deal to learn about which pitchers threw what, when and how. There are some rookies who absorb everything thrown their way, and in a hurry. Some don't, and that has its own consequences, meaning another hitch in the minors. Señor Pedro Oliva didn't need that trip.

Tony followed the Twins' May 2 homerfest with a grand slam against the Angels several days later. It was the first of

million-plus fans (the 1964 attendance mark, however, was down by over 200,000) were concerned, was disappointing, to say the very least.

But there was no disappointment registered over Tony O. By May everybody in the Twin Cities knew their new right fielder was there to stay. One day in the merry month of May was all Tony needed to set the Twins' faithful into ecstasy. Leading off in the top of the 11th on May 2 against Kansas City, he sent one of Danny Pfister's best into the far reaches of the ballpark to get things going. That was followed by a baseball rarity. Bob Allison followed the Oliva blast with one of his own. Jimmie Hall, the next batter, hit a Pfister pitch into the cheap seats as well, making it three straight. Royals manager Eddie Lopat next replaced Pfister with reliever

Box Score

Minnesota Twins at Kansas City, May 2, 1964

Minnesota	AB	R	H	BI	E
Rollins, 3b	5	1	1	0	0
Oliva, rf	5	2	4	3	0
Allison, 1b	5	1	1	1	0
Hall, cf	5	1	1	1	0
Killibrew, lf	5	2	2	2	0
Green, lf	0	0	0	0	0
Battey, c	5	0	2	0	0
Versalles, ss	5	0	0	0	0
Allen, 2b	4	0	0	0	0
Stange, p	3	0	0	0	0
Dailey, p	0	0	0	0	0
Fischer, p	0	0	0	0	0
Pleis, p	0	0	0	0	0
Mincher, ph	1	0	0	0	0
Arrigo, p	0	0	0	0	0
Totals	43	7	11	7	0

Kansas City	AB	R	H	BI	E
Mathews, cf	5	0	0	0	0
Causey, ss	5	0	0	0	0
Charles, 3b	5	2	3	0	0
Gentile, 1b	2	0	0	0	0
Colavito, rf, lf	4	1	1	1	0
Lau, c	4	0	2	2	0
Reynolds, lf	2	0	1	0	0
Jiminez, ph	1	0	0	0	0
Cimoli, rf	1	0	0	0	0
J. Tartabull, rf	1	0	0	0	0
D. Green, 2b	3	0	0	0	0
Alusik, ph	0	0	0	0	0
G. Williams, 2b	1	0	0	0	0
Monteagudo, p	2	0	1	0	0
Wyatt, p	0	0	0	0	0
Bryan, ph	1	0	0	0	0
Pfister, p	0	0	0	0	0
Handrahan, p	0	0	0	0	0
Totals	39	3	8	3	0

```
Minnesota     002  000  001  04   7-11-0
Kansas City   000  000  201  00   3-8-0
```

2BH	Battey, Charles
3BH	Lau
HR	Oliva 2, Killibrew 2, Allison, Hall
SB	Charles
LOB	Minnesota 4, Kansas City 8
DP	Monteagudo, Causey, D. Green; Allen, Versalles, Allison; Rollins, Allen, Allison
BB	Stange 3, Fischer 2, Monteagudo 1; Dailey, Pleis, Arrigo, Wyatt, Pfister, Handrahan 0
K	Stange 4, Pleis, 1, Arrigo 2, Monteagudo 2, Wyatt 3, Handrahan 1; Dailey, Fischer, Pfister 0
PB	Battey
WP	Arrigo (1–0)
LP	Pfister (0–1)
Umpires	Flaherty, Carrigan, Hall, Hurley
Time	3:13
Att	8,159

three he hit during his 15-year career with the Twins.

By the end of May the Minnesotans stood at the 24 and 19 mark, and as they headed into July the team was still above the .500 level at 39 and 35. However, during the month of July that less than sensational pitching began to register in the win-loss column as they were winners only 11 times in 29 tries. Tony Oliva, however, was headed in the opposite direction, putting together a 17-game hitting streak between July 16 and August 1. He was up there leading the hitting pack, piling up a record number of at-bats, hits and total bases en route to his batting championship. One of the special events along the way was an inside-the-park dinger on

- At bats/runs/hits   672/109/206   all rookie records
- Total Bases   374   club and rookie record
- Games/2-Base Hits   161/43   rookie record and league leader
- Bill Boni Award   club rookie of the year
- C. R. Griffith Award   club MVP
- RY Award   BBWAA, AL Rookie of the Year
- *TSN* Award   *Sporting News* RY Award

Uncle Sammy's Day that got the month of July underway with an appropriate display of power and speed.

Ultimately, the Twins wound up in a sixth-place tie with Cleveland, a disappointing 20 games behind New York's AL champions. But just as the Twins' fans thought the team was headed farther south, along came 1965 and a complete turnaround, and voilà, a World Series came to Bunyanland, spurred by another Oliva batting crown. The young Hispanic hero had moved from Cuba to Rookie of the Year to pennant winner — all in the space of a few short years.

Among the many outstanding numbers and honors registered by the Twins' rookie sensation, these few, shown above, will help spell out the special year that 1964 was.

Tony Oliva's distinguished 15-year career was honored in many ways, but principally by the retirement of his number 6 on July 14, 1991. It's safe to say that his ambitions and goals as a baseball player were realized in an indescribably fulfilled way. It couldn't have happened to a nicer fellow.

1964: Ten Top Rookies

Nm/Pos/Tm	GP	W–L/BA	SH/SV//RBI	PR/BR	ERA/FR	TPR
R. Allen/3b/Phl-N	162	.318	91	52	7	5.8
Oliva/of/Min-A	161	.331	94	42	5	4.1
Carty/of/Mil-N	133	.330	88	37	1	3.3
Knoop/2b/LA-A	162	.216	38	-23	37	2.8
Hart/3b/SF-N	153	.286	81	23	4	2.7
R. Lee/RP-RHP/LA-A	64	6–5	0/19	27	1.51	2.5
Stottlemyre/RHP/NY-A	13	9–3	2/0	17	2.06	2.5
Bunker/RHP/Bal-A	29	19–5	1/0	21	2.69	2.2
R. Green/2b/KC-A	130	.264	37	-5	17	2.1
Alley/ss/Pit-N	81	.211	13	-8	24	2.0

Note: Fred Newman, RHP, LA-A, missed rookie status by one out, completing 50 and one-third innings for the Angels. His 2.1 TPR was fashioned as follows: 32 GP; won 13 and lost 10; 2 shutouts, no saves; 11 pitching runs; and a 2.75 ERA.

Stephen Douglas "Steve" Rogers

TPR: 4.1

1973 Montreal, NL

Born: October 26, 1949, Jefferson City, MO
RHP, 6'1" 182 lb. Major League Debut: July 18, 1973
1973: W10, L5; .667 W%; 3/0 SH/SV; 9.6 Ratio; .199 OBA; .276 OB%; 34 PR; 1.54 ERA

The number one metropolis in that awesome land to the north of the American border became the home of baseball's first foreign entry into the major leagues. The National League expansion team that debuted at Jarry Park in Montreal on an unseasonably warm and sunny day and beat the St. Louis Cardinals, 8 to 7, on April 14, 1969, was promptly dubbed "Les Expos Nos Amours" by Montreal's sportswriters. And after hosting the first major league game in a championship season played on foreign soil, the Canadians said, "Oui!"

The new franchise opened with three 1969 farm clubs: Vancouver's Mounties of the AAA Pacific Coast League; the West Palm Beach Expos of the Class A Florida State League; and the Expos of the Gulf Coast Rookie League in Florida. It was a modest beginning. However in their first full season the parent Expos wound up with a wretched 52 and 110 record under their long-suffering skipper, Gene Mauch. Those hardy Canadians must have wondered if it might not have been better to go right back to the old days of the International League. Of this much all were convinced: there was a mountain to climb on the way to major league respectability. The tedious and tireless work of drafting, trading, mentoring, contracting and training ballplayers was underway.

During the Expos' first several seasons a number of rookies played well enough to make solid contributions. During that first wearisome season Puerto Rican Coco Laboy won the *Sporting News* Rookie of the Year honors, and the very next year, 1970, Carl Morton copped the BBWAA's Rookie of the Year Award with a staff-leading 18 and 11. That season the ballclub improved from its inaugural season's 52 wins to 73. Though it still wasn't good enough to escape the divisional cellar, there was definitely improvement.

The Expos' hard-throwing Steve Rogers. (Dennis Colgin.)

In 1971 Montreal made the rangy right-hander a top draft choice and dispatched him to their AAA farmclub at Winnipeg. As the rest of the 1971 season unfolded Rogers didn't exactly burn up the International League. Nor did the Whips, who finished dead last and won but 44 games. Steve Rogers pitched about the way the farm club played, finishing the season with a downright lousy 3 and 10 record.

But he had made a start, and the good news was that his control of the strike zone, the zip on his fast one, his command of the pitching game and his competitive fire made him a strong candidate for the big team's roster despite his limited experience and poor record. The Expos' brain trust opted for another crack at the International League level, and though they didn't know it at the time, their decision to stick with their young engineer was a decision for pitching excellence in the long run. Rogers would be their man for many years to come.

During the 1972 season Rogers, assigned once again to the Expos' Triple A farm club, the Whips (for that season they played under the name of the Peninsula Whips), missed seven weeks between April and June, having been placed on the temporarily inactive list. The rest of the season wasn't much of an improvement over his very shaky start in 1971, as he wound up his season with two wins, six losses and a 4.08 ERA.

There was obviously a problem. The intense young hurler just had too much talent to go on limping along as he had

During the 1971 season the Expos came up with another rookie of some merit, a right-hander by the name of Ernie McAnally, who fashioned an 11 and 12 record for Montreal, helping the team move out of the divisional cellar for the first time in its three-season history. That was accomplished by a slight backward skid to 71 wins, but good enough to outdistance a weak Philadelphia team.

However, 1971 was indeed a noteworthy year. Down in Oklahoma there was a Missourian who was completing his degree in petroleum engineering. The young man's name was Stephen Douglas Rogers, and he also pitched for the Tulsa University team with the kind of precision one might expect from an engineer. In fact his career record for Tulsa was a sparkling 31 and 5. And the Expos had their eyes on him.

been. But at least the interruptions in his career, caused by military service commitments, were a thing of the past. Now he could concentrate on the task at hand.

The task at hand was an assignment to the Quebec Carnavals of the Class A Eastern League. In 11 games there his record with a dead last ballclub was 4 and 5. What stuck out, however, was Rogers' intensity. His pitching game was coming together. A workmanlike 2.69 ERA in 11 games was enough of a teaser to move him back into the Triple A arena with another crack at the International League's hitters. By the time four games had gone by Steve Rogers stood at 3 and 1 with an arresting 1.86 ERA. The Rogers portfolio was about complete, including pinpoint control, a slider and his out pitch, a sinker, to go along with his fast one, often clocked in the 90s. And there was another dimension to his game: fielding. Though it surprised him when told that his fielding needed work, he went right at it, simultaneously sharpening his entire pitching game.

As the 1973 season moved to its halfway point the Montreal Expos were discovering what a *real* pennant race was like. In their fifth major league campaign, they found themselves in an Eastern Division race that involved every team except the Phillies. The Expos were in the hunt. But their pitching began to sag as staff leaders Steve Renko and Mike Torrez faltered.

That's when the decision was made to bring Steve Rogers to Montreal. By mid–July the right-hander was ready to go, and Mauch started him on July 18 at Houston. Rogers responded with eight tough frames in a 2 to 2 ball game that went into extra innings. Though Jerry Reuss received credit for the Expos' 11-inning victory, Steve had done the job. His work had lifted the staff in a hurry.

In his second major league start the 23-year-old rookie threw a one-hitter, the

first of four in his major league career, but the one he most fondly remembers. The victory, also his first, completed 17 innings during which he gave up but two earned runs. The win came at the expense of future Hall of Famer Steve Carlton. Rogers' domination of the Phils was bound to get the attention of *les canadiens*, if not the baseball world. It certainly did.

The hottest hand in baseball had arrived. The next time out Rogers edged the Mets, eventual winners of the divisional race, by a spine-tingling margin of 1 to 0, spacing seven hits in a masterful evening's piece of work. Jarry Park fairly exploded in the seventh inning when their newly found hero came to bat. Expo fans had something to cheer about and they gave Steve a standing ovation. And quite suddenly the Expos had a National League Pitcher of the Week (July 26 to August 5) on their hands.

That was followed up by a first in Montreal baseball history: fans jamming the wires to find out when Steve Rogers would be pitching next. With each announcement came a full house. Just several weeks into his major league career young Mr. Roberts had become the team's stopper and most talked-about ballplayer.

During the next three weeks Rogers' shutout total moved to three with a whitewashing of the Dodgers, 4 to 0, on three singles. That inevitable first loss and a couple thereafter, by scores of 2 to 1 and 3 to 2, came at the hands of the Giants. But he had pitched 75 innings since his July arrival, and his ERA had nearly dropped out of sight at 1.20.

Skipper Gene Mauch's trenchant summation of the rookie phenom's work appeared in the September 15 issue of *The Sporting News*:

> Usually, when a man comes up and makes an instant splash, it's because he's a strikeout pitcher. That's happened on a number of occasions. But

Box Score

Montreal at Veterans Stadium, Philadelphia, July 26, 1973

Montreal	AB	R	H	BI	E		Philadelphia	AB	R	H	BI	E
Hunt, 2b	3	0	2	1	0		B. Robinson, rf	4	0	0	0	0
Mashore, lf	5	0	1	0	0		Doyle, 2b	4	0	0	0	0
Woods, cf	4	0	0	0	0		Montanez, 1b	3	0	0	0	0
Breeden, 3b	3	0	0	0	0		Luzinski, lf	3	0	0	0	0
Jorgenson, 1b	1	1	0	0	0		Unser, cf	3	0	0	0	0
Bailey, 1b	4	1	0	0	0		Pagan, 2b	3	0	1	0	1
Singleton, rf	5	1	1	1	0		Boone, c	2	0	0	0	0
Boccabella, c	3	1	2	0	0		Bowa, ss	2	0	0	0	1
Frias, ss	3	0	1	2	0		Rogodzinkski, ph	1	0	0	0	0
Rogers, p	2	0	1	0	0		Harmon, ss	1	0	0	0	0
							Carlton, p	2	0	0	0	1
							Schmidt, ph	1	0	0	0	0
Totals	33	4	8	4	0		Totals	27	0	1	0	3

Montreal	000	000	130	4-8-0
Philadelphia	000	000	000	0-1-3

2BH	Boccabella, Singleton
SH	Frias, Rogers
LOB	Montreal 11, Philadelphia 2
DP	Philadelphia 2
BB	Carlton 7, Rogers 2
K	Carlton 5, Rogers 3
WP	Rogers (1–0)
LP	Carlton (9–11)
Time	2:12
Att	34,459

Rogers isn't doing that. He isn't blowing anybody out of there. He has great confidence in his sinker ball. He has a great feeling for the game. He knows himself…. He has the poise of a complete pitcher (*The Sporting News*).

Steve Rogers' numbers repeated themselves during the remainder of the season. He went on to win five more times against two setbacks, working a total of 134 innings with a sterling 1.54 ERA. In 17 starts he had completed seven games and shut out his opponents three times. Those accomplishments did not escape the notice of *The Sporting News*, as the publication selected him as their Rookie Pitcher of the Year.

In 1973 the Expos hounded Chicago, St. Louis, Pittsburgh and divisional winner New York down to the last three weeks of play before bowing to the champions. It was their finest season even though there were more losses than wins. Steve Rogers' 10 and 5 was an instrumental part of their surge, and one of the reasons Gene Mauch was elected the National League's Manager of the Year.

A career Expo hurler, Steve Rogers was a 13-year major leaguer who set most of the Expos' lifetime pitching marks, accumulating six Montreal Player of the Month awards, five National League All-Star team selections (he was the winning pitcher in 1982), and three selections as the National League Pitcher of the Week.

Four one-hitters stand out in his 158–152 career: 4 to 0 at Philadelphia on July 26, 1973; 2 to 0 against St. Louis at Montreal on June 3, 1977; 4 to 1 over Los Angeles at Montreal on June 8, 1978; and 3 to 0 over the Phillies at Montreal on June 23, 1979.

For French-speaking Quebecers, and especially those who follow their Expos, a salute is in order for the inauguration, in the 25 anniversary year of 1993, of their Temple de la Rennommee des Expos, that is, the Montreal ballclub's Hall of Fame. The first players selected for induction were "Le Grand Orange," Rusty Staub, and catcher Gary Carter. The next year, 1994, Steve Rogers and manager Gene Mauch were elected. Four worthy selections had found a permanent place of honor in Canada.

1973: Ten Top National League Rookies

Nm/Pos/Tm	GP	W–L/BA	SH/SV/RBI	PR/BR	ERA/FR	TPR
S. Rogers/RHP/Mon	17	10–5	3/0	34	1.54	4.1
J. Grubb/of/SD	113	.311	37	19	7	2.2
R. Cey/3b/LA	152	.245	80	5	16	2.1
M. Schmidt/3b/Phl	132	.196	52	-4	21	1.9
R. Zisk/of/Pit	103	.324	54	20	2	1.9
G. Mathews/of/SF	148	.300	58	15	6	1.7
G. Scarce/RP-LHP/Phl	52	1–8	0/12	11	2.42	1.5
E. Sosa/RP-RHP/SF	71	10–4	0/18	6	3.28	0.9
P. Frias/ss/Mon	100	.231	22	-2	17	0.6
K. Griffey, Sr./of/Cin	25	.384	14	9	-3	0.5

Robert Gilman "Bob" Allen

TPR: 4.0

1890, Philadelphia, NL

Born: July 10, 1867, Marion, OH. Died: May 14, 1943, Little Rock, AR
SS, 5'11" 175 lb. Major League Debut: April 19, 1890
1890: 133 GP; 456-69-103, AB-R-H; .226 BA;
.356 OB%; 57 RBI; 87 BB; 13 SB; 0 BR; 39 FR

On October 30, 1871, the Philadelphia Athletics,* later renamed the Phillies, beat the Chicago White Stockings, 4 to 1, at Brooklyn's neutral Union Grounds to win baseball's first major league championship. It was an auspicious opening for the fledgling ballclub, ushering in a successful run in the National Association of Professional Baseball Players, the forerunner of the National League, which, in turn, was organized after the National Association's demise in 1875. The franchise in the City of Brotherly Love ultimately became one of the National League's more stable operations, with an almost uncanny knack for introducing fresh, young talent to the baseball world.

One of those new, young talents was Bob Allen, a slick-fielding, brainy shortstop who, at 22, replaced the 1889 Phils' short-fielder, Bill Hallman, a recent defector to Philadelphia's new Player's League entry. Allen, a nimble-footed speedster, soon made the Phillies' faithful forget about Hallman. Although the veteran Hallman and several of his former Phils' teammates stayed right in town to play with the new Philadelphia Quakers, skipper Wright's young team more than held its own with the new, crosstown rivals, outdrawing, as well as outplaying them.

Joining Allen at the beginning of the season were four other rookies who had made the squad: first baseman Al McCauley,

The name Athletics was picked up by another new Philadelphia team in 1901, this time in still another new league, the American League, where it has remained since, though the franchise moved from Philadelphia to Kansas City, and on to Oakland. The name Athletics was also used by Philadelphia's American Association team (1882–1891).

Ed Mayer, who played third base with the tenacity of a badger, Eddie Burke, who was flanked in the Phillies' outfield by two Hall of Famers, Sliding Billy Hamilton and the veteran slugger Sam Thompson, and 20-game winner Vinegar Tom Vickery. While it is true that the ranks of top-flight ballplayers were thinned by a third major league, it must be said of Bob Allen that his rookie season was every bit the equal of the shortstops in all three leagues — if not better. The top shortstops in 1890 are shown below.

Allen's Range Rating, at 6.29, was a full point above the League Range for shortstops (5.29). Another sabermetric calculation, this figure reveals a player's ability to get to the ball and throw base-runners out. In 1890 Bob Allen led the league in putouts (337), assists (500), and double plays (68). Each of those figures is a superior achievement, contributing to the huge 39 rating he stacked up in Fielding Runs, the highest figure in each of the three leagues that season. His overall TPR rating was undeniably hurt by an anemic stick, which cost him more than a full point. With a more robust offensive showing, Allen's TPR might easily have reached into the 5.5 to 6.0 range.

Beyond his acrobatic and frequently amazing fielding feats (Allen's specialty was throwing out hitters from the outer edges of the infield), there was another facet of his game that was clearly evident early in the season. He was a born leader, and that would be tapped soon after his 23rd birthday.

In August of his rookie season Bob

The Phillies' rookie-manager, Bob Allen. (Brace Photo.)

Allen was called on by the front office to become the manager of the team. This astounding development, which made him the youngest manager, *all time*, albeit an interim arrangement, was nonetheless something just short of unbelievable, even for 19th century baseball. The Phillies had begun the season under the capable leadership of Harry Wright, the veteran baseball figure and Hall of Famer who was so respected and esteemed as one of baseball's pioneers. Into his seventh season as the Phils' major domo, he found it necessary

Pl/Tm	League	GP	BR	FR	BA	TPR
Jack Glasscock, NY	National League	124	27	22	.336*	4.9*
Bob Allen, Phila.	National League	133	0	39*	.226	4.0
Phil Tomney, Louisv.	American Association	108	9	18	.277	2.9
Billy Shindle, Phila.	Player's League	132	17	8	.324	2.9
John Ward, Brooklyn	Player's League	128	8	21	.335	2.9

*League leading figure

to step aside (Wright would return for the 1891 to 1893 seasons) because of failing eyesight. Wright gave way to the veteran catcher Jack Clements (13–6), who in turn gave way to Al Reach, the second baseman for the original, 1871 Athletics, and later Phils owner.

After Reach's 11-game, 4 and 7 record, it was time for the front office to do something sensible. Enter Bob Allen, who promptly saw the ballclub through the end of the season with a commendable 25 and 10 record. The final, third place finish, slightly miraculous in and of itself, was fashioned on a 78 and 54 mark under this quartette of club leaders. Allen, incidentally, came back to manage the Cincinnati Reds in 1900, after having led the Indianapolis Hoosiers to the Western League's pennant in 1899.

One of the more spectacular plays

that manager Allen turned in during his rookie campaign occurred on September 8, 1890, in a game against the pennant-winning Brooklyn Bridesmaids at the old Huntington Grounds in Philadelphia. On that day he initiated the first triple play in the franchise's history on a fly ball hit by George "Germany" Smith down the left-field line. After spearing it, he turned and threw to second base, nailing Brooklyn catcher Tido Daly. Second baseman Cod Myers then relayed the ball to Al McCauley at first to complete the triple play. That play, plus a last-ditch, ninth-inning rally for three tallies saved the day for Allen's Phillies, 4 to 3. Those ninth inning heroics showcased Philadelphia's rookies, with a leadoff triple by Eddie Mayer that stoked up the Philly fire. Al McCauley reached on an error, putting runners on first and third. That brought up the youthful skipper, who

Box Score

Brooklyn Bridesmaids at Philadelphia, September 8, 1890

Brooklyn	AB	R	H	O	A
Collins, 2b	5	1	1	1	3
Pinckney, 3b	4	0	2	2	0
O'Brien, cf	3	0	0	1	0
Foutz, 1b	2	1	0	9	1
Burns, rf	4	1	1	1	0
Terry, lf	3	0	1	5	0
Daly, c	3	0	1	5	1
Smith, ss	3	0	1	2	3
Lovett, p	4	0	0	0	4
Totals	31	3	7	26	12

Philadelphia	AB	R	H	O	A
Hamilton, lf	4	1	1	3	1
Sunday, cf	2	0	0	4	2
Myers, 2b	3	0	0	3	2
Thompson, rf	4	0	1	1	0
Clements, c	4	0	0	7	1
Mayer, 3b	4	1	1	0	3
McCauley, 1b	3	0	1	5	0
Allen, ss	4	1	1	4	1
Vickery, p	4	1	0	0	4
Totals	32	4	5	27	14

Brooklyn	001	002	000	3-7-2
Philadelphia	001	000	003	4-5-3

2BH	Pinckney; Burns
3BH	Mayer
SB	Hamilton, 2; Sunday; Allen; Vickery, 2
SH	Pinckney; Myers; Sunday
DP	Sunday and Clements
TP	Allen, Myers and McCauley
LOB	Brooklyn, 7; Philadelphia, 7
BB	Lovett, 5; Pinckney, 6
K	Lovett, 2; Pinckney, 4
WP	Vickery, 2
PB	Clements
Ump	Powers

singled sharply to right, scoring Mayer. Vinegar Tom Vickery, closing in on a 20-win season, then grounded to the Bridesmaids' first baseman, Dave Foutz, who threw out McCauley at the plate. That brought up Sliding Billy Hamilton with one away. Billy singled to center, scoring both Allen and Vickery and knocking in the two Phillie rookies for the win.

The young Philly short-fielder moved on through the early stages of his career as the glue that held together a superb Phils infield. By 1894 the team, with its three Hall of Fame outfielders (Ed Delehanty had replaced Eddie Burke, and Sam Crawford and Billy Hamilton were still there), two 20-game winners from the 1893 club (Cannonball Weyhing and Kid Carsey), and hard-hitting Lave Cross at third base, was ready to make a serious run at both the Boston and Baltimore clubs for the National League's blue ribbon.

That all fell apart one early spring day when Bob Allen was felled by a beanball that, to all intents, wrote fini to his major league career. He never fully recovered from the beaning and the inner defense of the Phillies promptly went south. It was also the end of the line for any realistic hopes the Phillies had of shouldering aside the mighty Orioles for the pennant.

All told, there are nine Phillies on the honors list of the greatest rookie seasons, more than any other major league franchise. Among them Bob Allen's number 19 represents that legion of relative unknowns who came along to surprise their contemporaries with a truly fine season that didn't receive the recognition it deserved.

1890: Ten Top Rookie Seasons

Nm/Tm/Pos	GP	W–L/BA	SH/SV//RBI	PR/A//BR	ERA/FR	TPR
Charles "Kid" Nichols, Bos-N, RHP	48	27–19	7/0	72	2.23	6.7
Billy Rhines, Cin-N, RHP	46	28–17	6/0	72	1.95	6.5
Bob Allen, Phl-N, ss	133	.226	57	0	39	4.0
Pat Luby, Chi-N, RHP	34	20–9	0/1	14	3.19	1.7
Jesse Burkett, NY-N, OF	101	.309	60	19	3	1.3
Jimmy Cooney, Chi-N, ss	135	.272	52	5	1	1.2
George Davis, Clv-N, OF	136	.264	73	6	12	1.2
Jack Sharrott, NY-N, RHP	25	11–10	0/0	13	2.89	1.2
Jack Virtue, Clv-N, OF	62	.305	25	16	0	1.2
Vinegar Tom Vickery, Phl-N, RHP	48	24–22	2/0	9	3.44	0.3

Russell William "Russ" Ford

TPR: 4.0

1910, New York, AL

Born: April 25, 1883, Brandon Ontario, Canada.
Died: January 24, 1960, Rockingham, NC
RHP, 5'11"' 175 lb. Major League Debut: April 28, 1909
1910: W26-L6; .813 W%; 33/29 GS/GC; 8/1 SH/SV; .188 OBA; 4 PHI; 34 PR; 1.65 ERA

At the height of the deadball era, two to four runs were, more often than not, enough to win a ball game. League ERAs were down around the 2.70 to 2.80 range between 1904 and 1909, and the ERA crown usually went to pitchers with marks under 2.00. Low-hit, low-run games were the rule, and base-to-base offense was the norm, with teams trying to make do on bunts, scratch singles, sacrifices and oodles of stolen bases. It was a pitcher's game. And that's where the Canadian emery-ball hurler Russ Ford entered the world of the more celebrated pitchers of the day. Ed Walsh, George Mullin, Jack Coombs, Christy Mathewson, Three Finger Brown, Chief Bender, Deacon Phillippe and Addie Joss were among the names of note.

Well seasoned at 27, Russ Ford made his way north from the Yankees, née Highlanders, training base at Athens, Georgia, hoping to shed the variety of minor league uniforms he had worn the previous six seasons. If ever there was a golden opportunity to crack the starting rotation, this was it. According to New York Press reporter Ernie Lanigan, manager George Stallings' ballclub was definitely a question mark, and his pitching staff was characterized as middle-of-the-road as the season opener approached. In his report to *The Sporting News* for the March 24, 1910, issue, Lanigan rated the Yanks as unlikely pennant winners. Further, there were no advance rave notices on the fellow who had mastered the art of scuffing the ball with a piece of emery board stashed inside his glove. Though the word soon made the rounds that the new Yankee spitballer, Ford, was someone to keep an eye on, "the book" on the right hander was only partially right. He did throw a spitter, but his strikeout pitch was doctored by emery — not moisture. As the summer wore on,

Ford put his hand to his mouth merely to disguise his pet pitch, rarely using the spitter. It was a successful ruse, as his final 26 and 6 mark shows. So doing, Russ Ford became the only rookie pitcher ever to win 20 more games than he lost, and it wasn't until several seasons later that the truth about his scuffed-up offerings came out.

The 1910 season opened in the nation's capital on April 14. It was the day President Howard Taft put 300 pounds of heft behind the ceremonial opening pitch to inaugurate a new and endearing spring ritual. The stands in Washington were packed, and Walter Johnson bested the Philadelphia A's with one of his seven Opening Day calciminings, 1 to 0.

Just a week later those same Athletics hosted New York, and Mr. Ford was slated to pitch. And he pitched, all right. On April 21 trick-pitch artist Ford put the league on notice with a brilliant 1 to 0 conquest, giving up five strung-out singles while whiffing nine A's and walking none.

Russ Ford, New York Highlanders' emory-ball twirler. (Brace Photo.)

Showing surprising strength, the Stallingsmen forged to a strong challenging position behind the front-running Athletics. They were doing it with just enough timely hitting to complement a starting rotation that included veterans Jack Quinn, Tom Hughes and Jack Warhop, and they were ably assisted by rookies Jim "Hippo" Vaughn and the Canadian Ford.

By May 23 Ford had negotiated his third shutout, and by mid–June his record would soar to an eye-popping 8 and 1. That coincided with the Yanks' push to the top of the standings, virtually tied with Philly's Mackmen. Ford's first lost came on June 10

in Tigertown as Detroit's ace, George Mullin, bested the Yankees in ten innings, 4 to 3, and though it did not cost them the league leadership, their fall from the top spot came soon after. The A's were the classiest ballclub in the major leagues, soon afterward recapturing the league lead, and moving on, ultimately, to pennant and World Series victories. Ford and his teammates would have to content themselves with a second-place finish.

Meanwhile, in the Big Apple, Russ Ford had established himself as the staff ace and had made the move from surprisingly good to absolutely dominating in nothing flat. A July 14 victory over venerable Cy Young, still in search of his 500th big time conquest (that one came after three tries) was followed by two shutouts at the expense of the Browns and another white-

Date	Opponent	Win No.	Record	Comment
Aug 9	St. Louis	1	15–6	8–0, 3-hitter
Aug 13	Chicago	2	16–6	1–0, 4-hitter, beating Doc White
Aug 19	St. Louis	3	17–6	6–0, 3rd straight shutout
Aug 23	Detroit	4	18–6	Scoreless streak ends at 30 IP
Aug 29	Cleveland	5	19–6	Beat Cy Young, tripled
Sep 5	Philadelphia	6	20–6	Beat Cy Morgan, 5–2
Sep 10	Boston	7	21–6	6–3, beat Eddie Cicotte at Boston
Sep 13	Boston	—	21–6	Relieved, credited with save
Sep 17	St. Louis	8	22–6	Won at St. Louis, 5–1
Sep 22	Cleveland	9	23–6	2–1 victory over rookie George Kahler
Sep 29	Detroit	10	24–6	Beat George Willett, 10–2
Oct 1	Washington	11	25–6	Beat Dolly Gray, 3–1
Oct 6	Philadelphia	12	26–6	Won 12th straight over Jim Dygert

washing on August 13, over the White Sox. By this time, he was the talk of the town and into a stunning streak of 12 straight victories. Above is the record-setting rookie skein.

The streak unofficially came to an end in the New York City Championship Series after the season when the Yankees and Giants faced off for "Bragging Rites," both teams having placed second in their respective leagues. Ford hooked up in a tight opening game duel with Christy Mathewson, only to have the game blown open in the seventh inning, when the Giants scored four times. Matty also won the other three, thus winning all four in the series as New York's Giants emerged victorious, four games to one. Ford lost his first game in 1911 to close out his streak officially at 12. That year he went on to a 21 and 11 season.

Russ Ford's rookie season has gone down in the Yankee history book as a record-setting extravaganza, and his achievements that season also rearranged major league all-time listings. In the following list below "NY" represents a Yankee record and "ML," a major league record.

Despite the introduction of a more lively ball early in the 1910 season, Russ Ford and his fraternity brothers in the pitching profession dominated the game, as his numbers indicate. Beside Ford and his teammate Hippo Vaughn, there were 11 other hurlers in the American League whose ERAs were *under* 2.00, and there were four more in the National League. That adds up to a mind-bending 17. And more: 10 of the 14 league teams sported *staff* ERAs under 3.00. Among American

Category	Record and Ranking		
• Shutouts	8	NY and ML Rookie Record	ML 52
• Hits per 9 IP	5.83	NY, 1st	ML 15
• ERA	1.65	NY, 2nd lowest	ML 72
• Wins	26	NY and ML Rookie Record	
• Strikeouts	209	NY, 6th	
• Wins Above Team	9.7	NY, 2nd	ML 56(t)
• Winning %	.813	NY Rookie Record;	ML 43(t)
• Opponents' BA	.188	NY, 1st	ML 23
• Opponents' OB%	.245	NY, 1st	
• Career ERA	2.54	NY, 1st	
• Consecutive Wins	12*	NY Rookie Record and NY #3(t)	

*Another Ford, Whitey, heads the Yankee list of pitchers with consecutive wins, 14, achieved in 1961.

League twirlers, Russ Ford's 1.65 ERA ranked a mere sixth. Connie Mack's big three, Jack Coombs, Chief Bender and Eddie Plank, *each* logged ERAs under 1.60.

1910 was the kind of season in which one would expect to see two titans like Big Ed Walsh of the White Sox and the Athletics' Jack Coombs go head to head in one of those 0 to 0 battles going into the ninth inning. On August 4 they did, and then some. The two locked up in a scoreless tie that went on for 16 innings before the winner was declared. The winner was Darkness. That was the kind of year during which Russ Ford came along to pitch his eight shutouts and lead his team in almost every pitching category, standing out among standouts.

Hypothetical honors, as formulated under the direction of Bill Deane, who was referred to in previous profiles of players active before the BBWAA began its rookie award presentations, were accorded to Philadelphia's 31-game winner Jack Coombs for both Cy Young and MVP awards, and to Russ Ford as the Rookie of the Year. Neither pitcher left any room for argument over those selections.

During his 22-victory sophomore season in 1911, Ford, by then 28, noticed a growing, achy weariness in his arm, and by season's end he had developed what in those days was called a chronic sore arm. It persisted throughout the 1912 season, a disaster as far as both Russ Ford and the Yankees were concerned. After having finished second in 1910 the club slipped to sixth in 1911 and tumbled into the American League cellar in 1912. Ford's record paralleled the New York descent, as he experienced a disastrous 1912 season with a league-leading 26 losses, pitching through his pain and the club's ineptitude. Though in full command of his emery ball and other pitches, there were only flashes of his former dominance, coming on days that the strain of throwing hard didn't get to

his arm. He nonetheless logged 281.1 innings and 13 victories that year. Considering the circumstances, that was still a better-than-middling performance. But Yankee owner Frank Farrell didn't see it that way, and, for that matter, Russ Ford didn't either.

The official parting of the ways came with the formation of the Federal League, when the Buffalo Blues persuaded Russ to give it another try. He agreed to a new start and a new contract that brought with it some of the liberally dispensed dollars that the fledgling league brandished in an attempt to get off to a solid start. Both the league and Ford got through the season in great shape. There were new ballparks for every entry and a franchise in four former minor league cities, including Indianapolis (the league's first champion), Kansas City, Baltimore and Buffalo, accompanied by four franchises located in major league cities: Brooklyn, Pittsburgh, Chicago and the tail end St. Louis Terriers. Fan support (though not overwhelming) and a tightly bunched set of contenders convinced all involved that it would be worth it to get into another season. That one, however, proved to be the end of the line, both for the league *and* for Russ Ford.

Although he had gone through a tolerably pain-free season in 1914, the emery-board whiz from Brandon, Manitoba, found that there was no way to repeat his 21 and 6 record for the Blues. He had led the new league in winning percentage at .778 and was one of the star hurlers in the league. But he just did get by. In 1915 his record at Buffalo was only 5 and 9, and his workload was reduced from 247.1 innings to half as many in 1915. Russ Ford had reached the end of the trail.

But the Russ story is really not about his last two years in the Federal League. His story is about an overwhelming rookie campaign during which he blitzkrieged the American League with an emery ball that absolutely befuddled American League hitters and paved the way for one of the great single-season performances in major league baseball. That season, 1910, merits a spot among the 20 greatest rookie seasons of all time.

1910: Ten Top Rookies

Nm/Pos/Tm	GP	W–L/BA	SH/SV//RBI	PR/BR	ERA/FR	TPR
R. Ford/RHP/NY-A*	36	26–2	8/1	34	1.65	4.0
L. Cole/RHP/Chi-N *	33	20–4	4/1	29	1.80	3.0
G. Suggs/RHP/Cin-N	35	20–12	2/3	15	2.40	2.1
F. Snodgrass/of/Ny-N	123	.321	44	32	-8	2.0
J. Vaughn/LHP/NY-A	30	13–11	5/1	20	1.83	2.0
G. Lewis/of/Bos-A	151	.283	68	14	10	1.9
L. Drucke/RHP/NY-N	34	12–10	0/0	12	2.74	1.7
Z. Wheat/of/Brk-N	156	.286	55	13	6	1.2
E. Barger/RHP/Brk-N	35	15–15	2/1	5	2.88	1.0
T. Clark/c/Cin-N	64	.278	20	6	-1	1.0

*Hypothetical Rookie of the Year Award winner

John Andrew "Nig" or "Johnny" Beazley

TPR: 4.0

1942, St. Louis, NL

Born: May 25, 1918, Nashville, TN. Died: April 21, 1990, Nashville, TN
RHP, 6'2" 190 lb. Major League Debut: September 28, 1941
1942: 43 GP; W21, L6; .778 W%; 3/3 SH/SV; 10.7 Ratio; .226 OBA; 31 PR; 2.13 ERA

In the minor leagues there were a few important rules to follow, and they didn't necessarily have to do with playing the game: keep your eyes and ears open and your mouth shut; do as you're told; and don't unpack your suitcase. The last of those commandments is especially important.

For Johnny Beazley the minor league map, particularly the southeastern part of it, was worn pretty thin. Before he had ever set foot in a major league ballpark he had played in eight different leagues, and by the time he was 22 he had played for teams in nine different cities all over the southland. He had a lot of practice on that third rule, and probably a good deal less on the other two.

That aside, it wasn't until the last stop on his nomadic journey that he became a pitcher. Before reaching the Big Easy and manager Ray Blades, he was, by his own admission, just a thrower. It was his New Orleans Pelican skipper, the sage veteran Blades, who got after the young flame-thrower often enough and long enough to register the most important piece of information he needed to make a big league pitcher out of him. That was, simply put, that it took more than blazing speed to win in the Bigs, or even in the Southern Association, for that matter. It's a lesson that seems to be hard to learn to this very day. When things fall into place for the talented few who have enough determination and enough common sense to follow the rules, good things start happening. Nig Beazley was certainly determined, and there was just enough common sense deep down inside him to realize that skipper Ray Blades knew what he was talking about. As 1941 moved along so did Beazley's game. He was still walking too many, hitting too many batters for lack of concentration, and offering up fat pitches when he fell behind on the count. But both Blades and Beazley stuck with it.

By mid-season the Beazley bag had in it a slicing curve ball, speed changes, and the mainstay, a crackling heater. He began hitting corners, offering hitters less and less to swing at, and he finished the season at 16 and 12. For the first time he could say, "I think I've gotten the hang of it." No less than the old Mahatma, Branch Rickey himself, was interested in the Pelican star, and after consulting with both Ray Blades and St. Louis Cardinal manager Billy Southworth, it was agreed to bring Beazley up for a look-see.

The last series of the season had begun. The Cardinals were finishing up the year's work as the second-place team behind Brooklyn's Dodgers, who had won their first pennant since 1920. The Cards were in Chicago to meet the Cubs. Billy Southworth scheduled Johnny Beazley to pitch on September 28. In his first try Beazley was a winner. He had gone the route, and though he had given up 10 hits, he won his game 3 to 1. Everyone in the Cardinal organization thought that merited a solid crack at the varsity level in 1942. That meant that it would take more than a bad start or two, or an inning of bad pitches to cause a reassignment and another hitch in the minors, as was often the case with minor leaguers who were on the edges. Beazley's Chicago game took him off those edges, and as he worked with the Cardinal coaching staff the next spring at St. Petersburg, he moved into a solid position on the pitching staff. Perhaps he wasn't yet ready to be moved into the starting rotation, but his improvement day by day suggested that might not be far away. And it wasn't.

Although Ray Blades deservedly received a good deal of credit for Nig Beazley's rise to stardom, Billy Southworth's handling of the Cardinals' rookie wonder is just as praiseworthy. Spotting Beazley first in relief assignments, and then a start here and there, the well-traveled (but still youthful) pitcher gained confidence and poise under the Cardinal manager's careful guidance. That paralleled Southworth's handling of Ernie White, who in 1941 turned in a big freshman season after a late 1940 call-up. The two, portsider White and righthander Beazley, travelled similar paths through ill-starred careers that were marked by huge first year successes, military service and career-ending arm injuries. But in 1942 Billy Southworth led both to strategic conquests that ultimately put the St. Louisans in the World Series.

Before it was all said and done Tennessee's pride and joy had won 21 ball games in only 215.1 innings. (For trivia buffs, that produced an interesting record: most rookie wins in the fewest innings pitched.) He was second in wins (21) to Mort Cooper's 22, and second in the following departments: ERA (2.13); Pitching Runs (31); pitcher TPR (4.0); and winning percentage (.778). Further, he gave up only 7.57 hits per nine innings pitched, placed third in the National League with a 114 Clutch Pitching Index, and wound up making 43 appearances, three of which resulted in saves. The final totals, then, recorded a Beazley hand in 24 Cardinal victories. Two of those marks endure as franchise rookie records, his 21 wins and 2.13 ERA.

During spring training, helmsman Southworth had noticed a slight difference in the action of the balls being put into play. There didn't seem to be quite as much "pop" in them. There was nothing wrong with the feel of the ball or the seams, but it just didn't seem to have as much sting in it. He marked if off to the war, but made the decision to revise his offensive game plan for the coming season. The Cardinals would run, emphasize speed, and take the extra base, not relying as much on power as in former years. Since there was an unusually strong contingent of young speedsters in camp, the skipper's plan was well suited to his personnel. Ray Sanders, Harry Walker, Stan Musial, Whitey Kurowski, Creepy Crespi, Marty Marion and Johnny Hopp were all 25 or under — and they could move. Added to swifties like Enos Slaughter and Terry Moore, Southworth's pesty ballclub would test the league's defensive mettle at every turn.

The new look was an instant hit. Combined with a strong defense based, again, on speed, and a starting rotation that featured Mort Cooper, Max Lanier, Howie Krist and the Cardinals' freshman prodigy, Johnny Beazley, all of whom won in double figures, it made enough difference in 1942 to turn a mid-season runnerup spot into a pennant. And that was followed up, incredibly, by a convincing conquest of the high-flying Yankees in the October Classic, four games to one. Had there been a Manager of the Year Award at the time, Cardinal boss Southworth would surely have won it.

World Series Yankee-tamer Johnny Beazley. (Brace Photo.)

The Cardinals didn't win the bunting in a walk, however. As late as mid–August "Dem Bums" were out in front of the pack by 10.5 games. But a trademark Cardinal surge crested right under Brooklyn's nose when the runnin' Red Birds tripped up the Dodgers in a twin-killing that narrowed the gap. The Cards were, in fact, in the midst of a 21 and 5 run in September, spurred on by their doubleheader conquest on the 13th. Two weeks later Mort Cooper threw his 10th shutout of the season and it was all over. The Birds had salted it away.

As in 1941, Southworth called on Johnny Beazley to pitch in the year-ending series with the Cubs. Beazley, at that point, was a 20-game winner and had lost only six times all summer. This time, however, Southworth would make Beazley work for his win. The Cardinal manager benched the regulars and put Beazley out there for a few innings of comic relief. That was all the new Red Bird hero needed. He scalped the Cubbies, 4 to 1, to win his 21st game, lowering his ERA to 2.13.

Bring on the Yanks! That was the war chant of the brash young National League pennant winners. The Big Show got underway in St. Louis. Unfortunately, there was no curtain call the first time around. Red Ruffing and his Yankee pals dampened Cardinal spirits with a 7 to 4 whipping, beating ace Mort Cooper. But Ruffing's victory turned out to be a fleeting moment of New York supremacy.

World Series-savvy Joe McCarthy picked Tiny Bonham, 21 and 5 on the season, to face the Cardinals in game two. Southworth's choice was Johnny Beazley. Weathering a three-run Yankee eighth, the Birds got to Bonham for a run in their half of the eighth to go ahead, 4 to 3. The Cardinals and Beazley made that run stand up to win the game and even the series. But Beazley's best was yet to come.

When the series moved into Yankee Stadium the smart money moved to the New Yorkers. St. Louisans, especially those wearing Cardinal uniforms, thought that was ridiculous. Those hinterland folk were right. Their beloved Birds went right at the Yanks and whipped them, first behind Ernie White, who shut them down in a 2–0 whitewashing, and then the NL champs pounded out 12 hits to beat the Yankees again, 9 to 6. Max Lanier picked up the win in relief. Could this really be? St. Louis, three to one, and only one away from the pot of gold? And in New York?

Beazley wrapped it all up, with the final tally, 4–2, going against the old master, Red Ruffing, and despite four Red Bird errors. With help from another rookie, Whitey Kurowski, who homered in the ninth to put the Cards up by two, Beazley

brought the Cardinals home a World Series winner. Roy Stockton, St. Louis sportsscribe, caught up with Beazley for a postgame comment that, he insisted, went like this, word for word: "Hot damn. I can't believe it's all true. But I guess it is. And won't Mom get a helluva kick out of this!" (*St. Louis Post-Dispatch*).

Between his immense 1942 achievements and another baseball season, Johnny Beazley traded uniforms. As an Air Force man he served principally in the Pacific theater. Pitching for service teams, he, like many another pitcher during those years, injured his arm. He never really recovered after his return. As it turned out, that 1942 season represented the whole of his major league career. Be that as it may, it was enough for Mr. Beazley.

In 1945 he was officially welcomed back to his native Nashville, where, amid

Box Score

World Series Game Five
St. Louis Cardinals at Yankee Stadium, New York, October 5, 1942

St. Louis	AB	R	H	PO	A
Brown, 2b	3	0	2	3	4
T. Moore, cf	3	1	1	3	0
Slaughter, rf	4	1	2	2	0
Musial, lf	4	0	0	2	0
W. Cooper, c	4	1	2	2	1
Hopp, 1b	3	0	0	9	2
Kurowski, 3b	4	1	1	1	1
Marion, ss	4	0	0	3	5
Beazley, p	4	0	1	2	0
Totals	33	4	9	27	13

New York	AB	R	H	PO	A
Rizzuto, ss	4	1	2	7	1
Rolfe, 3b	4	1	1	1	0
Cullenbine, rf	4	0	0	3	0
DiMaggio, cf	4	0	1	3	0
Keller, lf	4	0	1	1	0
Gordon, 2b	4	0	1	3	3
Dickey, c	4	0	0	4	0
Stainback, pr	0	0	0	0	0
Priddy, 1b	3	0	0	5	1
Ruffing, p	3	0	1	0	1
Selkirk, ph	1	0	0	0	0
Totals	35	2	7	27	6

St. Louis	000	101	002	4-9-4
New York	100	100	000	2-7-1

HR	Rizzuto, Slaughter, Kurowski
LOB	St. Louis 5; New York 7
SH	T. Moore, Hopp
DP	Gordon, Rizzuto, Priddy; Hopp, Marion, Brown
BB	Ruffing 1, Beazley 1
K	Ruffing 3, Beazley 2
Umpires	Magerkurth (NL), Summers (AL), Barr (NL), Hubbard (NL)
Time	1:58
Att	69,052

gala festivities Nig was commissioned an "Honorary Colonel" by Governor Cooper. The popular Nashvillian had returned home to a hero's welcome.

The Best of the World War I and II Rookies

Nm/Pos/Tm/Yr	GP	W–L/BA	SH/SV//RBI	PR/BR	ERA/FR	TPR
J. Pesky/ss/Bos-A/1942	147	.331	51	14	18	4.2
J. Beazley/RHP/StL-N/1942	43	21–6	3/3	31	2.13	4.0
S. Perry/RHP/Phl-A/1918	44	20–19	3/2	35	1.98	3.9
J. Berry/RHP/Phl-A/1944	53	10–8	0/12	19	1.94	3.6
N. Andrews/RHP/Bos-N/1943	36	14–20	3/0	27	2.57	3.4
D. Ferriss/RHP/Bos-A/1945	35	21–10	5/2	13	2.96	3.3
H. White/RHP/Det/1942	34	12–12	4/1	25	2.91	2.6
J. Kerr/2b/NY-N/1944	150	.266	63	-3	17	2.6
S. Musial/of/StL-N/1942	140	.315	72	31	1	2.5
W. Voiselle/RHP/NY-N/1944	43	21–16	1/0	22	3.02	2.5
C. Gillenwater/of/Bos-N/1945	144	.288	72	9	24	2.5
A. Brazle/LHP/StL-N/1943	13	8–2	1/0	18	1.53	2.4
A. Carter/LHP/Cin-N/1944	33	11–7	3/3	15	2.60	2.4
J. Harris/1b/Clv-A/1917	112	.304	65	16	10	2.3
V. Trucks/RHP/Det-A/1942	28	14–8	2/0	23	2.74	2.3
K. Burkhart/RHP/StL-N/1945	45	18–8	4/2	20	2.90	2.2
H. Brecheen/LHP/StL-N/1943	29	9–6	1/4	17	2.26	2.1
L. Cadore/RHP/Brk-N/1917	37	13–13	1/3	10	2.45	1.4
J. Hannah/c/NY-A/1918	75	.238	20	-7	-9	1.0
E. Martin/RHP/Chi-N/1918	9	5–2	1/1	6	1.84	0.9

George Watt McQuillan

TPR: 3.9

1908, Philadelphia, NL

Born: May 1, 1885, Brooklyn, NY. Died: March 30, 1940, Columbus, OH
RHP, 5'11.5" 175 lb. Major League Debut: May 8, 1907
1908: 48 GP; W23, L17; .575 W%; 7/2 SH/SV; .207 OBA; 36 PR; 1.53 ERA

In 1908 pitching was the dominant feature of the game. Overwhelmingly. National League pitchers posted a 2.35 ERA, a 20th century low point, and American League hurlers were mere percentage points behind at 2.39. Those were the lowest league ERA marks since 1878, when the six-team National League forged the 2.30 record. Sub–2.00 marks were commonplace. The top 10 hurlers in the majors recorded these marks in 1908:

Addie Joss, Clv-AL	1.16
Cy Young, Bos-AL	1.26
Ed Walsh, Chi-AL	1.42
Christy Mathewson, NY-NL	1.43
Mordecai Brown, Chi-NL	1.47
George McQuillan, Phl-NL	1.53
Howie Camnitz, Pit-NL	1.56
Ed Summers, Det-AL	1.64
Walter Johnson, Was-AL	1.65
Andy Coackley, Cin-Chi-NL	1.78

This list bears a number of legendary names. The top five are all distinguished members of the Hall of Fame. Each was a veteran campaigner by the time 1908 went into the record books. There are two in the next five who are worthy of special mention: Walter Johnson, who in 1908 was into his sophomore season at 20, and George McQuillan, 23, the Philadelphia phenom, who had exploded onto the major league scene in 1907 with 25 consecutive innings of scoreless pitching and an overall 4–0 record with a 0.66 ERA. Walter Johnson, one of the Hall of Fame's first class of honorees in 1936, needs no introduction. George McQuillan, of the Phillies, does.

1908 marked McQuillan's first full season in the major leagues. Having pitched 41 innings during that stunning career opener in 1907, he hadn't yet pitched enough innings to disqualify him for 1908 rookie status by present requirements, which stipulate that a pitcher is a rookie if he has formerly totalled less than 50 innings. That, of course, makes the Brooklynite eligible for our honors list of outstanding rookie seasons. And George McQuillan's 1908 certainly qualifies. Let's start from the beginning as we unravel the whys and wherefores.

George McQuillan possessed the strength of a bull and was about as single-minded. A tough six-footer, he loved to throw a baseball hard enough to knock over anyone brave enough to catch it. By the time he was 20 he had hooked on with a Patterson, New Jersey, semi-pro team, and had aroused the interest of several professional teams. One of them was the Jersey City Skeeters managed by Billy Murray, a soft-spoken mentor-type who saw enough potential in the hard-throwing McQuillan to get him into a Skeeters uniform. With a 5 and 2 Jersey City record and a 14 and 7 record with New Bedford of the Northeastern League, where he was sent to learn more about his craft, he wound up the 1905 season with a 19 and 9 mark. Moved back up to the Class A Eastern League with Jersey City, he spent the entire season there and fashioned a respectable 15 and 9 in 31 games and 224 innings of additional prepping before moving on to a trial with the 1907 Philadelphia Phillies at their spring training camp in Savannah, Georgia.

The man in charge at Savannah was no less than Billy Murray, who had been appointed the new Phils manager, replacing Hugh Duffy. Murray was sufficiently impressed with his former pupil, assigning him a Phillies' uniform and a spot on the pitching staff.

By mid–May Murray had seen enough to realize that although McQuillan wasn't quite ready for the Bigs, it wouldn't take much. So the young hurler was optioned to Providence where Duffy, the 1907 Phils manager, could see to it that the big fellow would get the necessary finishing touches.

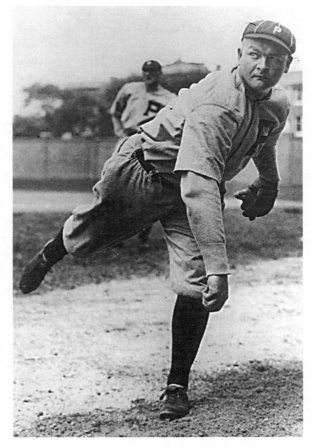

The Phillies' flame-throwing George McQuillan. (Brace Photo.)

Both of them, McQuillan and Duffy, came through.

By the Labor Day milestone McQuillan had run up a 19 and 7 record, had fashioned a no-hitter at the expense of Rochester, 2 to 0, on June 4, and had recorded a super 2.31 ERA in 225 innings of work. A ticket to Philadelphia was his payoff.

What happened next caught just about everyone off guard, including Murray and McQuillan. In his first outing on September 9 he matched goose eggs through nine innings with St. Louis' Johnny Lush in a game called by darkness. He scattered six hits, fanned nine and issued nary a free pass. Big George had apparently learned a thing or two. Some of the rough edges had clearly been rubbed off, as he nipped corners and moved the ball around a bit with his blazer. Murray was sufficiently encouraged to start him a few days later.

Chick Fraser, a grizzled, 36-year-old veteran finishing his career with Frank Chance's pennant-winning Cubs, faced McQuillan on September 25. In a six-inning stint, halted this time by rain, the Phillies mustered a six-run attack (for the Phils in 1907 this was a real bombardment) and McQuillan once again administered a whitewashing. After 15 innings in two games he had allowed no runs and eight hits, giving up two walks and whiffing 13.

On September 29, George McQuillan faced the Cincinnati Reds and Bob Spade, up for a season-ending trial. Spade was no match for McQuillan, although he, too, pitched brilliantly in a losing effort 1 to 0. Big George had done it again. He had won his third straight with another blanking. Though the Phillies were off the pennant pace by more than 20 games, there was something to cheer about. They were assured of a third-place finish, several games better than McGraw's Giants. And then there was this McQuillan fellow. Including a one-inning relief assignment before having been sent down to Providence, he had worked through 25 consecutive scoreless innings, a major league record that had tongues wagging. That record stands to this day and serves as the Philly standard, as well.

On September 29 George took the hill once more, this time against the Pittsburgh Pirates, and proceeded to shut them down — but not entirely. Scoring a run in the first inning, the Pirates managed to bring the scoreless innings skein to a halt, but that's about all they managed. McQuillan beat them 4 to 1, allowing three hits. His record now stood at 3 and 0.

Christy Mathewson was next. That one went seven innings, and New York scored twice on McQuillan. But the final result was the same: a Big George conquest. This one, a 3 to 2 job, bested Mr. Giants himself. Here's the final 1907 tally: a 4 and 0 record, 25 consecutive scoreless innings, a minuscule 0.66 ERA, 20 hits allowed in 41 innings pitched, an opponent batting average of .141 and 28 strikeouts. Those are Mathewson-like numbers, and there were already murmurings that McQuillan was, indeed, the next Christy Mathewson, though he hadn't yet hurled a full season. Mathewson, in 1908 and the years following, would have something to say about that.

George McQuillan didn't turn out to be the next Christy Mathewson. But he did turn in a Giant-sized rookie season in 1908. He couldn't have been expected to move on endlessly without giving up a bundle of runs now and then. Nonetheless, before another season closed out he had once again fashioned an earned run average of microscopic proportions. In order to beat the Big Mac of a former day, a ballclub needed a pitcher out there who would give up no more than a couple runs because they knew aforehand that knocking McQuillan out of the box was improbable. And so it was. In 1908 his earned run average was almost a full run less than the league's niggardly 2.35 at 1.53, and two years later he led the league with a 1.60 ERA. Seven shutouts were an immensely impressive part of that 1908 ERA. Further, he was the losing pitcher in *five* 1 to 0 games, one of which was a Hooks Wiltse no-hitter on July 4, when he lost the morning game of a the holiday doubleheader at New York's Polo Grounds. McQuillan's own throwing error cost him that one.

On a brighter note, however, our showcase McQuillan game occurred on May 29, when the big flamethrower knocked off Boston's Beaneaters, shutting them out, 8–0. A one-line recap in the *New York Times* of May 30 went like this: "The Philadelphia National League club returned home today, and, by hitting three of Boston's pitchers hard while McQuillan was a mystery to the visitors, won by 8 to 0." The McQuillan "mystery" resulted in a two-hitter.

That Boston romp was one of the Phils' few laughers that summer as they put the game away with a five-run opening stanza. The box score is reproduced in the *Times*' customary style, showing runs and hits but no at-bats. Mickey Doolan, Sherry Magee and outfielder Silent John Titus, veteran Phillies stars, led the unusually heavy-hitting attack with three hits apiece. Big George could have used a little more of that during a Philadelphia season of weak-kneed offense. A few timely hits now and then might easily have produced more than 25 victories for the staff workhorse

(359.2 innings pitched ranked second to Mathewson's 390.2). As it was, his 23 wins rates a second spot next to Grover Alexander's 28 in 1911, and he established still-standing, club rookie marks in the following categories: games started/completed (42/32), appearances (48, including 2 saves), innings pitched (above), and ERA (above). Would all of that have been worthy of Rookie of the Year recognition? Bill Deane, often cited before regarding the Hypothetical Awards, thought so.

After 1908 George McQuillan's Achilles heel began to catch up with him. Strongly attracted to bright lights and that old professional athlete's nemesis, the bubbly, his pitching began to blur right along with his eyesight. In 1909 he dropped off to a less than adequate 13 and 16, and by 1911 he was

Box Score

Boston at Baker Bowl, Philadelphia, May 29, 1908

Philadelphia	R	H	PO	A	E
Knabe, 2b	1	2	2	2	0
Grant, 3b	0	1	1	1	2
Titus, rf	3	3	1	0	0
Magee, lf	1	3	1	0	0
Osborne, cf	0	0	5	0	0
Bransfield, 1b	3	1	13	0	0
Doolan, ss	1	3	1	5	0
Dooin, c	0	2	2	1	0
Jacklitsch, c	0	0	1	0	0
McQuillan, p	0	0	0	6	0
Totals	8	15	27	15	2

Boston	R	H	PO	A	E
Browne, rf	0	1	2	0	0
Beaumont, cf	0	0	1	1	0
Bates, lf	0	0	3	0	0
Kelley, 1b	0	0	4	3	0
Bowerman, c	0	0	1	0	0
Graham, c	0	0	5	2	0
Ritchey, 2b	0	0	1	4	0
Dahlen, ss	0	0	5	2	0
Sweeney, 3b	0	1	1	2	1
Young, p	0	0	1	0	1
Ferguson, p	0	0	0	0	0
Pfeffer, p	0	0	0	0	0
Totals	0	2	24	14	2

Boston	000	000	000	0-2-2
Philadelphia	500	020	01x	8-15-2

2BH	Doolan
3BH	Knabe
SH	Jacklitsch
SB	Titus, Osborne, Doolan
LOB	Boston 5, Philadelphia 7
K	Young 3, McQuillan 1, Ferguson 0, Pfeffer 0
BB	Young 2, McQuillan 2, Ferguson 0, Pfeffer 1
WP	Ferguson
Losing P	Young
Time	1:45
Umpire	O'Day

doing his pitching for the Pirates — at less than a .500 level. He hung on until 1915 when the Phils brought him back for a reprise with their pennant winners (he won four late season games that helped the Phillies win the flag), and by 1918, when he finished out his ten-year career with Cleveland, what might have been — those grim words that always warn of dire endings — simply wasn't. And despite all, he wound up, remarkably, with a career 2.38 ERA and an opposing hitter's average of only .241.

George McQuillan, unheralded and hardly remembered, heads a group of four

"Cum Laudes," the last of the rookies who rank in the top 20 of our all time rookie listing. The final four, McQuillan, pitchers Scott Perry and Cliff Melton, and outfielder Vada Pinson, each rated at 3.9 TPR, had rookie seasons that meant a four game difference in the final standings of their superb freshman seasons. In George McQuillan's case the Phillies would have wound up at 79 and 75 instead of their fourth place, 83 and 71. That's a considerable difference over the course of a season. And that's what makes seasons like McQuillan's the gems they are.

1908: Ten Top Rookies

Nm/Pos/Tm	GP	W–L/BA	SH/SV//RBI	PR/BR	ERA/FR	TPR
G. McQuillan/RHP/Phl-N	48	23–17	7/2	36	1.53	3.9
E. Summers/RHP/Det-A	40	24–12	5/1	26	1.64	2.8
C. Herzog/Inf/NY-N	64	.300	11	13	1	1.6
W. Burns/LHP/Was-A	23	6–11	2/0	11	1.70	1.4
A. Schweitzer/of/StL-A	64	.291	14	8	5	1.2
R. Bescher/of/Cin-NL	32	.272	17	5	4	0.8
W. Carrigan/c/Bos-A	57	.235	14	-4	6	0.6
W. Foxen/LHP/Phl-N	22	7–7	2/0	8	1.95	0.6
T. McCarthy/RHP/Cin-Pit-Bos-N	17	7–4	2/0	7	1.82	0.4
R. Hoblitzel/1b/Cin-N	32	.254	8	0	2	0.1

Herbert Scott Perry

TPR: 3.9

1918, Philadelphia, AL

Born: April 17, 1891, Denison, TX. Died: October 27, 1959, Kansas City, MO
RHP, 6'1" 195 lb. Major League Debut: May 13, 1915
1918: 44GP; W20, L19; .513 W%; 36/30 GS/GC; 3/2 SH/SV; 332.1 IP; 35 PR; 1.98 ERA

The 1918 baseball season, with its truncated, 130 game schedule, came to an end with the Labor Day holiday while the nation was involved in its most intense Great War effort. Despite President Wilson's late–July statement indicating that there was no need to cut the season short, baseball officials declared that the World Series would begin directly after completing the season in early September. Both leagues played out the season amid player losses, adjustments and readjustments to wartime necessities and, just for good measure, through a number of extraordinary and unexpected events.

A chunky, breaking-ball pitcher was the centerpiece of both the unexpected and the extraordinary. His name was Herbert Perry, a puckish gay blade who, at least for one summer, was a right-handed Rube Waddell for Connie Mack's woe-begone Athletics. Not that Mr. Mack needed another Waddell.

First, regarding one of those extraordinary, if not bizarre, events. The National

Commission, which up to 1920 was baseball's high court, met to consider a Boston Braves claim filed against the Philadelphia Athletics during the early part of the 1918 season. The A's were charged with "stealing" pitcher Herbert, better known as Scott, Perry. Perry was, according to the Braves, their pitcher because he had been sold by Cincinnati to their Atlanta farm club. They charged, further, that Connie Mack had illegally purchased Perry's contract and had brought him to Philadelphia while the pitcher was signed with the National League's Boston club. The commission, under the leadership of National League prexy John Tener, upheld the Boston franchises claim and ordered Perry to report to Boston.

Connie Mack might have been mild-mannered, but he was no namby-pamby. In the first case of its kind in baseball history, he took his case to court, and if he wasn't to win enough ball games to escape the cellar during that misery-laden 1918 season, he was indeed bound and

211

determined to be a winner in the courts. He was, and the Athletics were permitted to keep Perry provided they would pay the interleague waiver price of $2,500. It was a provision they met — promptly — and a ruling that at the same time was recognized by one and all as the death-knell of the commission. Within two years Judge Kenesaw Landis was on the scene as baseball's one-man commission, the new commissioner of organized baseball.

So Scott Perry, already into a solid season with his new team, kept right on winning some and losing some for one of Mack's weaker ballclubs. Ever since the Braves had whipped the A's in four straight World Series humiliations in 1914, the slippery slope had led farther into the darkness of the American League nether regions. The Mackmen were fated to finish dead last seven times in a row between 1915 and 1921 before putting together another winning ballclub in 1925. The last season played out during World War I was no exception. The team was less than awful.

Now then, as to the unexpected. Two rookies came along to brighten the otherwise leaden skies of Philadelphia. One was, of course, the aforementioned Scott Perry. The other was one of Connie Mack's all-time favorites, Jimmy Dykes, the affable plumber's son from Philadelphia.

Winning 20 games for a 52 and 76 ballclub that finished 24 games south of the border behind the champion Boston Red Sox was an accomplishment of rare

magnitude. It wasn't, however, the most sensational season among last-place 20-game winners. That distinction belongs to Steve "Lefty" Carlton of the 1972 Phillies. There have been only seven pitchers who have turned this exceptional trick since 1900 shown below.

Scott Perry's big moment, his August 24 conquest of the Chicago White Sox for victory number 20, came during the last week of the abbreviated season. It was a typical Perry win. He spaced eight hits, only one of which was an extra-base blow, walked several batters (the total on the season was 111, 30 more than he whiffed), but prevailed in the end, 2 to 1.

The victory brought Perry an $800 bonus, about which *Chicago Tribune* wrote "victory or defeat [was] but incidental to the day's doings at Shibe Park." Considering the chronically precarious state of the Athletics' treasury, if it can even be called that, the bonus must have been the highlight of the season in Philadelphia.

Through 1919 and 1920 Scott Perry labored on — quite unsuccessfully. Too much food, too much booze, and not nearly enough winning days during two seasons that netted him a total of 15 wins against 32 losses, combined with a 3 and 6 start in 1921, were eventually too much to bear; Perry's antics and poor performance exhausted even Connie Mack's patience. By that time his ERA had ballooned to 4.11, and it was time to send Mr. Perry along the same route followed by many another

Nm/Tm	Yr	Tm W–L	Wins	% Tm	Wins	LL*
S. Carlton/Phl-N	1972	59–97	27	45.8	7.4	30 CG; 346.1 IP; 310 K; 27 Wins; 1.97 ERA; 7.4 TPR
S. Perry/Phl-A	1918	52–76	20	38.5	3.9	30 CG; 332.1 IP
P. Niekro/Atl-N	1979	66–94	21	31.8	3.4	21 W; 23 CG; 342.0 IP
N. Garver/StL-A	1951	52–102	20	38.5	3.1	24 CG
F. Hahn/Cin-N	1901	52–87	22	42.3	1.9	41 CG; 375.1 IP; 239 K
H. Ehmke/Bos-A	1923	61–91	20	32.8	1.6	
H. Thurston/Chi-A	1924	66–87	20	30.3	1.6	28 CG

LL designates league leadership

Box Score

Philadelphia at Comiskey Park, Chicago, August 24, 1918, Second Game

Philadelphia	AB	R	H	PO	A
Jamieson, rf	3	0	1	3	0
Kopp, lf	4	0	1	0	0
Acosta, cf	4	0	0	1	0
Burns, 1b	4	1	3	10	0
Gardner, 3b	3	0	0	1	2
Perkins, c	4	0	1	3	2
Dykes, 2b	4	0	0	2	1
Dugan, ss	4	1	1	2	3
Perry, p	3	0	1	5	5
Totals	33	2	8	27	13

Chicago	AB	R	H	PO	A
Good, cf	5	0	1	4	0
Liebold, lf	5	0	1	0	0
Murphy, 2b	3	0	1	1	2
Gandil, 1b	3	0	1	9	0
S. Collins, rf	4	0	0	3	0
Weaver, ss	4	1	2	1	4
Pinelli, 3b	3	0	2	1	1
Jacobs, c	4	0	0	5	0
Benz, p	3	0	0	0	2
Russell, ph	1	0	0	0	0
Totals	35	1	8	24	9

Chicago	010	000	000	1-8-1
Philadelphia	000	110	00x	2-8-3

2BH	Dugan, Jamieson
3BH	Pinelli, Perkins
K	Benz 5, Perry 6
BB	Benz 2, Perry 6
LP	Benz (8–8)
WP	Perry (20–19)
Umpires	Nallin and Connolly

baseball meteor. Out of baseball from 1922 to 1925, he tried once again with Dallas of the Texas League, but that, too, came to an end after a pair of lackluster seasons.

One of the things Scott Perry loved to do was eat, and he spent the last years of his life in the food business. As a matter of fact, he died in the same general hospital in Kansas City where he was employed as a cook.

In his column *Playing The Game*, sportswriter Ed Pollock wrote this about Scott Perry shortly after the former player's death on October 27, 1959:

> Remember Scott Perry, former A's pitcher? Pretty good, too. So good, in fact, that, in order to retain him on his staff, Connie Mack defied the highest authority in baseball. Perry, 68, made news for the last time last week. He

Scott Perry, the Athletics' 1918 ace, pictured here in 1916 during a Cincinnati Reds tryout. (Brace Photo.)

died in a general hospital in Kansas City where he had been employed as a cook. It could be said that he was the Bobo Newsom of World War I, a big, colorful Southerner, complete with good looks and drawl. Everybody loved him, but no one could straighten him out. He had a compelling thirst that couldn't be quenched, not even by Mack who, having had Rube Waddell, was entitled to past master ratings in handling such characters.... [After his professional pitching career] it wasn't long before it was reported here that his arm had given out, but his thirst was still going strong.

Pollock's clever summation is to the point, pulling no punches. But there is also a tinge of sorrow as well as respect for the one shining season that Scott Perry won more than he lost. It was a season worthy of top billing among honor-roll rookie seasons.

1918: Ten Top Rookies

Nm/Pos/Tm	GP	W–L/BA	SH/SV//RBI	PR/BR	ERA/FR	TPR
S. Perry/RHP/Phl-A	44	20–19	3/2	35	1.98	3.9
J. Hannah/c/NY-A	90	.220	21	-1	3	1.0
E. Martin/RHP/Chi-N	9	5–2	1/1	6	1.84	0.9
J. Northrop/RHP/Bos-N	7	5–1	1/0	6	1.35	0.9
C. Hollocher/ss/Chi-N	131	.316	38	21	-19	0.8
D. Fillingim/RHP/Bos-N	14	7–6	4/0	6	2.23	0.7
J. Enzmann/RHP/Clv-A	30	5–7	0/2	10	2.37	0.6
E. Meusel/of/Phl-N	124	.279	62	3	8	0.6
F. Thomas/3b/Bos-A	44	.257	11	-1	5	0.6
R. Youngs/of/NY-N	121	.302	25	18	-6	0.5

Noteworthy Events of the 1918 Season

April 15   The season opened with a Babe Ruth victory over Philadelphia's A's on a 4-hitter, 7 to 1.

May 15   Walter Johnson won an 18-inning shutout over Chicago's Lefty Williams on a wild pitch that allowed the game's only run to score.

Later, on July 25, Johnson hurled a one-hitter for 11 innings and finally won on a 15th-inning run over Cleveland.

Johnson was also involved in a 15-inning thriller with Scott Perry, beating him by a 1 to 0 margin. Perry stated that the game was one of his two biggest baseball thrills, the other being his 20th victory in 1918.

May 19   Washington won a nail-biter over Cleveland in 18 innings, 1 to 0, on the first Sunday major league baseball was legalized in the nation's capital.

July 17   Mule Watson was one of five rookies on the Athletics' 1918 ballclub. His record that season was 7 and 10. However, there was another Mule Watson in town. This one pitched for the Phillies. On this date the Phils' pitcher hooked up with Lefty Tyler in Chicago in a 21-inning game that set a record: 21 errorless innings of baseball in a single game. The Cubs beat the Phils 2 to 1, both pitchers going the route. Incidentally, the Watsons were not related.

July 25 and August 6

Prince Hal Chase, the gambling-prone, slick-fielding first baseman (in 1918 he played for the Cincinnati Reds), was allegedly involved in two fixing schemes involving his Reds, the Braves and the Giants.

Ray Schalk, diminutive Hall of Famer and Chisox backstop, caught his 100th game of the season, marking the sixth consecutive year he had reached that plateau and establishing a new record for durability. He would extend his unprecedented streak to 11 years.

September 9 Babe Ruth extended his consecutive scoreless inning streak to 29.2 innings as he beat the Cubs in the fourth game of the World Series. Boston went on to win the Series in four games out of six.

October 5 Capt. Eddie Grant, former ten-year major leaguer, became the only casualty among big leaguers who served in the Armed Forces during World War I. He was killed in action in the Battle of the Argonne Forest.

Clifford George
"Mountain Music" Melton

TPR: 3.9

1939, New York, NL

Born: January 3, 1912, Brevard, NC. Died: July 28, 1986, Baltimore, MD
RHP; 6'5.5" 203 lb. Major League Debut: April 25, 1937
1937: 46 GP; W20-L9, .690 W%; 2/7 SH/SV;
10.1 Ratio; .233 OBA; 10 PHI; 35 PR; 2.61 ERA

He was lean and lofty. All arms and legs. Angular. And he had a prominent feature or two. For one thing, there were those big ears, right out of a Disney cartoon. For another, he came from the mountain country of North Carolina, a banjo player. And, *mirabili dictu*, he was a lefty — just perfect — fitting all the sports scribes' requirements for colorful copy. "Mountain Music" would be his name. Everyone, writers, players and fans would have a field day with this one.

But Clifford George Melton, the fellow they called Mountain Music, or "Mickey Mouse" (those ears made that inevitable), broke into New York's sophisticated whirl with such a bang that there wasn't any time or space left over to hail or josh him as a left-handed backwoodsman for all the heroics he provided Bill Terry's defending National League champions. Instead, Cliff Melton and King Carl Hubbell

of the Giants gave the 1937 ballclub the best southpaw twosome they had ever seen in *any* New York uniform.

It wasn't Mickey Mouse once the towering portsider got busy out there. His fast one seemed to come at the hitter from the top of one of those North Carolina mountain peaks, gaining speed as it neared the plate. And *this* lefty could put the pellet where he wanted to. Complimenting his hummer with a snapping curveball and a sidearm crossfire pitch reserved especially for left-handed hitters, Melton soon became the most pleasant surprise in Memphis Bill Terry's camp. But before getting at the particulars of Cliff Melton's remarkable rookie season, a look at his earlier and formative years will be helpful in providing some background and perspective.

Although he was both a high school basketball and baseball star, Melton knew right from the start that he wanted to be a

216

pitcher. Mowing 'em down on the high school circuit soon attracted the attention of a few semi-pro teams in and around the Asheville, North Carolina, area. He signed his first play-for-pay contract after graduating from high school and put in a 19 and 2 season.

In the summer of 1931, 19 and still growing, the budding star signed his first professional contract with the Asheville Tourists of the Class C Piedmont League, threw a five-inning no-hitter against High Point on August 29, got into 22 ball games, and wound up with a 5 and 5 record. He had made a start and found that even though there was more to pitching than he ever dreamed of, he just loved it.

Cliff "Mountain Music" Melton. (Brace Photo.)

Between 1931 and 1936 the lean lefty made his way through the maze of minor league systems and teams that put major league wannabes through their paces. It wasn't until 1936 that the Melton package took on a big time look, however. By that time the fully matured left-hander had developed a style and approach to pitching that was to produce 20 wins for Guy Sturdy's Baltimore Orioles. Featuring a deceptively slow and loose windup that preceded his delivery, his pitches seemed to be halfway to the plate before the hitters picked them up. The Oriole star fanned twice as many as he walked and was a durable workhorse, putting in 271 innings for his ballclub. He was ready.

Bill Terry was into his fifth full season as successor to John McGraw's Giants. Beginning in 1932, he had led the Giants to first place finishes in 1933 and 1936, to second in 1934 and third in 1935. The New Yorkers had things pretty much to themselves during this span, with the Yankees in the process of stacking up dynastic claims to major league supremacy, the Giants rivalling them, and Brooklyn's "Bums" beginning to make front-running noises toward the end of the 1930s. The Big Town was hopping. And Bill Terry was determined to get a big slice of the action out there on Coogan's Bluff.

In another of those Subway Series rivalries, the Yanks had taken down the Giants in the 1936 World Series, four games to two. The difference was pitching — as usual. The Yankees just had too much depth and defensive polish. If the Giants were to return to baseball's throne room, another strong starting arm would make a huge difference.

The 1937 Giants trained in Havana. Maybe the answer to Terry's pitching puzzle could be found in Cuba. Although he didn't know it at the time, the answer was right there in camp, and his name was Cliff Melton. The Giant pitching staff that came north was once again headed by staff ace Carl Hubbell, who, at 33, had shown no signs whatever of slackening his whirlwind pace. The plan was to back him up with veteran hurlers Freddie Fitzsimmons, Prince Hal Schumacher, Harry Gumbert and Clydell "Slick" Castleman. Relief chores were slated for Dick Coffman and Al Smith. It remained to be seen how Cliff Melton would fit into that picture, but skipper Terry knew that the staff still needed another strong, 200-plus innings from a winner.

The New Yorkers opened up their 1937 season with three straight wins. With the Giants in search of their fourth straight, and Cliff Melton in search of his first win in his major league debut, the Giants met Boston's Bees on Sunday, April 25. The time had come to put the 25-year-old southpaw to the test of a regular season game in front of New York's boisterous faithful.

It would be nice to be able to say that Melton's well-pitched game resulted in a victorious major league debut. But it didn't quite work out that way. The Bees sent home 25,000 fans somewhat disappointed, but not in their new lefty. For him there was a standing ovation as he left the mound in the ninth inning. That vote of confidence was repeated in the clubhouse after the game by the Giants' bossman, Terry.

Not only did Guy Bush, an inveterate Giant-killer, put the brakes on the New York attack, but the Giants' defense sprung a leak with errors in both the infield and outfield, one of which led directly to a run in the top of the ninth, as Boston pushed across a pair to take a 3 to 1 lead into the bottom of the ninth. When Bush set down the Giants in order, it was all over and Melton had lost his first game under the Big Tent, 3 to 1. Along the way he had fanned 13, walked only two and otherwise handled himself like someone who belonged just where he was. His first start assured one and all that there would be another assignment soon. Whether that would be as a spot starter or as a reliever would take a little while to determine.

Cliff Melton didn't know it, but Bill Terry had already seen enough. He had made up his mind that his young lefty would work into the starting rotation a little down the road, and further, that Freddie Fitzsimmons, a long-time Giant standby, had been made expendable by Melton's early spring showing. By mid–June Fitzsimmons was wearing a Dodger uniform, having been traded to Brooklyn for a young right-hander named Tom Baker. It was an atrocious trade, but there was at least some poetic justice in the move that brought "Fat Freddie" to Brooklyn in that he spent two and a half seasons there, winning more than he lost and endearing himself to Brooklyn's faithful.

The 1937 race looked at first as though Chicago's Northsiders would take home the bacon, thus qualifying to meet the Yankees in the Fall Classic. "Those other New Yorkers" were odds-on favorites to win the American League banner. Charlie Grimm's Cubbies not only matched the Giants stride for stride in the early going but gradually pulled away to a lead that took a furious late-season Giant rally to overcome. The race narrowed down to a late-season series at the Polo Grounds, when the man they called "Mountain Music," Cliff Melton, shut down the Cubs in the second game of the series and came to the rescue for his league-leading seventh save the next day. That win put the Giants in the driver's seat. After the last out of the season was penned in the scorebook, the Giants had a three game edge on Chicago and had won their second consecutive pennant.

But that gets us a little ahead of our story. What preceded the last couple crucial weeks of the season was the season-long emergence of a new Giant star, picking up confidence and steam as the weeks went by. For Cliff Melton those spot assignments and relief calls became fewer

Box Score

Boston Bees at the Polo grounds, New York, April 25, 1937

Boston	AB	R	H	PO	A
Garms, lf	2	0	0	0	0
Reis, ph, lf	1	0	0	2	0
Mayo, 3b	4	0	0	0	0
V. DiMaggio, cf	4	0	0	2	0
Cuccinello, 2b	4	0	0	1	7
E. Moore, rf	4	1	2	2	0
Lopez, c	3	2	1	3	0
Fletcher, 1b	4	0	2	15	1
Warstler, ss	4	0	1	1	7
Bush, p	2	0	0	1	3
Totals	32	3	6	27	18

New York	AB	R	H	PO	A
Bartell, ss	3	1	1	1	1
Chiozza, 3b	4	0	0	0	1
J. Moore, lf	4	0	2	1	0
Ott, rf	3	0	0	3	0
Leiber, cf	4	0	0	2	0
McCarthy, 1b	4	0	0	7	0
Mancuso, c	4	0	0	13	1
Whitehead, 2b	3	0	2	0	2
Leslie, ph	1	0	1	0	0
Davis, pr	0	0	0	0	0
Melton, p	2	0	0	0	3
Ripple, ph	1	0	0	0	0
Totals	33	1	6	27	8

Boston	000	010	002	3-6-2
New York	100	000	000	1-6-3

2BH	Fletcher
SB	Reis
SH	Bush, Melton
DP	Warstler, Cuccinello, Fletcher
LOB	Boston 5, New York 8
BB	Bush 2, Melton 2
K	Bush 2, Melton 13
WP	Bush (1–1)
LP	Melton (0–1)
Umpires	Stewart, Pinelli and Quigley
Time	2:15
Attendance	25,107

and farther between as the end of June approached.

In April and May the story out of the Polo Grounds was Carl Hubbell. The premier Giant screwballer was busy putting together his 24 game winning streak, which had begun during the 1936 season and carried over into 1937. On April 23 his three-hitter beat Boston for his 17th straight. By mid–May he was working on number 21 in St. Louis and nailed that one down over Dizzy Dean. On May 27 he posted number 24 at the expense of the Cincinnati Reds, before finally falling to, of all teams in the league, the Brooklyn Dodgers, who let the Giants know they were still in the league before Bill Terry even asked. The 1937 ending was part of his 22 and 8 season that led the Giants' staff.

About the same time Hubbell experienced his streak-ending, 10 to 3 loss, Melton was coming on like the New York Central's locomotives. After moving into the starting rotation he reeled off 10 wins and lost but one to go with his debut defeat, setting his record at 10 and 2. Then he won three out of his next seven decisions to level off his mark at 13 and 6 by mid–August. Among those defeats were three extra-inning losses and two games in which the Giants were themselves whitewashed. The rookie southpaw sensation then toured the rest of the 1937 circuit with seven more wins to tally a final 20 and 9 mark. Number 20 came against the

Phillies, the same team that so graciously provided Jim Turner and Lou Fette of Boston with their 20th wins.

The transformation was complete. Cliff Melton, the backwoodsman from North Carolina, had gone from the Piedmont League to the Big Apple, from six seasons of minor league ball to stardom in the Bigs, and from a wannabe to a full-fledged star. And he had the numbers to back up his hard-earned stardom:

- League leadership in Pitching Runs (35) and saves 7, tied for league lead

- 2nd-place rankings in on-base percentage (.280), ERA (2.80), and winning percentage (.690)
- 3rd-place ranking in Fewest Hits/Game (7.84), and opponents' batting average (.233)
- 4th-place ranking in Strikeouts (142)

In 1937 Carl Hubbell and Cliff Melton became the only two lefties to win 20 games for the same team in baseball history.

Rookie Seasons: The Best of the Big Apple

Nm/Tm/Lg	YR	W–L/BA	SH/SV/RBI	ERA/FR	TPR
Wilcy Moore/NY-AL	1927	19–7	1/13	2.28	4.8
Christy Mathewson/NYG-NL	1901	20–17	5/0	2.41	4.1
Russ Ford/NY-AL	1910	26–6	8/1	1.65	4.0
Cliff Melton/NYG-NL	1937	20–9	2/7	2.61	3.9
Joe Gordon/NY-AL	1938	.255	97	24	3.2
Willie Randolph/NY-AL	1976	.267	40	40	3.2*
Candy Cummings/NY-NAss'n.	1872	33–20	3/0	2.97	3.1
Jeff Tesreau/NYG-NL	1912	17–7	3/1	1.96	3.0
Joe DiMaggio/NY-AL	1936	.323	125	15	3.0
Jerry Koosman/NYM-NL	1968	19–12	7/0	2.08	3.0
George McConnell/NY-AL	1912	8–12	0/0	2.75	2.9
Jon Matlack/NYM-NL	1972	15–10	4/0	2.32	2.9
Dwight Gooden/NYM-NL	1984	17–9	3/0	2.60	2.9
Andy Carey/NY-AL	1954	.302	65	17	2.7
Buddy Kerr/NYG-NL	1944	.266	63	17	2.6
Ron Guidry/NY-AL	1977	16–7	5/1	2.82	2.6
Art Devlin/NYG-NL	1904	.281	66	7	2.5
Marius Russo/NY-AL	1939	8–3	2/2	2.41	2.5
Tiny Bonham/NY-AL	1940	9–3	3/0	1.90	2.5
Bill Voiselle/NYG-NL	1944	21–16	1/0	3.02	2.5
Ryne Duren/NY-AL	1958	6–4	0/20	2.02	2.5
Mel Stottlemyre/NY-AL	1964	9–3	2/0	2.06	2.5
Dave Orr/NY-Amer. Ass'n.	1884	.354	112	-5	2.4
Larry Jansen/NYG-NL	1947	21–5	1/1	3.16	2.4
Tom Seaver/NYM-NL	1967	16–13	2/0	2.76	2.3

NY-AL   New York Hilltoppers/Yankees, American League
NYG-NL   New York Giants, National League
NYM-NL   New York Mets, National League
NY-Natl. Ass'n   New York Mutuals, National Association
NY-Amer. Ass'n. New York Metropolitans, American Association

All ties arranged chronologically.

Vada Edward Pinson

TPR: 3.9

1959, Cincinnati, NL

Born: August 11, 1938, Memphis, TN. Died: October 21, 1995, Oakland, CA
OF; 5'11" 181 lb. Major League Debut: April 15, 1958
1959: 648-131-205 AB-R-H; .316 BA; 47 2BH;
84 RBI; .509 SA; 21 SB, 3 SBR; .984 FA; 20 FR

The bird dogs gather in the warmth of spring training's sunshine to look over the youthful hopefuls they've signed, while also leveling trained eyes on other prospects or veterans their clubs may need. During the 1958 spring training season a number of them were on hand, sitting together with stopwatches and notepads at the ready, to take a closer look at a jet-fueled Cincinnati prospect named Vada Pinson. The first game of the training season was on tap, pitting the Reds against the Chicago White Sox. With a little luck they might see him bounce one to one of the White Sox infielders and get a better fix on just how fast he could move down the line. They already knew that he could really move, but they wanted to know what it meant to be "Pinson-fast." The stopwatch would tack it down.

That day Vada Pinson gave them a thing or two to look at. He dragged a bunt just past the pitcher, which, of course set the stopwatches ticking. An unbelievable

3.2 seconds later he crossed first base. Four of the scouts who were sitting together compared their watches in disbelief. All four registered 3.2. Incredible. That's faster than "The Mick" made it down the line.

There was more. Later in the game he threw a White Sox runner out going from first to third on a shot to deep right center. And he hit. Speed, power, great arm and good baseball instincts. If this was a big beginning, who would want to miss what was still to come?

What followed was a training season full of base hits, spectacular catches, stolen bases and a ticket to Cincinnati. Manager Birdie Tebbetts found it hard to contain himself. Though he knew that a successful leap from the Reds' Class C farm club in Visalia, California, was just about more than could be expected, the evidence in front of him day after day had him convinced that Pinson should start the season with the big team.

Vada Pinson started his professional

baseball career in 1956 with the Wausau Lumberjacks of the Class C Northern league. He had been signed to a Cincinnati contract by scout Bobby Mattick after graduating from McClymonds High School in Oakland, California. That was the same high school for which both Frank Robinson and Curt Flood had played ball before moving on to brilliant baseball careers. Pinson was next in line. As he was beginning his trek from the bushes on up through the Cincinnati system, Frank Robinson was getting ready to move into the center ring and a career that eventually would lead to the Hall of Fame.

Hitting .278 as Wausau's first baseman in 75 ball games was sufficient incentive for the Reds to stay right with him, moving him to the Visalia club in another Class C circuit for 1957. This time he tore the league apart, leading it in enough categories to garner all-star honors and the league's MVP award. So impressive was his season that Visalia's skipper, Bruce Edwards, had no doubt his 18-year-old outfielder–first baseman would make the jump all the way to the Bigs. Edwards had it right. The Reds opened the season with Pinson, only halfway into his 19th year, in center field. In order to make room in the outfield for him, helmsman Tebbetts posted Frank Robinson at first base, a position he had played previously even though he was an exceptional outfielder.

It took only two games for Vada Pinson to provide Cincinnati's fans with the kind of thrills that he would keep on providing for more than a decade of superlative hitting, outfielding, baserunning and all-out hustle. Facing Pittsburgh's Ronnie Kline on April 18 with Reds on every last base, he jacked one into the seats for the first of his six Cincy grand slams, winning the game. But it didn't take long for him to find out that it was far from the best thing that might have happened, as much as he and everyone else in the ball park reveled

in that exquisite moment. That four-run shot caused him to change his hitting approach just enough to exceed his natural limits.

Vada Pinson always could hit. He was primarily a line-drive hitter, and had enough power to clear the fences over 20 times a season — but he was no Frank Robinson. "Robby" was an authentic home run threat (over 500 career big ones put him in the exclusive "500 Club"), and Pinson wasn't. Vada's homers would have to come on the kind of stinging shots that drilled holes in concrete walls.

As April moved into May, Pinson's hitting nose-dived almost out of sight, and all because he was trying to lift everything over the fences. By May 12 it was ticket time again. This time the destination was Seattle. So Vada took his .194 average to the Pacific Coast League where he would have time to think about the ABCs of major league baseball as they applied to a ball player named Vada Pinson.

It was with Seattle's Rainiers that the youthful speedster came to grips with his expectations and capabilities. Connie Ryan, his manager, saw to it that Pinson began hitting outside pitches to the opposite field, and that "Mr. Precocious," as Cincy scribe Bill Ford had dubbed him, began to be more selective at the plate, picking his spots and pitches much more carefully. Quick hands and powerful wrists soon began to move his line-drive rifle shots all over the outfield. It was just a matter of time before Vada began slashing Triple A pitching into fine pieces. With it came renewed confidence. Before he finished his postgraduate course on the West Coast he had his velvet-smooth stroke back, along with improvements in his outfielding. He was around long enough that summer to hit a solid .343 and lead the league in stolen bases, 37, even though he only played three quarters of Seattle's schedule. Vada Pinson was ready for another shot at Cincinnati.

Outstanding 1959 rookie Vada Pinson pictured with Hall of Famer Frank Robinson at Yankee Stadium. (Dennis Colgin.)

Spring training for Vada Pinson was literally all fun and games in 1959. He moved right into a starting lineup that began its ascent to the pennant two years later under "Old Stoneface," Freddie Hutchinson. Frank Robinson and Johnny Temple anchored the infield. At short and third it was position by committee with Eddie Kasko, Roy McMillan, Willie Jones and Frank Thomas taking turns in a situation all hands made the best of, but dissatisfying nonetheless. Gus Bell, Jerry Lynch and Frank Thomas, doubling in utility roles, were the outfielders who played alongside Vada Pinson (154 games played, a team-leading 21 stolen bases and team highs in batting average [.316], at-bats [648], and runs scored [131]). Within another couple seasons "Hutch" had settled on Gordy Coleman at first base, moving Frank Robinson back to the outfield, and Don Blasingame, who was brought in from the Giants, played second base. Consequently, Hutchinson had a super outfield corps led by Robby and Vada Pinson in his pennant-winning season of 1961, which showcased a starting rotation of Joey Jay, Jim O'Toole and Bob Purkey, with Jim Brosnan in the number one reliever's role. Though the Reds lost the World Series to the Yankees, it was a huge Pinson year. He hit .343, second to Roberto Clemente's league-leading average, and won a Gold Glove, contributing 19 Fielding Runs to Cincinnati's cause.

But before 1961 there was a 1959, sixth-place finish that brought on a change in Redleg skippers, from Birdie Tebbetts to Hutchinson, who took over at mid-season. It was a season of transition as far as the franchise and the team were concerned, but for a young ball player like Vada Pinson, who would not turn 20 until mid–August, it was like one long summer afternoon visit to the chocolate shop. Reunited with his old American Legion ball teammate, Frank Robinson, only 23 himself, the two of them romped through the schedule, hitting at .311 (Robby) and .316 (Pinson), while running bases with abandon as they stole 39 bases between themselves.

Vada started off 1959 with a flurry of hits that quickly moved him into the National League's top 10. Eight games into the season he encountered 20-game winner Warren Spahn, mastering the future Hall of Famer with four RBIs on a single, a double, and a triple that hiked his average to .353. He was a top 10 hitter all season long, winding up fourth behind another Hall of Famer, Hank Aaron, who won his second batting title at .355, with a 200-hit effort. Pinson's was the first 200-hit season in the National League since Reds' first baseman Buck McCormick's 209 in 1939.

Pinson's revised approach to hitting paid off. His play proved beyond doubt that he had learned his lessons well. On June 6 he was at the .327 mark with 69 hits, 40 RBIs and 42 runs scored. As the summer wore on his stats reflected the same consistency his day-to-day performance did. Near the end of August he hit a season high point at .342. That triggered a "Hats Off" salute in *The Sporting News'* September 2 edition, which extolled his steady play and a 15-game hitting streak.

The box score below presents the two McClymonds High alums at their rampaging best. In a wild, base-hit orgy at Philadelphia, the Reds beat the Phillies 15 to 13 in the first game of a doubleheader sweep in which both Pinson and Robinson trashed Phillie pitching with five hits apiece. Pinson doubled twice and Robby homered.

After the smoke had cleared Pinson was in third place in the hitting race at .329 on 159 hits (second to Aaron), and he became the first player in either league to move over the 100 mark in runs scored. Robinson's home run solidified his third-place ranking in circuit clouts at 27, eight behind league leader Ernie Banks (35).

According to the Rookie of the Year rules used by the BBWAA, Vada Pinson was six at-bats over the limit for eligibility in 1959. In 1971 the present ruling, which stipulates no more than a total of 50 innings pitched or 130 at-bats, was adopted. Under that ruling Pinson qualifies for honors in our listing. Willie "Stretch" McCovey, who hit .354, playing in 52 games

Box Score

First game of a Cincinnati-Philadelphia Twin Bill, August 14, 1959

Cincinnati	AB	R	H	RBI		Philadelphia	AB	R	H	RBI
Temple, 2b	4	3	2	2		Ashburn, cf	6	2	2	0
Pinson, cf	6	4	5	1		G. Anderson, 2b	5	2	2	2
G. Bell, rf	5	3	3	2		Philley, ph	1	0	0	0
F. Robinson, 1b	6	3	5	4		Bouchee, 1b	5	2	4	1
Lynch, lf	3	0	0	0		Post, rf	5	1	1	1
Whisenant, ph-lf	1	0	0	0		Drake, rf	1	0	1	1
Powers, lf	1	1	0	0		Freese, 3b	4	1	1	1
Bailey, c	5	2	2	3		H. Anderson, lf	3	0	1	2
Jones, 3b	5	1	4	3		Koppe, ss	2	1	0	2
Kasko, ss	6	0	1	0		Lonnett, c	5	1	1	0
Newcombe, p	1	0	0	0		Thomas, c	0	0	0	0
Acker, p	0	0	0	0		Conley, p	3	2	2	2
Lockman, ph	1	0	0	0		Phillips, p	1	0	0	0
Pena, p	2	0	1	0		Farrell, p	0	0	0	0
Thomas, ph	1	0	0	0		H. Robinson, p	0	0	0	0
Lawrence, p	0	0	0	0		Gomez, p	0	0	0	0
Brosnan, p	0	0	0	0		Hanebrink, ph	1	1	1	0
Totals	47	15	23	15		Totals	42	13	16	12

2BH	Bouchee, Conley, Ashburn, Pinson 2, Jones, Temple, F, Robinson
HR	Freese, F. Robinson
SF	Koppe, Temple
LOB	Cincinnati 12, Philadelphia 10
DP	Jones, Temple, F. Robinson; Kasko, Temple, F. Robinson, Gomez, Bouchee
K	Newcombe, Brosnan, Farrell and H. Robinson, 0; Acker and Lawrence 1; Conley and Phillips 2; Pena 5
BB	Newcombe, Pena, Lawrence, Brosnan, Farrell and Gomez 0; Phillips and H. Robinson 1; Conley 3; Newcombe 5
HBP	Joppe by Newcombe; Freese by Acker
WP	Lawrence (7–10)
LP	Farrell (1–4)
Umpires	Delmore, Barlick, Jackowski and Crawford
Time	3:45

after a midseason callup to San Francisco, was, rather incredibly, selected as the BBWAA's unanimous choice for 1959, receiving all 24 of the scribes' votes.

But for Vada Pinson, not being named the Rookie of the Year was of little consequence. He had arrived. And for the present, at least, that was more than enough. His productive season had merited a 3.9 TPR, earning a top 20 ranking to tie with pitcher George McQuillan of the 1908 Phillies, Scott Perry of the 1918 Athletics, and Cliff Melton of the 1937 New York Giants for the final spot among our *Cum Laudes*. Vada Pinson is the last, but certainly not the least, among our 42 profiled freshmen who make up the list of baseball's greatest rookie seasons.

1959: Eleven Top Rookies

Nm/Pos/Tm	GP	W–L/BA	SH/SV//RBI	PR/BR	ERA/FR	TPR
Pinson/of/Cin-N	154	.316	84	25	20	3.9
J. Perry/RHP/Clv-A	44	12–10	2/4	18	2.65	2.8
L. Sherry/RHP/LA-N	23	7–2	1/3	21	2.19	2.2
Owens/RHP/Phl-N	31	12–12	1/1	22	3.21	2.1
McCovey*/1b/SF-N	52	.354	38	24	-2	2.0
J. Walker/RHP/Bal-A	30	11–10	2/4	18	2.92	1.9
Romano/c/Chi-A	53	.294	25	8	1	1.0
R. Miller/RP-RHP/StL-N	11	4–3	0/0	7	3.31	0.8
Gibson/RHP/StL-N	13	3-5	1/0	8	3.33	0.7
Allison†/of/Was-A	150	.261	85	15	-2	0.5
Snyder/of/KC-A	73	.313	21	5	3	0.5

*Voted National League Rookie of the Year
†Voted American League Rookie of the Year

PART III

From the First in 1880 to the Last in 1999

This part of our review of baseball's greatest freshman seasons covers 22 outstanding rookies extending back to the turn of the 20th century, and then back still farther to the latter decades of the 1800s. There is Artie Irwin, a diminutive infielder who played for the Worcester, Massachusetts, Brown Stockings, way back in 1880. And there is also the Cuban right-hander Rolando Arrojo, who, in 1998, earned his ranking among the rookie greats with Tampa Bay's Devil Rays in his — and their — major league debut seasons. Each has his own interesting story, as well as the credentials to merit top billing.

Keeping in mind that upwards of 20,000 ballplayers have pulled on uniforms in seven different major leagues since the formation of the National Association in 1871, the ranking of these 22 exceptional athletes, with Total Player Ratings ranging from 3.4 to 3.8, takes on a very special significance. Scott Rolen, the Phillies' super third sacker, whose select 1997 freshman year completes the list, is the 64th profile presented in *Rookies Rated*, making him one of less than 75 thus honored out of the mass of ballplayers who broke into major league baseball over the past 129 years.

Three Hall of Famers, Pete Alexander, Elmer Flick and Rogers Hornsby, are included in this section's diverse list of 12 pitchers and 10 position players. Some are well known, like Ozzie Smith and Wes Ferrell, while others may very well be who-are-they? players like reliever Cy Acosta of the White Sox and Cincinnati's Elmer Riddle. Let's take a look at them.

George Joseph "Nig" Cuppy

TPR: 3.8

1892, Cleveland Spiders, NL

Born: July 3, 1869, Logansport, IN. Died: 1922, Elkhart, IN; RHP, 5'7" 160 lb.
1892: W28, L13; .683 W%; 1/1 SH/SV; 37 PR; 3 PD; 2.51 ERA

There was no lack of open fields in Logansport, Indiana, where three gunny sacks and a metal can top could mark off a baseball diamond in George Cuppy's younger years. And he was out there every chance he got, including times when he knew he shouldn't be. But he loved the game like few others and found his way into semi-professional baseball while still in his earlier teens. By the time he was 20, he had signed to play with the Dayton, Ohio, team of the Tri-State League in 1890. He was quickly rubbed up against the facts of minor league life, as the ballclub folded in mid-season during those uncertain times. But he had made a mark in his first try, pitching decently, while running up a creditable 14 and 8 mark for the last place Dayton Reds. Two shutouts were among his wins and at the time the club folded he was one of the league ERA leaders at 1.43.

Moving eastward, the young right hander hooked on with the newly formed Meadville team of the New York–Pennsylvania

The Spiders' right-hander George "Nig" Cuppy. (Brace Photo.)

League for the 1891 season. There, he really started getting down to business, posting a 2.05 ERA, winning 23 games while losing but 11 for another cellar dweller, and hitting at a strong .280. For a second consecutive year the team for which he was pitching disbanded, this time in mid–August, but this time around he had attracted enough attention to enable him to sign on with the Jamestown team of the same circuit without even losing a pitching turn.

Two things attracted the attention of major league ballclubs. Naturally, one was his record. The other was his style. A most deliberate sort, the hurler they sometimes called "The Cuban Warrior" gave hitters fits while he was taking his good-natured time getting ready to deliver a variety of junkball pitches. Breaking in at a time when the pitching rubber was still only 50 feet from home plate, the order of the day for pitchers was to hustle the batter not only with fastballs and hard curves, thrown more to achieve speed than a break on the ball, but with pitches that were thrown as soon as the usual preliminaries like signals and windups could be taken care of. Cuppy's style stood in stark contrast to the hurry-up, blitzkrieg approach.

Any manager willing to make Cuppy and his three-quarter time baseball pace a part of his team's pitching staff would have to put up with the little fellow's shenanigans. Manager Patsy Tebeau and his Cleveland Spiders, hoping to improve on their fifth-place 1891 finish, were willing. And in 1892 George Cuppy returned their patience and investment in his unique style in handsome dividends even though he was on a staff boasting luminaries like Cy Young and John Clarkson, who joined Cleveland midway into the 1892 season. That year Nig Cuppy pitched a man-sized 396 innings (Young went 453), won a career-high 28 ball games in 47 appearances and recorded a 2.51 ERA in a league that had absorbed the best of the disbanded

American Association's players and saw its membership swell to 12 teams. There were, indeed, a number of brand new things vying for attention in the National League during the 1892 season besides George Cuppy. However, none of them was distracting enough to deter the young Cleveland twirling sensation from one well-pitched game after another.

Cy Young and George Cuppy made a perfect one-two punch for the Spiders. Young was a power pitcher, tireless, fast-working, and well-nigh unhittable. When Cuppy came along the next day with his nothing-stuff, the hitters around the league, still focused on Young's laser shots from the day before, found themselves popping up, chopping grounders, or missing altogether. All the makings for a frustrating afternoon were in place, and George Cuppy made the most of it.

Over the course of the summer Cuppy took the measure of Philadelphia four out of five meetings, sent Baltimore reeling four straight times, and silenced the bats of the rest of the league's ballclubs either two or three times apiece, except for Boston, which beat him twice and lost only once. Between them, Young and Cuppy posted 63 of Cleveland's 93 wins as the Spiders wound up second to the pennant-winning Boston Beaneaters. Playing in a split season, Boston, paced by Kid Nichols and Jack Stivetts (each of whom won 35 games), was the winner of the first half, and Cleveland the second half. In the playoffs that followed regular season play Boston won five straight after an opening game standoff between Cy Young and Jack Stivetts, who matched zeros for 11 innings before darkness ended the game in a tie. In the fourth game of the championship series, played at Boston, George Cuppy pitched well, but ran afoul George Duffy's two-run shot that went for four bases. The Spiders went down by a 4 to 0 count when it was all over. There was, however, a Cuppy bright spot:

of the four runs scored against him in his only appearance, only one, which came on Duffy's four-bagger, was earned, as he registered a sparkling 1.13 ERA.

On July 7, only a year removed from his Meadville days in the New York–Pennsylvania League, George Cuppy pitched his first major league shutout in the first game of a doubleheader against the Brooklyn Bridegrooms. He walked only one man while scattering seven hits, only one of which went for extra bases, a Mike Griffin double, defeating Brooklyn's crafty veteran, Scissors Foutz.

There's not much doubt about the fact that 1892 was a Cy Young masterpiece. He was the big news in town, and justly so. But the little fellow who joined him on the pitching staff that summer, Nig Cuppy, snared his share of headlines with a rookie season that signalled several years of Cleveland pitching superiority. During Cuppy's first five seasons with the Spiders, the two young dynamos turned in 279 Spider victories, averaging right at 55 to 56 a season. And 120 of those wins belonged to George Cuppy.

The Rookie Class of 1892

After the demise of the American Association in 1891, the National League suddenly blossomed to a 12-team circuit. There simply wasn't much room for freshmen. Teams headed north for their season openers with lineups that were jammed with former American Association and

---

Box Score

Cleveland at Eastern Park, Brooklyn, July 7, 1892

Cleveland	AB	R	H	PO	A
Childs, 2b	5	0	0	2	4
Burkett, lf	5	1	2	3	0
Davis, rf	5	0	2	1	0
McKean, ss	5	1	0	1	1
Virtue, 1b	5	1	1	11	0
McAleer, cf	5	1	1	7	0
Tebeau, 3b	4	1	2	1	3
Zimmer, c	4	1	2	0	0
Cuppy, p	4	0	1	0	4
Totals	42	6	11	26*	12

Brooklyn	AB	R	H	PO	A
Ward, 2b	5	0	1	2	2
Corcoran, ss	4	0	1	2	5
Joyce, 3b	3	0	0	1	2
Burns, rf	4	0	0	0	0
Brouthers, 1b	4	0	0	13	0
Griffin, cf	3	0	2	4	0
T. Daly, lf	4	0	2	4	0
C. Daly, c	2	0	1	1	0
Foutz, p	1	0	0	0	0
Hart, p	3	0	0	0	3
Totals	33	0	7	27	12

Cleveland　021　200　010　6-11-0
Brooklyn　000　000　000　0-7-5

2BH	Tebeau, Cuppy, Griffin
3BH	Burkett
SB	Virtue
SH	Davis, McLean 2, Virtue, Zimmer, Hart
LOB	Cleveland 7, Brooklyn 10
BB	Cuppy 1, Foutz and Hart 0
K	None
WP	Cuppy
LP	Foutz
Umpire	Hurst
Time	1:50

*Baserunner hit by batted ball for automatic out

National League veterans. With the exception of George Cuppy, whose rookie season is light-years removed from the rest of the Class of 1892, those who did manage some playing time during the season made up one of the weakest groups of rookies in the history of professional baseball. Below are the best of the worst.

Nm/Pos/Tm	W–L/BA	PR/RBI	ERA/FR	TPR
G. Cuppy/RHP/Clv	28–13	37	2.51	3.8
A. Jones/LHP/Lou	5–11	1	3.00	0.1
F. Clausen/LHP/Lou	9–13	0	3.06	-0.3
J. McMahon/1b/NY	.224	24	-2	-0.4
B. Abbey/RHP/Was	5–18	-4	3.45	-0.5
S. Dungan/of/Chi	.284	53	-6	-0.5
W. Merritt/c/Lou	.196	13	-3	-0.8
W. Hawke/RHP/StL	5–5	-5	3.70	-0.9
C. Newman/of/NY-Chi	.192	3	-3	-1.0
E. Moriarity/of/StL	.175	19	2	-1.2
F. Genins/Ut/Cin-StL	.186	11	-3	-1.3
W. Moran/c/StL	.136	5	-4	-1.3
W. Kennedy/RHP/Brk	13–8	-15	3.86	-1.5
L. Camp/3b/StL	.207	13	-16	-1.7
W. Parrott/3b/Chi	.201	22	-2	-2.0

Kenneth Ray Tatum

TPR: 3.8

1969, California Angels, AL
Born: 1944, Alexandria, LA; RP-RHP, 6'2" 205 lb.
1969: W7, L2; .778 W%; 0/22 SH/SV; 20 PR; 9.8 Ratio; 1.36 ERA

There have been a number of years when BBWAA voting for Rookie of the Year was anything but conclusive. In 1968, for example, the National League award went to Johnny Bench with 10.5 votes. But he was hard-pressed by lefty Jerry Koosman's 9.5 votes. In 1961, the Red Sox' Don Schwall beat out Kansas City's Dick Howser by a single vote, 7 to 6. And in 1952, right-hander Harry Byrd of the Philadelphia Athletics won the coveted honors by a slim, one-vote margin over the St. Louis Browns' Clint Courtney, 9 to 8.

In 1969, Sweet Lou Piniella of Kansas City's first-year Royals was elected the Rookie of the Year with a bigger margin than those above, but his 9 votes outpolled pitcher Mike Nagy by only three votes. Behind Nagy came Carlos May, Chicago White Sox outfielder, with five, and then Ken Tatum, California reliever, with four. That's a tight, somewhat inconclusive ballot.

On the other hand, the Total Player Rating, shown below, is much more decisive. Now then, what's wrong with the BBWAA picture? Is there a case to be made for Kenneth Ray Tatum? His profile should provide some answers.

Scout "Red" Smith signed Ken Tatum to his first professional contract. Tatum's first assignment was to the Class A Midwest League after an outstanding career at Mississippi State University, where he led his alma mater to conference championships in 1965 and 1966. The young right-hander was a versatile ballplayer who pitched well, hit, and fielded his position like a fifth infielder. The California Angels organization was impressed. Through two more seasons of minor league baseball he

Rank	Name	W–L/BA	PR/BR	ERA/FR	TPR
1	Tatum	7–2	20	1.36	3.8
2	C. May	.281	19	–1	1.0
3	Piniella	.282	3	15	1.0
4	M. Nagy	12–2	15	3.11	0.8

Angels reliever Ken Tatum. (Brace Photo.)

tion. Bridges suggested changing to relief pitching. Tatum concurred. The Ponce skipper, who was on the Angels' coaching staff, brought his pupil along carefully and suggested to the new California manager, Lefty Phillips, that Tatum was just about ready for relief duty. It couldn't have come at a better time, either for the Angels, or for Ken Tatum. The new Angels manager inherited a chaotic bullpen situation, and though Eddie Fisher and Hoyt Wilhelm were on hand for the 1969 season, there was room for an effective arm out of the pen.

Tatum was assigned to Hawaii to start out the 1969 season, where he appeared in eight ball games, winning three, relieving in four, and sharpening up his limited assortment of pitches. With Tatum, who bluntly acknowledged that "the hitters knew what was coming," there were three basic tools in his relieving kit:

made sufficient progress to move on up to Triple A ball with manager Chuck Tanner at Hawaii in the spring of 1969. En route he had led the California League with his 2.12 ERA and his fielding during a 12 and 6 season in 1967. He was just about ready for the Bigs. But not before overcoming an injury to his pitching arm and the inevitable adjustments that have to be made.

While pitching for Ponce, in Puerto Rican winter ball, Ken came down with a strain that shelved him momentarily. Thanks to manager Rocky Bridges, however, there was a major change in direc-

a moving fastball that was often clocked in the 90s, a slider and a change of speeds. But the secret was location. His postgraduate studies in relief pitching were conducted by past-masters Fisher and Wilhelm, who, as he was quick to point out, "never complained about my pitching ahead of them in relief appearances."

During his rookie year in 1969, after a late–May callup, and again in 1970, Ken Tatum was among the top three relievers in the American League. In his freshman campaign, which began with a May 28 debut, his Relief Ranking, 30.9,* was second

*Jim Kern's 65.0 Relief Ranking in 1979 is the all-time single-season high. Mark Eichhorn, whose 1986 rookie Relief Ranking was 55.3, ranks number seven on this list; Doug Corbett's 1980 mark of 46.6 ranks 21; Todd Worrell had a 40.8 Relief Ranking in 1986; and Dick Radatz's 39.5 in 1962 is number 47 on the list of top single-season relievers. Each of these four is ranked on our rookies honor list.

to league-leading Ron Perranoski's. The anchor man and ace reliever out of division titlist Minnesota's bullpen rated a 41.3 Relief Ranking.

During that magic summer of 1969, Ken Tatum was particularly rough on Baltimore's pennant winners and the Boston Red Sox. A late season call came in an August 20 game at Los Angeles after an accident in a baserunning collision shelved starting pitcher Andy Messersmith in the seventh inning. That brought on Tatum, who shut down the O's with runless stanzas in the final two innings.

The California win stopped Baltimore dead in its tracks after a seven-game win skein, and marked only the third time Oriole ace Dave McNally, 17 and 2 going into

the game, lost in a 20 and 7 season. The two hitless innings Ken Tatum hurled enhanced a season record that featured a mere 51 hits in 86.1 innings pitched. By the time another season had gone by, the tally stood at an exceptional 119 hits in 175 innings.

There were still other indications that he might have worn a Rookie of the Year crown with distinction. American League hitters, with the exception of Tony Oliva, who seemed to have no trouble with Tatum's slants, could muster only a .172 batting average against him as he ran up a league-leading 22 Pitching Runs for relievers. Adjusted for home park and league factors, the pitching runs total came to 20, one behind Ron Perranoski's 21 in the Adjusted Pitching Runs category.

Box Score

Baltimore at Los Angeles, California, August 20, 1969

California	AB	R	H	BI	E		Baltimore	AB	R	H	BI	E
R. Alomar, Sr, 2b	4	1	1	0	0		D. Buford, 2b	5	0	1	0	0
Johnstone, cf	3	1	1	0	0		Motton, lf	3	0	0	0	0
Fregosi, ss	3	0	2	0	0		F. Robinson, rf	3	0	1	0	0
Morton, rf	2	0	0	0	0		Powell, 1b	3	0	0	0	0
Voss, rf	1	0	0	0	0		Hardin, p	0	0	0	0	0
Reichardt, lf	4	0	1	2	0		Hendricks, c	4	0	0	0	0
Rodriguez, 3b	4	1	2	1	0		Johnson, 2b	3	0	1	0	0
Spencer, 1b	4	0	1	0	0		Rettenmund, cf	3	0	0	0	0
Azcue, c	4	0	0	0	0		Belanger, ss	3	1	0	0	0
Messersmith, p	3	0	1	0	1		McNally, p	2	0	0	0	0
Tatum, p	0	0	0	0	0		Leonhard, p	0	0	0	0	0
							Salmon, 1b	2	1	1	2	0
Totals	32	3	9	3	1		Totals	31	2	4	2	0

Baltimore   000   000   200   2-4-0
California   000   120   00x   3-9-1

2BH	Johnson, Spencer
HR	Rodriguez, Salmon
SB	Motton, Johnstone
LOB	Baltimore 10, California 8
K	McNally 4, Leonhard 1, Hardin 0, Messersmith 5, Tatum 2
BB	McNally 3, Leonhard and Hardin 0, Messersmith 6, Tatum 2
Wild P.	Messersmith 2
PB	Hendricks
WP	Messersmith (12–8)
LP	McNally (17–3)
Time	2:38
Att	11.334

And lest it pass by without mention: on no less an auspicious date than July 4, Ken Tatum caught one of Seattle right-hander Gary Bell's pitches for the first of his two dingers in 1969. In a series against the Red Sox at Boston he also blasted a shot over the "Green Monster" off Jim Lonborg's first pitch in relief. In that series he registered two of his saves that season.

Ken Tatum wasn't voted the AL's Rookie of the Year in 1969, but there seems to be plenty of evidence that he racked up the kind of freshman season most rookie relievers would kill for. Too bad the BBWAA didn't see it that way, reflecting Tatum's super season in their voting. The guess from this corner is that Mr. Tatum had all the better of it.

1969: Ten Top Rookies

Nm/Pos/Tm	GP	W–L/BA	SH/SV//RBI	PR/BR	ERA/FR	TPR
K. Tatum/RP-RHP/Cal-A	45	7–2	0/22	20	1.36	3.8
M. Fiore/1b-of/KC-A	107	.274	35	21	10	2.3
W. Granger/RP-RHP/Cin-N	90	9–6	0/27	15	2.80	2.3
R. Hebner/3b/Pit-N	129	.301	47	18	3	2.3
L. Hisle/of/Phl-N	145	.266	56	14	11	1.9
D. Money/ss/Phl-N	127	.229	42	-14	17	1.6
C. Taylor/of-1b/Pit-N	104	.348	33	17	-1	1.3
C. May/of/Chi-A	100	.281	62	19	-1	1.0
L. Piniella*/of/KC-A	135	.282	68	3	15	1.0
M. Nagy/RHP/Bos-A	33	12–2	1/0	15	3.11	0.8

*Lou Piniella was voted Rookie of the Year in the American League, and Ted Sizemore (Los Angeles) was voted Rookie of the Year in the National League (0.3 TPR).

Timothy James "Tim" Salmon

TPR: 3.8

1993, California Angels, AL
Born: 1968, Long Beach, CA; OF, 6'3" 201 lb.
1993: .283 BA; 31 HR; 95 RBI; .536 SA; 30 BR; 15 FR

Tim Salmon was a unanimous Rookie of the Year choice in 1993. With National League award-winner Mike Piazza, whose brilliant rookie season sparked the Los Angeles Dodgers, the two young power hitters were the first BBWAA selections to be honored unanimously in the same year. And the numbers justified the choices in an unusually rare "double play" that brought the coveted awards, one for either league, to California's "City of the Angels."

Although manager Buck Rodgers' Angels (71–91) were mired in a fifth-place tie with the Minnesota Twins at season's end, their rookie phenom gave Angel fans something to cheer about, establishing franchise rookie marks for doubles (35), home runs (31), extra base hits (67), and walks (82). Salmon's 23 home runs at Anaheim Stadium established a club record, and his subsequent Rookie of the

The 1993 Rookie of the Year, Tim Salmon. (Dennis Colgin.)

237

Year Award was the first in franchise history, finally breaking a 32-year drought.

But there was more. Much more. Tim was one of the Topps Rookie All-Star selections and a co-winner of the franchise's Owner's Trophy with pitcher Mark Langston, awarded annually to the Angels player, or players, who exemplify the qualities of inspirational leadership, sportsmanship and professional ability. Symbolic of the team's MVP award, the selection was made by Salmon's teammates. And in 1993 he became only the fourth player in the history of baseball's individual awards to be named the Minor League Player of the Year and the Rookie of the Year in successive years.

Tim Salmon's 1993 sabermetric Total Player Rating thus ties him with George Cuppy, Ken Tatum (whose 3.8 rating for the Angels in 1969 preceded Salmon's by almost a quarter century), and Rolando Arrojo for the lead-off spot in the final segment of our rookie honor roll. The 3.8 rating, which may be rounded to four, represents a four-game contribution to his team's win column, and the net result is a four game difference in the standings, as you will recall. Salmon's stellar season, therefore, merits ranking, along with Cuppy, Tatum and Arrojo, at the number 21 spot among the top 25 rookie marks in the game's history. That's an imposing achievement.

Unfortunately, the Angels collectively did not match Salmon's individual brilliance. They stepped off to a strong April start that put their best opening month into the franchise record book. Winning 16 times in 23 tries, including a season-best six-game winning streak, they came down to the end of the month with a homestand windup against the Yankees. The Yankees' cagey veteran southpaw, Jimmy Key, summarily dispatched the Angels with a 5 to 0 one-hitter. The Eastern Division had left a calling card. The news would not get any better on their second trip east. Losing five straight to Boston and Cleveland, they

limped home around the .500 mark. By All-Star Game break time, they were still around that same .500 mark, still in contention for the Western Division title, but still, in reality, heading south. The second half of the 1993 season confirmed everyone's worst suspicions: the Angels were not a .500 ballclub, and they wound up losing 20 more than they won, settling for a disappointing fifth-place finish in the division.

One of Tim Salmon's more notable accomplishments during the 1993 season was a season-long barrage of extra-base hitting, which accounted for 35 two-baggers, a triple and 31 home runs, leaving a trail of game-winners in the wake of his steady slugging. Twelve times during the season his game-tieing RBI helped the Angels along and on 21 occasions he brought home the go-ahead run. There were nine, 3-RBI games plus another three with 4 RBI's. On the next page are some of the more significant of his four-ply blows during the season.

Tim Salmon's two-dinger ball game against Detroit was the second of his multi-homer games in 1993. In a ball game that found the home-standing Haloes ahead 6 to 2 going into the ninth inning, another of those late-inning losses befell the team as the Tigers laid on a six-run barrage to make off with an 8 to 6 victory. The box score follows on page 239.

Salmon followed up his great freshman season with a super effort in 1995, rocking American League pitching with a .330 batting average (good for third place in the batting crown derby), a .594 slugging average, and a league-leading 5.9 TPR. That season he hit career highs in home runs (34) and RBIs (105). He had become a steady, productive Angels star, enjoying a promising career in his native California.

But then the big test came. In 1997 his wife Marci was diagnosed with thyroid cancer, and her condition bored into the

HR#	Date	Rd/Hm	Inn.	Men On	Pitcher	Made Score	Final Score
1	4/14	Mil-R	9	2	Graeme Lloyd	12–2	12–2
5	4/28	NY-H	9	0	Jim Abbott	3–2	3–2
6	5/14	KC-H	7	0	David Cone	1–1	1–2
11	6/4	Det-R	3	1	David Wells	3–1	6–3
18	7/16	Clv-R	6	0	Mark Clark	2–1	2–1
20	7/19	Bos-R	8	1	Paul Quantrill	5–8	6–8
22	7/27	Oak-H	1	2	Bobby Witt	4–0	15–8
23	7/27	Oak-H	4	0	Joe Boever	9–3	15–8
26	8/18	Det-H	1	1	Mike Moore	2–4	3–9
27	8/18	Det-H	3	0	Mike Moore	3–2	6–8
31	9/15*	Sea-H	4	3	Tim Leary	9–1	15–1

Box Score

Detroit at Anaheim Stadium, California, August 18, 1993

Detroit	AB	R	H	BI	E		California	AB	R	H	BI	E
Phillips, lf-2b	4	1	0	0	0		Polonia, lf	4	1	0	0	0
Gladden, cf	4	1	0	0	0		Curtis, cf	5	1	2	0	0
Fryman, 3b	5	0	2	2	1		Salmon, rf	5	3	2	3	0
Fielder, dh	4	1	2	1	0		Davis, dh	5	1	2	2	0
Trammel, ss	5	1	1	2	0		Correia, pr	0	0	0	0	0
Tettleton, 1b	4	1	2	0	0		Myers, c	2	0	0	0	0
Deer, rf	4	1	1	0	0		Tingley, c	1	0	1	0	0
Rowland, c	2	0	1	0	1		Javier, ph	0	0	0	0	0
Kreuter, ph-c	1	1	1	1	0		Perez, 3b	5	0	0	0	1
Gomez, 2b	3	0	0	0	1		Van Burkleo, 1b	3	0	0	0	0
Whitaker, ph	0	0	0	0	0		Stillwell, 2b	4	0	2	0	0
Barnes, ph	1	0	1	2	0		DiSarcina, ss	4	0	1	0	0
Thurman, pr-lf	0	1	0	0	0		Finley, p	0	0	0	0	0
Moore, p	0	0	0	0	0		Nelson, p	0	0	0	0	0
Knudsen, p	0	0	0	0	0		Frey, p	0	0	0	0	0
Henneman, p	0	0	0	0	0		Butcher, p	0	0	0	0	0
Totals	37	8	11	8	3		Totals	38	6	10	5	1

```
Detroit      020  000  006   8-11-3
California   201  010  200   6-10-1
```

2BH	Fryman, Tettleton, Rowland, Hreuter
HR	Trammel, Salmon 2, Davis
SB	Curtis, Salmon, Stillwell
SF	Fielder
LOB	Detroit 6, California 9
DP	Detroit
K	Moore 3, Knudsen 1, Henneman 1, Finley 7, Nelson, Frey and Butcher 0
BB	Moore 2, Knudsen 1, Henneman 1, Finley 1, Nelson 0, Frey and Butcher 1
WP	Knudsen (2–2)
LP	Frey (2–2)
Save	Henneman
Umpires	Coble, Merrill, Welke and Cousins
Time	3:27
Att	21,544

Salmon's first career grand slam came on the night he fractured his ring-finger in a season-ending attempt to catch a sinking line drive. The homer was his ninth hit in his last 18 at-bats and raised his batting average to a final .283.

depths of Tim Salmon's being. She was to endure months of uncomfortable tests, treatment, and advice — and Tim's inability to prevent any of this was excruciating. After submitting to thyroid removal and follow-up treatment, though, their prayers were answered when a year later at another of Marci's frequent checkups, this one for the latest six-month period and a radiation scan, she got the thumbs-up report. It brought them both peace of mind and comfort during a trying period in their lives.

Overcoming that kind of ordeal makes hitting a sinker or a 95 mph heater look simple. Tim Salmon, 1993's American League Rookie of the Year, had his head screwed on straight, and, in a baseball sense, that was bad news for major league pitchers. It was also very good news on the Salmon home front.

1993: Ten Top Rookies

Nm/Pos/Tm	GP	W–L/BA	SH/SV//RBI	PR/BR	ERA/FR	TPR
Piazza/c/LA-N	149	.318	112	41	12	5.1
Salmon/of/Cal-A	142	.283	95	30	15	3.8
DiPito/RP-RHP/Clv-A	46	4–4	0/11	12	2.40	2.0
Reynoso/RHP/Col-N	30	12–11	0/0	16	4.00	1.9
McMichael/RP-RHP/Atl-N	74	2–3	0/19	20	2.06	1.8
Martinez/RP-LHP/LA-N	65	10–5	0/2	14	2.61	1.7
Stocker/ss/Phl-N	70	.324	31	11	-1	1.7
Bere/RHP/Chi-A	24	12–5	0/0	11	3.47	1.4
Rueter/LHP/Mon-N	20	8–0	0/0	14	2.73	1.3
Turner/RP-RHP/Fla-N	55	4–5	0/0	11	2.91	1.3

Delmer "Del" Ennis

TPR: 3.7

1946, Philadelphia Phillies, NL

Born: 1925, Philadelphia. Died: 1996, Huntingdon Valley, PA; OF; 6' 194 lb.
1946: 141 GP; 30 2BH; 73 RBI; .485 SA; 28 BR; 14 FR; .313 BA

When the Phillies won their first pennant in 1915, gas buggies were vying with grandpa's horse and buggy for room on the streets of Philadelphia. By the time the team got around to winning another pennant, a second World War had come and gone and the year was 1950. During the intervening 35 years the Phils finished in seventh or eighth place 24 times, exceeding 100 losses 12 times. Now that's futility.

The 1945 season was one of those eighth-place years. The year World War II ended the Phils lost 108 times, 52 games behind the Cubs' pennant winners. They almost finished *outside* the National League, ending up the season under the volcanic and vitriolic Ben Chapman, a former Yankee, whose dislike for losing was not only legendary, but likely to cause ballplayers to hunt up safe places while trying to protect life and limb.

Everyone in Philadelphia knew that in a brand new peacetime era, a fresh start had to be made. Herb Pennock, another Yankee, was brought in to make however many changes might be necessary to turn the ballclub around once and for all. His first move was to bring in still more Yanks as coaches for the ballclub to get the postwar effort going with a stern emphasis on fundamentals — and winning. Other changes were made in the club's farm system, the front office and scouting. The crafty old left-hander, a Hall of Famer who was no stranger to Philadelphia, presided over a pretty thoroughgoing house-cleaning.

As the 1946 season approached and GIs filtered back into major league spring training camps, manager Ben Chapman was looking for the kind of help — from *any*where — that would extricate his ballclub from the dank recesses of the National League basement. There was no lack of ballplayers, but were they the right ones? An over-30 infield, showing signs of wear and tear, needed help. The pitching staff was in tatters. But there were a few bright spots. One was the outfield and another was Andy Seminick, 25, entering his fifth Phils campaign as catcher. Recasting his pitching staff around veterans Schoolboy Rowe and Oscar Judd, a 38-year-old lefty,

Chapman might just pick up a young pitcher or two and some bullpen help from returning relievers Charley Schanz and Andy Karl.

Then too, there was a tough young Philadelphian who had put in a great minor league season with the Phillies' farm club at Trenton before heading off to military service. His name was Del Ennis. In 1943 with Trenton's Packers he had hit a robust .343, driven in 93 runs, poled 18 homers and led the league's outfielders with 24 assists. And the icing on the cake was his age, 18. But as with many a promis-

ing 18 year old, his development was halted right then and there when Uncle Sam called. In the spring of 1946 Ennis was due to be discharged from the navy. But he wasn't due to be mustered out in time for spring training, and he barely made it in time to join the ballclub for the opening of the season. When that day finally did arrive, skipper Chapman wasted no time getting him into the lineup. He was going to get a solid crack at making it despite his long layoff and his youthful years.

With Johnny Wyrostek, a rookie, and Ron Northey, a muscular power hitter, and

Box Score

Philadelphia at Wrigley Field, Chicago, May 5, 1946

Philadelphia	AB	R	H	PO	A		Chicago	AB	R	H	PO	A
Newsome, ss	3	2	1	1	8		Lowrey, 3b	4	1	2	0	5
Wyrostek, cf	4	2	4	1	0		Glossop, 2b	3	0	0	2	1
Ennis, lf	5	2	2	0	0		Waitkus, 1b	4	0	1	8	0
McCormick, 1b	5	0	0	12	0		Cavaretta, lf	3	0	1	2	0
Wasdell, rf	5	1	1	0	0		Pafko, cf	3	0	0	2	0
Hughes, 3b	5	0	4	0	0		Nicholson, rf	4	0	1	1	0
Seminick, c	4	0	1	6	0		Livingston, c	4	0	0	9	1
Verban, 2b	5	0	2	7	4		Jurges, ss	2	0	1	3	0
Mulligan, p	3	0	0	0	2		Passeau, p	0	0	0	0	0
							Kush, p	1	0	0	0	0
							Ostrowski, ph	1	0	0	0	0
							Bithorn, p	0	0	0	0	0
							Secory, ph	1	0	0	0	0
							Adams, p	0	0	0	0	0
Totals	39	7	15	27	14		Totals	30	1	6	27	7

Philadelphia   410   000   200   7-15-0
Chicago   100   000   000   1-6-1

2BH	Wyrostek 2, Hughes 2, Verban
3BH	Newsome
HR	Ennis 2
SH	Newsome
LOB	Philadelphia 10, Chicago 6
DP	Newsome, Verban, McCormick 2; Verban and McCormick
K	Mulligan 6, Kush 2, Bithorn 2, Adams 2, Passeau 0
BB	Mulligan 3, Kush 1, Adams 2, Passeau 1, Bithorn 0
Wild P.	Passeau
PB	Livingston 2
WP	Mulligan (1–0)
LP	Passeau (1–1)
Umpires	Stewart, Henline and Magerjurth
Time	2:10
Att	45,505

with reserve outfielders Jimmy Wasdell and Charlie Gilbert, the Phils' outfield would be one of the team's strong points. There would be nothing to lose in giving the hometown boy a shot at the starting lineup. That's all Del Ennis needed. By May he had settled into the number three spot in the batting order as the ballclub's right fielder. Not yet 21, he was the young phenom in a new Philadelphia outfield that had Wyrostek, 26, in center field and Northey, also 26, in left.

Although the team got off to a horrendous start, losing 11 of its first 13 ball games, by May it started to straighten out a bit. On the first Sunday in May they suited up for a doubleheader at Chicago's Wrigley Field, playing before a record crowd of over 45,000 Cub die-hards. After taking a 13 to 1 lambasting in the first game, they came back with Dick Mulligan, who was given his first starting assignment of the season.

In the only complete game effort of his major league career, Mulligan sat down Charlie Grimm's Bruins on five hits after a shaky first inning when the Cubs scored their only run. But even bigger news in the nightcap victory was the hitting of the Phillies. Del Ennis was the pacesetter with round-trippers in the first and seventh innings. The bleacher blasts were the first two of his 288 major league home runs. After an opening frame outburst of four tallies, the Phils went on to whip the Cubs, 7 to 1.

The Phillies' improved play over the course of the 1946 season paid off in their highest finish in the standings since 1917, and though there weren't enough players who played at Del Ennis' level day after day, that fifth-place finish was a quantum leap for a ballclub that seemed to be forever fated to tailend finishes. Chapman's team won 69 games, and though it wound up 28 games out of pennant contention, it had turned a corner with a 23-game improvement over its 108, 1945 losses.

The Sporting News' first Rookie of the Year selection, Del Ennis, 1946. (Dennis Colgin.)

Sparking a team that drew 760,190 more fans in 1946 than in 1945, an unprecedented outpouring of support that totalled more than a million fans for the first time in the franchises history, the young, hometown outfielder, boyish-looking Del Ennis, became the toast of Philadelphia. His consistency, which was to become an Ennis trademark, outfield play featuring strong, accurate throws that cut down the unwary, and a steady bombardment of enemy pitching resulted in a .313 average, 73 RBIs, a .485 slugging average (good for second place among National League hitters), and top five rankings in dingers, total bases, batting runs and fielding runs. The 1946 package amounted to a 3.7 TPR, which ties him with reliever Dick Radatz in the number 22 spot on our all-time rookie listing.

Del Ennis' play in his rookie season was worthy of recognition. Sad to say, however, there was none available. Noting that there had been exceptional rookies long before Ennis came along, the people at *The Sporting News* decided that a special award should be made each season for the very best of the freshmen. Accordingly, in 1946 *TSN* inaugurated its award by honoring Del Ennis, and since that time has awarded a position player and a pitcher each season. Ennis won out over a fine crop of players who had returned from the service, including teammate Johnny Wyro-

stek, infielder Benny Zientra, Ewell Blackwell, the Red's "Whip," who was a nemesis for Del Ennis throughout his 11-year Philly career, Carl Furillo of the Dodgers and Bob Lemon, who fashioned a Hall of Fame career with the Cleveland Indians.

As for the Phillies, they kept on climbing. Del Ennis was soon joined by the Whiz Kids, who in 1950 scaled the National League's Everest, with Liberty Town's first pennant in 35 years. And Ennis went on to a 14-year career that left enough markers along the way, like a 19-game hitting streak in 1947, league leadership in RBIs at 126 for the 1950 pennant winners, nine seasons of 20 or more home runs, and high ranking in many of Philadelphia's career categories. The composite earned him a 1982 election to Philadelphia's Baseball Hall of Fame.

Del Ennis died in 1996, leaving behind a rich heritage of Philly baseball, a Philadelphian to the very end.

1946: Ten Top Rookies

Nm/Pos/Tm	GP	W–L/BA	SH/SV//RBI	PR/BR	ERA/FR	TPR
Ennis/of/Phl-N	141	.313	73	28	14	3.7
Wyrostek/of/Phl-N	145	.281	45	12	17	2.4
Zientra/Inf/Cin-N	78	.289	16	-4	24	2.4
Blackwell/RHP/Cin-N	33	9–13	5/0	19	2.45	2.3
R. Adams/2b/Cin-N	94	.244	24	-8	24	2.2
Bahr/RHP/Pit-N	27	8–6	0/0	14	2.63	1.3
Lemon/RHP/Clv-A	32	4–5	0/1	9	2.49	1.3
Edwards/c/Brk-N	92	.267	25	0	6	1.2
Furillo/of/Brk-N	117	.284	35	4	9	0.9
Hetki/RHP/Cin-N	32	6–6	0/1	5	2.99	0.7

Richard Raymond
"The Monster" Radatz

TPR: 3.7

1962, Boston Red Sox, AL
Born: 1937, Detroit, MI; RP-RHP, 6'6" 237 lb.
1962: 62 GP; W9, L6; .600 W%; 0/24 SH/SV; 144/40 K/BB; .211 OBA; 26 PR; 2.24 ERA

In 1962, 20 major league teams welcomed 147 first-year men to their rosters. By 1998 the number of teams had risen to 30, and the tally on newcomers had risen to 361. A full 116 of the new players in 1998 were relief pitchers. That represents a 32 percent share of the total and tells its own singularly surprising story. A growing demand for relief pitching had emerged during the latter half of the 20th century. It was a new force in the development and strategy of the national pastime.

Although relief pitching had been around since the earlier days of the game, it was not until the 1950s and 1960s that it started to become a refined specialty. And since that time the role of the reliever has been honed and polished to a point of rare sophistication.

Among those who came directly to the major leagues as relief pitchers, spearheading the *avant garde* and signalling a new era in the decades of the '50s and '60s, were Ron Perranoski (LA-N), Don McMa-

hon (Mil-NL), Terry Fox (Det-AL), Joe Hoerner (Hou-NL), and Frank Linzy (SF-NL, heralded as our honor roll rookie #11), among others, and an out-sized goliath of a man named Dick Radatz, who would add to the growing lore of the pen men in 1962, his rookie season with the Boston Red Sox.

At 6'6", and weighing in around the 240 mark, Dick Radatz had the wherewithal to powder the ole pellet past just about anybody — including Mickey Mantle, whom he frustrated so often that one day the "Commerce Comet" blew a string of expletives Radatz's way, winding up with "you [expletive] monster." The "monster" part stuck, and Radatz was known from that point on as "The Monster." In many respects it suited him.

It was Johnny Pesky who converted the big Michigan State alum from a starter to a reliever. In 1961 Pesky was the boss-man of the Red Sox' top farm club, the Seattle Rainiers of the Pacific Coast League. At his insistence, and over Radatz's initial

The Red Sox' huge reliever, bullet-throwing Dick Radatz. (Dennis Colgin.)

Red Sox dropped into the American League's second division with six straight seasons under .500, including Dick Radatz's first three years, which turned out to be the biggest years of his career. A lot of fine relieving went up in smoke during those years, as the Bosox won only 76 games in the expanded 1962 schedule, following that with another 76 in 1963 and only 72 in 1964. During those three seasons the burly right-hander appeared in 207 games with an increased work load each year. Between 1962 and 1964 he played under Pinky Higgins, then under his former manager Johnny Pesky in 1963, and for both Pesky and Billy Herman in 1964. None could find any fault in his work except that he would on occasion groove a fat hard one, and that would mean the ball game because when Radatz was in there the game was up for grabs. During that three-year span he was tagged for 31 dingers, 13 in 1964 alone. Other than that he kept on getting the side out, and most of the time at the rate of at least a strikeout for every inning pitched and slightly over two earned runs per nine innings pitched.

In The Monster's rookie year it wasn't until his sixth appearance in Chicago on April 26 that he was scored on. His first major league save came on April 15 in relief of Galen Cisco in a 2.2-inning stint. By April 21 he had picked up his second save in a 4 to 3 victory over Detroit, and though the Carmine finished April at 7 and 7, their huge rookie was moving along at a much swifter pace.

As Independence Day rolled around Radatz was at the 6-save mark, and before the day was over, he had picked up number seven, preserving Gene Conley's 9 to 5

objections, the transformation took place during the course of the season. In his fourth minor league campaign after having signed with the Red Sox in June, 1959, the hulking flame thrower responded to Pesky's coaching. Before the summer was over Dick's mentor proclaimed him ready for the Big Show. Particularly noteworthy were his strikeout-to-innings-pitched numbers through the four prep seasons: more than one whiff per inning pitched. Heat was his strong point, and he never once varied his approach, which, in his own words, was "take the ball and blow it past 'em." He had once remarked that the game could be played for another 500 years and there still wouldn't be a better pitch than the fastball.

After a third-place finish in 1958, the

win over Minnesota. His record at the end of that month stood at 4 and 4 with 9 saves in 75 innings of work. More importantly, the big fellow's ERA was just under 2.00, and he had maintained a steady stream of low-hit appearances. His ballclub's record was not quite as lustrous. Boston's record had fallen to 45 wins and 56 losses, and the team would maintain about that same pace to the season's end, when the final count on 1962 read 76 and 84.

No accounting of a Boston or New York ballplayer is complete without at least one mention of baseball's most prickly rivalry. It should come as no surprise that Dick Radatz's most satisfying rookie game came at Yankee Stadium (see box score). It was a game that went 16 innings, and Dick Radatz pitched no less than nine of them.

The 5 to 4 Bosox victory hiked Radatz's record to 8 and 5. Featuring seven double plays and airtight pitching during the last ten frames, the Red Sox finally broke through for a run in the top of the 16th to move ahead of the Yanks. It only remained to shut down the Yankees in the

Box Score

Boston at Yankee Stadium, New York, August 7, 1962

Boston	AB	R	H	BI	E
Geiger, cf	7	1	4	2	0
Bressoud, ss	3	0	2	0	0
Yastrzemski, lf	7	0	0	0	0
Clinton, rf	6	0	1	0	1
Runnels, 1b	6	1	1	0	0
Malzone, 3b	7	1	1	0	0
Nixon, c	2	0	0	0	0
Hardy, pr	0	1	0	0	0
Tillman, c	3	1	2	0	0
Schilling, 2b	5	0	0	1	0
Delock, p	0	0	0	0	0
Kolstad, p	2	0	0	0	0
Green, ph	1	0	0	0	0
Radatz, p	2	0	0	0	0
Gardner, ph	1	0	1	1	0
Totals	52	5	12	4	1

New York	AB	R	H	BI	E
Kubek, ss	7	2	5	0	0
Richardson, 2b	6	1	2	0	0
Tresh, lf	7	0	4	2	0
Maris, cf	7	0	1	0	0
Lopez, rf	7	0	0	0	0
Berra, c	0	0	0	0	0
Howard, ph	0	0	0	0	0
Skowron, 1b	7	1	2	0	0
Linz, pr	0	0	0	0	0
C. Boyer, 3b	7	0	3	1	0
Bouton, p	2	0	0	0	0
Daley, p	0	0	0	0	0
Blanchard, ph	1	0	0	0	0
Bridges, p	3	0	0	0	1
Nichols, p	0	0	0	0	0
Totals	60	4	17	3	1

Boston	000	200	200	000	000	1	5-12-1
New York	210	000	100	000	000	0	4-17-1

2BH	Runnels, Geiger, Tillman, Kubek
3BH	Skowron
HR	Geiger
SB	Kubek
SH	Schilling 2, Bressoud
LOB	Boston 11, New York 10
DP	Boston 2, New York 5
K	Delock 2, Kolstad 1, Radatz 9, Nichols 2
	Bouton 2, Daley 1, Bridges 8
BB	Delock and Kolstad 0, Radatz 1, Nichols 2
	Bouton 4, Bridges 5, Daley 0
WP	Bridges
Balk	Bouton
Umpires	Soar, Smith, Rice, Paparella
Time	4:33
Att	36,151

bottom of the 16th to win it. Boston got the job done with the veteran Chet Nichols' relief of Radatz, who had been lifted for a pinch-hitter during the rally that put the Bosox ahead. Subsequently, Nichols got the save and Radatz the win. How sweet any win over a Yankee ballclub can be, much less a nail-biter during a Yankee pennant year!

On September 16, Boston beat New York and Whitey Ford 4 to 3 behind Gene Conley and Radatz, who garnered the save in a ninth inning, three up and three down appearance. His 24th and final save of the season was registered at Washington's expense, giving him the league's top numbers in saves, appearances (62) and Pitching Runs (26).

In 1962 New York's Tom Tresh was elected the American League Rookie of the Year. Dick Radatz finished a distant third, tieing with California's sensational rookie pitcher Dean Chance and Minnesota's Bernie Allen. Each of the three received one vote apiece. Both Chance and Eddie Charles of Kansas City had outstanding rookie seasons, to say nothing of Dick Radatz's brilliant performance for a very mediocre team. Charles, Chance and Radatz are among the Top 10 Rookies featured in the 1962 listing following this profile.

But the season did not pass by without recognition for Dick Radatz. He was named the Fireman of the Year for 1962, and he repeated in 1964. He would move on to set franchise records for strikeouts as a reliever with 162 in 1963 and 181 in 1964. Those figures rank in Boston's number one and two spots, all time.

1962: Ten Top Rookies

Nm/Pos/Tm	GP	W–L/BA	SH/SV//RBI	PR/BR	ERA/FR	TPR
Radatz/RP-RHP/Bos-A	62	9–6	0/24	26	2.24	3.7
Chance/RHP/LA-A	46	20–9	11/4	51	1.65	2.0
Charles/3b/KC-A	147	.288	74	9	4	1.8
Haller/c/SF-N	99	.261	55	17	-2	1.6
Fregosi/ss/LA-A	58	.291	23	2	4	1.1
Rollins/3b/Min-A	159	.298	96	13	-5	1.0
Tresh/of-ss/NY-A	157	.286	93	17	-11	1.0
Belinsky/LHP/LA-A	33	10–11	3/1	6	3.56	0.7
Clendenon/1b/Pit-N	80	.302	28	9	-1	0.6
Stenhouse/RHP/Was-A	34	11–12	2/0	8	3.65	0.6

Grover Cleveland "Pete" Alexander

TPR: 3.6

1911, Philadelphia Phillies, NL
Born: February 26, 1887, St. Paul, NE;
Died: November 4, 1950, St. Paul, NE; RHP; 6'1" 185 lb.
1911: W28, L13; .683 W%; 7/3 SH/SV; 35 PR; 3DEF; 2.51 ERA
Hall of Fame: 1938

Manager Red Dooin's Phillies opened the 1911 campaign with one of the best road trips in the franchise's history. They took four straight at the Polo Grounds against the haughty New York Giants and two out of three in Boston. Their 6–1 start was marred only by a single loss, and the loser was Grover Cleveland Alexander, who dropped his first major league decision by a 5 to 4 count.

Neither Alexander nor the Phils would continue along the path they started, because "Pete" started winning and the Phils soon found a variety of ways to lose. Alexander quickly became the Phils' king of the hill, closing out his rookie season with a record-setting 28 and 13 mark that signalled the arrival of a new Christy Mathewson in the world of baseball. The strong-armed right-hander had travelled the first mile toward Cooperstown with a virtuoso performance in his initial season

under the Big Tent. Even before the year had reached its midpoint he was being hailed as "Alexander the Great."

Alexander's career, gilded with innumerable awards and honors, including election to the Hall of Fame in 1938 as one of the first ten players to be so honored, began at full stride in Rookie-of-the-Year style. Following his first loss to Boston on April 15, he fashioned a six-game winning streak during a 13 and 3 stretch as the last week in June approached. By that time he had beaten every team in the league except the Giants, and they, too, soon fell victim to the pinpoint control and breaking slants of the Phillies' rookie sensation.

By the time Alexander had finished two minor league seasons there was heated competition for his services. In 1910 he had tossed a dozen shutouts in putting together a 29 and 14 record for the Syracuse Stars of the New York Class B League, including a doubleheader victory over Wilkes-Barre on July 20.

The scouts and tipsters got busy and though it took some convincing to pry open owner Horace Fogel's purse strings, the deed was finally done when Alexander was signed prior to the 1911 spring-training trip. Bringing Pete Alexander into the Phillie fold was the single most positive contribution Fogel made in a brief-but-stormy two-year stint (before his ousting) as the club's owner.

After opening the year with his first 13 wins, Alex added another 15 to establish a club rookie record with 28 in a single season. Those 28 wins led the National League and tied crosstown rival Jack Coombs of the pennant-winning Athletics for major league honors. Alexander's seven shutouts

paced the majors and his 367 innings pitched, 31 complete games and a .219 opponents' batting average all topped the Senior Circuit — reason enough for Bill Deane to award him with Hypothetical Rookie of the Year honors for 1911.

Beyond the proverbial shadow of a doubt the most sensational streak of the 1911 season occurred between September 7 and 21, when Pete ran off an amazing four straight shutouts while adding numbers 23 to 26 to his victory belt. During the skein he was touched for only 14 base hits as he knocked off Boston, 1–0, on September 7; Brooklyn, 2–0, six days later; Cincinnati's Reds, 6–0, on September 17; and the Cubs, 4–0, on September 21. The Cubs shutout came at the expense of Ed Reulbach, who in 1905 had authored the

Box Score

Phillies at Chicago Cubs, September 21, 1911

Philadelphia	AB	R	H	P	A	E
Walsh, 2b	3	1	2	2	6	0
Lobert, 3b	4	0	1	1	0	0
Titus, rf	4	0	1	3	0	0
Luderus, 1b	5	0	1	13	0	0
Paskert, cf	3	0	1	2	0	0
Beck, lf	4	0	0	1	0	0
Doolan, ss	4	1	1	1	5	1
Madden, c	4	1	3	3	0	0
Alexander, p	4	1	0	1	1	0
Totals	35	4	10	27	12	1

Chicago	AB	R	H	P	A	E
Sheckard, lf	4	0	0	1	0	0
Schulte, rf	4	0	0	2	0	0
Tinker, ss	4	0	2	3	4	0
Zimmerman, 1b	1	0	0	6	0	0
Saier, 1b	2	0	0	6	2	0
Doyle, 3b	4	0	1	1	8	0
Shean, 2b	4	0	0	3	3	1
Hofman, cf	3	0	0	2	0	0
Graham, c	3	0	1	3	1	0
Reulbach, p	2	0	0	0	0	0
Totals	31	0	4	27	18	1

Philadelphia   000   020   011   4-10-1
Chicago   000   000   000   0 — 4-1

2BH	Luderus
RBI	Lobert, Titus, Paskert, Madden
SB	Beck, Tinker, Lobert, Doolan
Sac	Reulbach, Walsh, Beck
Sac. Fly	Lobert
LOB	Philadelphia 12; Chicago 7
BB	Reulbach, 4; Alexander, 2
K	Reulbach, 1; Alexander, 2
Hit by P	by Reulbach: Paskert
Winning P	Alexander (26–12)
Losing P	Reulbach (14–10)
Umpires	Klem and Brennan
Time	1:38

12th best rookie season in his Chicago debut.

Alexander's 4 to 0 victory on September 21 came at Chicago's West Side Park in front of a full house against Frank Chance's contending Bruins (see box score). On this day, in the first game of a doubleheader, there wasn't much contention as Pete handcuffed Chicago with four harmless singles, a pair of Ks and but two free passes. "Old Low and Away," a sobriquet he picked up as the years passed on because it soon became evident that the hitters were going to have to subsist on the "almost-strikes" he allotted them, simply took control and carried the Phils to victory on the strength of his trusty right arm. That was to become a recurring pattern during the next six summers as Alexander led them to second-place finishes in 1913, 1916 and 1917, and the pennant in 1915. In the City of Brotherly Love, a new generation of baseball fans was learning that another Phillie pennant winner might just be on the way.

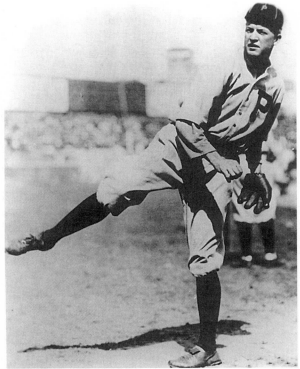

Grover "Pete" Alexander, Phillies Hall of Famer par excellence. (Brace Photo.)

Before the last pitch was thrown in Alexander's fabulous career, there were 373 victories, a number, no doubt decreed by the baseball gods, that was identical to the legendary Mathewson's victory total. Both made their way to baseball's Valhalla, though contrasting with one another radically in their approaches to both pitching and life.

Along with his career victory total, Grover Alexander left behind a host of club, league and major league records, some of which are, of course, remarkable, but most of which pale in comparison to the human-interest story involving his personal trials, tribulations, failures and storied shortcomings. For the record, however, there is added to his rookie player profile the Alexander Philadelphia Record Book in the place of the usual top 10 rookie review (for 1911), already presented in the Joe Jackson write-up.

Pete Alexander's Philadelphia Record Book: A Sampling

Club Rookie Records

Most Wins in a Single Season	28
Consecutive Shutouts	4
Shutouts in a Single Season	7
Fewest Hits per Game	6.99
Lowest Opponents' Batting Average	.219

Strikeouts	227
Innings Pitched	389.0

Club Records

Consecutive Pitching Triple Crowns	3	(1915-16-17)*
Low ERA, Single Season	1.22	(1915)
Wins, Single Season	33	(1916)
1–0 Wins, Single Season	4	(1916)
Complete Games in a Single Season	38	(1916)
One-hitters, Career	6	(4 in 1915)†
Philadelphia Career Shutouts	61	(90, ML career)†
Shutouts in a Single Season	16	(1916)*
Consecutive Scoreless Innings Pitched	41.2	(1911)

Major League Top 50 All-Time Rankings

Record	Number/Year		Rank
Single Season Shutouts	16	(1916)	1 (t)
ERA, Single Season (SS)	1.22	(1915)	11
Pitching Wins	7.1	(1915)	11
Total Pitching Index (SS)	8.6	(1915)	13 (t)
Ratio	7.82	(1915)	14
Opponents' On-Base % (SS)	.234	(1915)	26
Hits per Game (SS)	6.05	(1915)	30
Pitching Runs (SS)	64.1	(1915)	36
Opponents' BA (SS)	.191	(1915)	38

*Major League Record
†National League records

Elmer Ray Riddle

TPR: 3.6

1941, Cincinnati Reds, NL

Born: 1914, Columbus, GA. Died: 1984, Columbus, GA; RHP, 5'11.5" 170 lb.
1941: W19, L4; .826 W%; 4/1 SH/SV; .224 OBA; 3 PHI; 33PR; 2.24 ERA

The Cincinnati Reds entered the 1941 season as defending world's champions, having defeated the Detroit Tigers in seven games in the 1940 World Series. The National League's kingpins prepared to win their third straight pennant with one of baseball's finest pitching staffs. The 20-game winners Bucky Walters and Paul Derringer were back, and manager Bill McKechnie anticipated able support from Johnny Vander Meer (of double no-hit fame), Junior Thompson, and Jim Turner. It was a proven corps of veteran moundsmen.

There were also a number of younger pitchers who had been brought along with that special McKechnie touch. One of them, Elmer Riddle, had worked one inning in the 1940 World Series, tossing a hitless stanza at the Tigers while fanning two in a mop-up roll in game one of the Series. It just might be that the 25-year-old Georgian was ready. Joe Beggs, returning with a 12 and 3 mark in 1940, and Johnny Hutchings, another 25-year-old, were still other younger pitchers vying for a spot in the starting rotation.

But in a season marked by Brooklyn's resurgence, after a score of years, to capture the National League gonfalon, awesome individual exploits such as the DiMaggio 56-game hitting streak and the Splinter's .406 batting average, Bill McKechnie's well laid plans went astray. A combination of weak hitting, a noticeable drop-off in the effectiveness of stalwart Paul Derringer, and a terrible early season start felled the Reds, dropping them into third place.

There was one ballplayer who was totally unaffected by the Cincinnati power outage. That was the young man from Columbus, Georgia, Elmer Riddle, who, without any previous indication whatever that he might be able to take up the slack in the starting rotation, shouldered himself into a starting berth by dint of the sheer brilliance of his early season work in relief. By the end of May, Bill McKechnie had installed him in a starting roll, and before most of the league caught on it was nearing mid-season. By that time he was already perched at a jaunty 9 and 0 mark. Two more wins jacked up his record to 11

Country boy Elmer Riddle, Reds right-hander. (Brace Photo.)

and 0 before he tasted defeat. En route he had beaten every team in the league, including the Giants, both at the Polo Grounds and at Crosley Field.

Those two wins over the Giants early in the year, by Riddle's reckoning, were crucial not only to the success of his season, but even more so to his remaining in Cincinnati. It had developed that the Giants wanted to deal with the Reds, and their prime objective was Cincy's budding star. Figuring that he might be able to jar some hitting power or even another strong starter loose from the Big Apple, the wily McKechnie started his prize rookie at the Polo Grounds, where Riddle, who knew that something was brewing, threw a low-hit gem at the Giants. Elmer, who was soon dubbed "The Great," continued his mastery over the Giants at Crosley Field, beating them on his way to 11 straight victories.

Bill McKechnie was nobody's fool. He figured out in next to nothing flat that the

answer to some of the pitching staff's shortcomings was wearing a Cincinnati uniform, and the answer's name was Elmer Riddle. Consequently, when the time came to deal, Riddle's name was off the table. And that was the end of any trade talk either with the Giants or for Mr. Riddle.

Although he spent most of the 1940 season with the Reds, Riddle was rarely used. Why? According to Riddle, that was an unsolved mystery. McKechnie used him in relief here and there and he wound up putting in a mere 30-plus innings. He finished out the season with a 1 and 2 record, but a closer look at the innings he did pitch revealed a pair of saves and a sparkling 1.87 ERA. He surely wasn't getting roughed up when he did pitch. In fact, after his major league debut on the last day of the 1939 season, when he worked through his first inning of big league baseball without giving up a hit or a run, Elmer the Great reasoned that with a good spring training, he would be on his way in 1940. That simply didn't happen. What did happen was that Riddle spent the season watching pitchers and hitters, observing weaknesses and strengths, and, in a manner of speaking, taking a post–minor league graduate course in major league baseball. When the season began in 1941 he was ready to go.

After that slow start, when Elmer was just about resigned to another year in waiting, he picked up the first of his 11 straight wins as a reliever, this time against the Braves. The season was already a month old. It took three more wins, each in relief, to finally convince his skipper that the sun would still arise in the east even if his young right-hander might start a ball game. Seven starting shots later his season record was still unblemished. Finally, on July 23, Leo Durocher's Bums caught up with him, winning a white-knuckler, 4 to 3. At that point his won-loss record stood at 11 and 1.

There were to be but three more losses the rest of the way. One of them was at the hands of Lonnie Warneke and the Cardinals. On August 30, Warneke threw a no-hitter at the punchless Reds, who went down 2 to 0, putting the Cards momentarily in first place.

But there were victories — plenty of them. Going into a September 7 twinbill at St. Louis, Riddle's victory count stood at 15. McKechnie scheduled him to pitch against Cardinal ace Mort Cooper in the second game that afternoon (see box score).

The game, called after eight frames because of darkness, resulted in Riddle's 16th victory and gave the Reds a split for their day's work. Over 22,000 had seen Riddle's magic, and had begun to understand why the rookie Wunderkind with the sharply breaking curveball was riding along on a 15 and 3 record.

Before it was all over that season the Great One had upped his record to a gaudy 19 and 4, leading the league in both winning percentage and earned run average. His .826 winning percentage remains, to this very day, Cincinnati's number one single-season mark, and ranks at number 32 in the major league record book.

Elmer Riddle's 1941 numbers factor to a 3.6 TPR, the same number recorded by five other players, thus tying all six for the number 23 spot on the all-time rookie list. The six include Hall of Famer Grover Alexander, future Hall of Famer Ozzie Smith, Jittery Joe Berry and Cy Acosta

Box Score

Cincinnati at Sportsman's Park, St. Louis, September 7, 1941

Cincinnati	AB	R	H	PO	A	St. Louis	AB	R	H	PO	A
Koy, lf	5	0	0	1	0	Brown, 3b	4	1	1	2	2
Frey, 2b	3	2	1	2	6	Hopp, cf	4	0	1	2	0
Werber, 3b	3	2	2	0	2	Padgett, lf	4	1	1	1	0
F. McCormick, 1b	3	0	1	10	0	Mize, 1b	3	0	2	8	1
Gleason, lf	2	1	1	3	0	Crabtree, rf	4	0	0	1	0
Craft, cf	4	0	2	3	0	W. Cooper, c	4	0	1	6	2
West, c	3	0	1	2	0	Crespi, 2b	2	0	0	2	1
Joost, ss	3	0	0	3	6	Marion, ss	3	0	1	2	2
Riddle, p	3	0	0	0	1	M. Cooper, p	0	0	0	0	0
						I. Hutchinson, p	0	0	0	0	0
						Triplett, ph	1	0	0	0	0
						Gumbert, ›	1	0	0	0	2
Totals	29	5	8	24	15	Totals	30	2	7	24	10

Cincinnati   200   030   00   5-8-2
St. Louis   100   001   00   2-7-1

2BH	Mize, Craft
SB	Frey, West
SH	Werber, F. McCormick, Joost
DP	Cincinnati 2, St. Louis 1
LOB	Cincinnati 8, St. Louis 7
BB	Riddle 3, M. Cooper 4, I. Hutchinson 1, Gumbert 0
K	Riddle 2, M. Cooper 4, Hutchinson 1, Gumbert 2
Wild P.	M. Cooper
WP	Riddle
LP	M. Cooper
Umpires	Jorda, Barr and Sears
Time	2:05
Att	22,322

(both relief pitchers), and Cleveland's "Big Bear," Mike Garcia. The sixth, Elmer "The Great" Riddle, adds a touch of the Old South and a dash of country boy to this accomplished group.

1941: Ten Top Rookies

Nm/Pos/Tm	GP	W–L/BA	SH/SV//RBI	PR/BR	ERA/FR	TPR
Riddle/RHP/Cin-N*	33	19–4	4/1	33	2.24	3.6
E. White/LHP/StL-N	32	17–7	3/2	32	2.40	3.3
Stringer/2b/Chi-N	145	.246	53	-4	20	2.6
Rizzuto/ss/NY-A†	133	.307	46	-3	16	2.2
Muncrief/RHP/StL-A	36	13–9	2/1	15	3.65	1.5
Pollet/LHP/StL-N	9	5–2	2/0	14	1.93	1.5
Marchildon/RHP/Phl-A	30	10–15	1/0	14	3.57	1.3
Ferrick/RHP/Phl-A	36	8–10	1/7	6	3.77	1.2
Crespi/2b/StL-N	146	.279	46	-4	0	0.7
Branch/RHP/NY-A	27	5–1	0/2	6	2.87	0.6

*Named Hypothetical Rookie of the Year (Bill Deane awards), National League
†Named American League Hypothetical Rookie of the Year

Jonas Arthur "Jittery Joe" Berry

TPR: 3.6

1944, Philadelphia Athletics, AL

Born: 1904, Huntsville, AK. Died: 1958, Anaheim, CA; RP-RHP, 5'10.5" 144 lb.
1944: 53 GP; W10, L8; .556 W%; 0/12 SH/SV; .238OB%; 19 PR; 1.94 ERA

Deep in the throes of World War II, America, in 1944, bent its back to intensify its all-out war effort. Major League baseball rolled with the awesome punch, making adjustments wherever and whenever needed. Everything from schedules to equipment to travel, and especially manpower, was affected. And so was spring training, which for every team was, by mandate, completed north of the Mason-Dixon Line.

Connie Mack, entering his 50th anniversary year as a big league manager, gathered his Athletics at Frederick, Maryland, to prepare for the 1944 season. He, like so many other managers, had lost most of his 1943 squad either to military service or to full-time, war-related defense jobs. So the 83-year-old Philadelphia patriarch set about putting together a ballclub that he hoped would be more representative than his 1943 cellar-dwellers. Of

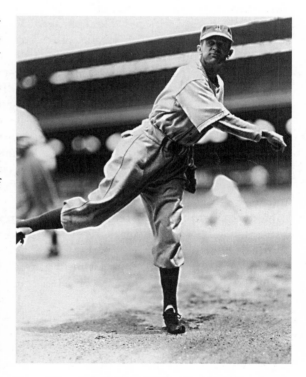

Jonas "Jittery Joe" Berry, 39-year-old rookie. (Brace Photo.)

257

course, with Connie Mack, that was a perennial hope. Since the dissolution of his early 1930s wrecking crews there hadn't been much to cheer about in the City of Brotherly Love, war or no war; but in the balmy spring breezes of 1944 everyone would start off as usual at 0 and 0. At that time 105 losses of 1943 would be history.

More than the normal number of newcomers made their way to the 1944 training camps. Connie Mack's recruits were typical among the first and second year players reporting. His entire infield for the 1944 season would be made up of rookies or sophomores, none of whom would be around after 1946, save one grand exception: George Kell, who came to camp after having led the entire minor league system in hitting with a .396 average for the Lancaster Red Roses in 1943. The future Hall of Famer was joined by Fibber McGhee, Mack's first baseman, a 38-year-old rookie. Mack's keystone combination, made up of Irv Hall, a sophomore, and rookie Eddie Busch, was joined by reserve infielders Joe Rullo and Bobby Wilkins, both of whom played only in 1944 and 1945. A good number of his other players had precious little major league playing time.

The rookie theme was repeated in the pitching staff. Mexican Jesse Flores, who pitched a few innings for the 1943 Cubs, came on as a 28-year-old rookie for the Mackmen in 1944. Don Black returned from a 6 and 16 season with the A's in 1943, and high schooler Carl Scheib, who debuted in 1943, was back for what would be his rookie season at age 17.

Typical of the slap-dash mixture of the very young, the very old, and the many who had limited or no experience along the big-time trail was another of Connie Mack's pitchers, a fellow they called "Jittery Joe." At 38 (he would turn 39 in December), Jonas Berry (a.k.a. Joe), climbed aboard the Philadelphia wagon to see what

life was like around the big league circuit east of the Mississippi.

Joe Berry had been around professional baseball since 1927, and in the 17 seasons he spent in 11 different minor league uniforms, he had already stacked up 231 victories and three 20-game seasons. His most recent hitch had resulted in an 18 and 8 mark with the 1943 Milwaukee Brewers. That got Connie Mack's attention. By the time training camp opened in Maryland, the Arkansan's name was on a Philadelphia contract.

Jittery Joe was an affable fellow who wasn't bothered one iota by being a career minor leaguer. He liked what he was doing, did it more than passably well, and particularly enjoyed his six seasons with the Los Angeles Angels of the Pacific Coast League, where he was fêted with an official "day" on August 11, 1938, and presented with an Arkansas mule branded "JB," christened "Hannah" after Berry's skipper, former major leaguer Truck Hannah. The festivities included an exhibition of mule-riding by the diminutive hurler, followed by his two-hit victory over the Portland Beavers. (The previous July 10 he had zeroed Oakland's Oaks with a 4 to 0, seven-inning no-hitter, which no doubt had at least a little something to do with the gala celebration.)

Jittery Joe, however, wasn't jittery. And he was unphased by 1944's major leaguers. He did what he had always done when it came time to pitch. He fussed, fidgeted, hitched, messed with the resin bag, gave it the old windmill windup in dirge-time, and finally, when the hitter had lost his concentration, delivered one of his knucklers, curves, sliders, or an off-speed "fast" one. It even got to Mr. Mack, known especially for his saintly patience. But the aged mentor stuck right with his rubber-armed reliever through two wartime seasons, calling on him 53 times in 1944 and a league-leading 52 times in 1945. That produced 18 victories and another 17 saves during the two seasons.

In one of his first appearances in 1944, April 28 at Fenway Park, he was called on to relieve in 33-degree weather. He threw less than ten fastballs and a curve or two in the bullpen, walked in, and retired nine Red Sox in a row. From that moment on Connie Mack knew a) that he could send for Berry, literally on a moment's notice, and b) that he would deliver. Any worries Mack might have had about the little fellow disappeared on that cold spring day in Boston.

One of the more typical Berry outings occurred at Yankee Stadium near the end of the season, when he preserved a 2 to 1, Don Black victory.

Entering the game in the seventh inning of what had been a 2 to 0 game with the Athletics holding the upper hand, Joe encountered the Yanks with none out, two men on and a 2 to 1 score. He then proceeded to herky-jerky his way to an Oscar Grimes strikeout, and induced Mike Garbark, the Yankee catcher, to hit into an inning-ending double play. The save was his 12th of the season, enabling him to tie Chicago's Gordy Maltzberger, another wartime reliever, and George Caster of the pennant-winning Browns for league supremacy in 1944.

Joe Berry moved on from Philadelphia in 1946, summoned by the Cleveland Indians' new owner, Bill Veeck, who brought him into "The Teepee" in 1946.

Box Score

Philadelphia at Yankee Stadium, New York, September 17, 1944

Philadelphia	AB	H	R	PO	A		*New York*	AB	R	H	PO	A
Hall, 2b	3	1	0	4	1		Stirnweiss, 2b	2	0	0	5	1
Garrison, lf	3	0	0	2	0		Metheny, rf	3	0	0	3	0
Epps, cf	4	0	0	1	0		Derry, lf	4	0	1	3	0
Hayes, c	4	0	1	6	3		Lindell, lf	4	1	2	4	0
Siebert, rf	3	1	1	0	1		Etten, 1b	4	0	2	7	3
Rosenthal, rf	0	0	0	0	0		Crosetti, ss	3	0	1	0	2
McGhee, 1b	4	0	1	10	0		Grimes, 3b	3	0	0	0	3
Kell, 3b	2	0	1	3	3		Garbark, c	3	0	0	3	0
Busch, ss	3	0	0	1	1		Dubiel, p	2	0	0	1	0
Black, p	3	0	0	0	0		P. Waner, ph	0	0	0	0	0
Berry, p	0	0	0	0	0		Borowy, p	0	0	0	1	1
Totals	29	2	4	27	9		Totals	28	1	6	27	10

Philadelphia	000 011 000 2-4-1
New York	000 000 100 1-6-0

2BH	Siebert
SB	P. Waner
SH	Garrison, Kell
LOB	Philadelphia 4; New York 5
DP	Hayes, Kell; Busch, Hall, McGhee; McGhee (unass.)
BB	Dubiel 2, Black 2, Borowy 0, Berry 2
K	Dubiel 3, Black 4, Borowy 0, Berry 2
HBP	By Black (Crosetti)
WP	Black
SV	Berry
LP	Dubiel
Umpires	Stewart, McGowan, Pipgras
Time	2:00
Att	55,536

The very evening of the day he arrived he was put to work in the fifth inning during a Brownie rally. He put down the uprising, following up with four flawless innings and a game-winning hit. It was vintage Berry.

Jonas Arthur Berry rounded out his 26-year pitching career at the tender age of 45, still going strong, and still enjoying every inning he pitched. He died in Anaheim in 1958, not too far from the site of the old Los Angeles Angels ballpark.

Age Before Beauty: The Oldest Rookie Pitchers — A Vintage Dozen

Nm/Tm	RY	Born	TPR	W–L	SH/SV	PR	ERA	Age
Diomedes Olivo/Pit-N	1962	1-22-1919	0.9	5–1	0/7	11	2.77	43
Satchel Paige/Clv-A	1948	7-7-1906	0.9	6–1	2/1	13	2.48	42
Joe Berry/Phl-A	1944	12-16-1905	3.6	10–8	0/12	19	1.94	38
Dixie Howell/Chi-A	1955	1-7-1920	1.7	8–3	0/9	8	2.93	35
George McConnell/NY-A	1912	9-16-1877	2.9	8–12	0/0	17	2.75	35
Jim Turner/Bos-N	1937	8-6-1903	4.5	20–11	5/1	34	2.38	34
Petie Behan/Phl-N	1922	12-11-1887	1.3	4–2	1/0	12	2.47	34
Joe Pate/Phl-A	1926	6-6-1892	1.8	9–0	0/6	18	2.71	34
Dazzy Vance/Brk-N	1922	3-4-1891	1.3	18–10	5/0	10	3.70	31
Ray Kremer/Pit-N	1924	3-23-1893	1.3	18–10	4/1	19	3.19	31
Tom Hurd/Bos-A	1955	5-27-1924	1.9	8–6	0/5	11	3.01	31
Curt Davis/Phl-N	1934	9-7-1903	7.8	19–17	3/5	54	2.95	31

Edward Miguel "Mike" or "The Big Bear" Garcia

TPR: 3.6

1949, Cleveland Indians, AL

Born: 1923, San Gabriel, CA; Died: 1986, Fairview Park, OH; RHP, 6'1" 210 lb.
1949: W14, L5; .737; 5/2 SH/SV; .308 OB%; 3 PHI; 32 PR; 2.36 ERA

Bill Veeck headed a syndicate that bought the Cleveland Indians in 1946, and by 1948 he had produced a World Series winner. Forest City denizens turned out in huge numbers to fill Cleveland's cavernous Municipal Stadium. That season a record 2,620,627 fans responded not only to Lou Boudreau's world champions, but to the many stunts, promotions and giveaways Veeck drummed up. One of the game's premier promoters, he also signed the American League's first black player, Larry Doby, and then brought the fabulous Satchel Paige to the Indians' pitching staff. Dull moments were few and far between with Veeck in the driver's seat.

On the last day of the 1948 season, amid the hoopla and excitement of pennant fever, the Cleveland Indians staged "Bill Veeck Appreciation Day." A crowd of 74,181 turned out on October 3 to see the festivities, *and* one of those classic rivalries between Hal Newhouser and Bob Feller. On this day, however, Bullet Bob

just didn't have it. Prince Hal and his Tiger teammates took the measure of the Boudreaumen, 7 to 1. The Tiger win plus a Boston loss to New York knotted the final day standings, forcing the famous playoff that ultimately made Cleveland an American League pennant winner for the first time since 1920.

However, a footnote should be added to Cleveland's last regularly scheduled game of the 1948 season. A brawny Californian by the name of Edward Miguel Garcia was brought into the contest by Boudreau. He hurled three innings that day in his major league debut, giving up three hits in three innings, fanning one and allowing no runs. Under the pressure-packed circumstances of that day in front of 70,000-plus fans (he had never seen such a spectacle before in his life), and in his first turn on a big league mound, one would have to say that it was an auspicious debut. It was, in fact, the first step toward a distinguished decade of pitching that

Mike "Big Bear" Garcia. (Dennis Colgin.)

ultimately resulted in a 142–96 record in an Indians uniform. Indeed, Mike Garcia turned out to be a member of what was arguably baseball's greatest pitching staff of all time, when Bob Lemon, Bob Feller and Early Wynn, each one a Hall of Famer, plus Mike Garcia, tamed the American League's best hitters, capturing another pennant with 111 AL victories in 1954.

Garcia, a muscular 200 pounder, began his professional baseball career in the Cleveland organization, assigned to their Appleton, Wisconsin, farm club in 1942. For a Southern Californian, that was like being shipped off to Alaska, but, by his own admission, he soon found life in the

Badger State most pleasant, and his pitching career, while not sensational at that point, made enough progress to warrant assignment to a higher classification for the 1943 season. "Higher classification" in 1943 for citizen Garcia meant military service, where he spent the next three seasons. Finally, in 1946 he was assigned to Bakersfield in his native state. His performance that summer netted ERA (2.56) and strikeout (186) honors, resulting in 22 victories, and a berth on the California League's all-star team. After a 17 and 10 season with Wilkes-Barre of the Eastern League in 1947, the Cleveland brain trust pronounced him ready for action under the Big Tent.

Lou Boudreau's 1948 MVP season — with more than a little help from Joe Gordon, Larry Doby, Gene Bearden (whose playoff victory capped an absolutely magnificent rookie season that landed him at number seven on our all-time list), peerless backstop Jim Hegan, and a sturdy pitching staff — captured the flag, and looked forward to repeating in 1949. However, New York and Boston didn't agree with that line of thought, and both finished ahead of the Indians in 1949. Nonetheless, it was in that tight 1949 race that Mike Garcia came on to record a scintillating rookie season of his own, succeeding Bearden on the Indians' staff as the Tribe's second straight freshman star. And with Bearden's falloff during his sophomore campaign, the Indians needed every last bit of Garcia's pitching prowess to pick up the slack.

Garcia's teammates soon found a nickname for the likeable Mexican. They called him "Bear" because of his broad, sloping shoulders and powerful, long arms. Picking up on the new name, the press soon referred to "The Big Bear" of Cleveland's mound staff, and as he moved into the 1949 season, Boudreau inserted Mike into the starting rotation. Bear's popularity with players and fans alike grew with his increasing success around the league. The Big Bear had arrived.

What brought him there was a sizzling fast ball that would rise as it moved toward the plate. Garcia was a power pitcher whose speed and hard slider were mainstays in his pitching assortment. Then, too, there was his battery mate, Jim Hegan, one of his closest personal friends, who was a hugely important part of his success. Not only did he call a brainy, well-tailored game for each of his pitchers, he was a superb fielder and was death on pop-ups, causing his teammates to remark that if a popup ever came down in foul territory, the batter was going to be out if Hegan was in the game—and he usually was.

On July 12, 1949, Big Bear's teammate, Larry Doby, was one of four blacks to break the All-Star Game color barrier in an American League victory, 11 to 7, at Brooklyn's Ebbets Field. Less than a week later, Doby, hitting cleanup, was in the Indians' lineup facing the Boston Red Sox on a hot, stuffy night at the Lake Erie lakefront. The pitchers slated for that evening were Mickey McDermott, the smooth Bosox lefty, and big Mike, looking for his seventh win against three defeats so far that season. After his first start on May 8, he had picked up six victories, several among them coming in taut, low-run ball games. The clash with Boston that evening of July 18 was another.

The story of the game was a stellar pitching duel that had the outcome in doubt all the way. Nursing a one-run lead in the seventh stanza, the big Californian had runners at second and third with Ted Williams coming up, but Garcia got him

Box Score

Boston at Municipal Stadium, Cleveland, July 18, 1949

Boston	AB	R	H	PO	A		*Cleveland*	AB	R	H	PO	A
O'Brien, cf	5	0	1	2	0		Mitchell, lf	4	0	1	2	0
Pesky, 3b	3	0	1	3	0		Boone, ss	4	0	1	2	4
Williams, lf	3	0	1	1	0		Vernon, 1b	3	0	1	13	1
Doerr, 2b	4	0	2	5	1		Doby, cf	3	0	1	1	0
Goodman, 1b	4	0	0	6	2		Gordon, 2b	3	0	0	2	5
Zarilla, rf	2	0	0	2	1		Boudreau, 3b	3	1	1	0	3
Batts, c	4	0	1	5	3		Kennedy, rf	3	0	0	2	0
D. DiMaggio, pr	0	0	0	0	0		Hegan, c	2	0	2	4	1
McDermott, p	3	0	0	0	3		Garcia, p	1	0	0	1	3
Tebbetts, ph	1	0	0	0	0		Stringer, pr	0	0	0	0	0
Totals	33	0	6	24	13		Totals	26	1	7	27	17

```
Boston      000  000  000   0-6-0
Cleveland   000  010  00x   1-7-1
```

2BH	Doerr, Hegan, Vernon
SH	Garcia 2, Kennedy, Vernon
LOB	Boston 10, Cleveland 8
DP	Zarilla, Goodman and Pesky
BB	McDermott 4, Garcia 4
K	McDermott 2, Garcia 4
LP	McDermott (3–2)
WP	Garcia (7–3)
Umpires	Hubbard, Berry and Paparella
Time	2:05
Att	34,632

on a wicked slider that sat down Teddy Ballgame and the Red Sox. Earlier he fanned dangerous Vern Stephens to retire the side with Pesky on third courtesy of Williams' single. The white-washing was one of five Garcia threw that season, ranking him second to league-leaders Virgil Trucks and Ellis Kinder (six each).

Garcia's statistics in 1949 included league-leading figures in earned run average (2.36) and the Clutch Pitching Index (123), which calculates the number of runs a pitcher actually gives up in a season compared to the number he might be expected to allow. The CPI, then, indicates overachievement. In 1949 Eddie Lopat, Bill Wight, Art Houtteman and Ellis Kinder joined Garcia as the American League's number one over-achievers. A CPI over the 120 mark is considered superior, an indication that the Big Bear had an outstanding year. The calculus on his year's work figured at a 3.6 TPR, placing Garcia among the 25 highest rookie TPRs in baseball history.

Between 1949 and 1954, Cleveland's next pennant winning year, Bob Feller, Early Wynn, Bob Lemon and Mike Garcia won 431 times for some of the greatest teams in the franchise's history. A full 106 of those victories belonged to the Big Bear. Along the way, he won another ERA crown in 1954 (2.64) and recorded two 20-game seasons. There was surely enough in the Garcia legacy to rate more than an add-on byline to the "Big Four" of Cleveland's halcyon years in the late 1940s and early 1950s.

1949: The Top Ten Rookies

Nm/Pos/Tm	GP	W–L/BA	SH/SV//RBI	PR/BR	ERA/FR	TPR
Garcia/RHP/Clv-A	41	14–5	5/2	32	2.36	3.6
Newcombe/RHP/Brk-N*	38	17–8	5/1	25	3.17	2.8
Glaviano/Inf/StL-N	87	.267	36	4	14	1.6
Sievers/of/StL-A†	140	.306	91	16	6	1.3
Banta/RHP/Brk-N	48	10–6	1/3	12	3.37	1.1
Groth/of/Det-A	103	.293	73	17	1	0.9
Restelli/of/Pit	72	.250	40	4	5	0.6
H. Thompson/2b/NY-N	75	.280	34	8	-7	0.4
Crandall/c/Bos-N	67	.263	34	-7	7	0.3
Coleman/2b/NY-A	128	.275	42	-4	1	0.2

*Newcombe was selected the National League Rookie of the Year by the BBWAA.
†Sievers was selected the American League Rookie of the Year by the BBWAA.

Cecilio "Cy" Acosta

TPR: 3.6

1973, Chicago White Sox, AL
Born: 1946, Sabino, Mexico; RP-RHP, 5'10" 150 lb.
1973: 48 GP; W10, L6; .625; 18 SV; .193 OBA; .289 OB%; 19 PR; 2.23 ERA

He was a Mexican meteor — and a tiny one at that. Frail-looking but wiry, the 150 pound tamale could certainly fire a baseball. He threw hard — and often — during a brief major league sojourn of three American League seasons plus a fourth with the Phillies in the National League that lasted but a few innings. And that was it.

His name was Cecilio Acosta. North of the Mexican border that was abbreviated to Cy, and he was the property of the Chicago White Sox when, during the 1970s, the Sox were heavy into Latin-American ballplayers. Jorge Orta, their second-year second baseman, infielders Eddie Leon and Luis Alvarado and Acosta formed the team's Hispanic contingent in 1973.

In 1974 Señor Acosta was stricken with a number of physical problems, the most significant of which was his ailing right arm. That was a culmination of many years of just too much work, summer *and* winter. He never recovered, disappearing from major league box scores as suddenly as he had appeared in 1972. But his work in 1972 and 1973 was about as spotless as a windexed window, and in 1973 — which was actually his rookie season — his 10–6 mark and 18 saves for a 77–85 ballclub fairly sparkled.

Cy Acosta's baseball journey started when the 18-year-old flamethrower's whiplike pitching motion attracted a number of professional Mexican teams. His pro career began with the Fresnillo Mineros of the Mexican Center League. Through eight seasons of minor league ball he played in summer and winter leagues. Nonstop. Six of those eight summer seasons were spent with teams in Mexico, and four of those, in turn, with the Triple A, Jalisco Charros. It was with Jalisco in 1972 that his early-season 5 and 3 record, with a 1.55 ERA, brought a transfer to the Pacific Coast

Cecil "Cy" Acosta, White Sox reliever. (Brace Photo.)

League where manager Gordy Maltzberger, a former White Sox reliever, was charged with the responsibility of sanding down the rough spots and readying the young right-hander for a closer look in the White Sox spring camp.

Still a youthful 24, Cy spent 1971 and the early part of the 1972 season with Tucson, playing for yet another former reliever, Larry Sherry, before he was called up to Chicago because Bart Johnson, a promising young hurler who had apparently regained his touch only to aggravate a back injury sustained earlier, had to be shelved. So it was on to New York, where Acosta was supposed to join the Pale Hose.

And that's when the fun began, because the young Mexican, who knew less than 10 words in English, quickly discovered that getting into Yankee Stadium was a rather formidable challenge for one with a severely limited vocabulary, to say nothing of getting to the visitor's locker room. Finally, after some frantic moments of gesticulation and near panic, someone brought him upstairs to where the Sox' Director of Player Personnel, Rollie Hemond, was watching the first game of a doubleheader with the Yanks, and said, "This could be your missing pitcher." And indeed it was.

In the second game Acosta, having settled down a bit, and trying to take in what it meant to be all dressed up in a big league uniform — with over 55,000 fans in the stands — was informed that his services were needed right there in the middle of Yankee Stadium. Chuck Tanner, White Sox manager, had sent out the call and met his new reliever for the first time on the mound, handed him the ball, and mumbled something like "Hasta la vista" before disappearing into the dugout. He knew as much Spanish as Acosta knew English.

As luck would have it, the little Mexican tamale got the side out and, in a more than Victorian ending to the last act of the play, Dick Allen, pinch-hitting in the ninth, drove a Sparky Lyle pitch into the far reaches of the stadium, putting the game on ice and turning Acosta into a winning pitcher.

There was an equally improbable encore played out the next Sunday against the Milwaukee Brewers. Tanner called on his Yankee-killer a second time to try to determine if lighting could strike again. And he found, much to his amazement, that it could.

The Sox' skipper called on Acosta to

face Dave May, George Scott and Johnny Briggs in the ninth-inning. Cy put Ks beside each name. And, once again, a ninth inning blow won the game. This time it was a Carlos May triple that brought home an Acosta victory.

So, in his first two appearances he won two ball games. Counting the 35,000-plus on hand in his second appearance, he had been introduced to big-time baseball before nearly 90,000 fans, had won two games, and still hadn't met all his teammates!

Inevitably, people asked, "Who is this guy and where did he come from?" There weren't many answers available from Cecilio Acosta. He was a quiet individual to begin with and then, of course, there was that language barrier. So he just let his arm do his talking while teammates like Luis Alvarado and Jorge Orta bridged the gap for him.

Acosta finished out the season with a perfect 3 and 0 and a microscopic 1.56 ERA. Then he headed back to Mexico for more winter ball. It was what he had always done. Only this time, his goal was a little different: stay in shape, don't overdo,

Box Score

Oakland at Comiskey Park, Chicago, June 24, 1973

Oakland	AB	R	H	BI	E
Campaneris, ss	3	0	1	0	0
Maxvill, ss	0	0	0	0	0
North, cf	4	0	0	0	0
Bando, 3b	3	0	0	0	1
McKinney, 3b	1	0	1	0	0
Jackson, rf	3	1	1	1	0
Mangual, rf	1	0	0	0	0
D. Johnson, dh	4	0	0	0	0
Tenace, 1b	3	0	0	0	0
Hegan, 1b	0	0	0	0	0
Rudi, lf	3	0	0	0	0
Kubiak, 2b	3	0	0	0	0
Hosley, c	2	0	1	0	0
Odom, p	0	0	0	0	1
Knowles, p	0	0	0	0	0
Lindblad, p	0	0	0	0	0
Totals	30	1	4	1	2

Chicago	AB	R	H	BI	E
Kelly, rf	5	0	1	0	0
Orta, 2b	5	1	1	0	0
R. Allen, 1b	2	0	0	0	0
Alvarado, 3b	2	1	1	1	0
Melton, 3b	2	1	0	0	0
Muser, 1b	1	0	0	0	0
C. May, dh	2	3	0	0	0
Reichardt, lf	3	2	2	0	0
Herrmann, c	4	2	3	7	0
Leon, ss	4	1	0	0	0
Sharp, cf	3	0	0	1	0
B. Johnson, p	0	0	0	0	0
Acosta, p	0	0	0	0	0
Totals	33	11	8	9	0

```
Oakland   000  001  000   1-4-2
Chicago   030  005  30x   11-8-0
```

2BH	Campaneris, Reichardt, Herrmann
3BH	Alvarado
HR	Herrmann, Jackson
SF	Sharp
LOB	Oakland 4, Chicago 4
BB	Odom 3, Knowles 1, Lindblad 0, B. Johnson 2, Acosta 0
K	Odom 1, Knowles 1, Lindblad 2, B. Johnson 2, Acosta 0
HBB	May by Knowles
PB	Hosley
WP	B. Johnson (1–0)
LP	Odom (1–9)
Time	2:21
Att	34,841

and keep the fine edge for spring training in 1973. He met all his goals except one: he had overdone it — again.

But the strain was not evident in 1973. Used judiciously in spot relief by Johnny Sain, the White Sox pitching coach, Acosta appeared in 48 games, winning 10 in relief and saving 18 more, thus having had a hand in 28 of Chicago's 77 victories. It was a significant achievement, considering that the Southsiders were not nearly as good a ballclub as they were in 1972, when Richie Allen was leading them to a second-place finish in his MVP year. Allen, capable of carrying a ballclub by himself, was sorely missed after a freakish accident in June at first base that put him on the sidelines the rest of the season.

One of Cy's better outings came against Oakland, 1973's World Series winners over the "Amazin' Mets," when, on June 24, in the second game of a doubleheader in Chicago, Acosta bullied the A's for three innings of shutout, one-hit ball.

By the All-Star Game break Acosta had run his record to 4 and 1 with a 1.94 ERA and a streak of 19 innings without having permitted an earned run. At season's end his 3.6 TPR was the fifth highest in the American League, and he ranked second in Relief Ranking behind John Hiller, who that season recorded a monstrous 64.9 (second on the major league all-time list) for the Detroit Tigers.

Sadly, by July of 1974 the year-in-year-out strain of pitching on Cy Acosta's arm began to tell. Unable to sustain the fire in his pitches, and with an arm that was simply "pitched out," the White Sox had little choice but to release him. He was sold to the Philadelphia Phillies at the waiver price in 1975, appeared in six games, and again released.

The end had come all too soon for one who had made such a promising beginning. The memory of his 1973 achievements would just have to do for the little Mexican flamethrower. At that, it was a great run while it lasted.

1973: Ten Top American League Rookies

Nm/Pos/Tm	GP	W–L/BA	SH/SV//RBI	PR/BR	ERA/FR	TPR
Acosta/RP-RHP-Chi-A	48	10–6	0/18	19	2.23	3.6
R. Reynolds/RP-RHP/Bal-A	42	7–5	0/9	22	1.95	2.5
Medich/RHP/NY-A	34	14–8	3/0	19	2.95	1.7
Porter/c/Mil-A	117	.254	67	16	-4	1.7
Bumbry/of/Bal-A*	110	.337	34	25	-10	1.2
Bird/RP-RHP/KC-A	54	4–4	0/20	13	2.99	1.0
Coggins/of/Bal-A	110	.319	41	16	-3	0.9
E. Rodriguez/RHP/Mil-A	30	9–7	0/5	4	3.30	0.9
Coluccio/of/Mil-A	124	.224	58	2	10	0.7
Sells/RP-RHP/Cal-A	51	7–2	0/10	-1	3.71	0.4

Al Bumbry was selected as the BBWAA's 1973 American League Rookie of the Year.

Osborne Earl "Ozzie" Smith

TPR: 3.6

1978, San Diego Padres, NL
Born: 1954, Mobile, AL; SS, 5'11" 150 lb.
1978: 159 GP; .258 BA; .312 OBA; 40 SB; 5 SBR; 26 FR; 5.75 Range

Bob Horner, the muscular Atlanta Braves third baseman, was awarded 1978 Rookie of the Year honors by the BBWAA. Danny Ozark, the Phillies' manager at the time, was afraid that might happen. He felt that the honor should go to Ozzie Smith of the San Diego Padres because of the outstanding job he had done at a difficult position *and* the difference he had made in the team. But when the votes were tabulated, the long-ball hitter won out over the little fellow who was the best shortstop in either league from the day he first set foot on a major league baseball diamond.

Nor was Danny Ozark the only person to take note of Ozzie's play. Cincinnati manager Sparky Anderson, Dodgers' boss-man Tommy Lasorda and Smith's manager, Roger Craig, were among other National League skippers who went on record to recognize the Padres' mid-fielder who popped up overnight as the best in the business. In the September 30 issue of *The Sporting News*, Craig proclaimed, "He's

one of the major reasons why we're second in the league in pitching, why we're still in contention for second place and why we lead the league in double plays. He makes plays I've never seen before, he gets on base, he steals bases and he sets up our offense."

Ozzie Smith's 19-year Hall of Fame career verified, with embellishments year after year, the initial rave notices his play drew. There seemed to be no limits to the variety, verve and sheer brilliance he brought to the difficult and demanding art of shortstopping. Tom Boswell, quoted by Jim Murray in the June 1981 issue of *Baseball Bulletin*, put it this way: "Instead of his number 1— it should be 8 but turned sideways because the possibilities he brings to his position are infinite."

It can hardly be said that the man they called "The Wizard of Oz" ("Wizard of Oh's" and "Wizard of Oooohs and Aaahhs" are but two of the familiar aliases) came up through the ranks. While attending California Polytechnic University at San

"The Wizard of Oz," Gold Glover Ozzie Smith, shown here as a Cardinal. (Dennis Colgin.)

sists, was in on 98 double plays, recorded a .970 fielding average, and led the league in Range at 5.11, which was almost a full point above the league average for shortstops in 1978 (4.25).

Because of Ozzie Smith's exceptional skills and achievements, prominently in evidence already during his freshman season, the chart on page 271, which presents the game's most accomplished rookie shortstops, replaces the usual box score and top 10 rookie displays.

Beyond the statistics indicating Range, Fielding Runs and the Fielding Factor, there are still other dimensions of the shortstop's play, including balance, throwing accuracy, speed and positioning. The great ones possessed each, and The Wizard of Oz was no exception to that rule. The respected Los Angeles sports scribe Jim Murray had this to say about Ozzie's defensive wizardry:

Luis Obispo he was a fourth-round draft selection and then played at Walla Walla, Washington, San Diego's farm club. That year, 1977, he was a league all-star selection. Then, after the Northwest League's 68-game mini-schedule, he made the jump from Class A ball directly to the majors in 1978.

The jump to the Bigs was not made on the strength of his shillelagh. The Wizard had to learn over the course of his first several big league seasons how to handle a bat. But he did, and the key factor here was his dedication to the task at hand. Conscientious and willing to practice long after the sun had set, the "Pods" not only had a wonderfully gifted athlete on their hands, but one who was ever and always looking for ways to improve his electrifying game.

What *did* bring Ozzie Smith to San Diego was his glove. During his rookie season he played in 159 games, had 548 as-

Asking Ozzie Smith to explain his deft talent is like asking the lion to explain his roar. He just woke up one day, and there it was. "I must see the ball the minute it comes off the bat," he admits. "I don't ever remember standing there thinking, 'Where is that going to go?' Somehow, I know where it's going to go, and I'm automatically moving in that direction." Smith is great because he can play deeper than most shortstops. He doesn't so much field a ball as pounce on it.... In baseball today, the Land of Oz is shortstop. And the way this Oz plays it, it's somewhere over the rainbow, all right! (*The Sporting News*)

The same speed that made him an offensive threat bunting or beating out dribblers, or stealing bases, or taking extra bases, also made him a defensive magician who routinely turned certain base hits into

6 to 3 outs. His career numbers fill a separate record book, providing all that's needed for Hall of Fame entry on the very first ballot.

The Top 20 Rookie Fielding Shortstops, Ranked by Rookie Year Range

Legend:

RY/GP	Rookie Year and Number of Games Played	
	(Note: Minimum number of games, 50)	
RYR	Rookie Year Range	
CHR	Career High Range	
RYA	Rookie Year Assists	
CA/G	Career Assist Average per Game	
RYFR	Rookie Year Fielding Runs	
CFF	Career Fielding Factor	
RY-TPR	Rookie Year Total Player Rating	

Nm-Tm — Lg	*RY/GP*	*RYR*	*CHR*	*RYA*	*CA/G*	*RYFR*	*CFF*	*RY-TPR*
1. H. Long-KC-AA	1889/136	6.36	6.36	479	3.52	32	+.131	3.3
2. R. Allen-Phl-NL	1890/133	6.29	6.29	500	3.76	39	+.118	4.0
3. Heinie Wagner-Bos-AL	1907/109	6.15	6.16	387	3.55	2	+.043	-0.5
4. E. Miller-Bos-NL	1939/77	5.95	5.95	275	3.57	12	+.058	1.3
4. G. Wright-Pit-NL	1924/153	5.95	5.95	601	3.93	11	-.037	2.3
5. H. Jennings-Lou-AA	1891/90	5.89	6.73	225	2.50	7	+.067	1.0
6. H. Sand-Phl-NL	1923/132	5.73	5.73	411	3.11	-2	-.006	-1.0
7. J. Tinker-Chi-NL	1902/131	5.61	5.85	453	3.46	4	+.093	0.9
8. D. Bush-Det-AL	1909/157	5.57	6.16	567	3.61	-4	+.091	2.3
9. W. Maranville-Bos-NL	1913/143	5.54	6.48	475	3.32	15	+.124	1.7
10. G. McBride-Pit/StL-NL	1905/108	5.47	6.06	293	2.71	-6	+.096	-2.4
11. E. English-Chi-NL	1927-87	5.45	5.76	281	3.23	7	+.012	0.7
12. M. Cross-Pit-NL	1895-108	5.43	6.41	327	3.03	-13	+.032	-1.3
13. L. Boudreau-Clv-AL	1939-53	5.42	5.74	184	3.47	8	+.048	0.6
14. M. Doolan-Phl-NL	1905-136	5.41	5.80	432	3.18	-9	+.077	-1.1
14. D. Bancroft-Phl-NL	1915/153	5.41	6.53	492	3.22	-2	+.144	-0.6
15. C. Hollocher-Chi-NL	1918/131	5.31	5.95	418	3.19	-19	-.001	0.8
16. G. Weaver-Chi-AL	1912/147	5.22	6.03	425	2.89	-6	+.064	-2.5
17. I. Olson-Clv-AL	1911/140	5.19	6.08	428	3.06	-16	-.008	-2.3
17. J. Sewell-Clv-AL	1921/154	5.19	5.64	480	3.12	-3	+.060	2.5
18. J. Cronin-Was-AL	1928/63	5.13	5.76	190	3.02	8	+.035	0.5
19. R. Chapman-Clv-AL	1913/141	5.12	5.64	408	2.89	-9	+.098	-0.2
19. E. Scott-Bos-AL	1914/144	5.12	5.90	408	2.83	-11	+.015	-2.4
20. O. Smith-SD-NL	1978/159	5.11	5.86	548	3.45	26	+.174	3.6

Elmer Harrison Flick

TPR: 3.5

1898, Philadelphia Phillies, NL
Born: January 11, 1876, Bedford, OH. Died: January 9, 1971, Bedford, OH
OF, 5'9" 168 lb.
1898: .302 BA; .430 OB%; 13 3BH; 8 HR; 81 RBI; 23 SB; 40 BR; 7 FR
Hall of Fame: 1963

When the Phillies broke up their 1898 spring training camp, a chilly affair staged at nearby Cape May, New Jersey, they were rather optimistic about their chances of unseating the kingpins of the National League, Boston's Beaneaters and the Baltimore Orioles. Into his second season as Philadelphia's manager, George Stallings had made several lineup changes and brought a number of impressive rookies to open the season at Baker Bowl. The changes included moving Larry Lajoie from first to second base and Monte Cross, an outstanding fielder with a rifle-like arm, from second base to shortstop. And it was encouraging to have back Hall of Fame-bound Sam Thompson, who was returning after a long layoff to restore his ailing back.

The rookie contingent included Wiley "Iron Man" Piatt, a 23-year-old lefty whose training season was good enough to persuade Stallings to use him in his regular rotation, and two other hurlers, Frosty

Bill Duggelby and George Wheeler. Another freshman, Billy Lauder, was installed at third base, replacing the veteran Bill Nash.

There was another rookie in camp who was just too good to farm out for another season of minor league ball. His name was Elmer Flick, an outfielder, and he presented skipper Stallings with the problem of where and when to use him in an outfield composed of headliners Ed Delehanty (who, like Larry Lajoie was Cooperstown bound), five-year veteran Duff Cooley and the hard-hitting Sam Thompson. Maybe the problem, one of his more pleasant, would work itself out as the season moved along. Francis Richter, the Philly sportswriter who had covered the Phils for a number of seasons described the line-drive hitting novice as "the fastest, most promising youngster the Phillies *have ever* had." Stallings' assessment was equally complimentary, especially for a crusty, hard-bitten veteran of the baseball wars.

He had determined that Flick would wear Philadelphia flannels in 1898.

Elmer Flick and Larry Lajoie both left home in 1896 to play professional baseball. Lajoie, over the disapproval of his parents for leaving his job, signed with Fall River, the New England pennant winners. That summer he hit a league-leading .429 and, before the 1896 season was over, wound up in a Phillies uniform, playing in 39 games and hitting .328 as a first baseman. That melted his parents' objections and started him off on a Hall of Fame career. His 1898 teammate "Elmer Flick, the demon of the stick," as he was later known, also started off his pro career with a rousing, 31-game season at Youngstown, in his native Ohio, hitting at a .438 clip. In 1897 he put in a full season with Dayton, again in the Interstate League, hitting .386, throwing out 25 baserunners and fielding .921. Though it took him one more year than it did Lajoie, the two made it to the Big Show in a hurry, convincing one and all that they could play in the Bigs. Their first seasons in the National League were unqualified successes. They were up there to stay.

Elmer Flick was a prototypical dead-ball-era hitter. His thickhandled bat (most of his bats were tailored to his liking by turning them out personally on his lathe) and smooth, level swing produced the kind of ropes that found their way to outfield fences for extra bases. And now and then he popped one *over* those distant barriers. Seven of those four-base blows left the park in his rookie year. The very first occurred not long after Stallings had settled on Flick as his right fielder, a move that was occasioned by the continuing physical miseries Sam Thompson was enduring. The popular Thompson, who had tried to play through the pain, finally left the game for good after a May 13 tilt that left him doubled-up in agony. From that point on, right field belonged to Elmer Flick.

Flick's rookie season started with a 2 for 3 game as an April 26 replacement for Thompson. A few days later he had the pleasure of seeing his first grand slam — from the bench. On April 21 rookie Frosty Bill Duggelby became the first and only pitcher in baseball history to hit a bases-loaded four-bagger in his first big league at-bat, leading the Phils to a 13 to 4 victory over the Giants.

Hall of Famer Elmer Flick, Phillies outfielder. (Brace Photo.)

Soon after, in Pittsburgh, the Phils' new right fielder snared a towering blow in deep right field at the Pirates' spacious Exposition Park that brought on a "silver shower" from the grandstands. In making his way around the league Flick was beginning to leave his calling card with superior defensive and offensive play.

On June 1, in a game with the Louisville Colonels, the left-handed hitting Flick cleared the right-field wall at Baker Bowl with a two-run dinger that won a 4 to 1 game for Al Orth (see box score, p. 274).

The victory was the Phils' fourth straight over the Colonels in the series and kept their hopes alive for surging on toward the pennant. But that was not meant to be in 1898, as the Phillies placed sixth, 24 games behind Boston's champions.

Elmer Flick's rookie season marks were just about all *A*s. He placed fourth among National League hitters in both walks (86) and on-base percentage (.430). He was a fourth place finisher in Batting Runs with 40. He also stole 29 bases and hit 14 triples, a category in which he would

Box Score

Louisville at Baker Bowl, Philadelphia, June 1, 1898

Louisville	AB	R	H	PO	A
Clarke, lf	2	1	0	4	0
Ritchey, ss	3	0	1	0	1
Hoy, cf	4	0	1	3	1
Dexter, rf	4	0	0	1	0
Wagner, 1b	4	0	1	6	0
H. Smith, 2b	4	0	0	2	1
Clingman, 3b	3	0	0	4	1
B. Wilson, c	3	0	0	4	1
Ehret, p	3	0	1	0	1
Totals	30	1	4	24	6

Philadelphia	AB	R	H	PO	A
Cooley, cf	4	1	0	2	0
Douglass, 1b	3	1	1	8	2
Flick, rf	2	2	1	3	0
E. Delehanty, lf	4	0	1	3	0
Lajoie, 2b	4	0	1	2	2
McFarland, c	4	0	0	5	0
Elberfeld, 3b	3	0	1	2	3
M. Cross, ss	4	0	2	0	1
Orth, p	4	0	0	2	3
Totals	32	4	7	27	11

```
Louisville      001  000  000   1-4-4
Philadelphia    003  100  00x   4-7-0
```

2BH	Elberfeld
HR	Flick (career first)
SB	Clarke 2, Delehanty, Lajoie
SH	Ritchey, Flick
DP	Hoy and Wagner
BB	Ehret 5, Orth 2
K	Ehret 3, Orth 2
WP	Orth
LP	Ehret
Umpires	Snyder and Curry
Time	2:00

later lead the American League three successive times for a share of the all-time record with two other players. Afield, the record was equally superior. He registered 242 putouts and 25 assists, fielding .954. The 1898 Philadelphia outfield boasted three .300 hitters in Ed Delehanty (.335), Duff Cooley (.312) and Flick (.302).

All told, the numbers for Elmer Flick's rookie season factored out at a 3.5 TPR, positioning the Buckeye at the leadoff spot among the honor rookies tied at 24. His fellow honorees include Detroit pitcher Roscoe Miller, the "Rajah," Hall of Famer Rogers Hornsby, Cincinnati's Bernie Carbo, and Britt Burns, the White Sox left-hander.

Elmer Flick's baseball odyssey, which wound its way through Philadelphia and then on to Cleveland (where he spent the better known part of his career), is a heartwarming story made of the stuff of pure American folklore. He was the barefoot boy who turned his own bat on his lathe, left the farm to play in the Bigs, made a success of it, and touched all the bases on the way to the Hall of Fame. Pure baseball Americana.

1898: Ten Top Rookies

Nm/Pos/Tm	GP	W–L/BA	SH/SV//RBI	PR/BR	ERA/FR	TPR
Flick/of/Phl-N	134	.302	81	40	7	3.5
Willis/RHP/Bos-N	41	25–13	1/0	30	2.84	2.5
J. Hughes/RHP/Bal-N	38	23–12	5/0	13	3.20	1.9

Nm/Pos/Tm	GP	W–L/BA	SH/SV//RBI	PR/BR	ERA/FR	TPR
Piatt/LHP/Phl-N	39	24–14	6/0	9	3.18	1.1
Kitson/RHP/Bal-N	17	8–5	1/0	4	3.24	0.8
A. McBride/of/Cin-N	120	.302	43	9	7	0.8
Woods/RHP/Chi-N	27	9–13	3/0	11	3.14	0.6
Ball/UT/Bal-N	32	.185	8	-7	9	0.2
Steinfeldt/UT/Cin-N	88	.295	43	2	-1	0.1
R. Wood/c/Cin-N	39	.275	16	-2	1	0.1

Roscoe Clyde "Roxy" or "Rubber Legs" Miller

TPR: 3.5

1901, Detroit Tigers, AL

Born: 1876, Greenville, IN; Died: 1913, Corydon, IN; RHP, 6'2" 194 lb.
1901: GP 38; W23, L13; .639 W%; 36/35 GS/GC; 332 IP; 33PR; 4 Def; 2.95 ERA

In 1887 Hall of Famer Big Sam Thompson pounded out 203 base hits to become the first major leaguer to record at least 200 safeties in a single season. His .372 average and 23 triples led the National League, and his Detroit Wolverines won the pennant, displacing Chicago's 1886 champions. In a challenge match the "Detroits," as they were also known, beat the American Association champs, St. Louis, and were crowned "Baseball Champions of the World." The Detroits were the toast of the town.

Incredibly, within the next two years Detroit, a bustling southeastern Michigan hub that was crazy about the new national pastime, was without a major league team and had to satisfy its hunger for the game by supporting sandlot and minor league baseball. However, as another century dawned, it brought with it a brash new entry to professional baseball that was already calling itself a major league.

The new challengers were Ban Johnson, Charley Comiskey and their cohorts, who had changed the name of their former league, the Western Association, to the American League, thus confronting the National League directly with a brand new competitor at the major league level. By 1901 the new league was ready to do battle, and though the National League owners despised their new rivals, waging all-out war with them over contracts, franchise locations, players and every other jot and tittle involved in breaking up their monopoly in professional baseball, they were forced to live with what for them was a grim new reality.

A vital cog in the new league was Detroit, and important parts of its franchise were team owners Jim Burns and George Stallings, the latter of whom was an abrasive, in-your-face survivor of baseball's crude earlier days. Stallings had been a part of the Detroit scene for a number of years, having led their minor league entries, and would manage the team he named the

Tigers (at least that was his version of changing the team's name from Wolverines or Detroits to Tigers) during 1901, the inaugural season of the American League.

Four teams that had as of 1900 signed on to the new league (now, in reference to that one year, called the *Early* American League) that were also a part of the 1901 American League's first season were Chicago, Detroit, Cleveland and Milwaukee. Four others would become members of the new American Association in 1902 at the minor league's highest level of competition. The newly renamed Western Association, now the American League, was clearly the best loop in the minor leagues in 1900, manned by upwards of 50 players who held their own in major league competition. Prominent names on the league's rosters included Rube Waddell, Wid Conroy, Dummy Hoy, Candy LaChance, Perry Werden, Socks Seybold, Honest John Anderson, and Tommy Dowd.

Detroit's roster included Roscoe Miller, virtually unknown except in Tigertown, where he was the ace of the 1900 pitching staff. His minor league career hit its zenith in 1899 when he led the Interstate League with 28 wins for the Mansfield club which finished a game behind the league's leaders, New Castle. That led to his acquisition by the Tigers, who in 1901 turned him into their pitching staff's workhorse, calling on the husky 24-year-old for 36 starts and 332 innings of work. The fastballer failed to complete only one of his starting assignments. Detroit's 1900 season was almost as interesting, and fully as eventful as its maiden voyage in the fledgling American League a year later. The team finished the season in fourth place behind champion Chicago on the strength of two 19-game winners (Roscoe Miller and Jack Cronin, who also lost 22 games) and Joe Yeager's 18 triumphs. One of Detroit's best pitching performances of the

Right-hander Roscoe Miller, Tiger 20-game winner, 1901. (Brace Photo.)

1900 season occurred on August 5, at Cleveland's League Park (see box score, p. 278).

Roscoe Miller muffled the Cleveland nine, scattering four hits and producing a pair of runs on his double, an extra-base blow that was enough to win his own game. The victory cemented the Tigers' hold on fourth place and upped their record to 49 and 46.

Turning to 1901, we find that George Stallings and his Tigers stepped up to American League competition with the same pitching mainstays that carried them through the previous season. Miller, Yeager, Cronin and Ed Siever, a portsider, formed Detroit's big four.

It took until the bottom of the ninth for the Tigers to find their roar in their first official American League game. In front of

Box Score

Detroit at Cleveland, August 5, 1900

Detroit	AB	H	PO	A		Cleveland	AB	H	PO	A
Casey, 3b	3	2	1	3		Pickering, cf	4	1	3	0
Holmes, rf	4	0	5	0		Frisbee, rf	3	0	1	0
Harley, lf	4	2	2	0		Genins, lf	4	2	0	0
Elberfeld, ss	4	1	3	2		LaChance, 1b	4	1	11	1
McAllister, c	2	0	8	3		Crisham, c	2	0	0	1
Dillan, 1b	4	0	7	0		Flood, 2b	3	0	5	0
Nicol, cf	4	3	1	0		Sullivan, 2b	3	0	2	1
Ryan, 2b	4	2	0	2		Shea, ss	3	0	2	4
Miller, p	4	1	0	1		McKenna, p	3	0	0	3
Totals	33	11	27	11		Totals	29	4	24	10

```
Cleveland*   000   000   000   0-4-2
Detroit      100   310   00x   5-11-2
```

2BH	Miller
SH	Frisbee
SB	Holmes, Harley 2, McAllister 2, Elberfeld, Crisham
LOB	Detroit 7, Cleveland 4
DP	Flood and Shea
BB	Miller 1, McKenna 2
K	Miller 5, McKenna 0
PB	McAllister
Wild P.	McKenna
Umpire	Sheridan

better than 12,000 shoehorned into tiny Bennett Field, they made their American League debut on April 25, 1901, scoring 10 times in the bottom of the final stanza to overcome Connie Mack's Milwaukee Brewers, 14 to 13. The Detroit newspapers gave it all they had with front page coverage, heralding the Stallingsmen and "real major league baseball's return" to what would become known by Detroiters as "The Corners." Those corners referred to the intersection of Trumbull and Michigan avenues, where Bennett Field was located, and where, in 1912, Tiger Stadium would be constructed on the Bennett Field site.

Aside from the acrimony, legal entanglements, and interleague conflagrations, the 1901 campaigns in both leagues were filled with standing-room-only crowds and interesting pennant races. Detroit set-

tled for a fourth-place finish but was a better ballclub than its 1900 predecessor. In Roscoe Miller they had one of the better pitchers in the American League. He won 23 games, fourth highest total in the league, his winning percentage of .639 was fifth, and his 33 Pitching Runs placed second. His 3.5 TPR tied him for fourth place among pitchers with stablemate Joe Yeager (12 and 11). During the course of the summer Miller came up with three shutouts and received credit for one save. His 2.95 ERA was some 70 percentage points better than the league earned run average (3.66).

Other hurlers on the Detroit staff chipped in with a total of five more whitewashings, one of which was Ed Summers' interesting blanking of Cleveland's Blues by a record 21 to 0 score on September 15, in a seven-inning game, mercifully short-

Home team (Cleveland) elected to bat first.

ened to enable the Blues to catch an early evening train. The staff completed 118 of its 136 starts that summer, an incredible number that was similarly repeated throughout the league.

Roscoe Miller was another of those meteoric rookies who flashed through Detroit skies during the first summer of American League baseball, only to fade and disappear from the major league scene about as quickly as he had emerged. By 1904 the remaining three years of his career in the Bigs had come to an end. But in 1901— well, that was a different story. It was a 3.5 Total Player Rating summer that put him among the elite of major league rookies, right up there with Hall of Famers Elmer Flick and Rogers Hornsby, and with Britt Burns and Bernie Carbo, all of whom rank in a prestigious 24th place slot on our all-time honors list.

Detroit's Top Fifteen American League Rookie Seasons

Nm/Pos	Yr	W–L–BA	SH/SV//RBI	PR/BR	ERA/FR	TPR
1. M. Fidrych/RHP	1976	19–9	4/0	38	2.34	5.0
2. R. Miller/RHP	1901	23–13	3/1	33	2.95	3.5
3. H. Pillette/RHP	1922	19–12	4/1	31	2.85	3.2
4. T. Fox/RP-RHP	1961	5–2	0/12	17	1.41	2.8
4. D. Rozema/RHP	1977	15–7	1/0	29	3.09	2.8
5. H. White/RHP	1942	12–12	4/1	25	2.91	2.6
6. F. Lary/RHP	1955	14–15	2/1	31	3.15	2.5
7. E. Summers/RHP	1908	24–12	5/1	26	1.64	2.4
8. D. Bush/ss	1909	.273	33	13	4	2.3
8. L. Whitaker/2b	1978	.285	58	3	12	2.3
9. V. Trucks/RHP	1942	14–8	2/0	-2	2.74	2.2
9. P. Trout/RHP	1939	9–10	0/2	23	3.61	2.2
10. I. Flagstead/of	1919	.331	41	22	2	1.9
10. M. Henneman/RP-RHP	1987	11–3	0/7	13	2.98	1.9
11. W. Louden/2b	1912	.241	36	-3	23	1.8
11. M. Nokes/c	1987	.289	87	22	-9	1.8
12. R. Johnson/of	1929	.314	69	17	14	1.7
13. W. Akers/ss	1930	.279	40	4	9	1.6
13. W. Horton/of	1965	.273	104	21	5	1.6
14. G. Dauss/RHP	1913	13–12	2/1	11	3.18	1.5
15. W. Wyatt/RHP	1930	4–5	0/2	12	3.57	1.4
15. S. Gibson/RHP	1926	12–9	2/2	13	3.48	1.4

Rogers "The Rajah" Hornsby

TPR:3.5

1916, St. Louis Cardinals, NL

Born: April 27, 1896, Winters, TX. Died: January 5, 1963, Chicago IL
2B, 5'11" 175 lb.
1916: .313 BA; .444 SA; 15, 3BH; 65 RBI; 17 SB; -2 FR; 29 BR
Hall of Fame: 1942

Latter day baseball statisticians, analysts and particularly sabermetricians are not much impressed with batting averages as a major standard for hitting excellence, but even they stand in awe of baseball's right-handed hitter *non pareil,* Rogers Hornsby. When a hitter *averages* .397 over a six-year span, as Hornsby did between 1920 and 1925 (there were five 200-hit seasons and 1,296 hits in 3,268 times at bat) while winning six consecutive batting titles and setting a modern batting average mark with .424 in 1924, there is a tendency to sit up and take notice no matter what one's preferences for superiority happen to be. The numbers are not only persuasive. They are simply overwhelming.

But the "Rajah," so named in his salad days because he *was* hitting royalty, didn't start out in orbit. He was, in fact, every bit the merely mortal, struggling rookie trying to make his way among the men of the big leagues. There were, after all, a few National Leaguers around in 1916 who knew a thing or three about hitting big-time pitching, fellows like Zack Wheat, Eddie Roush, Cy Williams, Gavvy Cravath, Heinie Groh and Bill Hinchman.

Yet, even in his first full season with the Cardinals, the rookie who played short and third (manager Miller Huggins used Hornsby in only one game at the position with which he was identified, second base), ended the year fourth in the hitting derby with a .316 average. His 15 triples tied for second and his .444 slugging average placed third behind Wheat's first place .461. For those interested in sabermetric figures, Hornsby's 28 Batting Runs were fifth best in the Senior Circuit. It was a year that merited a 3.5 Total Player Rating, far below Pete Alexander's 1916 7.3 rating, but good enough to get him into the 24th tier of all-time rookies.

A couple of things about Hornsby were apparent right from the start: One was his short, velvety stroke, elegant in its compact explosiveness; the other was the intensity of his concentration in the batter's box. And the start was made in the cattle country of Texas, where the young Hornsby was born in Winters, not too far from Abilene. There, during his high school years, he was a star for all seasons, football, basketball and baseball, the sport that possessed him day and night — especially that part of it that involved sending the little sphere to distant acres.

At 18, Hornsby's older brother Everett, who was pitching for Dallas "up north," talked his manager, Otto Jordan, into giving the kid brother

"The Rajah," Rogers Hornsby. (Dennis Colgin.)

a tryout. Jordan promptly sent the skinny infielder on up to Hugo, Oklahoma, where he took his first cuts at professional pitching in the class D Texas-Oklahoma League. When the Hugo club folded shortly after the young prospect arrived, he was moved on to the Denison Champions of the same league, where he spent the rest of 1914 and most of the 1915 season before the Cardinals brought him on up to the Bigs for his September 10, 1915, debut under Miller Huggins.

During his Class D days Rogers Hornsby soon discovered what it was like to be humiliated in the batter's box, something he decided he could definitely live without. A no-hitter thrown at his Denison club on July 25, 1914, by little Dickie Kerr of the league champion Paris Snappers proved to be an eye-opening experience, and it served admirably to sharpen his determination and concentration while

doing battle with the enemy, which in Hornsby's case meant *every* pitcher, and *every* pitch thrown his way. In Donald Honig's *Baseball America*, Wild Bill Hallahan, who was a rookie on the 1926 Cardinal world champions managed by Hornsby, would say, "Once he stepped into that batter's box he was in another world. His concentration was so intense you could have shot off cannons around him and he wouldn't have heard it."

At 19, then, Rogers Hornsby brought his immense, God-given talents to St. Louis, where over the next decade he would scale baseball's heights as the National League's answer to Ty Cobb, or Babe Ruth, or any of a number of American League hitters National League teams wished they had on their own rosters. It began in earnest with the 1916 season, starting off with a steady barrage of line drives that rattled the fences —*and the* inner defenses of NL ballclubs when his scorching missiles wound up wounding infielders who got in the way. Then came the four- and five-hit days that raised his average over the .300 mark. Here is one of them:

This game, played at Cincinnati's Crosley Field, went into the top of the ninth with the Redlegs ahead, 6 to 5. But a four-run rally took care of Cincinnati's slim margin, and when reliever Charley Hall came on to record his only save of the season, the Redbirds escaped with a 9 to 6 win. It was the Rajah's first five-hit game. He missed the cycle because he hit two triples that day. Adding a round-tripper and two singles, he completed his gala celebration with a good day at the hot corner. And speaking of home runs, Hornsby crushed a Jeff Pfeffer pitch about a month earlier for his first major league dinger, an inside-the-park-job against the Dodger ace at St. Louis' Robison Park. The date was May 14. Though Hornsby was primarily a

Box Score

St. Louis at Cincinnati, June 28, 1916

St. Louis	AB	R	H	PO	A
Betzel, 2b	5	2	2	4	4
Bescher, lf-cf	4	2	2	2	0
Smith, cf	2	0	0	1	0
Long, lf	1	1	0	0	0
Miller, 1b	4	1	1	13	0
Hornsby, 3b	5	2	5	3	2
Wilson, rf	3	0	1	0	0
Snyder, c	4	1	2	1	2
Corhan, ss	4	0	0	3	6
Ames, p	3	0	1	0	0
Meadows, p	0	0	0	0	0
Hall, p	0	0	0	0	0
Gonzalez, ph	1	0	0	0	0
Totals	36	9	14	27	14

Cincinnati	AB	R	H	PO	A
Groh, 3b	3	1	0	2	1
Herzog, ss	4	2	3	3	7
Neale, lf	4	0	1	0	0
Killifer, cf	4	0	1	3	0
Griffith, rf	3	0	1	3	1
Wingo, c	3	1	1	5	1
Mollwitz, 1b	4	0	1	7	1
Louden, 2b	2	0	0	3	1
Fisher, 2b	2	1	1	0	0
Toney, p	0	0	0	0	0
Dale, p	0	0	0	1	0
Knetzer, p	0	0	0	0	0
Schulz, p	0	0	0	0	0
Mitchell, ph	1	0	0	0	0
Clarke, ph	1	0	0	0	0
Mitchell, ph	1	0	0	0	0
Chase, ph	1	0	1	0	0
Emmer, pr	0	1	0	0	0
Schneider, ph	1	0	0	0	0
Totals	33	6	10	27	12

St. Louis	110	020	014	9-14-1
Cincinnati	100	000	140	6-10-1

2BH	Snyder, Herzog
3BH	Betzel, Bescher, Wingo, Hornsby 2, Miller
HR	Hornsby
SB	Herzog, Betzel, Griffith
SF	Bescher, Smith, Wilson
LOB	St. Louis 5, Cincinnati 4
DP	Betzel, Corhan and Miller; Corhan, Betzel and Miller
BB	Ames 2, Meadows 2, Toney 2
K	Hall 1, Dale 1, Knetzer 1
Wild P.	Ames
PB	Snyder 2
Time	2:02
Umpires	Klem and Emslie

line-drive hitter, there was enough pop in his stick to send 301 home runs on their way. Number 301 came some 22 seasons later when, in his last cameo appearance as the St. Louis Browns' major domo in 1937, he creamed his 301st.

When discussing hitters of Hornsby's stature, one goes right past the franchise record book to the all-time charts. That is one of the things that separate the Ruths and Cobbs and McGwires apart from the standard brand of baseball heroes. For example, on the all-time leaders list for single season records, you will find the Hornsby name listed among the top 25 in base hits, runs scored, total bases, batting average, on-base percentage, slugging average, Batting Runs, Batting Wins, Runs Produced and extra-base hits. That pretty much runs the gamut of baseball offense. Three seven-plus and three eight-plus seasons of TPR ratings in his career are extraordinary enough by themselves to shame fully 90 percent of Cooperstown's most honored.

While 1916 turned out to be a faint whisper compared to the roar of Rogers Hornsby's greatest years, it was still a noteworthy achievement.

The St. Louis Cardinals' Top Rookie Seasons

Nm/Pos	Yr	W–L/BA	SH/SV//RBI	PR/BR	ERA/FR	TPR
H. Haddix/LHP	1953	20–9	6/1	34	3.06	4.7
T. Worrell/RP-RHP	1986	9–10	0/36	18	2.08	4.2
J. Beazley/RHP	1942	22–6	3/3	31	2.13	4.0
R. Hornsby/3b-ss	1916	.313	65	17	-2	3.5
E. White/LHP	1941	17–7	3/2	32	2.40	3.3
A. Grammas/ss	1954	.264	29	-13	30	2.8
S. Hemus/ss	1961	.281	32	9	13	2.8
R. Bowman/RP-RHP	1939	13–5	2/9	28	2.60	2.7
A. Reinhart/LHP	1925	11–5	1/0	20	3.05	2.5
J. Dean/RHP	1932	18–15	4/2	20	3.30	2.5
J. DeLancey/c	1934	.316	40	18	5	2.5
J. Mize/1b	1936	.329	93	35	1	2.5
S. Musial/of	1942	.315	72	28	1	2.5
A. Brazle/LHP	1943	8–2	1/0	18	1.53	2.4
A. McBride/of	1974	.302	56	12	14	2.3

Bernardo "Bernie" Carbo

TPR: 3.5

1970, Cincinnati Reds
Born: 1947, Detroit, MI
OF, 6' 174 lb.
1970: 125 GP; .310 BA; .551 SA; 63 RBI; 21 HR; 10 SB; 40 BR; .979 FA

In 1993 Bernie Carbo and his wife Tammy founded the Diamond Club Ministry, a baseball program designed, as the Carbos put it, to "teach youth the fundamentals of the game while instilling religious values and encouraging relationship-building." Was this the same free spirit who roamed the outfield (and other environs) for the Cincinnati Reds and five other ballclubs during his major league career? As a matter of fact it was. Bernie Carbo at 45 had moved on, though still very much involved in the game he loved, and still very much dedicated to having fun while helping along another generation of ballplayers.

On a professional level, the Carbo baseball saga began in 1965 with a rare distinction. The young Detroiter, not yet finished with high school, became Cincinnati's number one selection in baseball's first free agent draft. Carbo's 1965 selection later caused even more of a sensation when it developed that Johnny Bench, who would ultimately become the recipient of

the Hall of Fame's prestigious plaque in 1989, was selected in a later round.

The Reds assigned both Bench and Carbo to their Tampa Class A farm club in the Florida State League where, as teammates, the two 17-year-olds became acquainted with Florida and pro ball. They were together again in 1966, playing for Pinky Mays and his Peninsula Grays, another Cincy Class A farm club in the Carolina League. This time around Johnny Bench took home league all-star team honors.

Carbo? Mays played him at third base, where he hit .269 and led the league in doubles with 30. Between them the teammates contributed 37 homers to the Grays' attack and were deemed worthy of promotions. Bench moved up to Buffalo's Triple A ballclub and Bernie Carbo was assigned to the 1967 Double A club at Knoxville. By 1970 both would be back together, this time with the big team in Cincinnati.

However, while Johnny Bench moved

along at a faster clip, donning the Reds'
flannels for a 26-game look-see at the end
of the 1967 season, it took Bernie a little
longer. But by the time he had put together
his 1969 MVP season with Indianapolis,
hitting a league-leading .369 with 37 doubles and 21 dingers, the parent Reds knew
he, too, was ready. The 1970 spring-training season confirmed his status. When
Sparky Anderson brought his lineup to
home plate on Opening Day, April 6,
Bernie Carbo's name was written into the
seventh spot of the batting order (see box
score, p. 286).

Carbo's fourth-inning bleacher blast
was also his first major league home run
shot and capped a four-run rally that put
Jim Merritt's first of 20 conquests on ice
and headed the Reds in the right direction.

The end of the line that season was a
National League pennant, a 102-victory
effort that eclipsed every other major
league team's winning total. They stormed
to their divisional title 14.5 games ahead of
their closest rival, Walter Alston's Los Angeles Dodgers. It marked the beginning of
Cincinnati's era of National League supremacy. The Big Red Machine was getting cranked up, and though they stumbled in the 1970 World Series, losing to
Frank Robinson and another of the Robin-
sons, Brooks, and their Baltimore Oriole
pals, this team and its wily leader, Anderson, would soon have its day.

The 1970 World Series was just as
humbling for Bernie Carbo as it was for
his team. At its conclusion he had been to
the plate eight times and was still in search
of something — anything — that resembled
a base hit. He had gone through the NLCS
and World Series hitless in 14 at-bats. But
there would be a brighter day in Boston
some years later, and against his old teammates, the Cincinnati Reds, when, on October 21, 1975, he hit the most famous
round-tripper of his career, a three run,
pinch-hit rocket in the bottom of the

Bernie Carbo, 1970 runner-up for Rookie of the
Year honors, pictured here in Red Sox uniform.
(Dennis Colgin.)

eighth that tied Game 6. It was his first
World Series hit and set up the even more
famous Fisk body-language dinger that
won the game in the 12th inning.

But those playoff and championship
disappointments take very little away from
Bernie Carbo's otherwise superb rookie
season. With another fine first year man,
pitcher Wayne Simpson, the Reds' new
sensations swept to Rookie of the Year contention, and though denied that honor by
the BBWAA, the two youthful Reds placed
second and fourth behind Montreal's Carl
Morton, who won 18 and lost 12. *The
Sporting News* saw things differently, however, giving their rookie award to Carbo.
And, judging by the comparative records
and the numbers that went into the season's TPRs, "Mr. Bernardo," as the Red
Sox' owner Tom Yawkey later called him
when he was with the Carmine, probably
had the better of it.

Carbo and Bench, voted the National

Box Score

Montreal at Crosley Field, Cincinnati, April 6, 1970

Montreal	AB	R	H	E
Sutherland, 2b	4	0	1	0
Staub, rf	4	1	1	0
Fairly, 1b	4	0	1	0
Bailey, lf	3	0	0	0
Laboy, 3b	3	0	0	1
Phillips, cf	3	0	0	0
Boccabella, c	3	0	0	0
Wine, ss	2	0	0	0
Sparma, p	1	0	0	0
Herrera, ph	1	0	0	0
Morton, p	0	0	0	0
Brand, ph	1	0	0	0
Waslewski, p	0	0	0	0
Totals	29	1	3	1

Cincinnati	AB	R	H	E
Tolan, cf	5	1	1	0
Helms, 2b	4	0	0	0
Rose, rf	2	1	2	0
Perez, 3b	3	0	0	0
Bench, c	4	1	1	0
L. May, 1b	3	1	1	0
Carbo, lf	3	1	2	0
Concepcion, ss	4	0	0	0
Merritt, p	4	0	1	0
Totals	32	5	8	0

```
Montreal     000  000  100   1-3-1
Cincinnati   000  410  00x   5-8-0
```

2BH	Rose, Bench
3BH	Staub, Rose
HR	L. May, Carbo, Tolan
SF	L. May
LOB	Montreal 3, Cincinnati 9
BB	Sparma 3, Morton 2, Merritt 2
K	Sparma 4, Morton 1, Merritt 8
WP	Merritt (1–0)
LP	Sparma (0–1)
Time	2:06
Att	30,124

League's MVP for 1970, had certainly done their share to get the Reds off and running into the '70s. And they were in on some exciting days in Cincinnati during their first championship summer. On April 21, for example, Bench and five other Reds had themselves a long-ball fest, lofting seven four-base shots out of the park in a 13 to 8 conquest of the Atlanta Braves. Bernie Carbo smacked two that day, joining Bobby Tolan, Tony Perez, Pete Rose and Dave Concepcion as the other homer hitters. Three Braves raised the total to 10 in the 21-run game.

On June 24 Bench connected again in the last game played at Crosley Field as the Reds subdued the Giants, and a week later Carbo and Bench were in the first River-front Stadium game, this time as losers to Atlanta. In that game Hank Aaron, just past 570 homers and 3,000 hits, and counting, added to his Hall of Fame totals with a four-ply blast. Two weeks later, on July 16, another stadium opening, this one in Pittsburgh, was on the docket, and Carbo, Bench and Company, beat the Pirates, 3 to 2, in the Three Rivers Stadium unveiling.

Throughout the eleven eventful years that followed, Bernie Carbo had his share of ups and downs, but it can be said that whatever may have happened along the way, he never denied himself a good time. Nonetheless, the time came all too soon when aspirin tablets rather than baseballs were being served when he was at the plate, and that, of course, meant that his career was about over. The end came with the Pittsburgh Pirates in 1980.

Some 13 years later Bernie Carbo found another way to continue in the game. This time *he* was to be the mentor. Further, it would be his aim to ground the good times through baseball in a sound moral and relational foundation among the players he would bring together. That's when, at Winter Haven, the Carbos established their Diamond Club Ministry. Fortunate are those who can enjoy what they're doing to the fullest. Bernie Carbo's got it down to a rare art!

The Cincinnati Reds' Top Rookie Seasons

Nm/Pos	Yr	W–L/BA	SH/SV//RBI	PR/BR	ERA/FR	TPR
W. Rhines/RHP	1890	28–17	6/0	72	1.95	6.5
V. Pinson/of	1959	.316	84	25	20	3.9
E. Riddle/RHP	1941	19–4	4/1	33	2.34	3.6
B. Carbo/of	1970	.310	63	40	0	3.5
M. Mitchell/of	1907	.292	47	12	22	· 3.2
F. Robinson/of	1956	.290	83	32	6	3.0
F. Hahn/LHP	1899	23–8	4/0	43	2.68	2.8
R. Egan/2b	1909	.275	53	3	24	2.7
C. Sabo/3b	1988	.271	44	2	19	2.7
M. Queen/RHP	1967	14–8	2/0	22	2.76	2.6
G. Nolan/RHP	1967	14–8	5/0	29	2.58	2.6
A. Carter/LHP	1944	11–7	3/3	15	2.60	2.4
B. Zientra/UT	1946	.289	16	-4	24	2.4

Robert Britt Burns

TPR: 3.5

1980, Chicago White Sox, AL
Born: 1959, Houston, TX
LHP, 6'5" 218 lb.
1980: W15, L13; 32/12 GS/GC; 133/63 K/BB; .241 OBA; 2.84 ERA; 31 PR

That lovable and peripatetic huckster, Bill Veeck, in his last round as franchise owner, innovator, promoter and baseball jack-of-all-trades, came back to Chicago in 1975 for one more crack at running the White Sox. While there were no pennants on his curtain-call watch, his five-year stewardship of the Sox' fortunes, if indeed they can be called fortunes, was anything but dull. Veeck managed to instigate a move here and there that helped pave the way for Chicago's 1983 divisional championship amid all the special stunts and promotions.

Two of the brighter stars of that championship ballclub were brought into the fold without any help from the scouting staff or other of baseball's cognoscenti. Typical Veeck unorthodoxy — of course.

One of them, Harold Baines, whose number 3 was eventually retired, was spotted by "Baseball's Barnum" himself on the Little League lots of Easton, Maryland. Baines was subsequently drafted as a number one selection in the June 1977 Free Agent Draft.

Just about a year later in the June 1978 Free Agent Draft, the White Sox opted for Robert Britt Burns in the third round. Young Burns, who answered to Britt, was made known to Veeck by one of his friends, Bob Cromie, a literary critic for Chicago's *Tribune* and a Chicagoland TV personality. Cromie tipped off Veeck after having read about Burns' exploits as a high school pitching sensation while on a trip to Birmingham, Alabama. Cromie's tip did not fall on deaf ears.

What the youthful Burns had accomplished as a high school pitcher was right out of an old-time pulp magazine baseball fantasy. The rangy portsider racked up a career 35 and 2 record at Huffman High in Birmingham while whiffing 292 preppies in 139 innings. That whiff-rate amounts to better than two per inning-pitched. With numbers like that, one would expect to have to get down on all fours to hunt up the young man's ERA, a barely visible 0.12.

After high school graduation there was just time to hustle the high school

288

whiz off to Appleton, Wisconsin, for his first taste of pro ball. There, his manager, Gordy Lund, was busily engaged in guiding his Foxes to the Midwest League title. His staff ace was LaMarr Hoyt, who that summer dazzled the league with 18 wins. Hoyt was joined by league all-star selection Dewey Robinson on a strong pitching staff that was primarily responsible for Lund's selection as the circuit's Manager of the Year. In six games Burns garnered three wins and a pair of losses, posting a 2.40 ERA and pitching with the poise of a veteran "Classman."

Only a few weeks removed from high school diamonds, the lefty was moved on to another league champion, this time the Knoxville Knox Sox, who were guided at the time by Tony LaRussa. Within another year, LaRussa would be calling signals for the White Sox. In faster, Class AA company, Burns logged in at 1 and 1, around just long enough to show his elders that there was major league stuff in both his arm and his head. In Chicago's front office the decision was made to put still another uniform on Burns. This one had *Sox* written across the jersey. Consequently, within the space of several months, Britt Burns had zipped along from prep baseball to Class A, on to Class AA, and finally to the Bigs. Was that improbable journey a bit much for an 18 year old? Probably. But through it all Burns' stuff, poise and an almost uncanny knack for the feel of the game, and especially for pitching, kept his head above the stormy waters of big league baseball. And, he was having the time of his life.

In what was left of the 1978 season, Britt was given the ball by manager Larry Doby, who was brought in for the latter part of the season, for two starts that resulted in two losses. Indeed, the differences between minor league and major league baseball were made painfully evident in this short round of exposure, but there would be another year. The memories of fanning three major leaguers and the thrills of moving from "nowhere" to "somewhere" sustained the Chicago southpaw until spring training.

For 1979 the full regimen of baseball training and a full year's play were in order. Burns' season started in Knoxville (6 and 10 with an almost 3 to 1 ratio of whiffs over walks) under Gordy Lund once again. Lund lost his budding star, as in 1978, to a higher-classification team in the Chicago organization, the Iowa Oaks. For the Oaks, Britt, just into his 20th year, logged 41 innings for Tony LaRussa, who left soon after Burns' arrival to take on the managerial reins of the White Sox. The two were reunited in Chicago late in the '79 season.

For the past two seasons LaMarr Hoyt, Burns and LaRussa, had bounced around the White Sox system, where, with Steve Trout, Rich Dotson, Ross Baumgarten, Mike Proly and Rich Wortham, they had more than nodding acquaintances with one another. These young players were to form LaRussa's pitching staff in his first full year as bossman of the Sox in 1980. Hoyt, Dotson and Burns would spearhead Chicago's drive to the divisional championship just ahead and Tony LaRussa would quickly gain stature as one of the bright young managerial brains in the major leagues.

In 1980 Britt Burns was named *The Sporting News'* Rookie Pitcher of the Year. Hoyt (9–3), Dotson (12–10), and Trout combined for 30 wins. Proly added five more victories along with eight saves, and Wortham, after a 14–14 log in 1979, came back with four wins and 41 appearances, many in relief. Although the Sox won only 70 games that season, LaRussa began turning the ship around. And without the sterling slants of Britt Burns, who enjoyed 15 conquests in his first full season under the Big Tent, LaRussa's Sox would have

Britt Burns, White Sox lefty who won 18 in his rookie year. (Brace Photo.)

wallowed in the West Division basement. *The Sporting News* Rookie Pitcher of the Year continued to demonstrate the exquisite control, throwing pitches that danced at the corners and chalking up a tough 2.84 ERA, a .241 opponents' batting average, and 31 Pitching Runs. The whole package had arrived.

The 33 votes BBWAA electors cast for Britt Burns were good for only fifth place in the annual Rookie of the Year voting, well behind the Indians' Joe Charboneau. No matter. Charboneau was soon gone from the scene, and had it not been for a chronic degenerative hip, Burns would have remained on the scene much longer than the eight productive seasons he provided the White Sox.

Big Britt was a winner in double figures from 1980 to 1983, and again in 1985 when, in his final season, he was an 18-game winner. He was one of the main cogs in the Sox' 1983 title year, and his 4 to 0 whitewashing of the Mariners on May 17, his only shutout of the season,* was a telltale indication of his arrival as a craftsman of the first order.

Box Score

Seattle at Comiskey Park, Chicago, May 17, 1980

Seattle	AB	R	H	BI	E
Cruz, 2b	4	0	0	0	0
Anderson, ss	4	0	0	0	0
Meyer, lf	3	0	0	0	0
Roberts, rf	4	0	1	0	0
Bochte, 1b	4	0	1	0	0
Horton, dh	2	0	0	0	0
T. Cox, 3b	1	0	0	0	0
Stein, 3b	2	0	0	0	0
Craig, cf	3	0	1	0	0
L. Cox, c	3	0	0	0	0
Honeycutt, p	0	0	0	0	0

Chicago	AB	R	H	BI	E
Bannister, lf	2	0	1	0	0
Bosley, ph-lf	1	0	1	2	0
Moore, 3b	3	1	1	0	0
Molinaro, ph	0	0	0	0	0
Bell, 3b	0	0	0	0	0
Lemon, cf	4	0	1	0	0
Johnson, 1b	3	0	1	1	0
Squires, 1b	1	0	0	0	0
Nordhagen, dh	4	0	1	0	0
Washington, pr-dh	0	0	0	0	0
Kimm, c	4	2	2	0	0

Burns threw a complete-game shutout on May 17, his only solo shutout of the season. On April 22, May 27, June 29 and August 22, he was the starting pitcher in games that resulted in White Sox shutouts, thus involving him in five.

Seattle	AB	R	H	BI	E
Heaverlo, p	0	0	0	0	0
Totals	30	0	3	0	0

Chicago	AB	R	H	BI	E
Baines, rf	3	1	1	0	0
Pryor, ss	3	0	2	1	1
Burns, p	0	0	0	0	0
Totals	31	4	11	4	1

```
Seattle   000  000  000   0-3-0
Chicago   001  001  20x   4-11-1
```

2BH	Roberts, Craig, Nordhagen
SH	Bannister
SF	Pryor
LOB	Seattle 5, Chicago 8
DP	Seattle 1, Chicago 1
BB	Honeycutt 1, Haeaverlo 1, Burns 2
K	Honeycutt 3, Heaverlo 0, Burns 7
HBP	Molinaro by Heaverlo
WP	Burns (5–2)
LP	Honeycutt (6–1)
Time	2:22
Att	8,419

The Chicago White Sox' Top Rookie Seasons

Nm/Pos	Yr	W–L/BA	SH/SV//RBI	PR/BR	ERA/FR	TPR
G. Peters/LHP	1963	19–8	4/1	32	2.33	4.5
E. Russell/LHP	1913	22–16	8/4	36	1.90	4.2
C. Acosta/RP-RHP	1973	10–5	0/18	19	2.23	3.6
B. Burns/LHP	1980	15–13	1/0	31	2.84	3.5
T. Agee/of	1966	.273	86	21	11	2.9
S. Minoso/of	1951	.326	76	41	-12	2.8
R. Thigpen/RP-RHP	1987	7–5	0/16	18	2.73	2.8
S. Rogovin/RHP	1951	12–8	3/0	31	2.78	2.8
R. Hernandez/RP-RHP	1992	7–3	0/12	17	1.65	2.8
W. Kamm/3b	1923	.292	87	8	8	2.5
T. Forster/LHP	1972	6–5	0/29	10	2.25	2.5
S. Fletcher/ss	1983	.237	31	-5	18	2.2
P. Ward/3b	1963	.295	84	27	-5	2.1
J. Whitehead/RHP	1935	13–13	1/0	22	3.72	2.0
R. Dent/ss	1974	.274	45	-7	9	2.0

Arthur Albert "Doc" or "Sandy" Irwin

TPR: 3.4

1880, Worcester Brown Stockings, NL
Born: February 14, 1858, Toronto, ON. Died: July 16, 1921, Atlantic Ocean
SS, "5.8.5," 158 lb.
1880: 85 GP; 19 2BH; 35 RBI; .259 BA; 53 Runs; -1BR; 31 FR

Worcester, Massachusetts, populated by only 58,000 people, was one of the smallest municipalities in the history of the national pastime to own a major league franchise. The city's team, the Brown Stockings, came into the National League in 1880 and lasted through the 1882 season when the team was unceremoniously dumped from the National League. The Worcester and Troy, New York, teams, then, became the first small market franchises to fall victim to the greater financial potential of larger metropolitan areas.

Small town team or not, however, the Brown Stockings had a passably decent ballclub that finished out its first season a tad below the .500 level in fifth place, having won 40 and lost 43. And the team had a wildly enthusiastic following. The local telephone company even offered running scores and final results for its subscribers at special rates.

The ballclub featured three "All-Star" caliber players. The first two were the hard-throwing southpaw, Lee Richmond, and a creative, baseball-smart shortstop named Art Irwin (a.k.a. "Sandy"). Those two were rookies, as were five other players on the Worcester roster. The star of the team in 1880, however, was another of the rookies, a chap named Harry Stovey who clubbed six round-trippers and 14 triples to lead the league in both categories while whacking National League pitchers for a .454 slugging average, good for the league's fourth spot behind the Chicago White Stockings' George Gore (.463 SA and .360 BA).

One other player on the team merits notice, Charlie Bennett, the able catcher who was in the second season of his 15-year career as one of the game's top receivers in the 19th century. In 1880 he was Worcester's catcher, and then he took up residence behind the plate for the next eight seasons in Detroit, where he was a member of the 1887 National League champions.

Artie Irwin was a Canadian, born in Toronto, where, after his playing days he owned and managed the Toronto team that won the International League pennant in 1902. Irwin's parents moved to the Boston area when he was still a young lad, and that is where the youth caught up with the game of baseball. From the very beginning he was challenged by the many possibilities, nuances and skills inherent in the game. His quick, incisive mind constantly sought new ways to field, hit, get on base, score and prevent opposing teams from scoring. Shortstop proved to be the ideal spot for his innovative spirit.

Irwin's baseball days had their beginnings with two of the Boston area's top semipro clubs, the Aetnas and the Amateurs of Boston. In 1879 he signed on with the Worcester independent club, hitting a respectable .271. He played short and several other positions for the team, and before another season had started he signed up to play for the Brown Stockings again, only to find that he had signed on to a National League team.

The ballclub got off to a fairly good start, pushing to the top of the league's standings in May. But they were neither experienced enough nor deep enough to maintain a first-place gait through a schedule that pitted them against teams like the White Stockings or Cleveland's Forest City ballclub. By June they had settled into a win-one–lose-one tempo that dropped them among the .500 teams like Troy and Boston.

But the Brown Stockings did have their moments. One of them came on June 12, when Lee Richmond tossed the first perfect game in baseball history. On that date he beat Cleveland, 1 to 0, shutting them down in Worcester while striking out five. In one of those rare twists, another perfect game was pitched only six days

Mustaschioed Artie Irwin, Worcester infielder, 1880. (Brace Photo.)

later by Monty Ward. The next time that happened during a regular season was in 1964, almost a century later, when Jim Bunning of the Phillies turned the trick.

On July 24, the Worcesters hosted the Chicagos of Cap Anson. It was a day Artie Irwin remembered for a long time. Not only did he enjoy a 4 for 4 day, he turned in a fine fielding afternoon, knocking down hard smashes and throwing out hitters in a 4 to 3 victory (see box score, p. 294).

During the 1880 season Art Irwin led major league position players with a 3.4 TPR, fashioned on the strength of his strong performance at shortstop. His 339 assists and 27 double plays in 85 games (Irwin played 82 games at shortstop, 3 at third base and 1 game as a catcher [our featured profile box score]) led the league, and he had an .895 fielding average. Irwin's 31 Fielding Runs were the class of the

Box Score

Chicago at Agricultural County Fair Grounds, Worcester, Massachusetts, July 24, 1880

Chicago	AB	R	H	PO	A
Kelly, 3b	4	1	2	1	1
Williamson, c	4	0	0	1	4
Anson, 1b	4	0	2	12	0
Burns, ss	4	1	1	1	1
Corcoran, p	4	0	1	0	5
Flint, rf	4	0	0	0	1
Quest, 2b	4	0	0	6	3
Gore, cf	4	0	2	2	1
Dalrymple, lf	4	1	1	1	0
Totals	36	3	9	24	16

Worcester	AB	R	H	PO	A
Stovey, cf	4	1	1	1	0
Irwin, ss-c	4	1	4	1	3
Whitney, 3b	4	0	0	2	1
Wood, lf	3	1	0	4	0
Bushong, c-rf	1	0	0	1	0
Bennett, rf-c	2	0	0	4	1
Richmond, p-rf-p	3	0	0	0	3
Corey, rf-ss-p-ss	3	0	0	1	4
Tobin, 1b	3	0	0	12	0
Creamer, 2b	3	1	1	2	1
Totals	30	4	6	27	14

```
Chicago      002   001   000   3-9-2
Worcester    100   000   12x   4-6-2
```

2BH	Irwin 2, Gore
3BH	Stovey, Irwin
DP	Whitney, Creamer and Tobin
BB	Corcoran 1, Richmond and Corey 0
K	Corcoran 3, Richmond 3, Corey 0
PB	Bennett, Williamson
WP	Richmond
LP	Corcoran
Umpire	Murphy
Time	2:30

league, edging out Wee Davy Force, Buffalo's tiny second baseman. The only other Worcester player who was among the circuit's leaders beside Irwin and Lee Richmond was pitcher Fred Corey, also a rookie, who won eight and lost nine, with top-five figures in opponents' batting average and on-base percentage, and in fewest hits allowed per game (7.95).

Irwin's 13-year-playing career occurred during a time when pro ball was experiencing growing pains, and not only from the standpoint of the cities to which franchises were awarded. More significantly, from a playing perspective, there were wholesale changes in equipment, game strategies and how positions were played. The game was evolving, and players like the diminutive Art Irwin were in the vanguard of those who were introducing new ways and means to play the game.

For starters, the scrappy infielder they called "Sandy" was, at least to hear him tell it, the originator of the first fielder's glove. He also claimed to have taken part in the first squeeze play and experimented with the hit and run long before the Baltimore Orioles ran wild with it in the 1890s. And there is enough evidence to support those claims. But that is another story among the many that could be told about this interesting fellow, one who was also a promoter (there seemed to be no limit to his sporting interests, each of which resulted in some kind of money-making scheme), the first college baseball coach, and the organizer of the first pro football team. Also to be recalled is his managing career during the 1890s with several teams, most notably Washington and Philadelphia.

Artie Irwin, with that promoter's touch and an eye for a quick buck, was a wealthy man in his later years. His death, probably a suicide, came under strange circumstances and was reported as a "death at sea." He was last seen aboard the steamer Calvin Austin bound for Boston from New York on July 16, 1921. That story, too, begs for some kind of closure, never having been satisfactorily explained. It was a bizarre ending for one whose varied talents had led him into an eventful and otherwise productive life.

1880: The National League's Top Rookies

Nm/Tm/Pos	GP	W–L/BA	SH/SV//RBI	PR/BR	ERA/FR	TPR
A. Irwin/ss/Wor	85	.259	35	–1	31	3.4
L. Corcoran/RHP/Chi	63	43–14	4/2	28	1.95	3.1
F. Dunlap/2b/Clv	85	.276	30	16	8	2.7
T. Keefe/RHP/Troy	12	6–6	0/0	19	0.86	2.2
L. Richmond/LHP/Wor	74	32–32	5/3	29	2.15	1.9
R. Connor/3b/Troy	83	.332	47	22	–10	1.4
P. Gillespie/of/Troy	82	.243	24	1	7	0.5
M. Welch/RHP/Troy	65	34–30	4/0	–1	2.54	0.3
S. Trott/c/Bos	39	.208	9	–4	6	0.2
H. Stovey/of/Wor	83	.265	28	11	–5	0.2

Wesley Cheek
"Wes" Ferrell

TPR: 3.4

1929, Cleveland Indians, AL

Born: 1908, Greensboro, NC; Died: 1976, Sarasota, FL; RHP, 6'2" 195 lb.
1929: 43 GP; W21, L10; .677 W%; 18 CG; 1/5 SH/SV; .279 OBA; 23 PR; 4 PHI

Monumental. White Hot. Outrageous. Wes Ferrell's temper was all of that and more. He tore gloves apart, dismantled lockers, stomped on watches and tried to throw anything he could lift about as far as he could throw a baseball. It happened nearly every time he lost, whether at cards or at any other kind of game, and especially after losing a ball game. That really lit his fuse, and, in particular, losing a close one signalled everyone on the ballclub to clear out the locker room in a hurry. The hurricane followed soon after. He was, in that respect, a right-handed Lefty Grove, another of those high-profile, low-boiling-point athletes who always expected to win.

But just like Grove, Wes Ferrell had athletic abilities to match his fury. He was a gifted, handsome ballplayer who won far more than he lost (there were those who were very thankful for that) in a 15-year major league career that was distinguished not only by his pitching, but by his hitting and all-around play, as well.

Wes Ferrell came from a North Carolina family of farmers. There were seven ball-playing brothers, including Hall of Fame catcher Rick (Wes' battery mate in both Boston and Washington) and an older brother, George, who was a 20-year career minor leaguer. The boys knew their way around a baseball diamond and played both local and semipro ball before heading off to professional careers.

For Wes, the start came in 1927 when one of the most respected baseball scouts at the time, Bill Rapp, spotted Ferrell playing for the Oak Ridge Academy team. A Cleveland Indians pact was ultimately arranged, and by the time the 1927 season was history, the rangy hurler with the blazing fastball had made appearances both for the academy and the Indians, for whom he debuted on September 9.

Brimming with the abundant confidence that carried him through his career, Wes Ferrell reported to the Indians' training camp at New Orleans in 1928, led by their new manager Roger Peckinpaugh, a no-nonsense, knowledgeable former Yankee and Senator star who replaced the 1927 skipper, Jack McAllister. There was an interesting exchange in the camp involving Ferrell, who responded to an order to do some batting practice pitching with "The hell with you. I didn't come up here for that." That ended the "conversation," but there was a response. It was a ticket to the Three-I League, where Ferrell spent his only minor league summer with the Terre Haute Tots. Having been rubbed up against the boys who called the shots, he swallowed his pride, stuck his glove in his hip-pocket and headed off to Indiana where he put in an I-told-you-so season, winning 20, losing 8, and posting a 2.73 ERA. Added to the Cleveland roster during the last two weeks of the 1928 season, he lost two ball games but showed Peckinpaugh and the front office that he was ready. In 16 innings of work his ERA was 2.25, and the zip on his ace made a huge impression on the seventh-place Indians.

Peckinpaugh's boys on the shores of Lake Erie bounced all the way from seventh and a dismal 62 and 92 record in 1928 to third place in Wes Ferrell's rookie season, logging an 81 and 71 mark. They were led by future Hall of Famer Joey Sewell, who on September 19 finally struck out after a record-setting 115 straight ball games in which no one was able to sit him down on a third strike. In 1929 he hit .315, moving from short to third in a revamped Peckinpaugh infield that also featured the league's batting champ, Lew Fonseca, at first base.

The Ferrell name made headlines in 1929 before the season even started when Rick became one of ten minor league players in various farm systems declared free by Commissioner Landis on February 28, meaning they could sign with other teams. Rick subsequently signed for the 1929 season with the St. Louis Browns as the two

Wes Ferrell, intensely competitive pitcher. (Dennis Colgin.)

brothers became rookies during the same year.

On the field of play still another rookie provided Cleveland Indian fireworks when on April 16 Earl Averill began his journey to the Hall of Fame with a circuit smash off Detroit lefty Earl Whitehill in his very first trip to the plate as a major leaguer. It didn't win the ball game, but did help the Tribe get off to a 1–0 start with an 11-inning, 5 to 4 win over the Tigers. He hit 215 home runs through an 11-year career in Cleveland.

Meanwhile, Wes Ferrell was busily engaged in putting together winning numbers on the mound. He was well on his way toward a 20-game season when on July 10 he found the range for a bleacher blast at the expense of Washington's Bump Hadley. He hit for the circuit nine times in 1931, and over the seasons Wes enjoyed, as only pitchers can, five two-homer games. His career tally on homers stands at 38. Each of those numbers is a record for pitchers.

In 1929 Wes Ferrell won 21 games. One of his best outings of the summer came in Cleveland on August 17, against the power-laden Athletics in a dramatic ninth victory (see box score below).

At just about the time Ferrell's Cleveland teammates must have been wondering what the locker room would look like after this one, Joey Sewell opened the ninth with a walk. Rube Walberg, an 18-game winner in 1929, nursing a four hit shutout through eight gritty innings, then surrendered a double to Earl Averill, sending Sewell to third. On Connie Mack's orders, Walberg walked Lew Fonseca to load up the bases with none away. Manager Roger Peckinpaugh then called on ancient Grover Hartley to hit for Bibb Falk, sending up a right-handed hitter in the place of Falk, a lefty. Hartley greeted Walberg with a line shot that scored Sewell from third,

tieing up the game. At that point Mack brought on the grizzled, but cagey, Jack Quinn, who promptly gave up a sacrifice fly to Johnny Hodapp, one of the Tribe's promising sophomores, sending Averill home with the winning run.

Wes Ferrell eventually pitched his way to 21 wins that season. Willis Hudlin, veteran Cleveland mainstay, won another 17, and with another pitcher on the staff capable of winning in the 20-game range, the Indians might have been able to overtake New York's defending world champions. But not Connie Mack's team. While they might have dropped a game like Ferrell's masterpiece here and there, they regularly belabored the AL's pitching staffs, and finally brought another pennant to Philadelphia. With Yankee-like power, Al Simmons, Jimmy Foxx, Mickey Cochrane and company complemented Mack's dynamic

Box Score

Philadelphia at League Park, Cleveland, Ohio, August 17, 1929

Philadelphia	AB	R	H	PO	A		Cleveland	AB	R	H	PO	A
Bishop, 2b	4	0	0	3	1		Morgan, rf	4	0	0	4	0
Summa, rf	4	1	1	4	0		J. Sewell, 3b	3	1	0	1	0
Cochrane, c	4	0	1	3	0		Averill, cf	3	1	1	2	0
Simmons, lf	4	0	0	4	0		Fonseca, 1b	3	0	1	8	0
Foxx, 1b	3	0	0	3	2		Falk, lf	3	0	0	1	0
Miller, cf	3	0	1	3	0		Hartley, ph	1	0	1	0	0
Hale, 3b	3	0	0	3	2		Hodapp, 2b	3	0	0	1	4
Boley, ss	3	0	0	1	1		Gardner, ss	3	0	2	3	5
Walberg, p	3	0	1	1	2		L. Sewell, c	2	0	0	7	0
Quinn, p	0	0	0	0	0		Ferrell, p	2	0	1	0	0
Totals	31	1	4	25*	8		Totals	27	2	6	27	9

Philadelphia   000 100 000   1-4-0
Cleveland   000 000 002   2-6-1

2BH	Gardner, Summa, Averill
SH	L. Sewell, Ferrell, Hodapp
LOB	Philadelphia 3, Cleveland 6
BB	Walberg 3, Ferrell 0, Quinn 0
K	Walberg 3, Ferrell 4, Quinn 0
WP	Ferrell
LP	Walberg
Umpires	McGowan, Mallin and Dinneen
Time	1:34

*One out when winning run scored

pitching duo, Lefty Grove and George Earnshaw (who with Wes Ferrell were the league's only 20-game winners), to initiate a three-year World Series spree, completely dominating the American League en route.

But for Wes Ferrell, life under the Big Tent couldn't have been better. He set a record in winning 20 four times in a row (1929–1932), threw a no-no at St. Louis on April 29, 1931, and won 13 straight during the 1930 season while staking claim to the number one spot on the Indians' pitching staff. There were a few losses to come, a few chairs to be thrown, and more homers to hit as the years rolled on toward his final 193–128 career mark, accomplished with the Red Sox, Senators and the Yankees. Finally, in 1941, he wound up in the National League, winning two out of three for the Boston Braves. Even on his last lap, he was a winner at the accustomed .600 pace he had maintained throughout his career, fussing, stewing, battling and tearing up gloves all the way.

The Cleveland Indians' Top Rookie Seasons

Nm/Pos	Yr	W–L/BA	SH/SV/RBI	PR/BR	ERA/FR	TPR
J. Jackson/of	1911	.408	83	70	8	6.8
E. Bearden/LHP	1948	20–7	6/1	42	2.43	5.5
V. Gregg/LHP	1911	23–7	5/0	44	1.80	4.7
M. Garcia/RHP	1949	14–5	5/2	32	2.36	3.6
W. Ferrell/RHP	1929	21–10	1/5	23	3.60	3.4
M. Pearson/RHP	1933	10–5	0/0	32	2.33	3.3
K. Lofton/of	1992	.285	42	6	17	3.3
E. Camacho/RP-RHP	1984	5–9	0/23	18	2.43	3.2
A. Rosen, 3b	1950	.287	116	38	1	3.1
J. Perry/RHP	1959	12–10	2/4	18	2.65	2.8
J. Heath/of	1938	.343	112	32	1	2.6

Billy Cordell
"Grabby" Grabarkewitz

TPR: 3.4

1970, Los Angeles Dodgers, NL
Born: 1946, Lockhart, TX
IF, 5'10" 172 lb.
1970: .289 BA; 84 RBI; 92 R; .403 OB%; 30 SB; 30 BR; -1 FR; .959 FA

Grbkwtz, the common box score abbreviation for Grabarkewitz used in the nation's sports pages, was the 1970 Dodgers' jack of all trades, a tough little Texan who played in 97 games at third base, 50 at shortstop and in another 20 at second base. Described by Tommy Lasorda, "Grabby's" manager at Spokane in 1969, and Al Campaneris, the Dodger Director of Player Personnel at the time, as one of those players who could do it all as an infielder, he enjoyed a career year in his freshman season in The Bigs. Unfortunately, it wasn't good enough to poll one Rookie of the Year vote. Not even from the

Los Angeles scribes. Below shows how the votes were distributed.

While it never bothered the LA handyman in the least, those Rookie of the Year tallies do present cause for some concern. The 1970 list does indeed have three or four top-drawer candidates. Certainly, Carl Morton's Montreal debut season, one of his finest, deserves consideration. Cincinnati rookie Bernie Carbo, previously profiled, was a strong contributor to the Reds' pennant drive under Sparky Anderson. And the Reds gave Wayne Simpson strong support, enabling him to chalk up a glittering 14 and 3 season.

Nm/Tm	GP	W–L/BA	SH/SV//RBI	PR/BR	ERA/FR	TPR	Votes
C. Morton/Mon	43	18–11	4/0	24	2.14	2.6	11
B. Carbo/Cin	125	.310	63	40	0	3.5	8
L. Bowa/Phl	145	.250	34	-34	-21	-3.9	3
W. Simpson/Cin	26	14–3	2/0	20	3.02	1.6	1
C. Cedeno/Hou	90	.310	42	6	3	0.7	1
B. Grbkwtz/LA	156	.289	84	30	-1	3.4	0

That leaves Billy Grabarkewitz at the end of the list, added along with his zero votes, somewhat facetiously, but nonetheless for purposes of comparison. And by comparison the numbers stack up. Nicely. Perhaps not quite well enough to merit the famed rookie award, but at least well enough to give pause in trying to understand just what was going on in the minds of the writers as they cast their votes.

If the Rookie of the Year Award is symbolic of the freshman who made the most valuable contribution to his team, then one would expect that the names of Carbo and Grabarkewitz would weigh heavily on the voters' minds. Apparently neither caused the necessary spark to light up the coveted award's candle. But the sports scribes notwithstanding, there is some appreciable distance between Morton's 2.6 TPR and Carbo's 3.5, or, for that matter, Grabby's 3.4. A closer look at the Grabarkewitz record is definitely in order.

Grabby was a baseball player almost from day one, making the rounds of Little League, Babe Ruth and American Legion baseball before moving on to college and semipro baseball, and finally on to professional baseball with a Dodger contract that ticketed him for assignment to the Northwest League, where he broke in under Dodger hero Duke Snider as the Tri-City and league all-star second baseman in 1966. On August 30 of that season the fleet-footed infielder stole four bases in a seven-inning game against Lewiston.

The next season, 1967, was another all-star campaign, this one played out in a Class A, Santa Barbara uniform in the California League. In 1968 the Dodger orga-

Billy Grabarkewitz, Dodgers handyman. (Dennis Colgin.)

nization moved Grabarkewitz up to Double A ball for another year of seasoning with Albuquerque. Once again he was voted to the league's all-star team, this time as a shortstop. But there were mixed blessings in 1968. On August 3, at a time when the Dodgers had decided to bring him to Los Angeles, he crashed into the Dallas–Fort Worth catcher, Hal King, with a sickening thud that almost completely demolished his ankle. Dr. Frank Jobe, the attending physician who performed extensive surgery afterward, expressed serious doubt about Grabby's ever being able to play again.

Hard-bitten, 23-year-old Grabby

would have none of it. Although the 1969 season was almost totally lost to rehabilitation, he did manage to crack the Dodger lineup for 34 games, though he hit poorly and was still hobbled by an ankle that needed continuing attention. Even at that, getting as far as he did was a major accomplishment.

Walter Alston's Dodgers returned to spring training in 1970 with a mission: to move up from the doldrums of their 1969 fourth-place finish in the Western Division. Although some of their veterans, like Maury Wills, were beginning to show a little tooth, Alston was fairly optimistic about the team's chances. What brought a gleam to his eye, in particular, was a strong contingent of rookies and second-year players. Out of that pool would surely come enough players to blend with the talent and experience of veterans like Manny Mota, Wes Parker, Willie Davis and catcher Tom Haller. Younger pitchers like Don Sutton and Alan Foster and a promising rookie, Sandy Vance, were on hand to bolster one of the 1969 20-game winners, Claude Osteen.

In camp preparing for the 1970 season were enough good young players to create a logjam of contenders for the Dodgers' infield and outfield positions. The 1969 Rookie of the Year, second baseman Ted Sizemore, Grabarkewitz's chum and roommate, led the infield hopefuls. Two Bills, Buckner and Russell, both of whom played in the 1970 outfield and were later infielding stalwarts with championship Los Angeles teams, were on hand. So were Bill Sudakis, Tom Paciorek, catcher Joe Ferguson, Bobby Valentine and Steve Garvey, who bided his time at third and second until he was moved over to first base in 1973. Von Joshua, an outfield prospect, and Charlie Hough and his knuckler were also in camp. So was Billy Cordell Grabarkewitz, and he was not about to get lost in the shuffle.

The Dodgers' first win of the 1970 season came on April 12 at Dodger Stadium.

The third baseman was a replacement for Steve Garvey. The replacement hit the first Dodger dinger of the season. His name should come as no surprise: Grabby. Within days he was a lineup fixture, playing equally well at second, third and short, literally as needed. Alston was delighted. His infield had versatility, speed and enough hitting punch to enable him to spread his hitters around the batting order, thus making it difficult for opposing pitchers to coast through the bottom of the order. Young Grabby was listed at eighth, leadoff, fifth, and sixth in the order from time to time, and by the time the fans began voting for their National League All-Star team he was up there among the league's hitting leaders.

It was the 1970 All-Star Game played at Cincinnati's Riverfront Stadium that provided the Dodgers' jack-of-all-infield-trades with his biggest thrill of the season. A lot could be, and was, written about that game, but for Grabarkewitz, a practically unknown and certainly unheralded All-Star, there was only one inning in the whole game. That was the 12th, when after two outs, Pete Rose singled. Up stepped Grabby, who rifled a Clyde Wright pitch into left field for a hit. Moments later the Cubs' Jim Hickman singled to send Rose on his famous crash course with Indians catcher Joe Fosse. The run Rose scored won the game, making Dodger Claude Osteen the winning pitcher.

Making that All-Star team, let alone getting a hit when it counted most, provided enough momentum for Grabarkewitz to move on through the rest of the season as one of the main cogs in Alston's ballclub. Without league leaders in any of the important statistical categories of the season, the sage Buckeye mentor, Walt Alston, had maneuvered his Dodgers into a second-place divisional finish. It was quite an accomplishment. So was the comeback rookie season of Billy Grabarkewitz.

The Brooklyn–Los Angeles Franchise's Top Rookie Seasons

Nm/Pos	Yr	W–L/BA	SH/SV//RBI	PR/BR	ERA/FR	TPR
M. Piazza/c	1993	.318	112	41	5	5.1
B. Grabarkewitz/UT	1970	.289	84	30	-1	3.4
J. Black/RHP	1952	15–4	0/15	24	2.15	3.3
J. Pfeffer/RHP	1914	23–12	3/4	31	1.97	3.1
H. Casey/RHP	1939	15–10	0/1	28	2.93	3.1
D. Newcombe/RHP	1949	17–8	5/1	25	3.17	2.8
D. Anderson/ss	1984	.251	34	-5	19	2.6
F. Valenzuela/LHP	1981	13–7	8/0	18	2.48	2.5
R. Perranoski/RP-RHP	1961	7-5	0/6	17	2.65	2.3
L. Sherry/RP-RHP	1959	7–2	1/3	21	2.19	2.2
R. Cey/3b	1973	.245	80	5	16	2.1
O. Hershiser/RHP	1984	11–8	4/2	18	2.66	2.1

Michael James "Mike" Boddicker

TPR: 3.4

1983, Baltimore Orioles, AL
Born: 1957, Cedar Rapids, IA
RHP, 5'11" 172 lb.
1983: W16, L8; 5/0 SH/SV; 120/52 K/BB; .216 OBA; 3 DEF; 2.77 ERA; 24 PR

It really couldn't be called a palm ball. Nor was it a knuckler. Actually, it was a cross between the two that Mike Boddicker called his "fosh ball." What ever it was, it got the job done in 1983. He used the pitch, among others in his off-speed arsenal, to win 16 regular season games, another in the ALCS and still another in the World Series, where his Game 2 shutout victory over the Phillies helped the Orioles bring the world's championship to Baltimore once again.

The O's brought in Joe Altobelli to lead the ballclub after Earl Weaver's 1982 retirement, and that meant there would be a stark contrast in management styles. Altobelli was neither as colorful nor as combative as Weaver was, but he was no less a competitor and, in his own way, every bit as tough. Any fears about how this would work out soon disappeared as the Orioles became a well-knit contender early in the season. Using a September hot streak to salt away the divisional banner in the AL East, they survived serious injuries to pitching staff stalwarts Jim Palmer, Mike Flanagan and Tippy Martinez, their southpaw reliever.

Staying in contention requires someone to step up when a player or two goes down. In the case of Altobelli's starting rotation, it was veteran Scotty McGregor, who led the staff with an outstanding season, sophomore Storm Davis and the "Fosh Ball Kid," Mike Boddicker. These three accounted for 47 wins — almost half of Baltimore's 1983 victories.

Mike Boddicker was another of those Baltimore pitchers during the Weaver era who paid his dues in the organization's system and then surfaced with super freshman or sophomore seasons.* Dennis

*A notable exception to this "Weaver Rule" was Jim Palmer, who came to the Baltimore staff after his 1964 professional debut with Aberdeen's Class A club in the Northern League. Following his 11 and 3 season he (cont.)

Martinez, Tom Phoebus, Mike Flanagan, Sammy Stewart and Dave McNally are other prime examples.

Mike developed his pitching philosophy around a single concept. That was to know what the batter was looking for and then to throw his pitch at a different speed than the batter expected. In other words, the key as he saw it was to disrupt the hitter's timing. Off-speed pitchers can be successful only if they can keep the batter off balance. Thus Boddicker followed a long line of hurlers who used breaking balls, trick pitches and off-speed pitches to get the job done. There are a few Hall of Famers in that category, by the way, including Teddy Lyons, Herb Pennock and Whitey Ford. In 1983 and 1984, especially, Mike Boddicker was successful enough to contribute 3.3 (1983) and 4.2 (1984, with league-leading figures in wins [20] and ERA [2.79]) TPR seasons to Baltimore's pennant teams. His 3.3 season in 1983 ranks among the top 75 on the all-time rookie list.

When the time came to step up, Mike answered the call. He turned in his second big league victory, and first of the 1983 season, in the second game of a double-header with the White Sox at Baltimore on May 17.

Boddicker's five-hitter was the first of his five shutouts in 1983, a league-leading figure. Only Rudy Law of the Sox got as far as third base in an 8-K effort. He would meet those same Sox again several months later in the ALCS in an October 6 night game at Memorial Stadium, firing a five-hit shutout at them while fanning 14 White Sox hitters (see box score, p. 306).

Mike followed up his ALCS victory with another in the World Series. Against the Phillies and their famed "Wheeze

Mike Boddicker, *Sporting News* Rookie Pitcher of the Year, 1983. (Brace Photo.)

Kids," he came up with a three-hit effort for a 3–1 victory in Game 2 of the Series. His win was pivotal in that it evened out the Series at a game apiece. There was no need for another Boddicker appearance because when the series moved to Philadelphia, the O's blew the Phillies away with three straight conquests, as Scotty McGregor came on in the fifth game to hand the Phils a 5–0 pasting. That gave the trophy to the O's. For Mike Boddicker it was a rookie's dream-come-true. He had been a part of a world's championship team.

came to Baltimore as a 19-year-old rookie. Whether or not his age and limited experience had anything to do with the constant fussing that marked the Weaver-Palmer years is of course debatable, but the future Hall of Famer's talent could not be denied, and "Count Earl" certainly knew it.

Box Score

Chicago at Baltimore, ALCS Game Two at Memorial Stadium, October 6, 1983

Chicago	AB	R	H	PO	A
R. Law, cf	4	0	2	2	0
Fisk, c	3	0	0	6	0
Baines, rf	4	0	0	1	0
Dybzinski, ss	0	0	0	1	1
Luzinski, dh	3	0	0	0	0
Paciorek, 1b	3	0	1	9	0
Kittle, lf	3	0	1	2	0
V. Law, 3b	2	0	0	0	3
G. Walker, ph	1	0	0	0	0
Rodriguez, 3b	0	0	0	0	0
Squires, ph	1	0	0	0	0
Fletcher, ss	2	0	0	1	3
Hairston, ph-rf	1	0	0	0	0
J. Cruz, 2b	4	0	1	2	1
Bannister, p	0	0	0	0	0
Barojas, p	0	0	0	0	1
Lamp, p	0	0	0	0	0
Totals	31	0	5	24	9

Baltimore	AB	R	H	PO	A
Shelby, cf	4	0	1	0	0
Landrum, rf	4	0	0	2	0
Ripken, Jr, ss	4	1	2	0	0
Murray, 1b	4	0	0	6	0
Roenicke, lf	2	3	2	1	0
Singleton, dh	4	0	1	0	0
Dauer, 2b	3	0	0	2	3
T. Cruz, 3b	3	0	0	1	3
Dempsey, c	3	0	0	15	1
Boddicker, p	0	0	0	0	1
Totals	31	4	6	27	8

Chicago	000	000	000	0-5-2
Baltimore	010	102	00x	4-6-0

2BH	Roenicke, Singleton, Ripken
HR	Roenicke
SB	R. Law 2, Shelby
LOB	Chicago 9, Baltimore 5
DP	Chicago 1, Baltimore 1
BB	Bannister 1, Lamp 1, Boddicker 3
K	Bannister 5, Boddicker 14
HBP	Paciorek and Luzinski by Boddicker
WP	Boddicker
LP	Bannister
Umpires	Merrill, Bremigan, Evans, Phillips, Reilly and Mckean
Time	2:51
Att	52,347

Among the many rookies appearing in 1983, Mike Boddicker appears to have been the best of the lot. The BBWAA tally disagrees with that assessment. However, he *was* selected for *The Sporting News'* Rookie Pitcher of the Year Award. On the next page is a listing of 1983's best freshmen with their BBWA status (V/R stands for how many votes, if any, each player listed received and his RY ranking) in the year's voting.

Mike Boddicker followed up his great rookie season with another outstanding effort in 1984, leading the staff with a 20-game season. Coupled with Scott McGregor's 15–12 and Storm Davis' 14–9 records, the Orioles might have taken a second straight title for manager Joe Altobelli, but they ran into a Detroit ballclub that rattled off a 35–5 early season start, making a shambles of the pennant race.

Logging 78 victories after his rookie season, Boddicker moved on to the Red Sox, posting a fine 17–8 mark with Boston's AL Eastern Division champions in 1990. His final victory as a Milwaukee Brewer

Nm/Pos/Tm	V/R	ERA/BA	PR/BR	SH/SV//FR	TPR
Boddicker/RHP/Bal-A	70/#3, AL	2.77	31	5/0	3.3
Young/LHP/Sea-A	-	3.27	22	2/0	2.8
Strawberry/of/NY-N	106/#1, NL	.257	17	6	2.3
Doran/2b/Hou-N	7/#5, NL	.271	11	5	2.0
McMurtry/RHP/Atl-N	49/#2, NL	3.08	20	3/0	2.0
Redus/of/Cin-N	8/#4, NL	.247	10	9	1.9
Ladd/RP-RHP/Mil-A	-	2.92	6	0/25	1.6
DiPino/RP-LHP/Hou-N	6/#6, NL	2.65	6	0/20	1.0
Dawley/RP-RHP/Hou-N	-	2.82	5	0/14	0.8
DeLeon/RHP/Pit-N	-	2.83	10	2/0	0.8
Fontenot/RHP/NY-A	-	3.33	6	1/0	0.8
Hall/of/Chi-N	32/#3, NL	.283	13	0	0.8
Jurak/Inf/Bos-A	-	.277	-1	9	0.8
Scherrer/RP-RHP/Cin-N	-	2.74	11	0/10	0.8
Franco/ss/Clv-A	78/#2, AL	.273	-11	-7	-0.1
Kittle/of/Chi-A	104/#1, AL	.254	10	-9	-0.3

in 1993 raised his career mark to 134–116. His off-speed pitches and that mysterious fosh ball had carried him a long, long way.

The St. Louis Browns-Baltimore Orioles Franchise's Top Rookie Seasons

Nm/Pos/Tm	Yr	W–L/BA	SH/SV//RBI	PR/BR	ERA/FR	TPR
M. Boddicker/RHP/Bal	1983	16–8	5/0	24	2.77	3.4
L. Newsom/RHP/StL	1934	16–20	2/5	29	4.01	3.2
G. Stone/of/StL	1905	.296	52	26	2	2.9
H. Pruett/RP-RHP/StL	1922	7–7	0/7	24	2.33	2.9
D. Pratt/2b/StL	1912	.302	69	16	14	2.8
N. Garver/RHP/StL	1948	7–11	0/5	25	3.41	2.7
G. Olson/RP-RHP/Bal	1989	5–2	0/27	20	1.69	2.7
R. Hansen/ss/Bal	1960	.255	86	8	6	2.5
E. Wingard/LHP/StL	1924	13–12	0/1	24	3.51	2.4
H. Rice/of/StL	1925	.359	47	9	7	2.4
C. Blefary/of/Bal	1965	.260	70	25	2	2.3
W. Bunker/RHP/Bal	1964	19–5	1/0	21	2.69	2.2
A. Mills/RHP/Bal	1992	10–4	0/2	16	2.61	2.1

Scott Rolen

TPR: 3.4

1997, Philadelphia Phillies, NL
Born: 1975, Evansville, IN.
3B, 6'4" 196 lb.
1997: .283 BA; 93 R; 92 RBI; 21 HR; 16 SB; .469 SA; 22 BR; 144 PO; 13 FR

The Philadelphia Phillies' organization selected 18-year-old Scott Rolen in the second round of the June 1993 draft. They made a very wise choice.

In young Rolen the Phils had a player with major league talent — and then some. At a time when most players, even the young ones, are filled with themselves and their pursuit of the outrageous sums of money baseball owners are willing to commit to sign them, Scott Rolen has, in effect, said, "Thanks, but enough is enough."

Hard to believe? This is what he told feature writer Paul Hagen shortly before signing a new, four-year contract in the spring of 1998: "I wasn't trying to get top dollar. I'm not trying to break the Philadelphia Phillies." Now that's a refreshing change.

Those who say he could well have afforded to say that, considering the seven-figure pact he signed, would do well to remember that his pay was modest beyond reason compared to his "market worth," or the sums being demanded — and being

given — around the major leagues. The youthful third baseman seemed determined not to get all caught up in the hype and folderol of the pop culture that so affected baseball in the 1990s.

Scott Rolen didn't forget or forsake his roots. Nor did he set aside his priorities when it became evident that his magnificent athletic gifts would thrust him into the glare of the major league's spotlights. Born into a humble Hoosier home of teachers, his first order of business has been family. Putting his newly signed contract to work, he saw to it that mom and dad would be able to retire in Florida. His comment: "(My contract) gave me the opportunity to help them.... They have worked 40 years and now they don't have to work anymore. You can't ever repay what your parents have done, but I'm going to try. They're the most unselfish people in the world. They've gone without so we could go with."

The muscular Rolen, instinctive and highly focused on a baseball diamond, got his start in pro ball with the Martinsville Phils of the Appalachian Rookie League, hitting .313 in 25 games after his drafting in 1993. The next season the Phillies moved him up to Class A ball in the South Atlantic League with their Spartanburg farm club. In his first full season he garnered all-star honors as the league's top third baseman, hitting .294 with 72 RBIs and a slugging average of .462. Rolen spent the next two seasons shuffling between the Reading and Scranton-Wilkes Barre farm clubs before being brought to Philadelphia for 37 games at the end of the 1996 season. His 130 at-bats were right at the limit of the rookie year requirement for position players. As a matter of fact, on September 7, 1996, he was hit on the arm with a pitch that put a premature end to his season. Had he completed that at-bat, it would have meant that 1996 rather than 1997 would have officially been his rookie season.

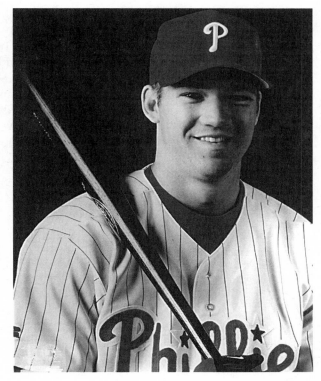

Hard-hitting Scott Rolen, 1997 Rookie of the Year. (Dennis Colgin.)

The wait for 1997 was a long one in view of the untimely ending to Scott Rolen's 1996 season. But when it finally did come he was ready.

So were the Phils as far as their third base situation was concerned. Charley Hayes, Dave Hollins and Todd Zeile all had a hand in manning the hot corner after Hall of Famer Mike Schmidt's departure in 1989. While it couldn't be expected to replace him with another third sacker of Schmidt's consummate abilities, the Phils, after several seasons of experimentation, decided that Scott Rolen would get every chance to settle in as their resident hot-sacker.

Rolen took the challenge, responding with a 3.4 TPR season that was rated a Rookie of the Year achievement by the BBWAA. His award was only the third in the Phils' history, the first having gone to pitcher Jack Sanford in 1957 and the second to another third baseman, Dick Allen, in 1964. (Allen's 5.8 TPR positioned him in the number five spot on the rookies honor list.) Consequently, following players like Allen and Schmidt has presented Rolen with a man-sized challenge.

Playing in Philadelphia in front of those testy Phillies fans is not always a piece of cake. They've been known to rile the home-town team with as much invective and orneriness as the players wearing road uniforms. That tends to complicate life for players who often get into foul territory after pop-ups, sliced grounders or line smashes. Scott's answer to the added pressure has been to play through it, and his brief career has been a masterpiece of restraint and cool perseverance.

The Phillies gave their fans plenty to get steamed over in 1997. They careened southward, hitting a 24 and 61 low point at the All-Star Game break. Nor was that all. On May 31, Scott suffered an injury to his hand that took him out of the game briefly. On June 11, sent in as a pinch runner, he reinjured the hand in a sliding mishap. He had played through a fracture, refusing to ride the bench, but it cost him, as his average slid. It was only after his hand began to respond to treatment that he put together two hitting streaks, one of eight and a second of 14 that culminated in a 3 for 4 day in Miami.

Scott's big day against "The Fish" sparked a 13 to 3 slaughtering of Florida's 1997 World Series champions. He was back near the .300 mark, and more importantly, as far as he was concerned, the Phils were

Box Score

Philadelphia at Miami, Florida, July 11, 1997

Philadelphia	AB	R	H	BI	E
M. Cummings, cf-rf	5	0	1	0	0
Morandini, 2b	4	2	1	0	0
Sefcik, ph-2b	1	0	1	0	0
Dalton, rf	3	2	2	0	0
Otero, pr-cf	0	1	0	0	0
Rolen, 3b	4	3	3	5	0
Jeffries, lf	3	0	0	0	1
Spradlin, p	0	0	0	0	0
K. Jordan, ph	1	1	1	1	0
Brewer, p	0	0	0	0	0
Brogna, 1b	4	1	1	2	0
Lieberthal, c	4	1	1	2	0
Stocker, ss	4	1	1	1	0
Schilling, p	3	0	1	0	0
Amaro, lf	2	1	2	2	0
Totals	38	13	15	13	1

Florida	AB	R	H	BI	E
L. Castillo, 2b	3	0	1	0	0
Renteria, ss	4	0	0	0	0
Kotsay, cf	4	0	0	0	0
Sheffield, rf	3	0	1	0	0
M. Alou, lf	4	0	1	0	0
Bonilla, 3b	3	1	1	0	0
A. Arias, 3b	1	0	0	0	0
Eisenreich, 1b	4	1	1	0	0
C. Johnson, c	4	1	2	3	0
K. Brown, p	1	0	0	0	0
K. Abbott, p	1	0	0	0	0
Helling, p	0	0	0	0	0
Cook, p	0	0	0	0	0
Cangelosi, ph	1	0	0	0	0
Hutton, p	0	0	0	0	0
Whisenant, p	0	0	0	0	0
F. Heredia, p	0	0	0	0	0
Zaun, ph	1	0	0	0	0
Totals	34	3	8	3	0

Philadelphia   203 000 008   13-15-1
Florida   000 020 001   3-8-0

2BH	Daulton 2, Stocker, Sefcik, C. Johnson
HR	Rolen, C. Johnson
SF	Rolen
SB	Daulton, Amaro
LOB	Philadelphia 10, Florida 7
DP	Eisenreich, Renteria; Eisenreich, C. Johnson and A. Arias
K	Schilling 10, Spradlin 3, Brewer 1, K. Brown 9, Helling 1, Cook 1, Hutton 1, Whisenant and F. Heredia 0
BB	Schilling 3, Spradlin and Brewer 0, K. Brown 2, Helling 1, Hutton 1, Whisenant and F. Heredia 0
HBP	Otero by F. Heredia
Wild P.	K. Brown
WP	Schilling
LP	K. Brown
Umpires	Hirschbeck, C. Williams, Vanover, Rippley
Time	3:38
Att	22,255

playing better ball. Before the season was over they had turned around an absolutely lousy 24 and 61 reading the first half of the schedule to a 44 and 33 finish that raised their seasonal mark to 68 and 94.

"The book" on the sensational young Philadelphian says his skills include exceptional baserunning, tremendous range for a third baseman, and a super arm. Stronger than he appears, he is also gifted with exceptional hand-eye coordination and a compact swing that allows him to hit the ball to all fields. All of that was in evidence as his outstanding freshman season wore down to its conclusion, leaving behind a league-leading number of putouts (144) to go along with 291 assists and a Range Rating of 2.81 (the league Range Rating for third basemen in 1997 was 2.19). Thirty-six multi-hit games paved the way for a strong season at the plate, and his 92 RBIs paced the Phils.

The Philadelphia Phillies' Top 16 Rookie Seasons

Nm/Pos	Yr	W–L/BA	SH/SV//RBI	PR/BR	ERA/FR	TPR
C. Davis/RHP	1934	19–17	3/5	54	2.95	7.8
R. Allen/3b	1964	.318	91	52	7	5.8
B. Sanders/RHP	1888	19–10	8/0	33	1.90	4.2
Bob Allen/ss	1890	.226	57	0	39	4.0
G. McQuillan/RHP	1908	23–17	3/0	36	1.53	3.9
D. Ennis/of	1946	.313	73	5	14	3.7
G. Alexander/RHP	1911	28–13	7/3	35	2.57	3.6
E. Flick/of	1898	.302	81	40	7	3.5
S. Rolen/3b	1997	.283	92	22	13	3.4
C. Passeau/RHP	1936	11–15	2/3	26	3.48	3.3
R. Ashburn/of	1948	.333	40	17	18	2.8
E. Bouchee/1b	1957	.293	76	32	4	2.7
R. Thomas/of	1899	.325	47	35	4	2.6
D. Carman/RP-LHP	1985	9–4	0/7	15	2.08	2.5
E. Dailey/RHP	1885	26–23	4/0	28	2.21	2.4
J. Wyrostek/of	1946	.281	45	12	17	2.4

PART IV

The Honorable Mentions

Six pitchers and four position players make up our honorable mention listing. Each logged a 3.3 TPR rookie season. They are arranged chronologically beginning with Pat Malone's 1928 season and winding up nearly three-quarters of a century later with Nomar Garciaparra's Rookie of the Year season in 1997.

There really isn't much to choose from between these ten outstanding seasons and the last ten of our honorees, whose 3.4 and 3.5 seasons qualified them for the Big List. But these final ten are not simply add-ons. There were notable achievements in each, adding up to rookie years too significant to pass by without mention. Prime examples include Dave "Boo" Ferriss' 1945 season, cited in Bill Deane's list for Hypothetical Rookie of the Year honors; Joe Black, one of the first BBWAA Rookies of the Year; Mark McGwire, selected for the 1987 rookie award; and Nomar Garciaparra, who was presented with a unanimous Rookie of the Year Award in 1997.

Let's close out our look at the very best of baseball's freshman stars with a brief review of these 10 players who left behind a few records that will take a little time to rewrite.

Perce Leigh
"Pat" Malone

1928, Chicago, NL
Born: 1902, Altoona, PA. Died: 1939, Altoona, PA
1928: RHP, W18, L13; 2.84 ERA, 28 PR; 2 SV

Things did not go very well at first in Pat Malone's rookie season. He lost seven straight before winning one for Joe McCarthy's Chicago Cubs. The tonic came in the form of a pitcher's delight: a four-bagger on July 14 against the Phillies' Augie Walsh at Wrigley Field.

Malone recovered from his wobbly start to finish out his rookie season with 18 wins plus two saves against only six more losses with commendable readings in ERA (among the top 10 in the National League), whiffs (a runner-up total of 155) and opponents' batting average (.236, third in the league).

During the next two seasons Malone was the NL's leader in victories with 22 in 1929 and 20 in 1930. With a league-leading 166 Ks in 1929 and a third-place total of 142 in 1930, he continued to dominate the league's bash-monsters as he had done with the Minneapolis Millers of the American Association during the 1927 season. That was what led the Wrigley-Veeck-McCarthy brain trust to bring him into the Cubs' fold.

Burly Pat Malone, the Cubs' 1928 ace. (Brace Photo.)

Pat Malone was a tough competitor, a no-monkey-business type of person on the field of play. The night hours were a different story. Chicago's (and other) watering holes were regular stops on his evening rounds. When that got to be a little much for the Cubs' front office, Pat was moved on to the Cardinals, who promptly sold him to the Yanks, where he spent the last three seasons of his career coming out of the bullpen, still effective, and still a winning pitcher. He was a winner three out of five times he was called on during his career, winning 134 games while losing only 92. And the 18 and 6 part of his rookie season was the catalyst.

Montgomery Marcellus "Monte" Pearson

1933, Cleveland, AL

Born: 1909, Oakland, CA. Died: 1978, Fresno, CA
1933: RHP, W10, L5; 2.33 ERA; 32 PR; 16/10 GS/GC; .260 BA

The Cleveland Indians found it necessary to make some changes several weeks into the 1933 season. The living pitching legend Walter Johnson was brought on to succeed Roger Peckinpaugh as manager. There were several position-player, pitching-rotation and batting-order changes. And after impressing the Cleveland front office with his work at Toledo, Monte Pearson was added to the Indians' roster. Pearson's addition was the best player move the Indians made that season.

At 19 Pearson started out his career in his native Oakland with the Oaks of the Pacific Coast League in 1929, putting in parts of three seasons there before notching 11 wins against only 5 losses for the 1933 Toledo Mud Hens of the American Association. After a 1932 cup of coffee resulting in eight appearances, the Indians shipped him to the Mud Hens for more seasoning, and shipped him right back there to start the 1933 season. But shortly after Walter Johnson found his way to the Cleveland locker room so did Monte Pearson, and the Indians put him right to work.

Monte Pearson, able Cleveland rookie pitcher. (Brace Photo.)

Pearson had excellent stuff. Perhaps a bit too much stuff, because he had a tendency to walk too many hitters. But that didn't get in the way of his outstanding rookie year. He won 11 games in 16 starts, racked up a league-leading 2.33 ERA and went on from there to win 18 in 1934 in his first full season in the Bigs.

Later in his career he threw a no-hitter for the Yankees on August 27, 1938, against, of all teams, his old Cleveland Indians, beating them, 13 to 0. During his first year with the Bronx Bombers in 1936, he recorded a league-leading .731 winning percentage while winning 19 and losing 7. He was also a four-time World Series winner for the 1936–1939 Bronx Bombers, nailing down a victory in each Fall Classic the team played in during the run.

Claude William Passeau

1936, Philadelphia, NL
Born: April 4, 1909, Waynesboro, MS
1936: RHP, W11, L15; 26 PR; 3.48 ERA; 9/2 CG/SH; .282 BA; 3 PHI

Between 1933 and 1945 the Phillies spent every season in the National League's seventh or eighth place. In 1936 they were eighth, and it would be understandable if a player would rather not have been traded to Philadelphia at that time. Claude Passeau didn't mind at all.

Passeau was a "throw-in" in a Pittsburgh-Philadelphia deal just before the 1936 season started. He preferred to play rather than to be shipped back to the minors, which is what Pittsburgh had intended to do with him. So the Louisianian joined the Phils in time to suit up for the season opener, and manager Jimmie Wilson began using him. Sparingly, if not reluctantly.

Passeau was called on five times in April, all in relief, and though he was not involved in a decision, the Phils lost each time. Then on May 11 he was called on again in relief and this time was tagged with his first major league decision, a loss. There came four more appearances, and then, on May 30, he was finally around when the Phillies, by this time burrowed

The Phillies' Claude Passeau. (Brace Photo.)

deep into the NL cellar, won a ball game. It took extra innings, but the lithe right-hander was on hand at the right time and was rewarded for three scoreless — and hitless — innings against Boston, with his first major league scalp.

Skipper Wilson finally gave Passeau his first start on July 4, a rather significant date, and Claude made the most of it with a shutout victory over Brooklyn, 4 to 0.

Passeau went on to an 8 and 8 record in the starts he was given throughout the remainder of the season, and he posted a 3.48 ERA for a pitching staff that gassed the league with a 4.64 ERA. His 3.3 TPR indicates that he was one of the few delights on a dismal ballclub that lost 100 ball games.

Ernest Daniel "Ernie" White

1941, St. Louis, NL
Born: 1916, Pacolet Mills, SC. Died: 1974, Augusta, GA
1941: LHP, W17, L7; 2.40 ERA; 32 PR; 3/2 SH/SV; .217 OBA

In 1938 the Portsmouth, Ohio, Red Birds were a part of the St. Louis Cardinals' vast 27-team minor league system. In an organization that controlled the fate of more than 500 ballplayers, only the very best moved up from the ranks of the lower minors. Ernie White, playing in a Class C league, was one of those poised for a move up the chain.

That summer Portsmouth vied with Boston's Canton club for first place honors, finally nipping them by a single victory margin for the league's crown. And White, the Red Birds' ace, was a young left-hander who ran up a 15 and 6 record, setting a league strikeout mark with 18 Ks in a seven-inning game as part of his summer's work. The Cardinals moved him up pronto.

After successful seasons at Houston, where he threw a no-hitter, and the Birds' top farm club at Columbus in the Triple A American Association, White completed the long route to the majors in 1941, when he became a member of Billy Southworth's St. Louis pitching staff.

Cardinal rookie pitcher Ernie White. (Brace Photo.)

It didn't take long for Ernie to make his presence felt. During one span of just 24 days he won eight straight ball games. By the time the season was over he had won

321

17 out of 24 decisions, saved two, and logged a super 2.40 ERA. Another rookie on that 1941 Cardinal club was Howie Krist, who ran off a stunning 10 and 0 record. That hoisted the Cards' rookie record to 27 and 7. Toss in Krist's two saves and the total runs to 31 winning decisions in which White and Krist were involved. To further ice the cake, Stan Musial came along in September, debuting with a 2 for 4 day. Even though the Dodgers won the pennant, Branch Rickey must have known that World Series Land was not far away. And it wasn't.

Ernie White combined with Johnny Beazley, Rickey's next first-year whiz, to defeat the Yankees in the 1942 World Series. White contributed a six-hit shutout in Game 3 of the Series at Yankee Stadium to help the Cards win the gold.

White's promising career was shut down by a shoulder injury in 1943 and two years of military service, but he remained in the game until 1964, managing in the minors, coaching and scouting. And the pleasant memories of 1941 were enough to carry him through a productive life in professional baseball.

David Meadow "Boo" Ferriss

1945, Boston, AL

Born: December 5, 1921, Shaw, MS
1945: RHP, W21, L10; 2.96 ERA; 5/2 SH/SV; 11 PHI; 5 DEF; 13 PR

In the delta country of Mississippi the Ferriss family raised a young man who made quite a name for himself with the Boston Red Sox. His name was Dave Ferriss, and family members called him "Boo" because as a little tyke he had trouble pronouncing the word brother, which came out "boo." A name like that is bound to stick, especially around nickname-crazy athletes — and it did.

Through high school and three years of college young Ferriss, a strapping, gifted athlete, stood out both on the mound and at the plate, attracting the attention of big league clubs hungry for pitching prospects. Signing with the Red Sox after his junior year at Mississippi State, the hurler's professional baseball career began in 1942 with Greensboro's Class B Piedmont League pennant winners.

After two years of military service in World War II, he was reassigned to the Louisville Colonels in 1945 and would have spent a full season there if the Bosox hadn't gotten off to a miserable start in 1945 with a pitching staff that, even for wartime, was

David "Boo" Ferriss, who opened his career with a shutout. (Dennis Colgin.)

less than adequate. So the call went out to Louisville manager Nemo Leibold to send up "that Ferriss fellow."

In his first start Boo was within a pitch or two of being sent back to Louisville. Debuting on April 29 against the Athletics, the first 11 pitches he threw were balls. Two were on with Bobby Estallela up, when Ferriss finally got a break on an Estalella pop up. Then Dick Siebert came up, rifling a shot back at Ferriss, deflecting it to the shortstop, who, in turn, converted the carom into a double play. The big power pitcher not only settled down, but proceeded to whitewash the Mackmen, winning his first game in the Bigs, 2 to 0. With all the debut jitters out of the way Ferriss got down to serious business.

His next start was another win and another shutout. And he kept right on winning, beating every team in the league while running amok with an 8 and 0 record. Before it was all over the 1945 log showcased a glittering 21 and 10 mark which at one point peaked at 17 and 4 before his 21 victory windup. A fistful of records fell in the wake of his 3.3 TPR season, and he went on to an even better 1946 mark, going 21 and 6 to lead the American League in winning percentage.

Dave Ferriss' 3.3, standing at the midpoint of our 10 honorable mentions, was a solid contribution to a Bosox club that recovered from a shakey start to play respectably the rest of the way. In 1946, with Boo pacing the pitching corps, they would make it back all the way, winning the pennant.

Joseph "Joe" Black

1952, Brooklyn, NL

Born: February 8, 1924, Plainfield, NJ
1952: RHP, W15, L4, .789 W%;
0/15 SH/SV; 2.15 ERA; .201 OBA; 24 PR; .262 OB%

Joe Black, a product of the Negro Leagues, broke into professional baseball with the Baltimore Elite Giants in 1943. He was a big, handsome, broad-shouldered right-hander who thought he was a shortstop. However, the Elite Giants' manager, Felton Snow, and their travelling secretary, George Scales, thought differently. They put the big fellow out on the mound and he thrived there, using a devastating slider and a blazing fastball to sit down the best in the business.

Although he wasn't among the very first blacks to crack baseball's color barrier, he was nonetheless among the first wave of pioneers during those crucial early years of baseball's integration. Black had spent two seasons in the Brooklyn farm system making the transition to the land of white baseball, and became the 25th black player to debut in the majors after Jackie Robinson's start in 1947 in the Dodgers' opener against the Boston Braves on April 15. And there was an almost immediate link between Robinson and Black, who became fast friends and roommates. When the end came for Robinson, it was Black who was called on to serve as one of his friend's pallbearers.

NL Rookie of the Year Don Black. (Dennis Colgin.)

Charlie Dressen's 1952 Dodgers had gaping holes left in the pitching department, both in starting and relieving, especially the one left by Don Newcombe's departure for military duty. Joe Black came along to plug them both, completing one of his two starts and providing more than

325

125 innings of absolutely incredible relief during a season in which he won 15, saved as many, and went on, in 1952, to become the first black pitcher to win a World Series game when he subdued Allie Reynolds and the Yankees in the series' first game.

Debuting on May 1, he entered a Dodger-Cub contest at Wrigley Field in the seventh inning and pitched a hitless and scoreless inning. After a two-inning shutdown of the Cincinnati Reds moved Da Bums into first place on June 1, skipper Dressen appointed him the go-to guy out of the pen. There followed more than 50 appearances, a slick 2.15 ERA and a minuscule .201 opponents' batting average.

Joe Black was the Rookie of the Year in 1952, an award he justly received over the stiff competition afforded by another rookie reliever, Hoyt Wilhelm, whose relief exploits would one day merit Hall of Fame honors. Joe Black's career did not match his freshman season, but that one, glorious season of 1952 was a glowing star that would shine through baseball's darker days of post-war integration and his own disappointment at not being able to sustain his brilliant start in the Bigs.

Ricardo Adolfo Jacabo "Rico" Carty

1964, Milwaukee/Atlanta, NL;
1973–1979, Texas, Cleveland, Oakland, Toronto, AL
Born: September 1, 1939, San Pedro De Macoris, Dominican Republic
1964: OF, .330 BA; 22 HR; 88 RBI; .554 SA; 37 BR; 1 FR; .978 FA

Big and sturdy, Dominican Rico Carty was a natural with a bat in his hands. A slashing, steady hit machine, he found hitting a ball much to his liking and did it exceedingly well, eight times eclipsing the .300 mark and winning the National League batting title with a .366 mark in 1970. Though he didn't possess the same finesse afield, he did have a strong throwing arm, which is what prompted him, as a young player, to harbor hopes of being a catcher. That, however, wasn't where he wound up. As he moved through Milwaukee's minor league system, he was used more and more as an outfielder, and that's where he played in the majors until the many injuries he sustained caused him to switch to the designated hitter's role in the American League, still potent with a bat, and still hitting in the .300 range.

Carty, who referred to himself as "The Big One," didn't start out his rookie year like a big-time player. Seldom used until mid–May, he finally caught up with major league pitching on May 12, 1964,

The Braves' Rico Carty. (Brace Photo.)

327

with his first home run, and became a lineup fixture for the next month until a slump pushed him from his .322 level on May 22 on down to the .280 mark a month later. But on June 25 a pair of hits, followed by a June 27 round-tripper helped turn things around. Within another week he was back up there among the league's top ten, hitting at the .330 level by the July 4 milestone. That's where he finally wound up at season's end, as runner-up to Roberto Clemente's .339.

Rattling high numbers of multi-hit ball games at National League teams, Carty placed fourth in on-base percentage (.391) and slugging average (.554). His season's work earned him a high 3.3 TPR rating, second only to Rich Allen's 5.8 mark.

The Big One's biggest day of that great rookie season came on August 24 in a Milwaukee-Philadelphia slugfest.

Rico Carty was named to the Topps Rookie All-Star Team, leading the fifth-place Milwaukee Braves in hitting, and although he picked a year in which Rich Allen's rookie award and Roberto Clemente's batting crown bettered his outstanding rookie marks, his was nonetheless a substantial achievement worthy of the honorable mention status accorded him among the best rookie seasons in baseball history.

Box Score

Philadelphia at County Stadium, Milwaukee, August 24, 1963

Philadelphia	AB	R	H	BI	E		Milwaukee	AB	R	H	BI	E
Gonzalez, cf	5	1	1	0	0		Carty, lf	5	4	5	1	0
Allen, 3b	5	2	2	0	1		Maye, cf	5	2	2	1	0
Callison, cf	4	1	2	0	0		Aaron, rf	3	3	1	3	0
Covington, lf	5	2	4	6	0		Mathews, 3b	4	1	3	2	1
Thomas, 1b	4	1	1	0	0		Torre, c	4	1	2	2	0
Rojas, ph	1	0	0	0	0		Oliver, 1b	5	0	2	2	0
Dalrymple, c	4	2	2	2	0		Menke, ss	4	0	0	1	0
Taylor, 2b	4	0	0	1	0		Woodward, 2b	4	0	0	0	0
Amaro, ss	4	0	1	0	0		Sadowski, p	4	1	0	0	0
Mahaffey, p	0	0	0	0	0							
Briggs, ph	1	0	0	0	0							
Bennett, p	1	0	0	0	0							
Culp, p	1	0	0	0	0							
Herrnstein, 1b	1	0	0	0	0							
Totals	40	9	13	9	1		Totals	38	12	16	12	1

```
Philadelphia   301   001   013    9-13-1
Milwaukee      230   203   20x   12-16-1
```

2BH	Gonzalez, Covington 2, Carty 3, Torre
3BH	Dalrymple
HR	Covington 2, Dalrymple, Carty, Aaron
SB	Taylor
LOB	Philadelphia 5, Milwaukee 9
SF	Aaron, Menke
DP	Milwaukee 1
HBP	Callison by Sadowski
Wild P.	Bennett
LP	Bennett
WP	Sadowski
Time	2:47
Att	11,726

Mark David
"Big Mac" McGwire

1987, Oakland, AL

Born: October 1, 1963, Pomona, CA
1987: 1b, .289 BA; .618 SA; 118 RBI; 49 HR; 97 R; 53 BR; .992 FA

There are defining moments in every career. Mark McGwire's came on September 27, 1998, when, on the season's last day, he creamed two bleacher shots for homers number 69 and 70, establishing a new single-season standard. No matter what came before or what would follow, those two home runs would forever mark his career with a searing brand of Hall of Fame achievement, and that necessarily includes other of his orbital accomplishments, like setting the round-tripper record for rookies at 49 in 1987.

"The Big Mac," a powerfully built giant with a gentle spirit, began his professional career with the Oakland A's' Modesto farm club. There he led the California League in 1985 with 24 of his specialties and 106 RBIs. By the end of the 1986 season he was in Oakland, where he debuted on August 22. Within a week he had registered his first major league dinger at the expense of Walt Terrell, a Detroit Tiger right-hander. Two more followed in his 1986 18-game "warmup."

McGwire really put the show on the road in 1987, capturing Rookie of the Year honors. He was the BBWAA's unanimous choice, and not only because he set a new rookie home run record. Teaming with Jose Canseco, the league's Rookie of the Year in 1986, the two accounted for 231 Oakland scores. Dubbed the Bash Brothers, the two combined for 82 homers and 608 total bases, providing a shuddering attack in the middle of Oakland's batting order.

Between Big Mac's first big-time home run and the last one of his famed 70 in 1998 there were 455 more, putting him well on the way to the 600 level. And it is well to remember that those numbers were achieved despite a three-season stretch, from 1993 to 1995, over which his playing time was cut to merely 178 games because of injuries of one kind or another.

During his orbital 1987 season McGwire's .618 slugging average led both leagues. Of the 49 homers he hit to spruce up that slugging average, his 39th, against the California Angels, set the new rookie standard, breaking the record set by Wally Berger in 1938 and later tied by Frank Robinson in 1956. The record-breaking box score is shown on the next page.

The A's Mark McGwire (right) and Jose Canseco (left). (Dennis Colgin.)

Box Score

Oakland at Anaheim Stadium, California, August 14, 1987

Oakland	AB	R	H	BI	E		California	AB	R	H	BI	E
Bernazard, 2b	6	1	2	0	0		Pettis, cf	4	0	0	0	1
Gallego, 2b	0	1	0	0	0		Miller, rf	2	0	2	1	0
Davis, rf	4	0	1	1	2		White, rf	4	0	0	0	0

Oakland	AB	R	H	BI	E
Canseco, lf	6	0	1	0	0
McGwire, 1b	6	3	3	2	0
Murphy, cf	4	1	2	0	0
Langford, 3b	4	0	1	2	0
Steinbach, c	5	1	2	2	0
Griffin, ss	4	0	0	0	0
Polonia, dh	2	0	0	0	0
Henderson, ph	0	0	0	0	0
Jackson, dh	3	0	0	0	0
Young, p	0	0	0	0	1
Jy. Howell, p	0	0	0	0	0
Cadaret, p	0	0	0	0	0
Lamp, p	0	0	0	0	0
Leiper, p	0	0	0	0	0
Rodriguez, p	0	0	0	0	0
Eckersley, p	0	0	0	0	0
Totals	44	7	12	7	3

California	AB	R	H	BI	E
Downing, dh	5	1	1	1	0
DeCinces, 3b	5	1	2	0	0
Hendrick, lf	4	1	2	0	0
Jones, ph	1	0	0	0	0
Boone, c	5	1	1	2	0
Ja. Howell, ph	1	0	0	0	0
Joyner, 1b	5	1	2	0	0
Schofield, 2b	3	1	2	1	0
Buckner, ph	1	0	0	0	0
McLemore, 2b	1	0	0	0	0
Polidor, ss	5	0	2	0	0
Sutton, p	0	0	0	0	0
Finley, p	0	0	0	0	0
Minton, p	0	0	0	0	0
Lucas, p	0	0	0	0	0
Buice, p	0	0	0	0	0
Totals	46	6	14	6	1

```
Oakland      000  032  001  001   7-12-3
California   030  001  101  000   6-14-1
```

2BH	Hendrick, Boone, McGwire, Joyner, Miller, Bernazard
HR	Steinbach, McGwire, Downing
SB	Davis
SH	Murphy, DeCinces
SF	Lansford
LOB	Oakland 6, California 9
DP	Oakland 2
BB	Young 1, Lamp 2, Leiper 1, Sutton 1, Minton 1, Lucas 1
K	Young 1, Lamp 1, Sutton 3, Finley 2, Minton 1, Buice 3
Balk	Young
Gm. Win. RBI	Davis
Umpires	Young, Shulock, McKean, McClelland
Time	4:07
Att	36,616

Kenneth "Kenny" Lofton

1992, Cleveland, AL;
1997, Atlanta, NL
Born: May 31, 1967, East Chicago, IN
1992: CF, .285 BA; .362 OB%; 66 SB; 96 R; 13 SBR; 6 BR; 17 FR

In *Best of Baseball*, by Paul Adomites and Saul Wisnia, two veteran baseball writers, there are 32 "Ten Best" lists on everything from baseball's craftiest pitchers to films about the game. Among the ten fastest baserunners, names like Cool Papa Bell, Mickey Mantle and Billy Hamilton

Speedy Kenny Lofton. (Dennis Colgin.)

stick out. Another on that list is Kenny Lofton, the Cleveland Indians' swiftie who moved from base to base in a blur.

Blessed with all the tools necessary to take extra bases, commit larceny on the base paths and disrupt defenses, distorting timing and defensive composure, the former University of Arizona basketball whiz ranks as one of baseball's very best leadoff hitters. Possessed of breathtaking speed, razor sharp reflexes and mercury-quick lateral movement, the Cleveland speed merchant moves from first to third in a heartbeat. And as if all that weren't enough, Lofton has a keen eye, hits for extra bases and gives the Indians its best center-fielder since the days of Tris Speaker.

In 1992, his freshman year, Kenny led the American League with 66 stolen bases, enabling him to log 13 Stolen Base Runs, tieing him for 35th place on the all-time major league list. His 17 Fielding Runs placed him fourth in the league, and he hit .285 with eight triples and a very good .362 on-base percentage. In Lofton the Indians had a catalyst who, with young players like Carlos Baerga, Albert Belle and hurler

Chuck Nagy, began turning things around for the Indians.

Some of Lofton's more significant dates in 1992 include:

- April 26   Lofton stole home for the first time in his career, and it was the Indians' first steal of home in 11 seasons.

- May 7   Lofton hit his first ML home run on a 3 for 4 day as the Indians beat the Texas Rangers.

- May 31   After 25 consecutive steals of second base, Angels catcher Lance Parrish threw him out.

- July 29   In a 3 for 3 game he stole his 35th base.

- September 15   Stole two bases, numbers 55 and 56, setting the new record for rookies.

- September 24   Broke the Cleveland season record with his 62nd steal. The old record was set by Miguel Dilone in 1980.

Kenny Lofton polled 85 votes for the BBWAA's Rookie of the Year Award in 1992, 37 less than Pat Listach's 122, but his 3.3 TPR is a strong enough credential to place him among the top rookie seasons in baseball's history.

Anthony Nomar Garciaparra

1997, Boston, AL

Born: July 23, 1973, Whittier, CA

1997: SS, 684 AB; .306 BA; 209 H; 11 3BH; 30 HR; 19 BR; 98 RBI

Nomar Garciaparra was an academic All-American at Georgia Tech, where his baseball coach, Danny Hall, knew just how

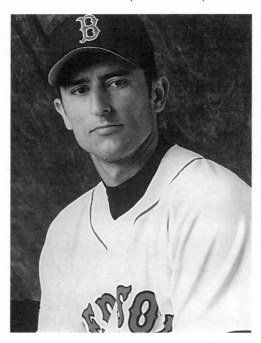

1997 Rookie of the Year Nomar Garciaparra. (Dennis Colgin.)

fortunate he was to have the superbly gifted Mexican-American in his lineup. Hall predicted that Garciaparra would hit .300, steal 30 bases and hit 20 home runs in the majors. The coach didn't miss by much. The Boston Red Sox' number one 1994 draft choice, who opened the 1997 season as their shortstop and leadoff hitter, hit .306, stole 22 bases and hit 30 home runs. His sensational break-in season earned him Rookie of the Year honors. Beyond even Danny Hall's expectations, Nomar drove home 98 runs, setting a new record for leadoff hitters. And on an even more noteworthy level, he hit safely in 30 consecutive games, another record for American League rookies.

But there is more to the Garciaparra envelope than hitting. When this fellow puts on his glove the Bosox' inner defense takes on a new luster. Nomar's exceptional range, soft hands and quick release make for extraordinary coverage from second base to third and beyond into foul territory. He put the league on notice with a play at Cleveland in April of 1997 that dumbfounded even grizzled veterans. Chasing down a ball that hit the third base bag and rolled into left field, he turned and threw a one-hop strike, without setting himself to make the throw, to catcher Bill Hasselman, cutting down the runner attempting to score. It was the most sensational of his 450 assists that season. There also were 249 league-leading putouts. He also led the league in total chances with 720 and was in on 113 double plays.

Nomar Garciaparra's 3.3 TPR is the last of our honorable mention rookies but certainly not the least. His 1997 season, which came within a hair's breadth of matching National League pace-setter Scott Rolen's, who was also a Rookie of the Year choice (3.4 TPR), outclassed Jose Cruz of Toronto and pitcher Jason Dick-son of the Anaheim Angels, his closest rivals in the BBWAA voting.

The honorable mention list, stretching from Pat Malone's exemplary 1928 season through the end of 20th-century baseball with Nomar Garciaparra's 1997 season, contains three contemporary players who might well be honored with more than rookie honors of one kind or another. Players like Kenny Lofton, Nomar Garciaparra and Mark McGwire may very well find their way to Cooperstown in due time. Like many another in our listing of the greatest rookie seasons in baseball's long and distinguished history, their careers began with a season that provoked wonder and, by hinting at what glory might follow, stirred the imagination.

Appendix A

Did They Get Better?

Among the rookie players reviewed, only 27 (37 percent) were able to improve on their freshman seasons. Eight Hall of Fame players on the rookie honors list (denoted by *) are among this elite group of 27.

Appendix A presents a listing of the players who bettered their rookie years, ranked according to the difference between their rookie season and their best TPR season.

Nm/Pos/Tm	ML Yrs	RY	TPR	Best Yr	TPR	Diff	W–L/BA	ERA/RBI
Mathewson*/RHP/NY-N	17	1901	4.1	1905	9.6	5.1	31–9	1.28
Alexander*RHP/Phl-N	20	1911	3.6	1915	8.6	5.0	31–10	1.22
Hornsby*/2b/StL-N	23	1916	3.5	1922	8.5	5.0	.401	152
McGwire/1b/Oak-A; StL/N†	13	1987	3.3	1998	7.2	3.9	.299	147
W. Ferrell/RHP/Clv; Bos-A	15	1929	3.4	1925	7.2	3.8	25–14	3.52
T. Williams*/of/Bos-A	19	1939	4.3	1942	8.1	3.8	.356	137
J. Morgan*/2b/Hou; Cin-N	22	1965	4.3	1975	7.1	3.8	.327	94
Salmon/of/Cal-A†	7	1993	3.8	1995	5.9	3.1	.330	105
Cuppy/RHP/Clv-N	10	1892	3.8	1895	5.8	2.0	26–14	3.54
Passeau/Phl; Chi-N	13	1936	3.3	1940	5.3	2.0	20–13	2.50
O. Smith/SD; StL-N	19	1978	3.6	1988	5.1	1.5	.270	51
Radatz/RP-RHP/Bos-A	7	1962	3.7	1964	5.1	1.4	16–9	2.29
Rolen/3b/Phl-N†	2	1997	3.4	1998	4.8	1.4	.290	110
Flick*/of/Phl-N; Clv-A	13	1898	3.5	1904	4.5	1.0	.306	56
Carty/of/Mil-Atl-N	15	1964	3.3	1970	4.2	0.9	.366	101
Lofton/of/Clv-A†	8	1992	3.3	1994	4.2	0.9	.349	57
Boddicker/RHP/Bal-A	14	1983	3.4	1984	4.2	0.8	20–11	2.79
Piazza/c/LA-N†	7	1993	5.1	1996	5.9	0.8	.336	105
Nichols*/RHP/Bos-N	15	1890	6.7	1897	7.3	0.6	31–11	2.64
McGinnity*/RHP/NY-N	10	1899	5.0	1904	5.6	0.6	35–8	1.61
Lynn/of/Bos-A	17	1975	4.7	1979	5.2	0.5	.333	122
R. Ford/RHP/NY-A	7	1911	4.0	1912	4.3	0.3	22–11	2.27
Oliva/of/Min-A	15	1964	4.1	1970	4.3	0.2	.325	107
J. Jackson/of/Clv-A	13	1911	6.8	1912	6.9	0.1	.395	90
Pesky/ss/Bos-A	10	1942	4.1	1946	4.2	0.1	.335	55
Mercer/RHP/Was-N	9	1894	5.0	1897	5.0	0.0	21–20	3.18
M. Garcia/RHP/Clv-A	14	1939	3.6	1952	3.6	0.0	22–11	2.37

*Hall of Famer
†Player is still active

Appendix B

The No-Hit Rookie Pitchers

Joe Borden, a 21-year-old rookie pitching for the Philadelphia Athletics on July 28, 1875, against the Chicago White Stockings, threw the first no-hitter in the history of organized baseball, winning 4 to 0. The two teams were members of the first major league in baseball history, the National Association, founded in 1871.

The National Association folded in 1875, and was succeeded by the National League, which began play in 1876. The first no-hitter in the new circuit was also thrown by a rookie, George Bradley of the St. Louis Brown Stockings, who whitewashed the Hartford Dark Blues on July 28, 1876.

The American League, founded in 1901, the fourth major league in the game's history (The American Association, The Union Association and the Player's League were, at one time or another, part of the major league scene during the 1880s and 1890s), along with the National League, have been the preeminent major leagues in organized baseball.

In this appendix are listed only the no-hitters thrown in the National League (from 1876 forward) and the American League (from 1901 forward). The list is arranged chronologically.

Nm/Tm/Lg	Date	Score	Opponent	Final Record	ERA
G. Bradley, StL-N	7-28-1876	2–0	Hartford	W33–L26	2.13
L. Richmond, Wor-N*	6-12-1880	1–0	Cleveland (perf. gm.)	W32–L32	2.15
L. Corcoran, Chi-N	8-19-1880	6–0	Boston	W43–L14	1.95
J. Hughes, Bal-N	4-22-1892	8–0	Boston	W23–L12	3.20
C. Jones,† Cin-N	10-15-1892	1–0	Pittsburgh	W1–L0	0.00
C. Phillippe, Lou-N	5-25-1899	7–0	New York	W21–L17	3.17
N. Maddox, Pit-N	9-20-1907	2–1	Brooklyn	W5–L1	0.83
J. Tesreau, NY-N	9-6-1912	3–0	Philadelphia	W17–L7	1.96
C. Robertson, Chi-A	4-30-1922	2–0	Detroit (perf. gm.)	W14–L15	3.64
P. Dean, Stl-N	9-21-1934	3–0	Brooklyn	W19–L11	3.43
V. Kennedy, Chi-A	8-31-1935	5–0	Cleveland	W11–L11	3.91
W. McCahan, Phl-A	9-3-1947	3–0	Washington	W10–L5	3.32
A. Holloman, St–L-A	5-6-1953	6–0	Philadelphia	W3–L7	5.23

*The Worcester, Massachusetts, National League franchise was moved after a three-year stay (1880–1882) to Philadelphia, where the Phillies have been ever since.

†Charles "Bumpus" Jones is the only player to pitch a no-hitter on the day of his major league debut. He pitched in the major leagues in parts of the 1892 and 1893 seasons, a total of only eight games.

Nm/Tm/Lg	Date	Score	Opponent	Final Record	ERA
R. Belinsky, LA-A	5-5-1962	2–0	Baltimore	W10–L11	3.56
V. Blue, Oak-A	9-21-1970	6–0	Minnesota	W2–L0	2.09
B. Hooten, Chi-N	4-16-1972	4–0	Philadelphia	W11–L14	2.80
S. Busby, KC-A	4-27-1973	3–0	Detroit	W16–L15	4.23
M. Warren, Oak-A	9-29-1983	3–0	Chicago	W5–L3	4.11
W. Alvarez, Chi-A	8-11-1991	7–0	Baltimore	W3–L2	3.51

Appendix C

The Twenty-Game Winners

Nm/Tm/Lg	Age	Yr Rec	ERA	TPR
T. Larkin, Har-N	*	1877, W29–L25	2.14	1.8
W. White, Cin-N	23	1878, W30–L21	1.79	0.7
J. Ward, Prov-N	18	1878, W22–L13	1.51	2.6
L. Corcoran, Chi-N	21	1880, W43–L14	1.95	3.1
M. Welch, Troy-N	21	1880, W34–L30	2.54	0.3
L. Richmond, Wor-N	23	1880, W32–L32	2.15	1.9
G. Derby, Det-N	24	1881, W29–L26	2.20	0.9
C. Radbourn, Prov-N	26	1881, W25–L11	2.43	0.9
J. Whitney, Bos-N	23	1881, W31–L33	2.48	1.9
C. Buffinton, Bos-N	22	1883, W25–L14	3.03	0.1
C. Ferguson, Phl-N	21	1884, W21–L25	3.54	-1.7
W. Stemmeyer, Bos-N	21	1886, W22–L18	3.02	1.2
J. Flynn, Chi-N	22	1886, W23–L6	2.24	4.1
M. Madden, Bos-N	20	1887, W21–L14	3.79	0.9
A. Krock, Chi-N	22	1888, W25–L14	2.44	1.6
C. Nichols, Bos-N	20	1890, W27–L19	2.23	6.7
P. Luby, Chi-N	21	1890, W20–L9	3.19	1.7
W. Rhines, Cin-N	21	1890, W28–L17	1.95	6.5
T. Vickery, Phl-N	23	1890, W24–L22	3.44	0.3
G. Cuppy, Clv-N	23	1892, W28–L13	2.51	3.8
W. Piatt, Phl-N	24	1898, W24–L14	3.18	1.1
V. Willis, Bos-N	22	1898, W25–L13	2.84	2.5
J. McGinnity, Bal-N	28	1899, W28–L16	2.68	5.0
C. Phillippe, Louv-N	27	1899, W21–L17	3.17	2.3
C. Mathewson, NY-N	21	1901, W20–L17	2.41	4.1
R. Patterson, Chi-A	24	1901, W20–L16	3.37	0.4
R. Miller, Det-A	24	1901, W23–L13	2.95	3.5
J. Weimer, Chi-N	29	1903, W20–L8	2.30	2.4
H. Schmidt, Brk-N	30	1903, W22–L13	3.83	-1.3
I. Young, Bos-N	28	1905, W20–L21	2.90	0.4
J. Pfiester, Chi-N	28	1906, W20–L8	1.51	2.8
G. McQuillan, Phl-N	23	1908, W23–L17	1.53	3.9
E. Summers, Det-A	23	1908, W24–L12	1.64	2.4
L. Cole, Chi-N	24	1910, W20–L4	1.80	3.0

*Terry Larkin's birth date is unknown and 1877 was the only year he pitched for the Hartford Dark Blues in a six-year career. He was a 20-game winner with Chicago in 1878 (29) and 1879 (31).

Nm/Tm/Lg	Age	Yr Rec	ERA	TPR
R. Ford, NY-A	27	1910, W26–L6	1.65	4.0
S. Gregg, Clv-A	26	1911, W23–L7	1.80	4.7
G. Alexander, Phl-N	24	1911, W28–L13	2.57	3.6
L. Cheney, Chi-N	26	1912, W26–L10	2.85	2.0
H. Bedient, Bos-A	22	1912, W20–L9	2.92	1.6
E. Russell, Chi-A	24	1913, W22–L16	1.90	4.2
J. Pfeffer, Brk-N	26	1914, W23–L12	1.97	3.1
S. Perry, Phl-A	27	1918, W20–L19	1.98	3.9
W. Ferrell, Clv-A	21	1929, W21–L10	3.60	3.4
M. Weaver, Was-A	26	1932, W22–L10	4.08	1.0
L. Fette, Bos-N	33	1937, W20–L10	2.88	2.5
C. Melton, NY-N	25	1937, W20–L9	2.61	3.9
J. Turner, Bos-N	34	1937, W20–L11	2.38	4.5
J. Beazley, StL-N	24	1942, W21–L6	2.13	4.0
W. Voiselle, NY-N	25	1944, W21–L16	3.02	2.5
D. Ferriss, Bos-A	23	1945, W21–L10	2.96	3.3
L. Jansen, NY-N	27	1947, W21–L5	3.16	2.4
E. Bearden, Clv-A	27	1948, W20–L7	2.43	5.5
A. Kellner, Phl-A	25	1949, W20–L12	3.75	1.3
H. Haddix, StL-N	27	1953, W20–L9	3.06	4.7
R. Grim, NY-A	24	1954, W20–L6	3.26	0.2
T. Browning, Cin-N	25	1985, W20–L9	3.55	0.8

Appendix D

Rookie Leaders in Home Runs and Runs Batted In

Rookie John "Buck" Freeman's 25 home runs in 1899 caused such a stir that the National League's leading home run hitter became the first player celebrity asked to endorse a non-sports article. "Buck's" picture appeared in newspaper ads touting Squinksquillet's Suspenders, a fashionable piece of men's clothing. Home runs ever since have captured the attention of fans — and marketers — everywhere.

Rookies who have hit 30 or more home runs:

Nm/Tm/Lg	Yr	HR	TPR
W. Berger, Bos-N	1930	38	2.2
H. Trosky, Clv-A	1934	37	2.5
R. York, Det-A	1937	35	0.9
T. Williams, Bos-A	1939	31	4.3
W. Dropo, Bos-A	1950	34	1.3
A. Rosen, Clv-A	1950	37	3.1
F. Robinson, Cin-N	1956	38	3.0
R. Allison, Was-A	1959	30	0.5
J. Hall, Min-A	1963	33	0.5
P. Oliva, Min-A	1964	32	4.1
J. Hart, SF-N	1964	31	2.7
E. Williams, Atl-N	1971	33	0.4
W. Montanez, Phl-N	1971	30	1.3
R. Kittle, Chi-A	1983	35	-0.3
P. Incaviglia, Tex-A	1986	30	-1.0
J. Canseco, Oak-A	1986	33	0.5
M. McGwire, Oak-A	1987	47*	3.3
M. Nokes, Det-A	1987	32	1.8
M. Piazza, LA-N	1993	35	5.1
T. Salmon, Cal-A	1993	31	3.8
N. Garciaparra, Bos-A	1997	30	3.3

*Rookie Record

In 1899 the Pittsburgh Pirates' third baseman, Jimmy Williams, became the first rookie to exceed the charmed 100 RBI mark. Rookie players who have driven in more than 100 runs are presented below:

Nm/Tm/Lg	R-Yr	RBI	TPR
J. Williams, Pit-N	1899	116	5.2
G. Wright, Pit-N	1924	111	2.3
A. Simmons, Phl-A	1924	102	-1.1
A. Lazzeri, NY-A	1926	114	-1.0
D. Bissonette, Brk-N	1928	106	2.0
D. Alexander, Det-A	1929	137	1.7
W. Berger, Bos-N	1930	119	2.2
S. Jolley, Chi-A	1930	114	-0.3
J. Vosmik, Clv-A	1931	117	0.1
H. Trosky, Clv-A	1934	142	2.5
H. Bonura, Chi-A	1934	110	1.4
J. DiMaggio, NY-A	1936	125	3.0
R. York, Det-A	1937	103	0.9
J. Rizzo, Pit-N	1938	111	1.6
K. Keltner, Clv-A	1938	113	-0.9
T. Williams, Bos-A	1939	145*	4.3
N. Young, NY-N	1940	101	0.0
A. Rosen, Clv-A	1950	116	3.1
L. Easter, Clv-A	1950	107	0.8
W. Dropo, Bos-A	1950	144	1.3
R. Jablonski, StL-N	1953	112	-3.0
J. Greengrass, Cin-N	1953	100	0.2
F. Lynn, Bos-A	1975	105	4.7
J. Rice, Bos-A	1975	102	1.2
R. Kittle, Chi-A	1983	100	-0.3
A. Davis, Sea-A	1984	116	2.5
J. Canseco, Oak-A	1986	117	0.5
W. Joyner, Cal-A	1986	100	1.4
M. McGwire, Oak-A	1987	118	3.3
M. Piazza, LA-N	1993	112	5.1

*Rookie Record

Appendix E

Rookies of the Year versus TPR Leaders

The Rookies of the Year (RY) chosen by the Baseball Writers Association of America (BBWAA), presented annually since 1947, are listed below with their Total Player Ratings (TPR). A comparison column appears to the right, indicating the year the award was given and the name of the rookie who achieved the highest TPR rating. Where no TPR rating appears in the comparison column, the BBWAA selection is the highest rating of that particular season.

BBWAA Choice			Player with Highest TPR	
Nm/Pos/TM	*TPR*	*Year*	*Nm/Pos/Tm*	*TPR*
J. Robinson/1b/Brk-NL	0.2	1947	L. Jansen/RHP/NY-NL	2.4
			F. Fain/1b/Phl-AL	1.8
A. Dark/ss/Bos-NL	0.4	1948	R. Ashburn/of/Phl-NL	2.8
			E. Bearden/LHP/Clv-AL	5.8
D. Newcombe/RHP/Brk-NL	2.8	1949		
R. Sievers/1b/StL-AL	1.3		M. Garcia/RHP/Clv-AL	3.3
S. Jethroe/of/Bos-NL	0.9	1950	D. O'Connell/ss/Pit-NL	2.0
W. Dropo/1b/Bos-AL	1.3		A. Rosen/3b/Clv-AL	3.1
W. Mays/of/NY-NL	1.9	1951		
G. McDougald/3b/NY-AL	1.2		S. Minoso/of/Clv-Chi-AL	2.8
			S. Rogovin/RHP/Det-Chi-AL	2.8
D. Black/RHP/Brk-NL	3.3	1952		
H. Byrd/RHP/Phl-AL	1.8			
J. Gilliam/2b/Brk-NL	1.7	1953	H. Haddix/LHP/StL-NL	4.7
H. Kuenn/ss/Det-AL	-0.9		J. Keegan, RHP/Chi-AL	1.9
W. Moon/of/StL-NL	0.4	1954	D. Jolly/RHP/Mil-NL	3.0
R. Grim/RHP/NY-AL	0.2		A. Carey/3b/NY-AL	2.7
W. Virdon/of/StL-NL	-1.0	1955	R. Crone/RHP/Mil-NL	0.4
H. Score/LHP/Clv-AL	2.2		F. Lary/RHP/Det-AL	2.5
F. Robinson/of/Cin-NL*	3.0	1956		
L. Aparicio/ss/Chi-AL	-0.6		W. Burnette/RHP/KC-AL	1.5
J. Sanford/RHP/Phl-NL	1.9	1957	E. Bouchee/1b/Phl-NL	2.7
T. Kubek/ss/NY-AL*	-0.2		W. Held/ss/Clv-AL	1.8
O. Cepeda/1b/SF-NL*	0.6	1958	G. Witt/RHP/Pit-NL	2.5
A. Pearson/of/Was-AL	-0.4		R. Duren/RP-RHP/NY-AL	2.5

*Unanimous RY choice

Nm/Pos/TM	TPR	Year	Nm/Pos/Tm	TPR
W. McCovey/of/SF-NL*	2.0	1959	V. Pinson/of/Cin-NL	3.9
R. Allison/of/Was-AL	0.5		J. Perry/RHP/Clv-AL	2.8
F. Howard/of/LA-NL	-0.7	1960	A. Mahaffey/RHP/Phl-NL	1.5
R. Hansen/ss/Bal-AL	2.5			
B. Williams/of/Chi-NL	0.2	1961	S. Hemus/ss/StL-NL	2.8
D. Schwall/RHP/Bos-AL	2.2		T. Fox/RHP/Det-AL	2.8
K. Hubbs/2b/Chi-NL	-1.0	1962	D. Clendenon/1b/Pit-NL	0.6
M. Tresh/of/NY-AL	1.0		R. Radatz/RP-RHP/Bos-AL	3.7
P. Rose/2b/Cin-NL	-1.3	1963	R. Hunt/2b/NY-NL	2.3
G. Peters/LHP/Chi-A	4.5			
R. Allen/3b/Phl-NL	5.8	1964		
T. Oliva/of/Min-AL	4.1			
J. Lefebvre/2b/LA-NL	0.5	1965	F. Linzy/RP-RHP/SF-NL	4.9
C. Blefary/of/Bal-AL	2.3		M. Lopez/RHP/Cal-AL	2.3
T. Helms/2b'Cin-NL	-2.8	1966	L. Jaster/LHP/StL-NL	0.6
T. Agee/of/Chi-AL	2.9			
T. Seaver/RHP/NY-NL	2.3	1967	G. Nolan/RHP/Cin-N	2.6
R. Carew/2b/Min-AL	0.2		R. Smith/of/Bos-AL	1.2
J. Bench/c/Cin-NL	2.6	1968	J. Koosman/LHP/NY-NL	3.0
S. Bahnsen/RHP/NY-AL	2.2			
T. Sizemore/2b/LA-NL	0.3	1969	L. Hisle/of/Phl-NL	1.9
L. Piniella/of/KC-AL	1.0		K. Tatum/RP-RHP/Cal/AL	3.8
C. Morton/RHP/Mon/NL	1.8	1970	B. Carbo/of/Cin-NL	3.5
T. Munson/c/NY-AL	3.0			
E. Williams/of/Atl-NL	0.4	1971	W. Montanez/of/Phl-NL	1.3
C. Chambliss/1b/Clv-AL	-1.4		P. Splittorf/RHP/KC-AL	1.5
J. Matlack/LHP/NY-NL	2.9	1972		
C. Fisk/c/Bos-AL*	4.4			
G. Mathews/of/SF-NL	1.7	1973	S. Rogers/RHP/Mon-NL	4.1
A. Bumbry/of/Bal-AL	1.2		C. Acosta/RP–LHP/Chi-AL	3.6
A. McBride/of/StL-NL	2.3	1974		
M. Hargrove/1b/Tex-AL	2.7			
J. Montefusco/RHP/SF-NL	2.0	1975		
F. Lynn/of/Bos-AL	4.7			
C. Metzger/RP-RHP/SD-NL	0.7	1976	P. Zachry/RHP/Cin-NL	1.4
M. Fidrych/RHP/Det-AL	5.0			
A. Dawson/of/Mon-NL	1.3	1977	S. Henderson/of/NY-NL	1.9
E. Murray/1b/Bal-AL	0.8		M. Page/of/Oak-AL	4.9
R. Horner/3b/Atl-NL	1.3	1978	O. Smith/ss/SD-NL	3.6
L. Whitaker/2b/Det-AL	2.3			
R. Sutcliffe/RHP/LA-N	0.8	1979	J. Fulgham/RHP/StL-NL	2.0
J. Castino/3b/Min-AL	1.3		R. Davis/RHP/NY-AL	2.3
S. Howe/RP–LHP/LA-NL	1.8	1980	A. Holland/RP-RHP/SF-NL	2.0
J. Charboneau/1b/Clv-AL	1.3		B. Burns/LHP/Chi-AL	3.5
F. Valenzuela/LHP/LA-NL	2.5	1981	T. Raines/of/Mon-NL	3.1
D. Righetti/LHP/NY-AL	2.0			
S. Sax/2b/LA-NL	0.0	1982	S. Bedrosian/RP-RHP/Atl-NL	2.0
C. Ripken, Jr./ss/Bal-AL	1.0		E. Vande Berg/LHP/Sea-AL	2.9
D. Strawberry/of/NY-NL	2.3	1983		
R. Kittle/of/Chi-AL	-0.3		M. Boddicker/RHP/Bal-AL	3.4
D. Gooden/RHP/NY-NL	2.9	1984	D. Gladden/of/SF-NL	2.9
A. Davis/1b/Sea-AL	2.5			
V. Coleman/of/StL-NL*	0.9	1985	C. Brown/3b/SF-NL	1.7
O. Guillen/ss/Chi-AL	0.6		S. Cliburn/RP-RHP/Cal-AL	2.9
T. Worrell/RP-RHP/StL-NL	4.2	1986		
J. Canseco/of/Oak-AL	0.5		M. Eichhorn/RP-RHP/Tor-AL	5.7
B. Santiago/c/SD-NL*	0.8	1987	M. Dunne/RHP/Pit-NL	2.3

Nm/Pos/TM	TPR	Year	Nm/Pos/Tm	TPR
M. McGwire/1b/Oak-AL*	3.3			
C. Sabo/3b/Cin-NL	2.7	1988		
W. Weiss/ss/Oak-AL	1.0		B. Harvey/RP-RHP/Cal-AL	2.7
J. Walton/of/Chi-NL	0.3	1989	G. Harris/RP-RHP/SD-NL	1.8
G. Olson/RP-RHP/Bal-AL	2.7			
D. Justice/of/Atl-NL	1.5	1990	L. Walker/1b/Mon-NL	1.5
S. Alomar/2b/Tor-AL*	0.0		K. Appier/RHP/KC-AL	2.3
J. Bagwell/1b/Hou-NL	2.1	1991		
C. Knoblauch/2b/Min-AL	0.2		D. Henry/RP-RHP/Mil-AL	1.9
			M. Timlin/RP-RHP/Tor-AL	1.9
A. Karros/1b/LA-NL	0.3	1992	M. Perez/RP-RHP/StL-NL	2.0
P. Listach/ss/Mil-AL	1.0		K. Lofton/of/Clv-AL	3.3
M. Piazza/c/LA-NL*	5.1	1993		
T. Salmon/of/Cal-AL*	3.8			
R. Mondesi/of/LA-NL*	1.1	1994	H. Carrasco/RP-RHP/Cin-NL	2.2
R. Hamelin/1b/KC-AL	1.3		J. Valentin/ss/Mil-AL	2.9
H. Nomo/RHP/LA-NL	1.8	1995	Q. Veras/2b/Fla-NL	2.2
M. Cordova/of/Min-AL	2.6		J. Tavarez/RP-RHP/Clv-AL	2.6
T. Hollandsworth/of/LA-NL	0.6	1996	E. Renteria/ss/Fla-NL	2.7
D. Jeter/ss/NY-AL*	1.3		J. Rosado/LHP/KC-AL	2.3
S. Rolen/3b/Phl-NL	3.4	1997		
N. Garciaparra/ss/Bos-AL	3.3			
K. Wood/RHP/Chi-NL	1.7	1998		
B. Grieve/of/Oak-AL	1.0		R. Arrojo/RHP/TB-AL	3.8
C. Beltran/of/KC-AL	0.7	1999	J. Zimmerman/RHP/Tex-AL	2.6
S. Williamson/RP-RHP/Chi-NL	4.7			

*Unanimous Rookie of the Year choice

Bibliography

Adomites, Paul, and Saul Wisnia. *Best of Baseball*. Lincolnwood, IL: Publications International, 1997.

Alexander, Charles. *Our Game*. New York: Henry Holt, 1991.

Aylesworth, Thomas, Benton Minks and John S. Bowman, eds. *The Encyclopedia of Baseball Managers*, New York: Brompton Books, 1990.

Benson, John, and Tony Blengino. *Baseball's Top 100*. Wilton, Conn.: Diamond Library, 1995.

Bjarkman, P.C., ed. *Encyclopedia of Major League Baseball*. New York: Carroll and Graf, 1993.

Brown, Warren. *The Chicago Cubs*. New York: G.P. Putnam's Sons, 1946.

Cairns, Bob. *Pen Men*. New York: St. Martin's Press, 1992.

Carmichael, John P. *My Greatest Day in Baseball*. New York: Grosset and Dunlap, 1951.

Dewey, Don, and Nicholas Acocella. *The Ball Clubs*. New York: HarperCollins, 1996.

Dickson, Paul. *Baseball's Greatest Quotations*. New York: Edward Burlingame Books, 1991.

Falls, Joe. *The Detroit Tigers*. New York: Walker, 1989.

Gallagher, Mark. *The Yankee Encyclopedia, #3*. Champaign, Ill.: Sagamore, 1997.

Hines, Rick. "Harvey Haddix: Former Lefty Hurler Discusses Career." *Sports Collectors Digest* 19 (November): 200–203.

Honig, Donald. *Baseball America*. New York: Gallahad Books, 1985.

_____. *A Donald Honig Reader*. New York: Simon and Schuster, 1988.

Hynd, Noel. *The Giants of the Polo Grounds*. New York: Doubleday, 1988.

Irwin, Arthur. *Practical Ball Playing*. New York: American Sports, 1895.

Ivor-Campbell, F., R. Tiemann and Mark Rucker, eds. *Baseball's First Stars*. Cleveland, Ohio: Society for American Baseball Research, 1996.

Johnson, L., and M. Wolff, eds. *The Encyclopedia of Minor League Baseball*. Durham, N.C.: Baseball America, 1997.

Johnson, L., and B. Ward. *Who's Who in Baseball*. New York: Barnes and Noble, 1994.

Lanigan, Ernest. *The Baseball Cyclopedia*. New York: Baseball Magazine, 1922.

Lindberg, R.C. *Stealing First in a Two-Team Town*. Champaign, Ill.: Sagamore, 1994.

Linn, Ed. *The Great Rivalry*. New York: Ticknor and Fields, 1991.

Longert, Scott. *Addie Joss: King of Pitchers*. Cleveland, Ohio: Society for American Baseball Research, 1998.

Mathewson, Christy. *Pitching in a Pinch*. New York: Grosset & Dunlap, 1923.

Mazer, Bill, with Stan and Shirley Fischler. *Bill Mazer's Amazin' Baseball Books*. New York: Simon and Schuster, 1988.

Nemec, David. *The Great Encyclopedia of 19th-Century Minor League Baseball*. New York: Donald Fine Books, 1997.

_____, and Pete Palmer, eds. *Fascinating Baseball Facts*. Lincolnwood, Ill.: Publications International, 1994.

Peary, Danny, ed. *We Played the Game*. New York: Hyperion, 1994.

Reichler, Joseph. *Baseball's Greatest Moments*. New York: Crown, 1981.

_____. *The Great All-Time Baseball Record Book*. New York: Macmillan, 1993.

Schoor, Gene. *Christy Mathewson: Baseball's Greatest Pitcher*. New York: Julian Messner, 1953.

Seymour, Harold. *Baseball: The Early Years*. New York: Oxford University Press, 1960.

Shatzkin, Mike, ed. *The Ballplayers.* New York: William Morrow, 1990.

Solomon, Burt. *The Baseball Timeline.* New York: Avon Books, 1997.

Spalding, Albert. *America's National Game.* New York: American Sports, 1910.

Thorn, John, and Pete Palmer, eds. *Total Baseball.* 5th ed. New York: Total Sports Publications, 1999.

_____, _____, and Michael Gershman, eds. *Total Baseball.* Editions I–VI. New York: Viking and Total Sports, 1989–1998.

Tiemann, Robert L., and Mark Rucker, eds. *Nineteenth Century Stars.* Cleveland: The Society for American Baseball Research, 1989.

Trachtenberg, Leo. *The Wonder Team.* Bowling Green, Ohio: Bowling Green State University Press, 1997.

Walton, Ed. *The Rookies.* New York: Stein and Day, 1982.

Wright, Marshall D. *Nineteenth Century Baseball.* Jefferson, N.C.: McFarland, 1996.

Baseball Guides

Beadles Dime Base-Ball
Spalding's Official Base Ball Guide, 1885–1896
The Sporting News' Baseball Registers, 1975–1999

Circulars

Baseball Bulletin
Baseball Research Journal
National Pastime

Newspapers

Boston Globe
Chicago Inter-Ocean
Chicago Tribune
Detroit News
Milwaukee Journal
New York Times
Providence Journal
St. Louis Post-Dispatch
Sporting Life
The Sporting News
USA Today Baseball Weekly

Index